EXPLORING COLOR
PHOTOGRAPHY

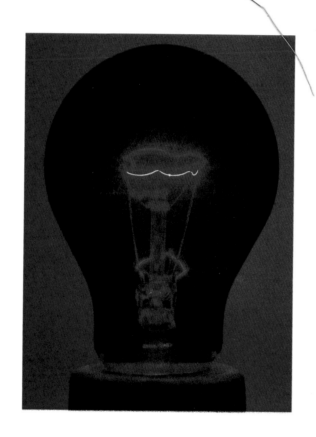

4TH EDITION

Exploring Color Photography

From the Darkroom to the Digital Studio

Robert Hirsch

McGraw-Hill

To my mother, Muriel Hirsch, for teaching me to read and my wife, Adele Henderson, for her inspiration and on-going support.

And to the memory of my father, Edwin Hirsch, for introducing me to photography; and Ernest Shackleton, explorer of the South Pole, and the crew of the Endurance, who provided me with insight into the nature of true exploration.

"The qualities necessary to be an explorer are, in order of importance: optimism, patience, physical endurance, idealism, and courage. Optimism nullifies disappointment. Impatience means disaster. Physical endurance will not compensate for the first two moral or temperamental qualities."

Ernest Shackleton

"We travel into or away from our photographs."

Don Delillo, *MAO II*
New York: Viking, 1991, p. 141

 Higher Education

Exploring Color Photography

Published by McGraw-Hill, an imprint of The McGraw-Hill Companies, Inc. 1221 Avenue of the Americas, New York, NY 10020. Copyright © 2005, 1997, 1993, 1989 by The McGraw-Hill Companies, Inc. All rights reserved. No part of this publication may be reproduced or distributed in any form or by any means, or stored in a database or retrieval system, without the prior written permission of The McGraw-Hill Companies inc., including but not limited to, in any network or other electronic storage or transmission, or broadcast for distance learning.

Printed in Singapore.

1 2 3 4 5 6 7 8 9 0   3 2 1 0 9 8 7 6 5 4

ISBN 0-07240-706-9

Editor-in-Chief: Emily Barrosse
Publisher: Lyn Uhl
Senior Sponsoring Editor: Joe Hanson
Editorial Assistant: Elizabeth Sigal
Marketing Manager: Lisa Berry
Media Producer: Shannon Gattens

A CIP catalog record for this book is available from the Library of Congress.

This book was designed and produced by
Laurence King Publishing Ltd, London
www.laurenceking.co.uk

Every effort has been made to contact the copyright holders, but should there be any errors or omissions Laurence King Publishing Ltd would be pleased to insert the appropriate acknowledgment in any subsequent printing of this publication.

Senior Editor: Samantha Gray
Assistant Editor: Eno Jebens
Copy Editor: Krystyna Mayer
Designer: Peter Ling
Cover Design: Price Watkins

Front cover: © James Crable. *Empire State Plaza*, Albany, NY, 1985. 28 x 28 ins. Chromogenic prints.
Half-Title page: © Amanda Means. *Light Bulb 0016C*, 2001. 5 x 4 ins. Diffusion transfer print. Courtesy of the Ricco/Maresca Gallery, New York.
Frontispiece: © Douglas Holleley. *Luna En-Trance*, Luna Park, Sydney, Australia, 1995. 20 x 24 ins. Chromogenic color print.
Back cover: © Joseph Scheer. *Automeris io*, 2002. 34 x 46 ins. Inkjet print.

CONTENTS

PREFACE

Color photography is an exciting amalgamation of aesthetics, culture, psychology, and science. *Exploring Color Photography*, Fourth Edition, is a stimulating introduction to the approaches, techniques, and history of color photography, illustrated with a wide range of imagery from photographers in the field. As photographic technology continues to change at a rapid rate, the text assumes a conceptual methodology that stresses the understanding of ideas from which aesthetic and technical explorations can be conducted. The coverage is based on the author's experiences as an image-maker, teacher, curator, and writer, who has an ongoing dialogue with the medium and its makers. The text is comprehensive and is structured to provide the fore-knowledge necessary to think about and comprehend photo-based color work. The approach is pragmatic, explaining how theory relates directly to the practice of making photo-based color images, in addition to presenting the means necessary to elaborate ideas through photography. It assumes a basic working knowledge and understanding of black-and-white photography, digital image processing, and photo history. In the midst of the digital transition, *Exploring Color Photography*, Fourth Edition, takes the position that digital imaging is another tool available to imaginative photographers and should be integrated into their creative processes whenever necessary to achieve the desired results.

The opening chapters provide the foundational information necessary to make intelligent work, the middle chapters furnish data covering technical processes, and the latter chapters offer numerous working approaches. Each chapter is organized into discrete units that help readers easily find major topics of interest. This arrangement also encourages skipping around and discovering alternative structures for the material. Two new chapters on digital imaging reflect its growing influence in photographic practice. Another improvement is the continued expansion of the index that covers ideas, images, people, processes, and terminology by directly referencing sources in the text, including image-makers and historical information that supply a context for the discovery of meaning. This system of amplification facilitates a clearer definition and a broader understanding that is only possible through personal interaction with the materials being questioned.

Exploring Color Photography, Fourth Edition, stresses visual thinking and encourages image-makers to select materials and processes that express their ideas. To be an explorer is to investigate the unknown for the purpose of discovering truth. Once truth is uncovered, it is possible to gain understanding. Understanding can lead to creation. From creation, meaning can be uncovered. This book presents a structured starting place for the exploration of ideas and techniques through guided paths that involve students in the spirit of discovery and provide the means to expressing their visions. Because this book is not intended to be a final authority, it provides additional sources of information throughout the text to encourage outside exploration.

Ultimately, the purpose of this book is to arouse curiosity and provide the tools and direction to make informed artistic decisions.

The illustration program in this fourth edition represents an overview of the diversity of approaches employed by artists, professionals, teachers, and students. It is valuable for people entering the field of color photography to be exposed to the varied practices and content that the medium offers. The images reflect the ways that contemporary photographers experiment and push the definitions and limits of what defines a color photograph. It promotes a vital curiosity that fosters an expansion of the boundaries of color photography. This edition incorporates images that both illustrate color photography techniques and show off the extraordinary rich interconnectedness of the sensory areas of the brain involved in making, viewing, and understanding color images.

The captions are based on the author's collection of statements, personal correspondence, e-mails, and conversations with photographers, in which they explain key aesthetic and technical choices that went into their work. Furthermore, the captions are a concise forum through which photographers relate their work to theories or techniques covered in the text. They are not intended as final closures of meaning, but as initial toeholds into the thinking behind each image. The captions spur thinking, encourage alternative explanation and evaluation, and promote questioning the limits of language.

Acknowledgements

The critic Northrop Frye commented, "Poetry can only be made out of other poems; novels out of other novels [photographs from other photographs]." This book is about the spirit of transmitting knowledge, and as such I would like to thank the teachers who have made a difference to me: Mr. Rice, my high school art teacher, for giving me the hope to pursue my dream amidst the sea of boring conformist expectations; Stan McKenzie, for encouraging me to think and write; Judy Harold-Steinhauser, for supporting experimentation and group interaction; Art Terry, for not being a hypocrite; and the numerous image-makers and writers who have shaped my thinking.

This book would not have been possible without the generosity of numerous individuals, especially the artists who have allowed me to reproduce their work. For this fourth edition I want to thank the contributors, expert consultants, and numerous readers of this and the previous editions for sharing their knowledge: David Allison, Stephen Babbitt, Brian Barsky, Greg Erf, Wendy Erickson, Harris Fogel, Stan Godwin, John Hooton, Keith Johnson, Ron Jude, Joe Labate, Isabella La Rocca, Daniel Larkin, Rob Littlefield, Karen Norton, Dan Overturf, Maria Politarhos, Peter Rad, Neil Rantoul, John Valentino, and Jack Wilgus.

Thanks to all the people at McGraw-Hill who have offered their cooperation, time, and knowledge in creating this book.

Special thanks are in order for the following people who have made important contributions to this fourth edition:

Greg Erf, with whom I co-created the digital chapters, and with assistance from John Valentino who co-authored the digital chapter in the previous edition. I worked with Greg Erf because of his varied expertise in photography and digital imaging. In addition, Greg and I have worked together creating and teaching the history of photography online: www.enmu.edu/photohistory, writing columns for *Photovision* magazine, and various other activities: www.negative-positive.com. After jointly creating a working outline, Greg wrote the drafts while I acted as editor and rewriter. Then John entered the process, reviewing all the digital areas and researching and writing new material. The final drafts were volleyed back and forth until all three of us were satisfied. Greg is also responsible for all the new illustrations in the digital chapters;

Molly Jarboe, who assisted with the art program, caption writing, and manuscript preparation;

Professor Michael Bosworth, Villa Maria College, Buffalo, NY, for technical assistance and preparing work for the art program;

Professor Adele Henderson, SUNY Buffalo, for manuscript preparation;

Professor Dan Larkin, Rochester Institute of Technology, for his color print ring-around model;

Keith Johnson, for on going manuscript suggestions and for making the images for color print ring-around.

Professor Hans I. Bjelkhagen, De Montfort University, Centre for Modern Optics, Leicester, UK for his expertise on Gabriel Lippmann's interference process;

Tod Gangler of Art & Soul for his illustrations of the pigment process;

To Mark Jacobs for sharing his expertise on early color processes, numerous examples from his collection, and reading drafts of the color history chapter;

Hugh Tifft for information about early color processes and providing examples from his collection;

The members of the PhotoHistory list serve: *PhotoHistory@yahoogroups.com* for answering numerous questions and providing valuable contacts;

Joe Hanson, Kari Grimsby, and Elizabeth Sigal, my editors at McGraw-Hill, for their support, understanding, and ideas;

Samantha Gray, my production editor; Krystyna Mayer, my copy editor; and Alison Worthington, my indexer; for their thoughtful efforts in making improvements to this fourth edition; and to all my reviewers.

A word of caution: in many color photography processes you will be working with materials that can be hazardous to your health if they are not handled properly. To prevent problems from occurring, read all directions, precautions, and safety measures (especially those outlined in the safety addendum) thoroughly before you begin working in any process. Preventative common sense will go a long way to ensure a safe, healthy involvement with color photography. Have fun in your explorations.

BOB HIRSCH
Buffalo, New York

Photographers

Koya Abe ○ Bill Adams ○ David R. Allison ○ Bill Armstrong ○ Shimon Attie ○ Steve Babbit ○ Jo Babcock ○ Pat Bacon ○ Darryl Baird ○ Jennifer Baker ○ Tina Barney ○ Uta Barth ○ Thomas Barrow ○ Steven H. Begleiter ○ Paul Berger ○ Audrey Bernstein ○ Laura Blacklow ○ Michael Bosworth ○ Marcie Jan Bronstein ○ Lawrence Brose ○ Jerry Burchfield ○ Larry Burrows ○ Edward Burtynsky ○ Diane Bush and Steven Baskin ○ Jeffery Byrd ○ Roger Camp ○ Kathleen Campbell ○ John Paul Caponigro ○ Ellen Carey ○ Christine Carr ○ James Casebere ○ Cora Cohen ○ Richard Colburn ○ Kelli Connell ○ Gregory Crewdson ○ Joyce Culver ○ Binh Danh ○ Eduardo Del Valle and Mirta Gómez ○ Brian DeLevie. ○ Pamela De Marris ○ Francois Deschamps ○ Allen deSouza ○ Deena des Rioux ○ Seze Devres ○ Rita DeWitt ○ Jean-Jacques Dicker ○ Jay Dunitz ○ Camilla Dussinger ○ Steve Dzerigian ○ William Eggleston ○ Olafur Eliasson ○ Mitch Epstein ○ Greg Erf ○ Janyce Erlich-Moss ○ Barbara Ess ○ Mark Lewis Essington ○ Terry Evans ○ Marion Faller ○ Robert Fichter ○ Bill Finger ○ Carol Flax ○ Robert Flick ○ Robert Flynt ○ Harris Fogel ○ Jennifer Formica ○ Nicole Fournier ○ Bill Frazier ○ Roger Freeman ○ James Friedman ○ Shauna Frishkorn ○ Adam Fuss ○ Tod Gangler ○ Gretchen Garner ○ Judy Gelles ○ Tyrone Georgiou ○ Ron Giebert ○ Peter Goin ○ Sheldon Goldberg ○ Judith Golden ○ Linda Adele Goodine ○ David Graham ○ Susan Kae Grant ○ Lorne Greenberg ○ Lauren Greenfield ○ Sally Grizzell Larson ○ Andreas Gursky ○ Jules-Gervais Courtellemont ○ Toni Hafkenscheid ○ Gary Hallman ○ Judith Harold-Steinhauser ○ Louis Ducos du Hauron ○ Stefan Hagen ○ Masumi Hayashi ○ Robert Heinecken ○ Adele Henderson ○ Linda Hesh ○ Rev. Levi L. Hill ○ Robert Hirsch ○ Rick Hock ○ David Hockney ○ Douglas Holleley ○ Suda House ○ Ambler Hutchinson ○ Birney Imes ○ Josh Iguchi ○ Fredrick Ives ○ Bill Jacobson ○ Molly Jarboe ○ Len Jenshel ○ Ron Jude ○ Richard E. Jurus ○ Tamarra Kaida ○ Jennifer Karady ○ Barbara Kasten ○ Misty Keasler ○ Tatana Kellner ○ Marie Kennedy ○ Gary Keown ○ Jon Kline ○ Viktor Koen ○ Barbara Kruger ○ Joseph Labate ○ Cay Lang ○ Erik Lauritzen ○ Frank Lavelle ○ Bovey Lee ○ Erika Leppmann ○ William Lesch ○ Laura Letinsky ○ David Levinthal ○ M. L. Lincoln ○ Jonathan Long ○ Martha Madigan ○ Stephen Marc ○ Antonio Mari ○ Paul Marlin ○ Pamela de Marris ○ Thomas McGovern ○ Dan McCormack ○ James Clerk Maxwell ○ Gerald C. Mead, Jr ○ Amanda Means ○ Pedro Meyer ○ Joel Meyerowitz ○ Marcel Meys ○ Sybil Miller ○ Gary Minnix ○ Richard Misrach ○ Akihiko Miyoshi ○ Rebekah Modrak ○ László Moholy-Nagy ○ Jim Moninger ○ Delilah Montoya ○ Yasumasa Morimura ○ Steven P. Mosch ○ Brian Moss ○ Nickolas Muray ○ Jeff Murphy ○ Patrick Nagatani ○ Patrick Nagatani and Andrée Tracey ○ Osamu James Nakagawa ○ Ellen Neal ○ Janet Neuhauser ○ Lori Nix ○ Peter Noble ○ Simon Norfolk ○ Michael Northrup ○ Carrie Notari ○ Jayme Odgers ○ Dinh Q. Lê ○ Arthur Ollman ○ Cheryl Opperman ○ Christine Osinski ○ Luis Gonzalez Palma ○ Laura Paresky ○ Bart Parker ○ Olivia Parker ○ Stephen Petergorsky ○ John Pfahl ○ Sheila Pinkel ○ Fred Payne Clatworthy ○ Kathleen Pompe ○ Eliot Porter ○ Nolan Preece ○ Janet L. Pritchard ○ Susan Ressler ○ John Reuter ○ Holly Roberts ○ J. Baylor Roberts ○ Joyce Roetter ○ Anne C. Savedge ○ Lynn Saville ○ Jeffrey Henson Scales ○ Joseph Scheer ○ Betsy Schneider ○ Collier Schorr ○ Larry Schwarm. ○ Fred Scruton ○ J. Seeley ○ Andres Serrano ○ Paul Shambroom ○ Christine Shank ○ Cindy Sherman ○ Steven Shore ○ Laurie Simmons ○ Jeffrey Silverthorne ○ Sandy Skoglund ○ Mark Slankard ○ Clarissa Sligh ○ Ursula Sokolowka ○ Alec Soth ○ Jan Staller ○ Mike and Doug Starn ○ Jim Stone ○ Evon Streetman ○ Stan Strembicki ○ Thomas Struth ○ Larry Sultan ○ Brian Taylor ○ David Taylor ○ Maggie Taylor ○ Deborah Tharp ○ Matthew Tisschler ○ Jessica Todd Harper ○ Terry Towery. ○ Dr. Arthur Traube ○ Marcia G. Treiger ○ Arthur Tress ○ Charlotte Trolinger ○ Linda Troeller ○ John Tuckey ○ John Valentino ○ Sandra Varry ○ Jeff Van Kleeck ○ Kathy Vargas ○ Jeff Wall ○ William Wegman ○ Jo Whaley ○ Jennette Williams ○ Annette Weintraub ○ Edwin Wisherd ○ Lloyd Wolf ○ Beth Yarnelle Edwards ○ Kent R. Younger ○ Dan Zaitz ○ Bryan Zanisnik ○ Charles C. Zoller

Chapter One

CONCEPTS OF COLOR PHOTOGRAPHY

Carey's image celebrates light and color photographic theory while referencing the origins of photography with the photogram. "The pins are placed directly and at random into the paper's surface in the color darkroom and the paper is exposed multiple times using a color enlarger."

© Ellen Carey. *Push Pin Photogram,* 2002. 24 x 20 inches. Chromogenic color print. Courtesy of Jane Baum Gallery, New York, NY.

Newton's Light Experiment

From the time of Aristotle, common wisdom held that the purest form of light was white. In 1666 Sir Isaac Newton of England debunked this belief by demonstrating that light is the source of color. In an elegantly simple experiment Newton passed a beam of sunlight through a glass prism, making the rainbow of colors that form the visible spectrum (red, orange, yellow, green, blue, indigo, violet, and the gradations in between). He then passed the rainbow back through a second prism, which converted all the hues back into white light (figure 1.1). From this experiment Newton determined that color is in the light, not in the glass prism as had been previously thought, and that the light humans see as white light is actually a mixture of all the visible wavelengths of the spectrum. This also served as a reminder against reductionism, for what appeared to be simple on the surface, a beam of white light, was, if examined more deeply, beautifully complex.

A prism such as the one Newton used separates the colors of light through the process of refraction. When light is refracted, each wavelength of light is bent to a different degree. This separates

1.2 A red object appears to be red because it reflects red wavelengths of light while absorbing most of the other wavelengths of light.

1.3 A white object looks white because it reflects all wavelengths of light that strike it.

light into individual bands that make up the spectrum. It is the wavelength of the light that determines its visible color.

Separating Light

The colors of light are also separated by the surfaces of objects. We perceive the color of an object by responding to the particular wavelengths of light reflected back to our eyes from the surface of the object. For example, a red car looks red because it absorbs most of the light waves reaching it but reflects back those of the red part of the spectrum (figure 1.2). An eggshell appears white because it reflects all the wavelengths of light that reach it (figure 1.3).

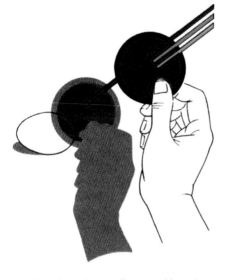

1.4 If a white object is illuminated by only a single-filtered source of light (for example red), it will appear to be only that single color. If only one color strikes an object, that color is the only color that can be reflected back.

If the light is filtered, it changes the color of any object that it illuminates. If the white eggshell is seen only by a red filtered light source, it appears to be red. This occurs because red is the only wavelength that strikes the eggshell, and in turn, red is the only color reflected back from the eggshell (figure 1.4). Objects that transmit light, such as color slides, also absorb some of the colors of light. They contain dyes that absorb specific wavelengths of light while allowing others to pass through. We perceive only the colors that are transmitted, that is that are allowed to pass through the slide.

Dual Nature of Light: Heisenberg's Uncertainty Principle

In 1803 Thomas Young, an English physician and early researcher in physics, demonstrated that light travels in waves of specific frequency and length. This had important consequences for it showed that light seemed to have characteristics of both particles and waves. This apparent contradiction was not resolved until the development of

1.1 Isaac Newton's experiment proved that colors exist in white light and that white light is made up of the entire visible spectrum of colors.

After observing his lawn changing color when a water hose was placed on it for long periods of time in the sun, Binh Danh began experimenting with the process he calls chlorophyll printing. With this process, images are created through the interaction of light, chlorophyll, carbon dioxide, and water. First, a negative is created in Photoshop. After several weeks in the sun, a positive image is contact printed to a leaf through photosynthesis. The process itself lends heavily to the meaning he wishes to convey in his work. Danh asserts: "This process deals with the idea of elemental transmigration: the decomposition and composition of matter into other forms. The images of war are part of the leaves, and live inside and outside of them. The leaves express the continuum of war."

© Binh Danh. *Lost and Found Story*, 2002. 21 x 18 inches. Chlorophyll print, cast in resin.

quantum theory in the early decades of the twentieth century. It proposes a dual nature for both waves and particles, with one aspect predominating in some situations and the other predominating in others. This led to Werner Heisenberg's uncertainty principle in 1927, which places an absolute theoretical limit on the accuracy of certain measurements. The result is that the assumption by earlier scientists that the physical state of a system could be exactly measured and used to predict future states had to be abandoned. These lessons were reflected in new, multifaceted ways of visualizing the world by artists from Pablo Picasso to Marcel Duchamp.

Young's Theory/RGB

In 1807 Young advanced a theory of color vision, which states that the human eye is sensitive to only three wavelengths of light: red, green, and blue (RGB). The brain blends these three primary colors to form all the other colors. Young's ideas later formed the basis of the additive theory of light: white light is made up of red, green, and blue light. Theoretically all the remaining colors visible to the eye can be formed by mixing two or more of these colors (see additive theory in Chapter 2, page 27). When all three of these primary colors are combined in equal amounts the result is white light. Young's theory has yet to be disproved, even though it does not seem to fully explain all the various phenomena concerning color vision (see section on color observation, page 20). It continues to provide the most useful model to date to explain all the principal photographic processes in which color images have been produced.

How We See Color

It is rare for us to see pure color, that is light composed solely of one wavelength. Almost all the hues we see are a mixture of many wavelengths. Color vision combines both the sensory response of the

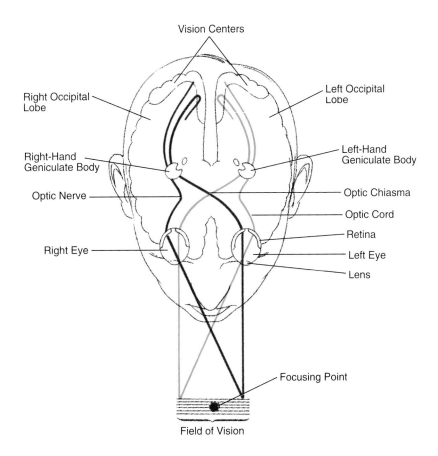

Vision Centers

Right Occipital Lobe

Left Occipital Lobe

Right-Hand Geniculate Body

Left-Hand Geniculate Body

Optic Nerve

Optic Chiasma

Optic Cord

Retina

Right Eye

Left Eye

Lens

Focusing Point

Field of Vision

1.5 This top cutaway view of the human skull reveals how color images are believed to be formed in the brain.

eye and the interpretive response of the brain to the different wavelengths of the spectrum. Light enters the eye and travels through the cornea, passing through the iris, which acts as a variable aperture controlling the amount of light entering the eye. The image that has been formed at this point is now focused by the lens onto a thin membrane at the back of the eye called the retina. The retina contains light-sensitive cells known as rods and cones, named after how they appear when viewed with a microscope. The cones function in daylight conditions and give us color vision. The rods function under low illumination and give vision only in shades of gray. The rods and cones create an image-receiving screen in the back of the eye. The physical information received by the rods and cones is sorted in the retina and translated into signals that are sent through the optic nerves to the nerve cells in the

back of the brain. The optic nerves meet at the chiasma. Visual images from the right side of the brain go to the left, and images from the left side of the brain go to the right (figure 1.5).

Humans can see a spectrum of about one thousand colors that range from red light, which travels in long wavelengths, through the midrange of orange, yellow, and greens, to the blues and violets, which have shorter wavelengths. The distance from wave crest to wave crest determines the length of the light waves. The difference between the longest and the shortest wavelengths is only about .00012 of an inch.

How the Brain Sees Color

In the brain this information is analyzed and interpreted. Scientists have not yet discovered the chemical and neurological reactions that actually let us perceive light

or color. It is currently believed that the effects of light and color on an individual are dependent on our subjective emotional, physical, and psychological states and our past experiences, memories, and preferences. It appears the brain is an active system where all data is constantly revised and recorrelated. There is nothing mechanical or cameralike in the brain, as every perception is a conception and every memory a reconception. There are no fixed memories, no "authentic" views of the past unaffected by the present.

Seeing color is a dynamic process, and remembering it is always a reconstruction as opposed to a reproduction. It has been proven that when a group of people views a single specific color, the responses of the individuals to it vary considerably (see colour is a personal experience, page 23). Although color can be defined objectively with scientific instruments, we lack this ability and see color subjectively rather than quantifiably. The act of experiencing color and light involves a participatory consciousness in which we feel identified with what we are perceiving.

This brings up the toughest problem in neuroscience: consciousness. We know what red is, but one person will never know the character of another's experience of red. This means that our understanding and interpretation of color is based on neurological phenomena, their relationship to physiological mechanisms, and their integration with philosophy of mind.

Color Blindness

We the sighted, who are able to build our own images so effortlessly, believe we are experiencing "reality" itself. Color-blind people remind us that reality is a colossal act of analysis and synthesis that involves the subjective act of seeing.

Irregular color vision commonly manifests itself as the inability to distinguish red from green, followed by the inability to tell blue from yellow, but rarely is there the inability to perceive any color. Color blindness affects approximately 8 percent of males and

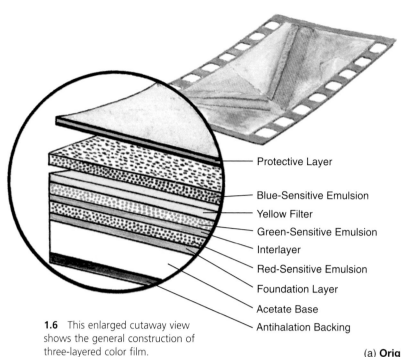

1.6 This enlarged cutaway view shows the general construction of three-layered color film.

Protective Layer
Blue-Sensitive Emulsion
Yellow Filter
Green-Sensitive Emulsion
Interlayer
Red-Sensitive Emulsion
Foundation Layer
Acetate Base
Antihalation Backing

0.5 percent of females. A mother transmits the genes that affect color vision to her offspring. The reason for this anomaly is not certain because there appear to be many causes. It is possible to learn how to color print with mild color blindness, but it is not advisable for people with severe anomalous color vision to take on situations where precise evaluation is of critical importance.[1]

Young's Theory Applied to Color Photography

Current techniques for creating color photographs make use of Thomas Young's theory that almost any color we can see may be reproduced optically by combining only three basic colors of light: red, green, and blue (RGB). For example, color film is typically made up of three emulsion layers supported by an acetate base (figure 1.6). Each emulsion layer is primarily sensitive to only one of the three additive primary colors. The top layer is sensitive to blue light, the middle to green light, and the bottom to red light. Blue light is only recorded on the layer of film that is sensitive to blue, green light on the green-sensitive layer,

and red light on the red-sensitive layer. All other colors are recorded on a combination of two or more of the layers. Some films have a fourth emulsion layer that improves the film's ability to record the green portion of the spectrum, which can be valuable under fluorescent, artificial, and mixed-light situations.

How the Film Produces Color

During development each layer makes a different black-and-white image that corresponds to the amount of colored light that was recorded in each individual layer during the exposure (figure 1.7). The developer oxidizes and combines with the color chemical couplers in the emulsion to create the dyes. The green-sensitive layer forms the magenta dye, the blue-sensitive layer the yellow dye, and the red-sensitive layer the cyan dye. During the remaining stages of the

(a) Original Scene

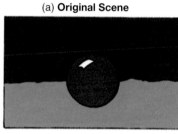

(b) After Exposure

Blue-Sensitive Layer of the Emulsion

(c) After Processing

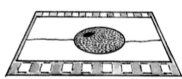

Green-Sensitive Layer of the Emulsion

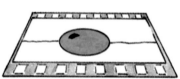

Red-Sensitive Layer of the Emulsion

1.7 This is a representation of how color negative film produces an image from a scene. (a) The original scene. (b) How each layer of the film records the colors. (c) How each layer responds to processing. (d) The final makeup of the color negative that is used to produce a color print.

(d) Final Negative

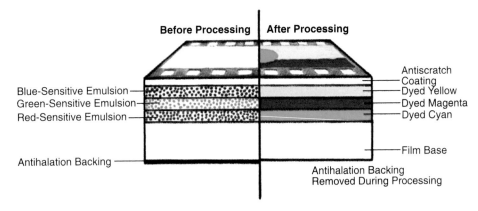

Before Processing | **After Processing**

Blue-Sensitive Emulsion
Green-Sensitive Emulsion
Red-Sensitive Emulsion

Antihalation Backing

Antiscratch Coating
Dyed Yellow
Dyed Magenta
Dyed Cyan

Film Base

Antihalation Backing Removed During Processing

1.8 A cross-section of a typical contemporary color film before and after processing.

process, the silver is removed from each of the three layers. This leaves an image created solely from the dyes in each of the three layers (figure 1.8). This is a significant difference from black-and-white films in which—in the latter case—the image is physically formed by clumps of silver in the emulsion. The

color film is then fixed, washed, and dried to produce a complete color image (see chapter 5 for details).

How Digital Cameras Record Color

One-shot digital-image capture, as in commonly used digital cameras, is also based on RGB. At this time a one-shot

sensor that cannot fully distinguish between colors usually captures image data. Therefore, most sensors use a color filter array, a pattern of RGB squares known as a mosaic filter, so each pixel is covered by a red, green, or blue filter. One common array is the Bayer pattern, invented at Kodak, in which 25 percent of the pixels are red, 25 percent blue, and 50 percent green. This formula favors the more sensitive green range of human vision by sacrificing the data in the red and blue ranges. To fill in the gaps of missing information, a computer-imaging program in the camera or host computer takes an average of the neighboring pixels, utilizing algorithms based on visual perception to fabricate an acceptable representation known as interpolation. Interpolation works because the eye is more sensitive to variations in luminance (brightness) than to variations in color. Using a scanner to

Images such as this remind us that color is a highly subjective experience and that photographic methods can offer expressionistic associations that are outside the boundaries of the Renaissance tradition of imitating nature through continuity in time and space.

© Robert Hirsch. *Thinking Elvis*, 1991. 16 x 20 inches. Gelatin-silver print with paint, colored pencil, and collage materials. Courtesy of CEPA Gallery, Buffalo, NY.

capture an image from film or a print provides more accurate and complete data because it makes multiple exposures, one for each RGB color, which limits it to recording still subjects. There are also cameras that make use of the multi-shot method.

Color Reality

Color has not always been synonymous with truth and reality. In the past Plato and Aristotle both attacked the use of color in painting because they considered color to be an ornament that obstructed the truth. Even the word color contains a snub against it. The Latin *colorem* is related to *celare*, to hide or conceal; in Middle English to color is to embellish or adorn, to disguise, to render specious or plausible, to misrepresent. Today most people prefer color pictures to black-and-white pictures. They claim that color photographs are more "real" than black-and-white photographs. This implies that people tend to confuse color photography and reality to an even greater extent than they do with black-and-white photographs. Many people have had the experience of someone pointing to an 8- x 10- inch color glossy and saying: "There's Mary. She sure looks good, doesn't she?" We know that it is not Mary, but it acts as a vivid reminder of how we expect photography to duplicate our reality for us. This expectation reveals an entire series of problems dealing with the construction of photographic color materials and our own powers of description and memory. The photographer and the audience must face these problems when working with color.

1.9 The complete spectrum is made up of all forms of electromagnetic energy. Only an extremely limited range of the entire spectrum, known as the visual spectrum or white light, can be detected by the human eye. When white light is broken up into its various wavelengths, the eye sees these wavelengths as separate colors.

Standards in Color

In all color processes, the final outcome hinges on how successfully the synthetic dyes replicate a "natural" color balance. Each film manufacturer makes emulsions that emphasize different color balances. Certain colors are overemphasized in some and in others their degree of saturation is exaggerated. While these colors may look good, they are not accurate, and there is a loss in delicate and subdued colors. There is *no standard*! Some films tend to create a cool, neutral, or even detached look. They emphasize blue and green. Other films give a warm look, favoring red and yellow. These colors seem more intense and vivid. The warmth tends to draw people in and create more involvement.

This lack of a standard color balance affects all color films, whether negative or slide films. The dyes simulate the look of reality, but they do not reproduce true colors. What you get is an interpretation of the scene. For this reason it is imperative that the photographer work personally with many of the available materials to find one that agrees with his or her personal color sense. By learning the characteristics of films, the photographer will also know what film works best in a given situation.

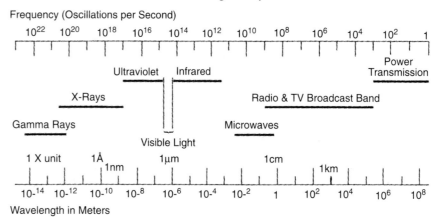

The Electromagnetic Spectrum

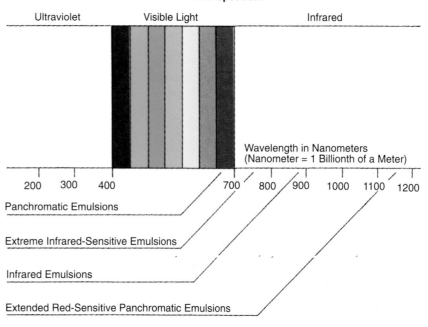

The Visible Spectrum

Talking about Color

Have you ever noticed how few words there are in the English language to describe colors? Some languages have up to 20 words to distinguish slight differences within one color. Without words to describe them, we have a very limited ability to see and distinguish subtle variations in color. Most people simply say a car is red. This covers a great deal of territory. A car dealer may call the same car "candy apple red." Neither term is an accurate description, nor does it give another person much sense of what we are attempting to describe. These vague generalizations cause problems translating into words what we see in pictures.

Color Description— Hue, Saturation, and Luminance

Each color can be defined by three essential qualities. The first is hue, which is the name of the color, such as blue or yellow. It gives the specific wavelength that is dominant in the color source. The second quality is saturation, or chroma, which indicates the apparent vividness or purity of a hue. The spectrum shows

perfectly saturated hues (figure 1.9). The narrower the band of wavelengths, the purer the color. Strong, vivid hues are referred to as saturated colors. Almost all colors we see are desaturated by a wider band of other wavelengths. When different wavelengths are present, the hue is said to be weaker, or desaturated.

The third quality of color is luminance, or brightness. Luminance deals with the appearance of lightness or darkness in a color. These terms are relative to the viewing conditions. They describe color as it is seen in individual situations.

Hue, saturation, and luminance can be applied to color description in any situation. Take as an example the specific hue of red, which has the longest wavelength of visible light. Mix it with a great deal of white light and it produces pink, which is desaturated red. Now paint this color on a building that is half in sunlight and half in shadow (figure 1.10). Each side of the building has the same hue and saturation, but each side has a different luminance. If a beam of sunlight strikes an object and makes a "hot spot," then that area is said to be desaturated since the color has been diluted with a large amount of white light. White is a hue with no saturation but has a high luminance. Black contains no

saturation and a very small amount of luminance.

Understanding these three basic concepts helps the photographer to translate what is seen by the eye into what will be recorded through photographic means. It also provides a common vocabulary of terms that we can employ in accurately discussing our work with others.

Color Relativity

Our perception of color is relative. Hue does not exist for the human eye without a reference. A room that is lit only by a red light will, after a time, appear to us as normal. Household tungsten lights are much warmer than daylight, yet we think color balance appears normal under these conditions. When a scene is photographed in tungsten light on a daylight color-balanced film, it will be recorded with an orange-red cast.

Stare at a white wall through a red filter. In time, your eyes will stop seeing the color. Now place an object of a different color into this scene. The red reappears along with the new color.

This point is important to remember when attempting to color balance prints. If you stare at the print too long, the color imbalances will appear correct.

1.10 This is an example of color description for red. Notice how this hue's saturation and luminance have been altered, producing a wide variety of color effects.

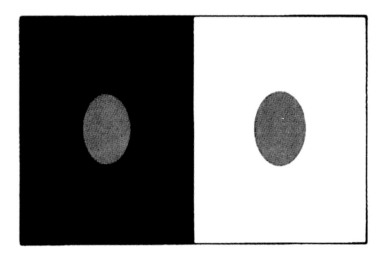

1.11 The circles in this illustration are the same color. The circle on the right appears to have a greater luminance than the circle on the left because both color luminance and saturation are subjective and dependent on the surrounding colors.

For this reason it is recommended that color-management software or a standard reference, such as the Kodak Color Print Viewing Filters with a piece of white paper, be used for determining color balance (see chapter 6, page 124).

The color luminance and saturation of an object within a scene appear to change depending on the colors surrounding it. A simple experiment can be performed to see how luminance is relative. Cut two circles from a piece of colored paper. Put one of the circles in the center of a bigger piece of black paper and the other on a piece of white paper (figure 1.11). The circle on the black paper will seem to have a greater luminance than the circle on the white paper, demonstrating how color luminance and saturation are subjective and dependent on the surrounding colors.

This phenomenon, also called simultaneous contrast, will cause the hue and brightness of a color to change. For example, a gray circle will appear yellowish on a purple background, reddish on a green background, and orange on a blue background.

Color Contrast

Color contrast happens when complementary colors, opposite colors on the color wheel, appear next to each other in the picture (figure 1.12). Blue next to yellow is an example. The appearance of great contrast is given, even if the color intensity is identical.

The human eye helps to create this impression. Every color has a different wavelength of light. Blue has the shortest wavelength and red the longest. When two primary colors appear next to each other, the eye cannot properly process the color responses. Thus, the colors appear to vibrate, creating contrast. Contrast is the major element that influences balance and movement in a composition. In color photography, unlike in black-and-white photography, contrast does not depend solely on light reflectance.

Color Harmony

Color harmony is a product of both reflected light and the relationship of the colors to each other on the color wheel. A low-contrast picture has colors that are next to each other on the color wheel (figure 1.13). These harmonious colors

1.12 Color contrast is created when complementary colors (opposite colors on the color wheel) appear next to each other. This presents the appearance of greater contrast, even if the color intensity is the same. The closer the colors are to each other on the color wheel, the less color contrast will be produced.

© Roger Camp. *The Race,* 1985. Variable dimensions. Dye-destruction print.

was always disagreement. To Albers this indicated that we have a short color memory span. Albers's book will help you gain a deeper understanding of how color interacts with our perceptions.

Color Deceives

To begin to see and use color effectively, it is first necessary to recognize the fact that color continually deceives us. It is possible for one color to appear as two different colors. In figure 1.14, the two halves of the circle are the same color, yet the human eye does not see them as the same.

This tells us that one color can and does evoke many different readings depending on the circumstances, which indicates that it is necessary to experience color through the process of trial and error. Patience, practice, and an open mind are needed to see the instability and relativity of color. Observation will reveal the discrepancy between the physical fact of color perception and its psychological effect. In any scene there is a constant interplay between the colors themselves and between the viewer and his or her perceptions of the colors.

1.13 In this image of a fictional archaeological dig, Nagatani simulates the subtle sense of New Mexico's desert environment color harmony by using colors that are next to each other on the color wheel. Dealing with issues of archaeology, history, the culture of the automobile, and how a photograph is considered to be a window on the real, Nagatani explores the elements of archaeological evidence and questions how scientific discourse and the photographic record claim to hold the truth.

© Patrick Nagatani. *BMW, Chetro Ketl Kiva, Chaco Canyon, New Mexico, U.S.A.*, 1998. 17 3/4 x 22 7/8 inches. Chromogenic color print. Courtesy of the Andrew Smith Gallery, Sante Fe, NM.

Color Changes

Colors are in a continuous state of change, depending on their relationship to their neighboring colors and lighting and compositional conditions. The following sections provide a series of visual examples that reveal the flux of color.

can reflect greatly varying amounts of light yet still not provide as much visual contrast as complementary colors with closer reflectance values.

In color photography contrast is the result of the amount of light reflected, the colors present, and the relationship of the colors on the color wheel. Complementary colors create a higher contrast and more vibrancy. Harmonious colors produce a more placid scene with lower contrast.

have a poor memory for color. Albers asked an audience to visualize a familiar color, such as the red on the Coca-Cola logo. Then he showed different shades of red and asked the audience to pick which one was "Coca-Cola red." There

1.14 The two halves of the circle are the same color, yet the human eye does not see them as the same color. This phenomenon is an example of color relativity.

Color Observations

Color Memory

Josef Albers, who wrote *Interaction of Color* (1963), discovered that people

Subtraction of Color

In figure 1.15 the two circles in the centers of the rectangles appear to be the same color. To get the best comparison, do not look from the center of one to the center of the other but at a point midway between the two. The small, elongated semicircles at the top and bottom of the figure show the actual colors of the circles in the rectangles. The circle on the white ground is an ocher yellow, while the one on the green ground is a dark ocher. This shows that any ground subtracts its own color from the hues that it possesses.

Experiments with light colors on light grounds indicate that the light ground subtracts its lightness in the same manner that hue absorbs its own color. The same is true for dark colors on a dark ground. This indicates that any diversion among colors in hue or in the light–dark relationship can be either visually reduced or obliterated on grounds of equal qualities.

The conclusion is that color differences are caused by two factors, hue and light, and in many instances by both at the same time.

Afterimage

Stare steadily at the marked center of the green circle in figure 1.16 for a minimum of 30 seconds, then rapidly shift your focus to the center of the white circle. Red or light red will appear instead of white. This example reveals how color can appear differently from what it physically is.

Eye Fatigue: Bleaching

Why does this happen? No one knows for certain, but one theory is that the nerve endings of the human retina, the cones and the rods, are set up to receive any of the three primary colors, which in turn make up all colors. This theory implies that by staring at green, the blue- and red-sensitive parts of the eye become fatigued, causing the complement, red,

1.15 The subtraction of color shows how two different colors can be made to look the same.

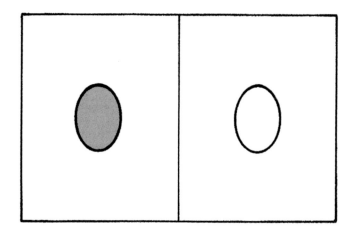

1.16 Look steadily at the circle on the left for 30 seconds, then look immediately at the circle on the right. Do you see the afterimage? In an afterimage a color may appear to be different than it is in reality.

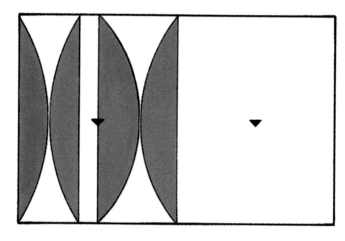

1.17 Stare steadily at the black inverted triangle on the left, then quickly shift your focus to the inverted triangle on the right. In the reversed afterimage the white areas of the original will appear as blue and the blue areas as pale orange.

to be visible. When the eye quickly shifts to white, which is the combination of blue, red, and green, only red is seen, due to the fatigue. Thus red, which is the complement of cyan, is the color seen.

Another theory is that the photopigments of the retina are bleached by bright light. This bleaching process (which is not understood) stimulates the nerves and it takes time for the photo-

chemical to return to normal. When a region of photopigment is bleached, this part of the retina is less sensitive than its surrounding regions and produces visual afterimages.

Reversed Afterimage

Stare at the blue figures with a black inverted triangle in the center in figure

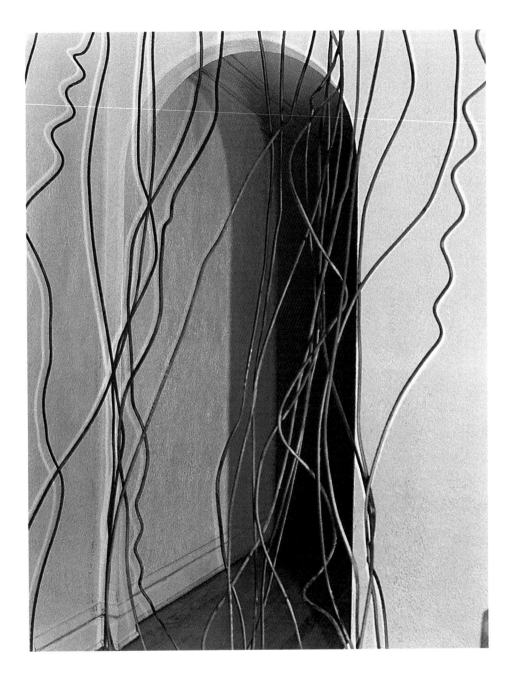

1.18 To create the effect of seeing an afterimage, Minnix first made a straight color print that was used as a paper negative in the making of the final image. This was accomplished in the following manner. A new sheet of color paper was exposed to the original negative in the enlarger for a predetermined time. This paper was left in the easel. The first straight print was then laid over the top of this newly exposed print. The enlarger was turned on for a brief time with the straight print lined up with, and then slightly offset from, the projected image. The negative was then removed and replaced by a clear orange negative mask. A brief exposure was made through the paper negative (the straight print) onto the paper in the easel. This created a light exposure of the image in reversed tone and negative color.

© Gary Minnix. *Untitled*, 1985. 24 x 20 inches. Chromogenic color print.

deceived by color. The conclusion is that colors cannot be seen independently of their illusionary changes by the human eye (figure 1.18).

Cooking with Color

Learning to work with color has many similarities to learning how to cook. A good recipe is no guarantee of success; the secret is often in preparation. The cook must constantly sample, taste, and make adjustments. The colors in a scene can be thought of as the ingredients that make up the picture; their arrangement and mixture will determine the final result. Two cooks can start off with the same ingredients yet produce a completed dish that tastes quite different. Simply by making small changes in quantity, one of the ingredients will lose its identity while another dominates. Cooking teaches that a successful meal involves more than reading a recipe. The same holds true for the photographer. Changes in color placement within a composition cause shifts in dominance, which can alter the entire feeling or mood of the picture. Also remember that properly presented food/photographs show that the cook/photographer has thought about every stage of the dining/visual experience and set the psychological stage for the diner's/viewer's response.

1.17 for at least 30 seconds, then quickly shift your focus to the square on the right. Instead of seeing the afterimage of the blue figures in their complement, the leftover spaces will predominate, being seen in blue. This double illusion is called reversed afterimage, or contrast reversal.

Positive Afterimage

When the eye has been "adapted" to a bright light (a light bulb viewed with the eye held steady or an electronic flash) a dark shape, of the same form as the adapting light, appears to hover in space near the light source. This floating shape appears dark when seen against a light-colored background. It may appear very bright during the first few seconds, especially if it is viewed in darkness. This is known as positive afterimage and is caused by the continuing firing of the retina and optical nerve after stimulation.

The phenomena of afterimage, reversed afterimage, and positive afterimage show us that the human eye, even one that has been trained in color, can be

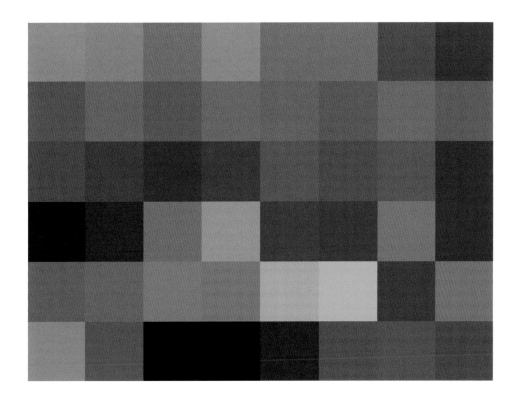

Color Is a Personal Experience

Learning about color is a step-by-step process of observation, memory, and training that teaches us that seeing is a creative process involving the entire mind. What is ultimately learned is that color continues to be private, relative, elusive, and hard to define. Our perception of color is hardly ever as it actually appears in the physical world. There are no standard rules because of mutual influences colors have on one another. We may know the actual wavelength of a certain color, but we hardly ever perceive what the color physically is. Although a group of people may be simultaneously looking at the same color, there is no way to know how each individual actually perceives the color.

In photography this problem is compounded by the fact that the registration and sensitivity of the retina in the human eye is not the same as that of photographic materials. In the world of human vision, colors are busily interacting with each other and altering our perceptions of them. This interaction or interdependence keeps colors in an active state of flux, and in spite of attempts to organize color, color remains unruly.

References

ALBERS, JOSEF. *Interaction of Color,* rev. ed. New Haven and London: Yale University Press, 1987.

ARNHEIM, RUDOLF. *Art and Visual Perception: A Psychology of the Creative Eye,* 2nd ed. Berkeley: University of California Press, 1974.

GREGORY, RICHARD L. *Eye and Brain: The Psychology of Seeing,* 5th ed. Princeton: Princeton University Press, 1997.

ITTEN, JOHANNES. *The Elements of Color.* New York: John Wiley & Sons, 1970.

LAMB, TREVOR AND JANINE BOURRIAU, eds. *Colour: Art and Science,* Cambridge: Cambridge University Press, 1995.

ROCK, IRVIN. *Perception.* New York: Scientific American Books, 1984.

VON GOETHE, JOHANN WOLFGANG. *Theory of Colours.* Cambridge, MA: MIT Press, 1970.

Endnotes

[1] For detailed information about the effects of losing the sensation of color see OLIVER SACKS, "The Case of the Colorblind Painter," *An Anthropologist on Mars: Seven Paradoxical Tales.* New York: Knopf, 1995, 3–41.

1.19 By studying the work of master photographers it is possible to gain insight into their sensitive handling of color relationships.

© Eliot Porter. *Waterfall Hidden Passage, Glen Canyon, Utah,* 1962. Dye Transfer print. Courtesy of Amon Carter Museum, Fort Worth, TX.

---

a s s i g n m e n t

Study the works of the visual masters of color to gain an artistic understanding of what they knew about color relationships and how they applied them (figure 1.19). This is not done to copy, compete, or revive the past. The aim of any study is to understand history and create new work that reflects present-day concerns, directions, and ideas.

Chapter Two

A Concise History of Color Photography

Gursky's super-formalistic and hyper-detailed images fit the Stephen Shore mold cast by MOMA in the 1970s by its former photography curator John Szarkowski. The major difference is that today a computer is used to imitate reality, resulting in a picture that appears more real than reality. Peter Galassi, MOMA's current photography curator, who trained under Szarkowski, declares Gursky's large-scale hybrids as finally giving photography the quality to compete with painting. Gursky's premeditated Olympian-sized spectacles of color and pattern present subjects not as they are, but as we think they should be. The gigantic work continues the belief in photographic detail, whose fundamental premise is that more information is good because clarity is the way we build our truths and it represents how we want to see the world. Gursky maintains the position that photography is best suited to be a cataloger of outward appearances because detail is emblematic of truth.

© Andreas Gursky. *99 Cent,* 1999. 81½ x 132 ⅝ inches. Chromogenic color print. Courtesy of Matthew Marks Gallery, New York, NY.

The First Color Photographs: Applied Color Processes

To understand what is happening in color photography today it is beneficial to know what has been accomplished. The quest for color photography can be traced to Louis-Jacques-Mandé Daguerre's 1839 public announcement of his daguerreotype, a finely detailed, one-of-a-kind, direct-positive photographic image, produced through the action of light on a silver-coated copperplate. Daguerreotypes astonished and delighted, but nevertheless people complained that the images lacked color. As we see the world in color, others immediately began to seek ways to overcome this deficiency. Not surprisingly, the first colored photographs made their appearance that same year. The color was applied directly on the daguerreotype's surface by hand (figure 2.1).

In the United States, four major methods were employed in the coloring of daguerreotypes: (1) applying paint directly to a gilded (gold-toned for appearance and stability) daguerreotype; (2) applying a transparent protective varnish over the plate, then hand coloring with paints; (3) applying transparent colors to specific areas of the image and fixing them by passing an electrical current through the plate with the aid of a galvanic battery; and (4) heating the back of the plate with a spirit lamp, instead of a battery, to fix colors that were selectively applied to the front of the plate.

By 1843 John Plumbe Jr. of Boston was advertising that his chain of six galleries in the Northeast could make colored daguerreotypes. Despite such rapid initial progress, it would take nearly a hundred years of research and development to perfect the rendition of color through purely photographic means.

Direct Color Process: First Experiments

In 1840 Sir John Herschel, renowned British astronomer and also the originator of many seminal ideas in photography, reported being able to record blue, green, and red on silver chloride-coated paper. These three colors corresponded to the rays of light cast on the paper by a prismed solar spectrum. Herschel's work suggested that color photographs could be made directly from the action of light on a chemically sensitive surface. Herschel was unable, however, to fix the colors on the coated paper. They could only be looked at very briefly under lamplight before they darkened into blackness. Other experimenters, including Edmond Becquerel in the late 1840s and early 1850s and Niépce de

Saint-Victor in the 1850s and 1860s, attempted to record colors directly on daguerreotypes. This was done through a process called Heliochromy, referencing the sun and color, which did not make use of any filters or dyes. Although the colors did not fade by themselves, Niépce de Saint-Victor never found a method to permanently fix them. When exposed to direct light, without a protective coating, they quickly turned gray.

Heliochromy: A Secret Direct Color Process

In early 1851 Levi Hill, a Baptist minister from Westkill, New York, announced a direct color process by which he was able to produce permanent color images (figure 2.2). Hill's announcement created quite a stir and temporarily brought the daguerreotype portrait business to a halt, since the public decided to wait for the arrival of the new color process. Everyone was clamoring to know how Hill had achieved this miracle. The public waited but nothing was forthcoming from Hill, and he was roundly denounced as a fake. Five years later, Hill finally published, by advance subscription, his method in *A Treatise on Heliochromy* (1856). It was a rambling tale of his life and experiments that did not contain any workable instructions for his secret process of making color photographic images. He did say the method was based on the use of a new developing agent (never stated) in place of mercury. At the time, the process was dismissed as a hoax that Hill had carried out by cleverly hand coloring his daguerreotypes. Just before his death in 1865, Hill still claimed to have made

color photographic images, but said he had done so by accident. He stated that he had spent the last 15 years of his life attempting to repeat this accidental combination without success. Recently there has been new scientific evidence suggesting that Hill may have stumbled onto a direct color process.[1]

The Additive Theory: First Color Photographic Image

The first true color photographic image was made in 1861 by James Clerk Maxwell, a Scottish scientist. Maxwell used the additive theory developed by Thomas Young and refined by the German scientist Hermann Helmholtz. The additive theory was based on the principle that all colors of light can be mixed optically by combining in different proportions the three primary colors of the spectrum: red, green, and blue (RGB). Just two primary colors can be mixed in varying proportions to produce many colors of light. For example, a mixture of the right proportion of green

and red light produces yellow. When all three of these primary colors of light are combined in equal amounts the result is white light (figure 2.3). When white light is passed through a primary-colored filter of red, green, or blue, the filter transmits only that particular color of light and absorbs the other colors. A red filter transmits red light, while absorbing all the other colors, which are combinations of green and blue light.

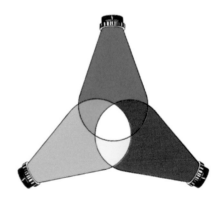

2.3 In the additive process separate colored beams of red, green, and blue light are mixed to form any color in the visible spectrum. When the three additive primaries are mixed in equal proportions, they appear as white light to the human eye.

Maxwell's Triple Projection Process

Making use of this theory, Maxwell made three separate black-and-white negatives of a tartan plaid ribbon through three separate blue-violet, green, and red filters. Black-and-white positives were made from the three negatives. These positives were projected in register (the three images perfectly coinciding) onto a white screen, each from a different projector. Each slide was projected through the same colored filter that was used to make the original negative. For example, the positive originally photographed through the green filter was projected through the green filter. When all three positives were simultaneously projected, the result was a projected color image (not a photograph) of the multicolored ribbon (figure 2.4). Maxwell's demonstration not only proved the additive color theory, but it also provided a method, known as the triple projection process, for producing photographic color images.

Later scientific investigation revealed that Maxwell's photographic emulsions were not capable of recording the full visible spectrum (neither orthochromatic—sensitive to all colors except red and deep orange—or panchromatic—sensitive to red, green, blue, and ultraviolet—emulsions had been invented). The experiment should have failed. The emulsion Maxwell used was not sensitive to red and only slightly sensitive to green. It took scientists a century to figure out why Maxwell's experiment worked with an emulsion that was not sensitive to all the primary colors. It turned out that Maxwell's experiment succeeded because of two other deficiencies in the materials that canceled out the effect of the nonsensitive emulsion: (1) the red dye of the ribbon reflected ultraviolet light that was recorded on the red negative, and (2) his green filter was faulty and let some blue light strike the plate. Both of these defects corrected for the lack of sensitivity of the emulsion to

red and green light. When done with today's panchromatic emulsions, sensitive to all the colors of the spectrum, Maxwell's method proves to be theoretically sound. This proves his experiment was theoretically sound. However, the first true panchromatic emulsions, which had their sensitivity extended through the use of dyes, did not become commercially available until the twentieth century.

Interference Method of Gabriel Lippmann

Sir Isaac Newton observed that colors could be produced by interference when a very thin film of air or liquid separates two glass plates. If a slightly convex surface of glass is placed on a flat surface, a thin film around the point of contact will produce colored circles known as Newton's rings. Also, the colors in certain beetles, birds, and butterflies, as well as the tints in mother-of-pearl and soap bubbles, are the result of the interference phenomena and not due to actual pigments. Another common example of this can be seen in gasoline or oil on a wet road.

In 1891 the French physicist Gabriel Lippmann introduced a color process based on wavelength interference principles that did not use dyes, pigments, or colorants, which gives the process excellent archival properties. Lippmann made color photographs by using a panchromatic emulsion and a mercury mirror that reflected waves of light, in a manner similar to how color is produced on oil slicks. In the camera, the emulsion plate was placed in contact with a mirror of liquid mercury, facing away from the lens. Light traveled through the plate and was reflected by the mercury, producing a latent image of the interference pattern on the plate. The plate was developed and the faint color image could be viewed by illuminating the plate with diffuse light from the side where the viewer was positioned. The light was reflected off the surface (emulsion side)

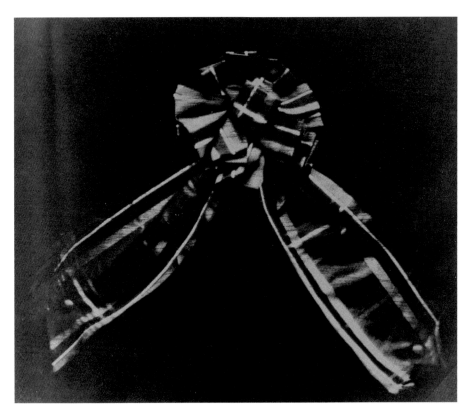

2.4 James Clerk Maxwell made the first true color photograph in 1861. Maxwell's success proved the additive color theory and provided the first path for the creation of a true color photographic process.

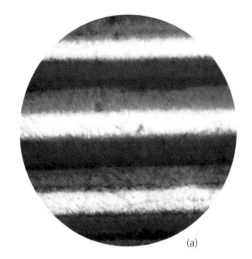
(a)

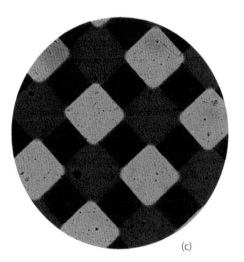
(b)

(c)

2.5 These photomicrographs of (a) Joly Color, magnified 20x, (b) Autochrome, magnified 50x, and (c) Finlay Colour, magnified 50x, allow a direct visual comparison of how each of these additive screen processes constructed a color image.

Courtesy of George Eastman House.

of the plate. In order to separate the directly reflected light from the light reflected from the recorded fringes in the emulsion, a glass wedge or prism was cemented on top of the emulsion. Although the colors could be surprisingly true, the process was impractical for general commercial use because it required scientific precision, extremely long exposure times, and complex viewing methods. The process, for which Lippmann won the Nobel Prize, is also considered to be a cornerstone for the future development of holography.

Additive Processes

In 1869 Louis Ducos du Hauron, a French scientist, published *Les Couleurs en Photographie—Solution du Probleme*, which anticipated most of the theoretical underpinning methods for making color photographs. Among the methods he proposed was one in which the additive

theory could be used to make color photographs in an easier manner than the method Maxwell had devised. He speculated that a screen ruled with fine lines in the primary colors (red, green, and blue) would act as a filter to produce a color photograph with a single exposure instead of three, as were needed in Maxwell's experiment (figure 2.5). Simultaneously, Charles Cros independently demonstrated how color images could be made using three-color separation negatives and positives.

Joly Color

In 1894 John Joly, a Dublin physicist, patented the first line-screen process for additive color photographs, based on Ducos du Hauron's idea. In this process, a glass screen with transparent ruled lines of blue, green, and red, about 200 lines per inch, was placed against the emulsion of an orthochromatic plate (not sensitive to red light). The exposure was

2.6 Joly Color, the first commercial line-screen process for additive color photographs, was introduced to the public in 1896. Although it had only limited success, it indicated that the additive method could become a commercially viable way of making color photographs.

Unidentified photographer, Irish (?). *Stuffed Birds,* circa 1895. 4 x 5 inches. Joly Color. Courtesy of George Eastman House.

made and the screen was removed. The plate was processed and contact-printed on another plate to make a positive black-and-white transparency. This was placed in exact register with the screen used to make the exposure. The final result was a limited-color photographic transparency that was viewed by transmitted light. This method was introduced in 1896 as the Joly Color process (figure 2.6). It enjoyed only a brief success, because it was expensive and the emulsions that were available were still not sensitive to the full range of the spectrum, so that the final image was not able to achieve the look of "natural" color. However, Joly's work indicated that the additive screen process could be a commercially practical way to make color photographs.

Autochrome

In Lyon, France, Auguste and Louis Lumière, the inventors of the first practical motion-picture projector, patented a major breakthrough in the making of color photographs in 1904. Autochrome was their improved and modified additive screen process. In the Autochrome system, a glass plate was dusted, in a random fashion, with microscopic grains of potato starch that had been dyed red-orange, green, and blue-violet. A fine powder of carbon black was used to fill in any spaces that would otherwise allow unfiltered light to pass through this filter screen, eliminating the need for colored lines to act as filters. A newly developed panchromatic emulsion, which greatly extended the accuracy of recording the full range of the visible spectrum, was then applied to the plate. With a deep yellow filter in front of the camera lens, the exposure was made with the filter layer pointed toward the lens, so that the plate with the dyed potato starch acted as tiny filters. The plate was then developed, re-exposed to light, and finally redeveloped to form a positive transparency made up of tiny dots of the primary colors. The Autochrome was a new method of utilizing the principle articulated by Ducos du Hauron and Charles Cros, in which the eye mixed the colors in a fashion much like George Seurat's pointillist painting *Sunday Afternoon on the Island of La Grande Jatte* (1884–86), to make a color-positive image (figure 2.7). Alfred Stieglitz sang its praises in *Camera Work*, Number 20, October 1907: "Color photography is an accomplished fact. The seemingly everlasting question whether color would ever be within the reach of the photographer has been definitely answered. … The possibilities of the process seem to be unlimited. … In short, soon the world will be color-mad, and Lumiére will be responsible."

Autochrome was successfully used from 1907 to 1932, though it did have its limitations. Autochromes were often dark due to the habitual underexposure caused by the density of the potato starch grains. Since the light had to travel through this filter, exposure times were longer than with black-and-white films. In all the additive processes, it was not uncommon for 75 percent or more

2.7 Meys was known as the "photochromist" because of his artistic and technical abilities, which enabled him to use "special effects" to create artistic and moody compositions. Meys can be considered a forerunner of modern multimedia presentations with his image projections that were done to poems and even to singing and dancing.

Marcel Meys. *Rocky Coastline at Night*, circa 1908. 4 ¼ x 3 ½ inches. Autochrome. Courtesy of Mark Jacobs Collection.

of the light to be absorbed by the filters before reaching the film. Recommended starting exposure time was between one-fifth and one second at f/4 in direct sunlight at midday in the summer and six times longer on a cloudy day, although over time there were many suggestions on how to increase the plate's sensitivity. When they were marketed in New York (circa 1910), a box of four 3 ¼- x 4-inch plates cost $1.20 and a box of 7- x 14-inch plates sold for $7.50, making them pricey for an average working person.

The randomly applied potato grains tended to bunch up in places, creating blobs of color. Also, Autochromes that were not made for lantern projection were difficult to see and were generally looked at in specially designed viewers called diascopes (figure 2.8).

The advantages of this process, however, were numerous. Autochromes could be used in any regular plate camera with the addition of a special yellow-orange filter; the image was made in one

2.9 The marketing of the Autochrome plate in 1907 offered serious amateurs such as Charles C. Zoller of Rochester, New York, who often projected his Autochromes to audiences, the opportunity to make their own color snapshots of vernacular scenes.

© Charles C. Zoller. *World War I Support Parade,* circa 1918. 3 ¼ x 4 inches. Autochrome. Courtesy of George Eastman House.

2.8 Autochromes were difficult to see and were often looked at in specially designed viewers called diascopes. The 13th edition of the instruction booklet *Color Photography with Autochrom* [sic] *Plates* stated: "Diascopes are reflectors so arranged that the light first passes through the picture, which is then reflected into a mirror. When closed they **fold like a book** and protect the picture; when open they are neat and **decorative** as a table ornament. They are made for either **upright** or **landscape** (horizontal) pictures." The image in the diascope is 5- x 4- inch autochrome by an unknown photographer.

Diascope No. 1, circa 1908. 7 x 6 x 1 ½ inches (flat). Folding door style covered in black leather with a mirror. Unidentified photographer. *Girl with Flowers,* circa 1912. 5 x 4 inches. Autochrome. Courtesy of Mark Jacobs Collection.

exposure, not in three; the cost was not overly prohibitive; it gave serious amateurs access to color (figure 2.9); and while the colors were not accurate by today's standards, they did produce a friendly, warm, soft, pastel image that was considered to be quite pleasing.

World War I was the first major conflict to be covered in color. Autochromes became the basis for publications such as *L'Histoire Illustrée de la Guerre de 1914* (figure 2.10). By the end of World War I, magazines such as *National Geographic* were using Autochromes to make color reproductions for the first time. Between 1914 and 1938, *National Geographic* published a reported 2355 Autochromes, more than any other journal, thus taking

Les Champs de Bataille de la Marne

20
photographies
en couleurs
par fascicule

❧

N° 8

Le 1er et le 15
de chaque mois

Récit
technique
et
documenté

❧

1 franc

Le 1er et le 15
de chaque mois

Photographies directes en Couleurs
et TEXTE de GERVAIS-COURTELLEMONT

(Les illustrations de cet ouvrage sont faites directement d'après des plaques autochromes et non d'après des photographies coloriées)

Le plus bel ouvrage publié sur la Guerre : **240** photographies en couleurs. Complet en **12** livraisons

L'EDITION FRANCAISE ILLUSTREE

2.10 World War I (1914–18) was the first major conflict to be photographed in color. It saw 65 million people under arms, and produced about 10 million dead and another 20 million wounded without a single decisive battle. This image was made as part of series of 240 autochromes that appeared in one of the earliest books published in color chronicling the Battle of Marne, one of the bloodiest battles of the war.

Jules-Gervais Courtellemont. *Les Champs de Bataille de la Marne*, from *L'Histoire Illustrée de la Guerre de 1914*, 1915. 9 ½ x 13 inches. Color halftone from an autochrome.

2.11 This autochrome was published as *The Glass of Fashion in Hopi Land* in the June 1929 issue of *National Geographic* with the following caption: "Natural color photograph by Fred Payne Clatworthy. Few of the North American Indians attained as high a degree of civilization as did the cliff-dwelling tribes of the Southwest. Among these are the Hopi, a peace-loving people who are industrious, quick to learn, and have a well-developed sense of artistry. The blanket, beads, and silver belt worn by this brave are examples of their craftsmanship."

Fred Payne Clatworthy. *Hopi Man*, 1923. 5 x 7 inches. Autochrome. Courtesy of Mark Jacobs Collection.

a leadership role in bringing the "realism" of color photography into mass publication (figure 2.11). Autochrome was the first color process to get beyond the novelty stage and to be commercially successful. It cracked a major aesthetic barrier because it was taken seriously for its picture-making potentialities. This enabled photographers to begin to explore the visual possibilities of making meaningful photographs with color.

Finlay Colour Process and Paget Dry Plate

Other additive screen processes followed on the heels of Autochrome. Finlay Colour was an additive screen process patented by Clare L. Finlay of England in 1906 and introduced in 1908 as the Thames Colour Screen. This screen was made up in a precise checkerboard fashion of red, green, and blue elements, rather than in the random mosaic pattern used in Autochrome. This separate screen could be used with any type of panchromatic film or plate to make a color photograph. In 1909, the Thames Colour Plate was released, which contained an integral screen in which the screen and emulsion were combined to form a single plate. Both of these processes were abandoned after World War I, but improved versions were marketed under the name of Finlay Colour in 1929 and 1931 (figure 2.12). The Finlay Colour processes were to be the major rivals to Dufaycolor until the introduction of the subtractive materials in the mid-1930s.

G.S. Whitfield also obtained a patent in 1912 for screen-plates that were marketed by the Paget Dry Plate Company (figure 2.13). In 1920 it was renamed Duplex, but it was discontinued after a few years.

Dufaycolor

The French firm of Louis Dufay, beginning about 1910, made the Dioptichrome Plate. The process was improved and renamed Dufaycolor in the 1920s. Dufaycolor was produced as a roll film, which gave wider public access to color. Dufaycolor eventually became more popular than Autochrome because people preferred the structure of its screen. The screen was a mosaic of alternating blue-dye and green-dye squares that were crossed at right angles by a pattern of parallel red-dye lines. This design offered greater color accuracy and a faster emulsion; by the mid-1930s exposures of f /8 at 1/25 of a second on a sunny day were possible (figure 2.14). Dufaycolor was marketed until the 1940s. By this time, the quest for an easier to use process that would provide more realistic and natural colors brought about technical discoveries that made all the additive screen processes obsolete.

Polachrome

Between 1983 and 2002 Polaroid marketed Polachrome, an instant 35-mm color slide film, which could be used in any 35-mm camera and was based on additive-color, line-screen, positive-transparency film similar to Joly Color (see diffusion-transfer process later in this chapter, page 41). The film was inserted with an individual chemical pod into a small tabletop Polaroid AutoProcessor for processing.

Additive Enlargers

Today the additive method is occasionally employed in color printmaking. It is in limited use because the additive enlarger systems are more complex and expensive. To make a full-color print with the additive process, the enlarger is used to make three separate exposures, one through each of the three primary-colored filters. The blue filter is used first to control the amount of blue in the print, next the green filter is used to control the green content, and last the red filter is used to control the red in the picture. Some people prefer this additive technique, also known as tricolor printing. This is because it is relatively easy to make adjustments in the filter pack, with each filter controlling its own color.

2.12 *National Geographic* photographers such as Edwin Wisherd regularly used the reintroduced Finlay Colour process to illustrate their stories and continued to do so through the mid-1930s, when Kodachrome replaced all the screen plate processes.

© Edwin Wisherd. *Circus Performers,* circa 1932. Finlay Colour. Courtesy of Volkmar Wentzel Collection.

2.13 The modestly successful Paget color screen process used a regular mosaic color screen-plate. It was commercially available as the Finlay plate and Duplex Color Plate after 1929. Paget was one of the few additive color processes used for a brief time (circa 1912–14) to make paper reflection type prints.

Unidentified Photographer. *3 Flowers,* circa 1914. Paget process. Courtesy of Hugh Tifft Collection.

2.14 Dufaycolor, introduced in the 1920s, became the most popular of the additive screen processes because it was faster, had an improved screen that provided more realistic color and, since it was like cut film, was easier to use.

© J. Baylor Roberts. *Pennsylvania Boy Scouts at the World Jamboree in Washington, D.C.*, 1937. 5 x 7 inches. Dufaycolor. Courtesy of Volkmar Wentzel Collection.

Digital Enlargers

A major change in additive color printing is the use of digital enlargers in photo labs that continue to make chemical prints on silver halide paper. Instead of the older bulb-based printers, this combination of chemical-based color printing and digital imaging relies on rapid bursts of laser light in three colors—red, green, and blue—to expose the photographic paper. The laser light is bounced off a rotating six-sided mirror that reflects the light dots onto the paper. As the mirror turns, it draws a line across the paper in light, making extremely sharp images. These digital enlargers also have the advantage of high-speed scanners and the ability to work from a digital file, which allows each image to be analyzed by software that adjusts color, contrast, and exposure as needed. They also have facial recognition software for smoothing facial features so that every skin pore is not apparent. Other systems use LED light printers instead of lasers.

Television

The additive system is the ideal vehicle for color television since the set creates and then emits the light-forming picture. The color television tube has three electron guns, each corresponding to one of the additive primaries. These guns simulate red, blue, or green phosphors on the screen to create different combinations of the three primaries. This creates all the colors that form the images we see on the television set.

The Subtractive Method

Louis Ducos du Hauron not only proposed a method for making color photographs with the additive process in *Les Couleurs en Photographie*, but also suggested a method for making color photographs using the subtractive process.

The subtractive process operates by removing certain colors from white light while allowing others to pass. The modern subtractive primaries (magenta, yellow, and cyan) are the complementary colors of the three additive primaries (green, blue, and red). When white light is passed through one of the subtractive-colored filters it transmits two of the primaries and absorbs (subtracts) the other. Individually each subtractive filter transmits two-thirds of the spectrum while blocking one-third of it. For example, a magenta filter passes red and blue but

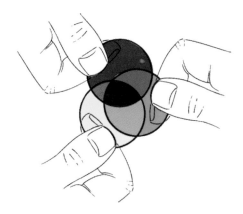

2.15 The subtractive process allows almost any color to be formed by removing certain colors from white light while permitting other colors to pass. The subtractive primary colors in photography are magenta, yellow, and cyan. They are the complementary colors of the additive primaries, green, blue, and red. Black is formed when equal amounts of all three of the subtractive primaries overlap.

blocks green. When two filters are superimposed, they subtract two primaries and transmit one. Magenta and yellow filters block green and blue, allowing red to pass. When all three subtractive primaries overlap in equal amounts, they block all the wavelengths and produce black. When they are mixed in varying proportions they are capable of making almost any color (figure 2.15). The advantages of the subtractive method over the additive process are twofold: a full-color reproduction on paper is possible, and it dispenses with the previous need for expensive and cumbersome viewing equipment.

Primary Pigment Colors

When working with pigments, as in painting, instead of light, the colors are also formed subtractively. The different colors of pigments absorb certain wavelengths of light and reflect others back for us to see. However, there is a major distinction between the primary pigment colors and those of light, with painters generally using red, blue, and yellow as their primary colors. These colors cannot be mixed from any other colors and in theory are used to make all the other colors with the assistance of black and

white. Red and yellow make orange, red and blue make purple, and blue and yellow make green. Green, an additive primary, cannot be used as a primary color in paint because it consists of two colors, blue and yellow. In practice, it is necessary to use secondary and intermediate colors, such as green and violet, because artist's pigment is not "pure color." The wavelengths of its minor components are different from the dominant wavelength and therefore affect the color produced.

The Assembly Process: Heliography

In Ducos du Hauron's patented subtractive method, known as Heliography, three separate negatives were made behind three separate filters. He used violet, green, and orange-red for his filters (the current modern subtractive filters had not yet been established). From these negatives, positives were made and assembled in register to create the final print, known as a Heliochrome. These positives contained carbon pigments of blue, red, and yellow, which Ducos du Hauron believed to be the complementary colors of the filters that were used to form the colors in the original exposure. Color prints or transparencies (figure 2.16) could be

made with the assembly process, depending on whether the carbon transparencies were attached to an opaque or transparent support. One of the first commercial subtractive assembly processes was the bichromated gelatin glue process, which was known as Tri-Chromatic or Tri-Cromie and was patented by the Lumière Brothers in 1895. The assembly process is the principle used in the carbro process (see chapter 16, page 340).

Though the subtractive process proved to be practical, it plagued photographers with long exposure times. Ducos du Hauron reported typical daylight exposures of one to two seconds with the blue-violet filter, two to three minutes with the green, and 25 to 30 minutes behind the red filter. If the light changed during the exposure process, the color balance would be incorrect in the final result. This problem was solved in 1893, when Frederick Eugene Ives perfected Ducos du Hauron's single-plate color camera.

The Photochromoscope Camera and Kromskop Viewer

Ives's apparatus, the Photochromo-scope camera, made three separate black-and-

2.16 In Louis Ducos du Hauron's Heliochrome process three separate negatives were made on black-and-white plates, using three separate subtractive filters. The negatives were used to make three positives, which were then superimposed to assemble a color photograph. The Heliography method was the first successful use of the subtractive process in the making of color photographs. The image on the left shows the transparency from the front. That on the right presents the transparency from the back, where the separation of the yellow layer of the assembly print can be seen.

© Louis Ducos du Hauron. *Stuffed Rooster and Parrot*, 1879. Assembly print. 8 ¼ x 8 ½ inches. Courtesy of George Eastman House.

2.17 The Kromogram was the name given to the transparencies used in the Ives Kromskop for projecting "photographs in natural colors."

Fredrick Ives. *Interior of Greenhouse*, No. 88, circa 1899. 10 ½ x 5 ¼ inches. Kromogram. Courtesy of Mark Jacobs Collection.

Carbro Process

In 1855 Alphonse Louis Poitevin patented a carbon process to make prints from photographic negatives and positives by using an emulsion containing particles of carbon or colored, nonsilver pigment to form the image. The original purpose of this process was not to make colored images but to provide a permanent solution to the fading and discoloration problems that plagued the early positive silver print processes. The carbro process, considered the most versatile of the carbon processes, evolved from Thomas Manly's Ozotype (1899) and Ozobrome processes (1905). The name carbro was given to an improved version of the process in 1919 by the Autotype Company to signify that carbon tissue was used in conjunction with a bromide print (car/bro).

Separation negatives were exposed through red, green, and blue filters and white negatives simultaneously on a single plate through blue-violet, green, and red filters. Positives were made by contact printing. The three glass positives were cut apart and placed on Ives's Kromskop viewer. This viewing system had the same type of colored filters as the camera and a system of mirrors that optically superimposed the three separations, creating a color Kromogram (figure 2.17). The completed color image could only be seen in this viewer (there was no actual object), hence it was called a direct viewing process. While Ives's methods did work, they were complex, time consuming, and expensive.

Numerous other one-shot cameras followed, such as the Sanger-Shepherd in the first decade of the twentieth century, which used black-and-white plates to simultaneously make three exposures through three separate color filters that were later combined to form a color image (figure 2.18). Improvements followed, and these one-shot cameras were used for advertising and portrait work until the advent of multilayered films like Kodachrome, Agfacolor, and Kodacolor.

2.18 Sanger Shepherd got involved in color photography as an assistant to Fredrick Ives. By the early part of the twentieth century, Shepherd was advertising his own spin-off process and camera. Shepherd continued to work on simplifying ways of making color photographs until his death in 1937.

Unidentified Photographer. *English Estate?* circa 1904. Sanger-Shepherd Process. Courtesy of Hugh Tifft Collection.

2.19 Muray was a highly accomplished commercial photographer and carbro printer. In addition to his advertising work, Muray did color celebrity portraits of people including Joan Crawford, Elizabeth Taylor, and Marilyn Monroe. This formally informal rooftop portrait uses color to capture the style, mystique, and allure surrounding Kahlo. The original photograph was a Kodachrome transparency in the Kodak Bantam format that was scanned and produced as a color carbon print.

© Nickolas Muray. *Frida Kahlo in New York,* 1946. 11 x 8 inches. Carbro print. Courtesy of the Nickolas Muray Photo Archives and Art & Soul Studio, Seattle, WA.

used to make a matched set of bromide prints. In the carbro process the image is formed by chemical action when the pigmented carbon tissue is placed face to face with a fully processed black-and-white print on bromide paper. When the print and the tissue are held in contact, the gelatin of the tissue becomes insoluble in water in proportion to the density of the silver on the bromide print. After soaking, this sandwich is separated. The tissue is transferred onto a paper support, where it is washed until only a pigment image remains. This is repeated for each of the three pigmented tissues, and the final print is an assemblage of cyan, magenta, and yellow carbon tissues in register, producing a full-color print. Autotype's tricolor carbro process produced splendid color prints from cyan, magenta, and yellow pigmented tissues. Using a bromide print created numerous advantages, including the following: (1) enlargements could be made from small-format negatives (figure 2.19); (2) ordinary exposure light sources could be used instead of high-intensity ultraviolet; (3) contrast was determined by the bromide print; and (4) regular photographic printing controls such as burning and dodging could be used. The perfecting of the carbro process demonstrated that it was possible to make full-color images from black-and-white materials and was an important step on the path toward a practical chromogenic method for making color images (see following section, Subtractive Film and Chromogenic Development, page 40). Other variations of this three-color subtractive assembly printing method, such as the affordable Vivex process (1931–39), followed (figure 2.20).

Color Halftones

The first color images to receive widespread viewing were not made by direct photographic means. They were created indirectly by applying the subtractive principles of color photography on William Kurtz's photoengraver's letterpress in New York in 1892. Using an early halftone process, a scene of fruit on a table was photographed, screened, and run through the press three times (a separate pass for each of the three subtractive colored inks—cyan, magenta, and yellow). The halftone process is a printing method that enables a photographic image to be reproduced in ink by making a halftone screen of the original picture. The screen divides the picture into tiny dots that deposit ink in proportion to the density of the original image tones in the areas they represent. These color reproductions were bound into the January 1, 1893, issue of *Photographische Mittheilungen*, published in Germany. Even though it was still not possible to obtain color prints from color film in an ordinary camera, this printing procedure pointed to a way in which color images could be photographically produced (figure 2.21).

2.20 Bauhaus master László Moholy-Nagy conducted experiments in color as part of his quest to find purely photographic forms of representation and urged investigation into "the new culture of light." He wrote: "This century belongs to light. Photography is the first means of giving tangible shape to light, though in a transposed and—perhaps just for that reason—almost abstract form."

© László Moholy-Nagy. *Study with Pins and Ribbons,* 1937–38. 13 ¾ x 10 ⅜ cm. Assembly (Vivex print). Courtesy of George Eastman House.

Dye-Imbibition Process/
Dye-Transfer Process

In the imbibition process, a dye image is transferred from a gelatin relief image to either a paper or film-receiving layer, usually of gelatin. Charles Cros described this method of "hydrotypie" transfer printing in 1880 and suggested it could be used to transfer three dye images in register. The Hydrotype (1881) and the Pinatype (1905) were examples of the early use of this process. One of the notable, but not widely used, relief matrix processes was developed by Dr. Arthur Traube and introduced as the Uvatype in 1929 (figure 2.22). This was an improved version of his earlier Diachrome process (1906) and the dye mordant Uvachrome process (1916). The widest commercial application of the imbibition process was the Technicolor process for producing motion-picture release prints. The Eastman Wash-off Relief process (1935) was a refinement of the imbibition process, until it was replaced by the improved Dye-Transfer process (1946–93).

2.21 Nickolas Muray asserted "Color calls for a new way of looking at people, at things, and a new way of looking at color." His 1931 illustration of models in beachwear for the *Ladies Home Journal* became the first color photograph to be published in a popular American magazine. Muray also produced color domestic scenes and portraits for the covers of *McCalls Magazine, Modern Screen Magazine,* and *Time* throughout the 1940s and 1950s.

© Nickolas Muray. *McCalls Magazine Cover,* 1939. 11 x 14 inches, approx. Carbro process. Courtesy of George Eastman House.

2.22 The Uvatype, developed by Dr. Arthur Traube, is an example of the imbibition process. In this method, a dye image is transferred from a gelatin relief image to a receiving layer of paper or film.

© Dr. Arthur Traube. *Female Nude,* circa 1920s. Uvatype. Courtesy of Volkmar Wentzel Collection.

Subtractive Film and Chromogenic Development

Between 1911 and 1914 Rudolph Fisher of Germany, working closely with Karl Schinzel of Austria, invented a color film that had the color-forming ingredients, known as color couplers, incorporated directly into it. This discovery, that color couplers could produce images by chromogenic development, laid the foundation for most color processes in use today. In this type of film, known as an integral tripack, three layers of emulsion are stacked one on top of another, with each layer sensitive to red, green, or blue.

Through a process known as chromogenic development, the color couplers in each layer of the emulsion form a dye image in complementary colors of the original subject. During chromogenic development, the dye image is made at the same time as the silver halide image is developed in the emulsion. The silver image is then bleached away, leaving only the dye, which is fixed to form the final image. The problem with this tripack film was that unwanted migration of the dyes between the three layers could not be prevented, causing color inaccuracies in the completed image.

Some black-and-white films, such as Ilford's XP2 SUPER, also make use of this system to make various densities of black dye.

Kodachrome

In 1930 Kodak Research Laboratories hired Leopold Godowsky Jr. and Leopold Mannes, who had been experimenting with making color films in makeshift labs since they were teenagers. By 1935 they were able to overcome the many technical difficulties and produce the first truly successful integral tri-pack subtractive color reversal film. This film was called Kodachrome and was first marketed as a 16-mm movie film. It was said, only half jokingly, that it took God and man (Godowsky and Mannes) to solve the problem of the color couplers' unwanted migration between the emulsion layers. Their ingenious solution to this problem was to put the color couplers in separate developers during the processing of the film, rather than building them into the film emulsion itself.

In Kodachrome film, only one exposure was needed to record a latent image of all three primary colors. The top emulsion layer was sensitive only to blue. Under this was a temporary yellow-dye filter that absorbed blue light, preventing it from affecting the emulsion below. This temporary yellow filter, which dissolved during processing, allowed the green and red light to pass through and be recorded in the proper emulsions below.

The Kodachrome Process

Kodachrome was first developed into a negative and then, through reversal processing, into a positive. During the second development, the colors of the original subject were transformed into the complementary dyes of cyan, magenta, and yellow, which formed the final color image. Then the positive silver images were bleached away and the emulsion was fixed and washed. This left a positive color image that was made up only by subtractive-colored dyes, with no silver.

In 1936 Kodachrome was made for the 35-mm still photography market. Kodak was concerned that no one would want a tiny slide that had to be held up to the light to be seen. In a shrewd move, by 1938 Kodak was returning each processed slide in a 2- x 2-inch cardboard "Readymount" that could be projected onto a screen. At this time Kodak also introduced the Kodaslide project, re-invigorating the Victorian-era Magic Lantern slide exhibitions, which had been in decline. By the late 1930s the union of the small-format Leica camera with Kodachrome launched the modern color boom and signaled the end of the additive screen processes such as Autochrome.

Kodachrome was the first film to achieve the dream of an accurate, inexpensive, practical, and reliable method for making color photographs (figure 2.23). The major drawbacks of Kodachrome were its slow speed (its original ISO of 8 was eventually increased to 200), and its complex processing meant the film had to be sent to a special lab. Kodachrome's legendary characteristics, which were even commemorated in a popular song by Paul Simon, allowed it to reign as the benchmark in color accuracy, rendition, contrast, and grain until it finally succumbed to improved and much faster chromogenic films in 2001.

Chromogenic Slide Film

In 1936 Agfa released Agfacolor Neu film, which overcame the problem of migrating the color couplers by making their molecules very big. In this manner, they would mix easily with the liquid emulsion during the manufacturing of the film. Once the gelatin that bound them together had set, the color coupler molecules would become trapped in the tiny spaces of the gelatin and would be unable to move. This was the first three-layer, subtractive-color reversal film that had the color couplers built into the emulsion layers themselves and employed a single developer to make the positive image. This simplified process allowed the photographer to process the film. Kodak countered with its own version of the Agfacolor process in 1946, Ektachrome.

Chromogenic Negative Film

Agfa brought out a color negative film in 1939 from which positive color prints could be made directly on a special companion paper. Kodak followed suit in 1942 with Kodacolor. Kodacolor is considered to be the first subtractive color negative film that completely solved the problem of the color couplers migrating from layer to layer in the emulsion.

Kodacolor overcomes the limitation of each image being one of a kind since any number of positive prints can be made from a color negative film.

Chromogenic Negative Development

The processing method used for Kodacolor is, with many improvements, the basis for all color negative film processes utilized today (see chapter 6). In this process, currently called C-41, a single developer produces a negative silver image and a corresponding dye image in all three layers of the emulsion at the same time. Bleach is used to remove all the silver, leaving only the dye. The film is fixed, washed, and dried, which completes the process.

When making prints from a chromogenic negative with the subtractive method, the light is filtered in the enlarger before it reaches the negative. Correct color balance can thus be achieved in a single exposure. One of the three dye layers in the negative is usually left unfiltered. Printing is simplified because it is not necessary to use more than two filters at one time to make a print. The subtractive method also enables pictures to be made directly from slides in a reversal printing process such as Ilfochrome Classic.

2.23 The introduction of Kodachrome marked the modern era in color photography of accurate, reliable, affordable, and easy-to-use color films. Kodachrome gave a wider variety of photographers the ability to respond in color to subject matter from new points of view and to represent previously unseen subjects and situations.

Unidentified photographer. *Untitled*, circa 1936. 3 ¼ x 4 inches. Kodachrome. Courtesy of George Eastman House.

Other Color Processes

Silver Dye-Bleach: Dye-Destruction Process

The silver dye-bleach, also known as the dye-destruction process, is a method of making color prints from positives or negatives. Bleach is used to remove the unnecessary dyes from the emulsion, rather than using chromogenic development to produce dyes in the emulsion. This method was commercially introduced by Hungarian chemist Bela Gaspar as Gasparcolor in 1933 for color motion-picture work. Today's Ilfochrome Classic materials, introduced as Cibachrome in 1963, make use of this process to make

prints directly from transparencies (see chapter 6).

Internal Dye Diffusion-Transfer Process

Modern "instant" photography, or more accurately self-processing film, began in 1948 with the marketing of Edwin Land's first Polaroid process. In 1963 Polacolor, the first full-color peel-apart color print film that developed itself and produced a color print in 60 seconds was introduced. In 1976 Kodak launched its own line of instant products but 10 years later was forced to withdraw them when Polaroid won patent infringement suits against Kodak's design. Polaroid and Fuji collaborated on

a Fuji peel-apart instant film that was sold in Japan. By 1991, when many of the original Polaroid patents had expired, Fuji began selling this instant film in Europe.

Self-processing materials such as Polaroid use the internal dye diffusion-transfer process, often called the diffusion-transfer process. It operates by causing the dye-formers to transfer out of the negative emulsions layer(s) to a single receiving layer (also in the material), where the visual positive image forms. The three phases of the process—negative development, transfer, and positive development—happen simultaneously, so that the positive images begin to form almost immediately (see chapter 16, page 306).

(a)

Colors in the Original Scene

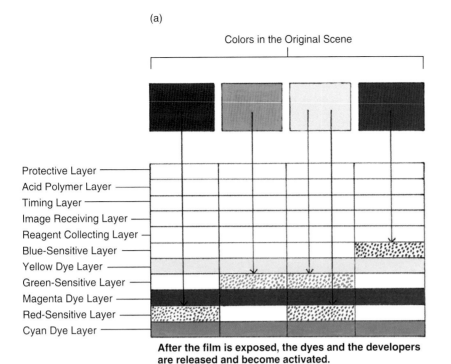

Protective Layer
Acid Polymer Layer
Timing Layer
Image Receiving Layer
Reagent Collecting Layer
Blue-Sensitive Layer
Yellow Dye Layer
Green-Sensitive Layer
Magenta Dye Layer
Red-Sensitive Layer
Cyan Dye Layer

2.24 Typical diffusion-transfer process: (a) Film exposure; dye developers begin to diffuse upward. (b) The exposed silver blocks upward diffusion of corresponding dyes. For example, the exposed blue-sensitive layer blocks the yellow dye. (c) The dyes not restrained by the silver continue diffusing upward to form the image.

After the film is exposed, the dyes and the developers are released and become activated.

(b)

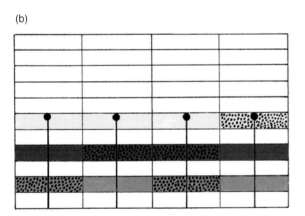

Exposed silver blocks upward diffusion of corresponding dyes. For example, exposed blue-sensitive layer blocks yellow dye.

(c)

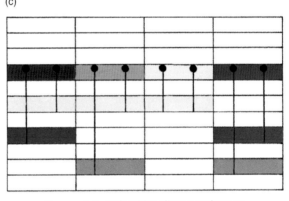

Dyes not restrained by silver continue to diffuse upward to form the image.

The Polaroid Process: Diffusion-Transfer

The Polaroid SX-70 camera and film, introduced in 1972, and the later Spectra camera and film called Time Zero, make use of the diffusion-transfer method (figure 22.4). After the shutter is pressed, the motor drive, which is powered by a battery in each film pack, automatically ejects the film through a set of rollers that break a pod of reagent located at the bottom of each piece of film. Development is then automatic and

requires no timing. The best results are obtained at about 75°F (24°C). If it is colder, the color balance can shift to the cool direction. Development can take place in daylight because the light-sensitive negative is protected by opaque dyes in the reagent. Both the positive and negative images are contained within each sheet of film.

As the picture forms, a number of things occur at once. First the silver halides are reduced to metallic silver in the exposed areas of each of the three additive primary light-sensitive layers. As this happens, the complementary

subtractive primary dye developers move through the layers of the negative and the opaque reagent to form a white background for the picture. Now the dye developers are prevented from moving up to the positive image area by the developing silver. This layer will now only pass certain colors through. For example, the blue layer blocks the yellow dyes but not the cyan and magenta. Within a few minutes all the dyes that have not been blocked travel through the white opaque layer and become visible. The process automatically completes and stabilizes itself, resulting in a com-

2.25 Levinthal creates an imaginary miniature world by placing this landscape on a screen through a video camera and then recording scenes from it on Polaroid SX-70 film.

© David Levinthal. *Modern Romance*, 1985. 3 ¼ x 3 ¼ inches. Diffusion transfer process. Courtesy of Paul Morris Gallery, New York, NY.

None but a very literal person would fail to see that color is his music, that there is melody line, counterpoint, harmony, dynamics, voicing, and phrasing all there for those who will listen. There is absolute pitch, too—absolute color pitch. As we looked at the dye-transfer prints in Porter's exhibit … we were quietly amazed by what this man knows about color.[3]

By the late 1960s, a few fine-art institutions and galleries had begun to recognize color photography as a legitimate way of working. A key breakthrough occurred when John Szarkowski, the curator of photography at the Museum of Modern Art, New York, presented the show *William Eggleston's Guide* in 1976 (figure 2.26). In the exhibition catalogue Szarkowski proclaimed the images to be "perfect: irreducible surrogates" of understated, vernacular views dealing with the social landscape of the New South. Others, like critic Hilton Kramer who called them "perfectly boring," saw them as overblown, trivial snapshots of the mundane that confronted viewers with an insipid emptiness. Nevertheless, the prohibition against color as too crass and commercial to be art had been cracked, granting photographers such as Joel Meyerowitz (figure 2.27) and Stephen Shore (figure 2.28) the freedom to begin to use color for its descriptive qualities. In his book *Cape Light* Meyerowitz said: "When I committed myself to color exclusively, it was a response to a greater need for description … color plays itself out along a richer band of feeling—more wavelengths, more radiance, more sensation. … Color suggests more things to look at [and] it tells us more. There's more content [and] the form for the content is more complex."[4] Today with digital cameras and desktop printers, color is ubiquitous.

pleted unique, dry print—which also made it acceptable to collectors in the art world (figure 2.25). The diffusion transfer process was also the basis for Polaroid's Polachrome, an additive color screen film.

Color Gains Acceptance in the Art World

Since the 1930s color photography was equated with advertising, while black-and-white photography was associated with both art and authenticity. This attitude is expressed in *Camera Lucida* (1980), where Roland Barthes wrote:

"color is a coating applied later on to the original truth of the black-and-white photograph. For me, color is an artifice, a cosmetic (like the kind used to paint corpses)."[2] But vast improvements in color film technology, especially in terms of rendition, film speed, and archival qualities, led more photographers to work with color in new and challenging situations. In turn, this produced a shift in attitudes about how and what color photography could communicate, as seen in Eliot Porter's *In Wildness Is the Preservation of the World* (1962). This seminal project was published by the Sierra Club, and in the preface the club's Executive Director, environmentalist David Brower, wrote:

Amateur Systems Propel the Use of Color

The 1963 introduction of the Kodak Instamatic with its drop-in film cartridge generated a tidal wave of amateurs mak-

2.26 The 1976 debut of *William Eggleston's Guide* at the Museum of Modern Art, New York, marked color photographs' entrée into the world of fine art. Critics of Eggleston claim he is a slumming aristocrat whose photographs are not worthy of a frame of film. His fans counter by saying he possesses the gift of being able to make photographs out of nothing. At his best the seemingly casual and dispassionate manner of his images masks his adroitness as a caustic yet affectionate memoirist of the banality and strangeness of everyday America, in which objects take on a personality and become portraits.

© William Eggleston. *Untitled*, from *Troubled Waters Portfolio*, 1980. 16 x 20 inches. Dye-transfer print. Courtesy of Cheim and Read, New York, NY.

ing color snapshots. This democratization of color led more professionals to work with it, as everyday people had come to expect color photographs. The photography industry has tried to duplicate this success with the creation of other formats such as the 110 in 1975, the Disk in 1982, and the Advanced Photo System (APS) in 1996. Designed for amateurs, APS film is about 40 percent smaller than 35 mm, which allows camera manufacturers to make less bulky cameras and lenses. The reduction in film size produces more visible grain in enlargements of 8 x 10 inches or greater. The APS format has a magnetic layer that allows a camera to record a variety of information linked to each frame; this includes format type (regular or panoramic), text, and exposure, and allows photo-finishing equipment to recognize and correct a photographer's errors. APS never took hold and now amateurs are going digital.

Digital Imaging

In 2002 CNET.com estimated that about 100 billion photographs were made, and that of these 25 percent were digital and almost all were in color. Computer images, like their sister analog images, are shaped by technology. Knowing the challenges early computer imagemakers faced can deepen appreciation of their work and provide a space to contemplate the evolution of the medium. Although the first electronic digital computers were built between 1937 and 1942, text and images had already been digitized and electronically transmitted for over 40 years by fax. Scottish physicist Alexander Bain created a proto facsimile machine in 1843, but it was not until 1902 that Arthur Korn demonstrated a practical photoelectric scanning facsimile. The system used light-sensitive elements to convert different tones of an image into a varying electric current. Using the same basic principles as those employed by scanners today, these early fax machines digitized an image by assigning the area a number such as "0" for white or OFF and "1" for black or ON. The fax then transmitted the signal via telephone lines to another facsimile receiver that made marks on paper corresponding to the area on the original image. Commercial use of Korn's system began in Germany in 1908 by means of two synchronized, rotating drums, one for sending and the other for receiving, which were connected via the telephone. An image was mounted on the sending drum, and scanned by a point light source that converted the image to electrical impulses that were then transmitted to the receiving unit. By 1910 Paris, London, and Berlin were all linked by facsimile transmission over the telephone network. Facsimile then made slow but steady progress through the 1920s and 1930s, and in 1935 the Associated Press introduced a wire photo service.

The Birth of Computing

The first electronic computers, such as Britain's Colossus of 1943, were used to decipher codes and calculate weapons trajectories. In 1946 the Electronic Numerical Integrator and Computer (ENIAC), the first large-scale, general-purpose electronic digital computer, was built in the United States. ENIAC weighed 30 tons, had 500 miles of wire, and used 18,000 vacuum tubes, which burned out at the rate of one every seven minutes.

2.27 The publication of Meyerowitz's *Cape Light* (1978) brought more widespread public interest to the art of color photography. His sincere, romantic 8- x 10-inch contact prints concentrating on the color of light and atmosphere were a radical departure from his often-ironic, black-and-white 35-mm street photography. Meyerowitz said: "Color suggests that light itself is a subject ... the work here on the Cape is about light. ... [Now] we have color and it tells us more. There's more content! The form for the content is more complex, more interesting to work with." [4]

© Joel Meyerowitz. *Long Nook Beach*, 1983. 8 x 10 inches. Chromogenic color print. Courtesy of Ariel Meyerowitz Gallery, New York, NY.

2.28 Shore's 8- x 10-inch recording of vernacular spaces radiates a sense of nostalgia for ordinary scenes that are fading out of existence. These shapely focused, familiar, peopleless scenes of the human-altered landscape were indicative of the New Topographics style of the mid-1970s and follow Shore's axiom "Attention to focus concentrates our attention." Shore's passive yet circumspect approach to atmosphere, color, and light contemplates the secular world with the utmost clarity and detail. His work was exhibited by the Museum of Modern Art in 1976 and thus was instrumental in the acceptance of color photography as an art form.

© Stephen Shore. U.S. 97, *South of Klamath Falls, Oregon, July 21, 1973*, 2002. 20 x 24 inches. Chromogenic color print. Courtesy of 303 Gallery, New York, NY.

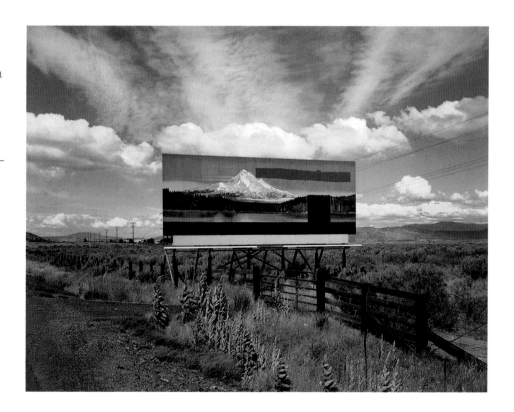

The computers of the early 1950s were room-sized machines marketed to the government, the military, and big business. Even though access to the machines was limited, early scientist-artists found ways to create art. In 1950 Ben F. Laposky made the first artistic electronic image, *Oscillon Number Four—Electron Abstraction*, which was an analog wave pattern photographed from an oscilloscope. In the mid-1950s Russell A. Kirsch and his colleagues at the National Bureau of Standards made a proto drum scanner that could trace variations in intensity over the surfaces of photographs. These recordings of light and shadow were converted into binary digits, but unlike the facsimile machines of the time this information was processable electronic digital information. Such activities reveal the unintended consequences that accompany new ideas, as it is doubtful that these scientist-artists, who were developing new technologies mainly for military applications, imagined that their work might one day revolutionize photography.

By 1957 IBM was marketing the disk drive, a stack of 50 disks that could store five million characters. By the end of the decade transistors made computers cheaper, smaller, faster, and more readily available. An important innovation for artists was the 1959 introduction of the first commercial ink output printing device, the plotter. Plotters used a pen that moved across a sheet of paper to draw lines. The pen was controlled by two motors that moved the pen on an x and y axis in a manner similar to an Etch-a-Sketch. Plotters could not draw curves, so images were composed of lines and broken curves and were generally black and white. Geometric shapes were the dominant visual language and compositions were frequently made up of rotated and scaled copies of themselves. Like the pioneering photographers had before them, scientist-artists looked to painting for inspiration, and many of these early computer artworks resembled Cubist and Constructivist art.

The 1960s: Art in the Research Lab

In the 1960s anyone wishing to create computer-generated artwork needed to either be a programmer or work closely with one. Working blind, unable to see their work until it was output, scientist-artists mathematically mapped out an image before beginning to work on the computer. Mathematical instructions were input into another computer using 4- x 7-inch punch cards that contained information to drive a plotter. It could take boxes of cards to represent a single image and if the image did not come out as planned, the whole process had to be repeated.

During the 1960s, NASA developed digital technology for recording and transmitting images from outer space. By 1964 NASA scientists were able to use digital image-processing techniques to remove imperfections from the images of the lunar surface sent back by spacecraft.

The 1970s and 1980s: Computers Get Personal

In 1970 a Xerox research team at the Palo Alto Research Center (PARC) divided the computer screen into a mosaic of phosphor dots that were turned on or off by a beam of electrons that swept the screen methodically row by row. They called the rows *raster* after a row of type. Raster graphics were revolutionary because they allowed users to fill in selected areas of a screen, creating realistic-looking computer images. Xerox researchers took advantage of raster graphics to develop an interface that used image icons to create a virtual desktop, the forerunner of the Macintosh and Windows operating systems. The interface worked best with a device called a mouse, which had been invented a decade earlier.

In the 1970s personal computers became available as kits, which led to the creation of information-sharing clubs. In 1975 Steve Wozniak brought a circuit board that he had constructed to a meeting of the Homebrew Computer Club.

Friend and fellow member Steve Jobs was so impressed that he proposed a partnership that eventually became the Apple Computer Company. Their Apple II computer was a breakthrough in terms of its cost, superior color graphics capabilities, and art applications. Apple's combination of art and business applications paved the way for the desktop computer transformation of the 1980s that brought sophisticated machines to the home, office, school, and artist's studio. By the end of the 1980s, new equipment and software designed for artists resulted in the appearance of books, magazines, and exhibitions of computer art, and digital imaging.

In 1981 Sony introduced the Mavica, the first electronic camera to record an image in analog signals (a continuously variable scale) rather than in digital form. Its high cost, low quality, and expensive output kept its use limited. Since then manufacturers have introduced greatly improved, lower-cost digital cameras and backs for film cameras. The research firm Gartner Dataquest projects that half of all US households will have digital cameras by 2006, which will effectively end the dominance of silver-based photography.

The 1990s: Digital Imaging Enters the Mainstream

In the 1980s and early 1990s the rapid spread of personal computers, and of consumer imaging software such as Photoshop, made computer-generated and manipulated imaging an option for others besides the scientist-artist. Again computer artists looked to older forms of artwork for inspiration. The computer coupled with a scanner and/or digital camera was the perfect tool for montage, a favorite technique of Dadaist and Surrealist artists. Coupled with these advances was the development of affordable desktop inkjet printers for the making of photographic-quality color prints at home or in the studio.

The Internet, which had since its inception in 1969 only been used by research labs and universities, was now

Wall's canvas-size fabricated photograph, situated on the divide between chemical and digital practice, meditates on war. This giant lightbox tableau, inspired by Goya, imagines 13 dead Russian soldiers who appear totally uninterested in the living. This is significant, for it acknowledges the role of the artist in representing physical and psychic pain. It dismantles the lingering and limited notion that a photograph is an objective mirror, instead of an expressive medium capable of portraying multiple realities. In her book *Regarding the Pain of Others* (2003), Susan Sontag used this image to conclude that we, who have not directly experienced "their" specific dread and terror, cannot understand or imagine their suffering.

© Jeff Wall. *Dead Troops Talk (A Vision after an Ambush of a Red Army Patrol near Mogor, Afghanistan, winter 1986)*, 1991-92. 90 x 164 inches. Dye-destruction transparency. Courtesy of David Pincus, Philadelphia, PA.

hosting the World Wide Web. People were using computers during the day in their places of work and in the evening at home to balance their checkbook, send e-mail, look at photographs, and play games. An average person now had access to a single device that was simultaneously their bank, post office, movie theater, art gallery, newspaper, playground, and artist studio.

As more artists started using the computer a debate began about whether digital imaging was simply another photographic tool that, combined with analog methods, would define the future of photography, or if it was a separate entity that would supplant previous notions about photography. As the debate continues, digital imagemakers have come to realize that they cannot escape the way computer-generated images are indelibly changed by the multiple characteristics of the computer. The challenge for digital artists is to develop an aesthetic that is uniquely digital and built on the abilities of the computer to combine media.

References

COE, BRIAN. *Colour Photography: The First Hundred Years 1840–1940*. London: Ash and Grant, 1978.

COOTE, JACK H. *The Illustrated History of Colour Photography*. Surbiton, Surrey: Fountain Press, 1993.

DERIBERE, M., ed. *Encyclopaedia of Colour Photography*. Watford, England: Fountain Press, 1962.

EDER, JOSEF MARIA. *History of Photography*, 4th ed., translated by Edward Epstean. New York: Columbia University Press, 1945; reprinted, New York: Dover Publications, 1978.

FRIEDMAN, JOSEPH S. *History of Color Photography*. Boston: American Photographic, 1944; reprinted, London and New York: Focal Press, 1968.

GERNSHEIM, HELMET, and GERNSHEIM, ALISON. *The History of Photography 1685–1914*. New York: McGraw-Hill, 1969.

HIRSCH, ROBERT. *Seizing the Light: A History of Photography*. New York: McGraw-Hill, 2000.

MEES, C. E. KENNETH. *From Dry Plates to Ektachrome Film*. New York: Ziff-Davis, 1961.

NEWHALL, BEAUMONT. *The History of Photography from 1839 to the Present*, 5th ed. New York: Museum of Modern Art, 1982.

OSTROFF, EUGENE, ed. *Pioneers of Photography: Their Achievements in Science and Technology*. Springfield, VA: The Society for Imaging Science and Technology, 1987.

PANTHEON PHOTO LIBRARY. *Early Color Photography*. New York: Pantheon Books, 1986.

ROSENBLUM, NAOMI. *A History of Women Photographers*. New York: Abbeville Press, 1994.

———. *A World History of Photography*, 3rd ed. New York: Abbeville Press, 1997.

SIPLEY, LOUIS WALTON. *A Half Century of Color*. New York: Macmillan, 1951.

STROEBEL, LESLIE and ZAKIA, RICHARD, eds. *The Focal Encyclopedia of Photography*, 3rd ed. Boston and London: Focal Press, 1993.

WALL, E.J. *The History of Three-Color Photography*. Boston: American Photographic, 1925; reprinted, London and New York: Focal Press, 1970.

WELLING, WILLIAM. *Photography in America: The Formative Years 1839–1900*. New York: Thomas Y. Crowell, 1978; reprinted, Albuquerque: University of New Mexico Press, 1987.

WOOD, JOHN. *The Art of the Autochrome: The Birth of Color Photography*. Iowa City: University of Iowa Press, 1993.

Endnotes

[1] SEE HERBERT KEPPLER, "The Horrible Fate of Levi Hill: Inventor of Color Photography," *Popular Photography* 58, no. 7, July 1994, 42–43, 140.

[2] ROLAND BARTHES, *Camera Lucida: Reflections on Photography*, translated by Richard Howard, New York: Hill and Wang, 1981, 81.

[3] DAVID BROWER in ELIOT PORTER, *In Wildness Is the Preservation of the World*. San Francisco: Sierra Club, 1962, 9.

[4] JOEL MEYEROWITZ, *Cape Light: Color Photographs by Joel Meyerowitz*. Boston: New York Graphic Society, 1978, unp.

Chapter Three
EXPOSING THE LIGHT

In his book *Juke Joint* (1990), Imes records the aesthetic character of back-road Mississippi Delta cafés and taverns. He used portable flash to light these dark, "mysterious interiors" and maintain their unique ambient character. Imes recalls: "I came to see these places as visual expressions of the same impulse that spawned the music—both products of a process that took the elemental and transformed it into something rare and wondrous."

© Birney Imes. *Royal Crown Café, Boyle Mississippi,* 1983. Dimensions vary. Chromogenic color print.

An Exposure Starting Place

Proper exposure technique, acceptable shadow and highlight detail, is the prerequisite to the process of transforming ideas into photographs. However, having the light match the subject is also essential to make a good photograph and this is where the art of photography comes into the fore. These exposure guidelines will produce acceptable exposures under a wide variety of conditions without an extensive amount of knowledge, testing, or frustration regardless of whether you are using a film camera or digital camera. Although digital imaging software offers many correction tools, it is preferable to make original exposures as accurate as possible to avoid compromising image quality. As you gain experience and confidence, more advanced exposure and development procedures can be employed as discussed at the end of this chapter.

Determining the correct exposure with color materials is essentially the same as it is for black-and-white ones. Transparency film requires the greatest accuracy because the film itself is the final product; its exposure latitude is not wide, so small changes can produce dramatic results. In general, underexposure of slide film by up to 1/2 f-stop produces a richer, more saturated color effect. With negative film, overexposure of up to a full f-stop produces similar results. Good detail in key shadow areas is needed to print well. Negative film has a much wider exposure range, plus the printing stage allows for further corrections after initial exposure of the film. The exposure latitude of digital cameras is similar to color transparency materials, making accurate metering essential.

Many cameras offer an exposure compensation dial that will provide you with the desired amount of correction automatically. For instance, if you photographed a dark figure against a dominant light background, the exposure suggested by an averaged meter metering will produce an unexposed image. By setting an exposure compensation of +1.5, for example, the result will be more natural.

Digital cameras usually have a saturation control for adjusting the intensity of color in the image for printing and/or manipulation in the computer. Most also have an image adjustment control for altering the image contrast and brightness at the time of exposure.

Camera Meters

Camera meters are the device most of us initially employ to make our exposure calculations. Almost every contemporary 35-mm and digital SLR camera has a sophisticated thru-the-lens (TTL) metering system. These systems provide accurate results under even light and they are convenient, but it is up to the operator to make them perform to obtain the desired pictures. The more you know about the camera's metering system, the greater the likelihood you will use it to achieve the desired exposure. All meters are partially blind; they see only the middle gray of 18 percent reflectance as it appears on film. (See the tear-out 18 percent gray card at the back of the book, which you can use to help determine the proper exposure.) The reflectance reading tells the photographer that if the object the meter is reading is a middle gray or averages out to be a middle gray, this is how the camera should be set for an average exposure. The meter is a tool that measures only the intensity of the light; it does not judge the quality of the light or the feeling and mood that the light produces upon the subject. The best exposure is not necessarily the one the meter indicates is the correct exposure. The meter is a guide that reads the signs. It is up to the photographer to see, respond to, and interpret the light and decide what exposure will deliver the color, detail, feeling, and mood needed to express and convey the situation to the audience. Some basic metering guidelines are summarized in table 3.1.

Reflective and Incident Light

There are two fundamental ways of measuring the amount of light in a scene. Virtually all in-camera meters are designed to read reflective light. Reflective light is metered as it bounces off the subject. This is accomplished by

---

Table 3.1 Basic Metering Guidelines

1. Check to see that the ISO film speed matches the meter setting or that the sensitivity selector (digital ISO) of your digital camera is at the desired setting.
2. Perform a battery check before going out to take pictures.
3. When taking a reflected light reading, point the meter at the most visually important neutral-toned item in the scene.
4. Get close to the main subject so that it fills the metering area. Avoid extremes of dark or light when selecting areas on which to base your general exposure.
5. If it is not possible to meter directly from the subject, place your hand in the same light as the subject and compensate the exposure by opening up one f-stop, or place the 18 percent gray card from the back of this book in the same type of light and meter off it.
6. In situations of extreme contrast and/or a wide tonal range, consider averaging the key highlight and shadow areas, or take a reading from an 18 percent gray card under the same quality of light.
7. For an incident reading, fit the light-diffusing dome over the cell and point the meter at the source of the light so that the meter is in the same lighting conditions as the subject in relation to the camera position.

3.1 A reflective light reading is made by pointing the light meter directly at the subject. A reflective reading measures the light that is bounced off, or reflected from, the subject. Most in-camera meters can only measure reflected light.

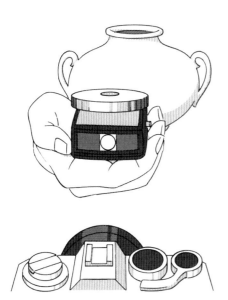

3.2 An incident light reading measures the light that falls on the subject. To make an incident reading, the photographer stands in front of the subject and points the meter at the camera or main light source. The meter is not pointed toward the subject. Most meters require a special light-diffusing dome attachment to read incident light.

pointing the meter directly at the subject (figure 3.1). A reflected reading from low midtones and high shadows delivers good general results with negative film.

Incident light is measured as it falls on the subject. The meter is not pointed at the subject but toward the camera or main light source (figure 3.2). Incident meters are not influenced by the multiple reflectance values of a subject; therefore they do not require as much expertise to achieve satisfactory results. Most in-camera meters cannot read incident light without a special attachment that fits over the front of the lens. This adapter permits incident reading with most TTL metering systems. Incident readings work well with slide film, as does reflected reading of key highlights, if areas containing shadow detail are not visually critical.

Gray Card

Both reflective and incident meters can be easily fooled if there is an unusual distribution in the tones of a subject. For this reason it is often desirable to ignore the subject completely and take your meter reading from an 18 percent gray card (like the one in the back of this book). The gray card provides a neutral surface of unvarying tone that is only influenced by changes in illumination. In this respect, it is like an incident reading; only it is measured by reflective light. The gray card is designed to reflect all visible wavelengths of light equally, in neutral color, and to reflect about 18 percent of the light striking it. To obtain accurate results, be certain the gray card is clean and not bent. Position the gray card to avoid highlight or shadow emphasis. Point your reflective meter to fill as much of the gray card as possible; avoid casting any shadows in the area being metered.

In color photography, the gray card can be photographed in the same light as the subject and included at the edge of the frame or on a separate exposure. This can provide a standard neutral reference guide for evaluating the filtration

requirements when making prints or additional slides, or in photomechanical reproduction. It is a popular misconception that the gray card represents the average reflectance of an ideal subject, for the average reflectance of a normal subject is about 9 percent.

Basic In-Camera Metering Systems

There are five basic metering systems with a wide variety of internal patterns that are currently in use (figure 3.3).

The Center-Weighted System

The center-weighted system has its light-sensitive cell located in the back of the pentaprism, providing the center of the frame with the greatest sensitivity to light. This sensitivity decreases toward the bottom and top of the frame.

The Overall System

In the overall system the cells read the entire frame as it is reflected from the shutter curtain or the film. It tends to provide a bias of sensitivity toward the center of the frame.

The Averaging System

The averaging system has two cells in the pentaprism that read different parts of the frame. Their readings are averaged together with a bias toward the center of the picture area.

The Spot System

The spot system measures light from a small zone in the center of the frame. It requires care and skill to make use of the spot. It must be pointed at crucial areas of detail in the picture to obtain proper results. Averaging is often employed when working with a spot meter. For instance, the light is measured in the key shadow and highlight areas, then these two readings are combined and averaged to get the exposure. When it is not practical for the photographer to get up close

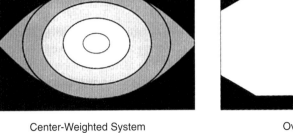

Center-Weighted System

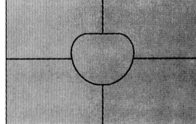

Overall System

Matrix System

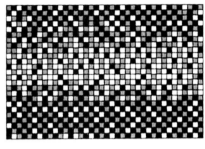

Averaging System

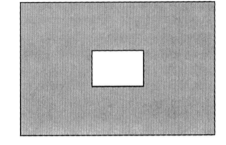

Spot System

3.3 How five basic in-camera metering system patterns are set up to determine exposure.

---

to measure the light on a subject, as in the case of a distant landscape, a sporting event, or an animal in the wild, the spot meter has the advantage of being able to measure the light from any number of key areas of the scene from a distance.

Matrix Metering

Most modern cameras have computer-assisted matrix metering. With this feature, the meter is programmed to recognize common lighting situations and adjust the exposure accordingly. Typically the camera's meter divides the scene into a series of weighted sectors and compares the scene being metered with the light patterns from numerous photographs in its memory. The meter may automatically shift between sensitivity patterns, depending on whether the camera is held horizontally or vertically. It can also choose between different meter programs depending on the light, such as center-weighted, highlight- or shadow-biased, or segment averaging, to automatically deliver highly accurate results.

Common Metering Problems

Having a TTL metering system does not guarantee good exposures. Unusual lighting conditions can still easily fool the meter. The most common errors occur when the subject is not in the main area that the system is reading, if there is a very dark or light place in the metered area, if the quality of the light is not even and is striking the subject from the front, or if the light is overly bright or dim. Knowing which type of metering system the camera uses allows the photographer to frame the proper areas within the metered zone to get the desired outcome.

How the Meter Gets Fooled

Scenes containing large amounts of light areas, such as fog, sand, snow, or white walls, give a meter reading that causes underexposure because the meter is fooled by the overall brightness of the scene. Additional exposure of between one and two f-stops is needed to correct the meter error.

Scenes with a great deal of dark shadow produce overexposures. This happens because the meter is designed to reproduce an 18 percent gray under all conditions. If the major tones are darker or lighter the exposure will not be accurate and must be corrected by the photographer. A reduction of one to two f-stops is needed for dark subjects. An incident reading performs well in these situations because it is unaffected by any tonal differences within the subject. Bracketing is a good idea in both situations.

Bracketing

Bracketing is done by first making what is believed to be the correct exposure, then an exposure 1/2 f-stop under that exposure, and finally one more exposure 1/2 f-stop over the original exposure, totaling three exposures of the scene, are made. In tricky lighting situations, bracket two 1/2 f-stops in each direction (over- and underexposure) for a total of five exposures of the scene. When using slide film, which has less tolerance for exposure error than negative film, critical results can be achieved by bracketing in

Dicker got this dramatic late-afternoon lighting effect by taking his light reading in the sunlit portion of the scene with his camera on a tripod. In so doing, extreme detail is achieved in the highlights and the darker areas of the room are underexposed, making them appear intensely dark.

© Jean-Jacques Dicker. *Window Light, New Delhi, India,* 1985. 8 x 10 inches. Dye-destruction print.

3.4 Treiger relied on a conversion chart, bracketing, and a Polaroid film back to arrive at her eight-minute exposure for this highly reflective still-life shot with a 4- x 5- inch pinhole camera. The illusionist composition was designed "to overcome the objective reality of a regular camera and show that an invisible web connects all things to each other."

© Marcia G. Treiger. *Looking Through Glass, #1,* 2003. 16 x 20 inches. Inkjet print.

3.5 Scenes containing larger areas of dark shadows or bright highlights can easily fool the meter. In this scene of great contrast, Noble used a handheld meter to take an incident light reading to help determine the exposure he wanted so the highlight areas would retain maximum detail.

©Peter Noble. *Pushkar Morning Shave*, 1990. 36 x 24 cm. Chromogenic color transparency.

1/3 f-stops. Many cameras have auto-bracketing that will make a series of three exposures: normal, under, and over (usually +/- 0.5 or +/- one f-stop) in rapid succession. Do not be afraid to shoot a few more frames. Bracketing can help a photographer gain an understanding of the relationship between light and exposure. Analyze and learn from the results so you can apply them next time a similar situation is encountered.

Photographers using cameras that can accommodate a Polaroid back can shoot Polaroid film tests to check exposure, lighting, and composition (figure 3.4).

Handheld Meters

When acquiring a handheld meter make certain it can read both reflected and incident light. Incident light readings are accomplished by fitting a light-diffusing attachment over the meter's cell. The meter can then be pointed at the light source rather than at the subject. Since it measures the light falling on the subject and not the light reflected by the subject, the incident reading is useful in contrasty light or when a scene has a large variation in tonal values (figure 3.5).

Handheld spot meters are also available. As with the in-camera spot system, the main danger of using the spot meter is that it reads such a tiny area that taking a reading from the wrong place can easily throw off the entire exposure. For this reason the spot meter should be used with care until confidence and understanding is gained of how and where to meter. Some handheld meters have attachments that allow them to make spot readings.

Manual Override

Cameras that have fully automatic exposure systems without a manual override reduce a photographer's options. The machine decides how the picture should look, how much depth of field it should have, and whether to stop the action or to blur it. If you only have an automatic camera, try fooling it by adjusting the

shutter speeds, altering the film-speed setting, or using the backlight control to change your lens aperture. Learn to control the machine and not be its prisoner.

Batteries

Small silver-oxide or lithium batteries power most in-camera meters. They tend to fail without much warning, so carry spare batteries when you go out to photograph. Silver-oxide batteries work well if the camera is used often. For the occasional user, lithium batteries have better cold weather performance and a longer shelf life; they can retain up to 90 percent of original service life capacity after 10 years in storage.

Since cold reduces the self-discharge that eventually runs batteries down while they are sitting on the shelf, all types of battery commonly used in photographic

equipment—alkaline, lithium, oxide, silver—will stay active longer if they are stored in airtight bags with silica-gel dryer packets in the refrigerator. Keep them in this wrapper while bringing them up to room temperature—an hour is usually about right. Batteries should never be frozen. Freezing can cause leakage or full-scale rupture. It is a good idea to change batteries about once a year to avoid risking a power failure as you are about to make your next masterpiece.

Older equipment designed to run on mercury batteries that are no longer made because of environmental concerns, can be powered by less toxic zinc-air batteries made specifically for photographic applications. They require special handling to extend their shorter life spans and avoid leakage. Read and follow each manufacturer's handling guidelines.

3.6 Under diffused light, colors appear to be muted and the difference between highlights and shadows is minimal. Trolinger's work not only shows the aftereffects of the great fire in Yellowstone National Park, but also reveals how even in color the combination of light and subject can produce a minimalist color palette—black and white in color.

© Charlotte Trolinger. *Swan Lake Flats*. Yellowstone National Park, September 11, 1988. 11 x 14 inches. Chromogenic color print.

Opposite page
3.7 In average bright daylight, contrast is greater, colors are more saturated, and there is good detail in both key shadow and highlight areas. Because all the satellite dishes in this area faced the southeast and Freeman didn't want any shadows on the dishes, he photographed only in the late afternoon. Freeman said the dishes opened up the communications frontier for rural areas. "It makes me think of when I was a kid in Chicago, in 1948. Our family had the first television set on the block and every Sunday night there'd be twenty people from the neighborhood sitting in our living room, watching 'Ed Sullivan.' That's what dishes have done for the country."

© Roger Freeman. *Satellite Dish Series: Allegeny County, NY*, 1984–85. 20 x 24 inches. Chromogenic color print.

Basic Methods of Reading the Light

The Brightness Range of the Subject

The brightness range of a subject (the difference in the number of f-stops between the key highlight and key shadow area of a scene) is one way to determine exposure. The brightness range method can be divided into four broad categories: diffused, even, or flat light; average bright daylight with no extreme highlights or shadows; brilliant, contrasty, direct sunlight; and dim light.

Diffused Light

Overcast days offer an even, diffused quality of light. Colors appear muted, quiet, and subdued. Both highlights and shadows are minimal (figure 3.6). Whenever the scene is metered, the reading usually remains within a range of three f-stops. The apparent brightness range and contrast can be increased through overexposure.

Average Daylight

In a scene of average bright daylight the colors look more saturated, the contrast is more distinct, the highlights are brighter, and the shadows are darker with good detail in both areas (figure 3.7). Meter reading from different parts of the scene may reveal a range of about seven f-stops. Care must be given to where meter readings are taken. If the subject is in direct sunlight and the meter is in shadow, overexposure of the subject is the result.

Brilliant Sunlight

Brilliant, direct sunlight causes the deepest color saturation while also producing conditions of maximum contrast (figure 3.8). The exposure range can be 12 f-stops or greater, which stretches or surpasses the ability of the film to record the scene. However, this can be corrected with a digitized image.

These conditions result in black shadows and bright highlights. Color separation is at its greatest; white appears at its purest. Determining which areas to base the meter reading on is critical for obtaining the desired results. These effects can be compounded when photo-

3.8 In brilliant sunlight, contrast and color saturation are at their maximum. The exposure must be carefully thought out so the needed detail is produced in the key subject areas.

© Eduardo Del Vaile and Mirta Gómez. *Ixtlan de los Hervores, Mexico*, 1989. 11 ¾ x 17 ½ inches. Chromogenic color print.

graphing reflections off glass, polished metal, or water. Selective exposure techniques such as averaging, use of incident light, or spot reading may be needed (see section on unusual lighting conditions later in this chapter, page 60).

Dim Light

Dim natural light taxes the ability of the film or digital media to record the necessary color and detail of the scene (figure 3.9). Colors can be flat and monochromatic, and contrast is often problematic. Digital images can have high levels of electronic "noise" that can show up as specks or mottling, especially in the shadows. Contrast can be extreme when artificial light sources are included within the scene. Contrast can also be lacking, with details often difficult to determine. Low levels of light mean long exposures, which entail the use of a tripod, a high-speed ISO or sensitivity, or additional lighting to make the picture.

Metering for the Subject

Metering for the subject is another way to determine proper exposure. When in doubt about where to take an exposure reading, decide what the subject is in the picture and take a reflected reading from it (figure 3.10). For instance, when making a portrait, go up to the subject and take the meter reading directly from the face, open up one f-stop for fair skin or close down one f-stop for dark complexions, and then return to the chosen camera position. When photographing a landscape in diffused, even light, an overall meter reading can be made from the camera position. If the light is hard (not diffused) or directional, the camera

---

3.9 Dim light can strain a film's ability to record the necessary color and detail. Colors can appear monochromatic and the contrast range is often extreme, with either not enough contrast or too much contrast. Artificial light sources can supply unusual and/or dramatic effects.

© Jan Staller. *Taxi, New York City*, 1985. 15 x 15 inches. Chromogenic color print. Courtesy of Lieberman and Saul Gallery, New York. NY.

3.10 When exposing for the subject, a reflective reading is made directly from the most important object in the scene. Proper detail is then retained where it is required and the meter is not fooled by areas of bright light or deep shadow. To make her circus series Saville used a handheld Nikon F with a 135-mm lens. The 200-speed negative film was intentionally overexposed for greater color saturation and shadow detail. Saville says: "I use slow shutter speeds and let the movement paint itself onto my film. ... The use of quick shutter speeds, to freeze the movement, would artificially separate these performers from their actions, leaving them high and dry in an *instant* that never really existed for the spectator."

© Lynn Saville. *White Liberty Horses*, 1991. 16 x 20 inches. Chromogenic color print.

meter can be pointed up, down, or sideways to emphasize the sky, the ground, the highlights, or the shadows. These readings can also be averaged.

Exposing for Tonal Variations

Exposing for tonal variations is another method that can be used in calculating the exposure. A scene that has large amounts of either dark or light tones can give incorrect information if the exposure is based on a single reading (figure 3.11). When making a picture of a general outdoor scene, the correct exposure can be achieved by taking two readings and then averaging them. For example, you are photographing a landscape, it is late in the day, the sky is brighter than the ground, and detail needs to be retained in both areas. First meter a critical highlight area (sky) in which detail is required. Let's say the reading is f/16 at 1/250 second. If the exposure was made at this setting, the sky would be rich and deep, but the ground detail would be lost and might appear simply as a vast black area. Now meter off a key area in the shadow area of the ground. Say it is f/5.6 at 1/250 second. This would provide an excellent rendition of the ground, but the sky would be overexposed and appear white, completely desaturated of color, and with no discernible detail. To get an average reading, take the meter reading from the highlight (sky) and the shadow (ground) and halve the f-stop difference between the two readings. In this case, an average reading would be about f/8 at 1/250 second. It is permissible to set the aperture in between the click stops with most cameras. The final result is a compromise between the two situations, with acceptable detail and color saturation in each area.

3.11 Goldin is known for using a seemingly casual snapshot aesthetic to photograph the private lives of her close circle of friends. In this image of herself and her lover in an intimate setting, subtle detail is important for a full appreciation of a sensitive moment. When a scene contains large amounts of dark and/ or light areas, taking an average reading for tonal variation is a good way to get a wide range of detail and retain the atmospheric flavor of the moment.

© Nan Goldin. *Nan and Brian in Bed, NYC, 1983*. 30 x 40 inches. Dye-destruction print. Courtesy of Matthew Marks Gallery, New York, NY.

When working with negative film, it is often possible to take the meter reading from the ground, let the sky overexpose, and correct by burning it in when a print is made.

If the subject that is being photographed is either a great deal darker or lighter than the background, such as a dark-skinned person against a white background or a fair-skinned person against a black background, averaging will not provide good results. If there is more than a five f-stop range between the highlight and shadow areas, there will be an unacceptable loss of detail in both areas. In a case like this, let the

background go or use additional lighting techniques such as flash fill to compensate for the difference.

Electronic Flash and Basic Flash Fill

Electronic flash operates by producing a veritable bolt of lightning between two electrodes inside a quartz-crystal tube that is typically filled with xenon gas. A quick discharge of high-voltage current from the system's capacitor excites the gas and a brief, intense burst of light is

emitted in the range of 5600 to 6000 K. Many cameras have built-in flash units that are convenient but have limited capabilities. Other cameras have dedicated external flash units designed to function with a particular camera that provide automatic exposure control and expanded versatility. Professional portable and studio flash units are synchronized with a camera by means of a sync cord or a "slave" unit. The shutter must be completely open at the time the flash fires. This is achieved at any speed with a between-the-lens shutter, but most focal plane shutters will not sync at speeds faster than 1/250 of a second (check your camera manual). If the shutter speed is too high, only part of the frame will be exposed. Systems can have multiple flash heads and variable power control that can be set to use only a portion of the available light. This allows you to control the intensity of the light, which is very useful for stopping action, bringing a subject forward in a composition, and creating atmospheric and flash-fill effects. Filters can be placed over the flash head(s) to alter the color of the light for purposes of correction or to create a mood.

A basic flash-fill technique involves first taking an available-light meter reading of the scene, setting your camera's shutter to the correct flash synchronization speed, and then determining the f-stop. Now divide the exposure f-stop number into the guide number (GN) of your flash unit. The result is the number of feet you need to be from your subject. Shoot at the available-light meter reading with the flash at this distance. For example, the meter reads f/16 at a synchronization speed of 1/125. Your flash unit has a GN of 80. Divide 16 (f/16) into 80 (GN). The result is 5, the distance you need to be from the subject with an exposure of f/16 at 1/125.

A second flash-fill method is to set the camera to make a proper ambient light exposure, using the correct synchronization speed. Note the correct f-stop that is required. Position or adjust the flash unit to produce light that is the equivalent of one or two f-stops less exposure, depending on the desired effect. If the flash produces an amount of light equal to the original exposure, the shadow areas will be as bright as the directly lighted areas, and the modeling effect will be lost (see section on flash and slow shutter speed in chapter 14, page 266).

A third technique is to determine the correct ambient light exposure at the proper flash synchronization speed and then vary the output of the flash by using the different power setting (half- or quarter-power) so the amount of flashlight is correct for the subject-to-flash distance. If the flash does not have a power setting, putting a diffuser or neutral-density filter in front of the flash head can reduce the output. You can also improvise by putting a clean white handkerchief in front of the flash head; each layer of cloth reduces the output by about one f-stop. Most dedicated flash units can make automatic flash-fill expo-

3.12 Colburn states: "With the exploration of small town events it becomes increasingly important to me to establish the sense of inclusion and membership that forms the structure of these events. The nature of the events and the context in which they occur presents an opportunity to make images that celebrate shared values and a sense of identity and membership. The images should be seen in contrast to the many exclusive experiences of contemporary life. These exclusive experiences reinforce the perception that we are, at best, members of a subgroup never to be a part of the whole. My photographs are premised on what we hold in common." Flash-fill was used in the early evening light to give a theatrical look, to provide more detail on the subjects, and to separate them from the background. The negative film was also overexposed one f-stop to give extra color saturation.

© Richard Colburn. *Mr. and Mrs. Nevis Pageant, Muskie Days, Nevis MN,* 1990. 18 1/4 x 18 1/4 inches. Chromogenic color print.

sures. Flash-fill can also be employed selectively to provide additional illumination or with filters to alter the color of specific areas in a scene (figure 3.12).

Red Eye

When photographing any living being with a flash unit attached to the camera or with a ring light around the lens, red eye can happen. If your subject looks directly at the camera and the light is next to the lens axis, light passes directly into the pupils of your subject's eyes and is strongly reflected back to the camera. With color film, this is seen as a pink or red spot in the center of the eye because the light illuminates the blood vessels in the retina of the eye. If this effect is not desired, try one of the following: have the subject look to one side of the camera, bounce the flash light, or move the

Neuhauser captured both the ambient light of the sunset and the details of the witch costume. She accomplished this by using a slow shutter speed with the camera on a tripod to capture the ambient light, and a fill-in flash during the exposure to bring out the details in the subject.

© Janet Neuhauser. *Jess as a Witch*, 1997. 14 x 11 inches. Chromogenic color print.

flash unit some distance (six inches or more) from the lens axis. This can be done by elevating the flash on a commercially available extender post, or by getting a long flash synchronization cord and holding the unit away from the camera with one hand. Bear in mind that most digital imaging software offers red eye correction.

Unusual Lighting Conditions

Unusual lighting conditions cause exposure problems: uneven light, light hitting the subject from a strange angle, backlight, glare and reflections, areas with large highlights, or shadows such as those produced inside doorways and windows, as well as light from computer and television screens (figure 3.13). The wide range of tones in such scenes is often greater than the ability of the film to record them. The photographer must decide what is important to record and how to get it done.

Subject in Shadow

When the subject is in shadow, decide what is the most important area of the picture, which colors have the most interest, and what details need to be seen. If the subject is in shadow, take a reflected meter reading from the most important shadow region. This provides the correct information for that key area. Other areas, mainly the highlights, will experience a loss of color saturation and detail due to overexposure, which can be corrected by burning in these areas when the print is made (figure 3.14). At other times, there may be a key highlight striking the subject in shadow. The exposure can be made based on the highlight reading, letting the remainder of the subject fall into obscurity. Additional light can be used to put more illumination on the subject by means of flash and/or reflective fill-cards.

Subject in Bright Light

Should the main point of interest be in a bright area, take a reflected reading from the key highlight area or use an incident reading. A contrasty subject dealt with in this fashion provides dramatic, rich, and saturated color, along with good detail in these bright areas (figure 3.15). The shadows will lack detail and not provide much visual information. Anything that is backlit becomes a silhouette with no

3.13 Yarnelle Edwards's series *Suburban Dreams* investigates her "fascination by the signs and symbols of contemporary life, by the relationships among people, the spaces they inhabit and their possessions." Here Yarnelle Edwards wanted the light from the television to illuminate this scene. To make this happen without losing detail in the shadow areas, she used a hot light close to the television to amplify its effects. The result is a hyper-real image that "creates a portrait of a culture, not of individuals."

© Beth Yarnelle Edwards. *Bruce, age 32, and Melissa age 43*, from Suburban Dreams, 2000. 30 x 38 ½ inches. Chromogenic color print.

3.14 Although the fighter was standing in the shade at the time of exposure, Lavelle was able to bring out the color of the fighter's bandages by taking a reflected meter reading from the most important shadow area in the scene.

© Frank Lavelle. *Fighter, Havana, Cuba*, 2001. 12 x 18 inches. Chromogenic color print.

Alternative Solutions

If it is not acceptable to lose the details in the shadows, there are other alternatives. These include averaging the reflective reading, bracketing, using additional lighting techniques such as flash fill, or combining both a reflective and an incident reading. This last method is done by taking an incident reading directed toward the camera of the light striking the subject. This reading is not affected by extreme highlights. Then take a reflected reading with the meter aimed at the key subject area. Now average the two and bracket for insurance. When in doubt, the best insurance is to bracket.

Reciprocity

What is the reciprocity law? It is the theoretical relationship between the length of exposure and the intensity of light. It states that an increase in one is balanced by a decrease in the other. For example, doubling the light intensity should be balanced exactly by halving the exposure time. In practical terms, this means that if you meter a scene and calculate the exposure to be f/8 at 1/250 second, you could obtain the same exposure by doubling your f-stop opening and cutting your exposure time in half. Thus, shooting at f/5.6 at 1/500 second should produce the same results as shooting at f/8 at 1/250. You could also double your exposure time and cut your f-stop in half, so that shooting at 1/125 second at

detail at all under these circumstances.

Inexpensive digital cameras often overexpose highlights, which results in a lack of detail. In contrasty situations, expose for the areas that you want to retain detail and texture by zooming in, locking the exposure, reframing, and then making the photograph.

Table 3.2 **Theoretical Exposure Equivalents** (based on a starting exposure of f/8 at 1/250 second)	
f-stop	*Time in Seconds*
f/16	1/60
f/11	1/125
f/8*	1/250*
f/5.6	1/500
f/4	1/1,000
*Starting exposure.	

3.16 Reciprocity failure creates the intense colors found in Zaitz's images. He has this to say about his work: "The technique I use for transforming my landscapes is time. On the average each exposure is one hour long, with some going 2 ½ hours. I never use any filters or lighting equipment with colored gels. All the light sources were different types of ambient street light mixing with the slowly changing early morning light."

© Dan Zaitz. *Places I've Dreamed of #18*, n.d. 16 x 20 inches. Chromogenic color print.

f /11 is the same as shooting at 1/250 second at f /8. Table 3.2 shows some of the theoretical exposures that would work the same if your exposure was f /8 at 1/250 second.

Reciprocity Law Failure

Unfortunately, the reciprocity law does not hold true in every situation. When using film to make either very long or very brief exposures, reciprocity failure can take place. Depending on the type of film used, exposures at about 1/5 second or longer and those faster than 1/10,000 second begin to show the effects of reciprocity failure. Depending on the film, starting at exposures of about one second or longer, the normal ratio of aperture and shutter speed will underexpose the film. Since only specialized cameras are capable of speeds higher than 1/10,000 second, most photographers do not have to worry about high-speed reciprocity failure. Some electronic flash units, when set on fractional power, can achieve exposures that are brief enough to cause

reciprocity failure. Some films can now tolerate exposures of up to 30 seconds without exposure compensation. Check the manufacturer's suggested guidelines for details.

Reciprocity Failure and Its Effect on Color Materials

In the case of black-and-white film we can simply increase the exposure time to compensate for the slow reaction time and avoid underexposure of the film. The problem with color materials is that the three emulsion layers do not respond to the reciprocity effect in the same manner. This can produce a shift in the color balance of the film or paper. If you wish to correct for reciprocity failure, follow the exposure and filtering instructions provided with the film or paper. These are merely starting points, and you must experiment to discover what works best in a particular situation.

The problem with filtering is that by adding filters you make the exposure even longer, which in turn can cause the

reciprocity effect to be even more pronounced. When using a single lens reflex (SLR) camera the filters add density, which can make viewing and focusing more difficult in a dimly lit situation.

Common Reciprocity Failure Situations

Some typical times that you will run into reciprocity problems are before sunrise, after sunset, at night, and in dimly lit interiors. Fortunately, the quality of light at these different times tends to be strange. That is, there is no standard by which we can judge whether or not you have succeeded in producing an acceptable color balance. Accurate color does not always mean good color. At times like these you may want to take a chance that the combination of light and reciprocity shift will work in your favor to create an unusual color balance, giving your picture impact that would be impossible to achieve in any other fashion (figure 3.16). Apply what you have learned from this experience to future situations.

Digital Noise

There is no equivalent reciprocity with digital sensors, but low light and long exposures do produce increased image noise. This noise is related to grain in film, but can be better described as "flecks" of visual static that appear as light snow in the image. These flecks are known as "artifacts," and although they do not produce global color shifts they can cause color tinges around their edges (see section on digital aberrations in chapter 7, page 155).

Advanced Exposure Techniques/The Zone System for Color

What Is the Zone System?

In the late 1930s Ansel Adams and Fred Archer devised the Zone System as a method of explaining exposure and development control to students of black-and-white photography. It is based on the old photo adage: "Expose for the shadows and develop for the highlights." Since then, the system has been continually refined and expanded. According to

Adams its purpose was "to provide a bridge between sensitometry and practical creative work by offering step-by-step working methods that do not require extensive training or equipment."

What Is a Zone?

A "zone" is not a place but a concept. It is the relationship between a subject's brightness and the density it is represented by in the negative and the corresponding tone in the final print. The grayscale of a full-range print has tones that have been divided into 11 zones (Zone 0–Zone X) and are identified with roman numerals to avoid confusing them with all the other numerical combinations used in photography. Each zone is equivalent to a one f-stop difference in subject brightness and negative exposure (see table 3.3 for a list of the basic zones and their physical equivalents).

Previsualization

The photographer measures the brightness range of the subject, "previsualizes" the print tonal range that is wanted to represent the subject, then picks a combination of exposure and development procedures to make this happen. Previsualization is a mental act in which the photographer imagines how the final print will look before the camera exposure is made. It involves combining technique and vision to realize the photographer's subjective response to the subject. The term can be found in the writings and work of Edward Weston and Ansel Adams, and has become the keystone of the Modernist, realistic approach to photography. The principles of the Zone System can be found in the curves and levels (histogram) functions of image-processing software.

In order to achieve maximum effect and control, a photographer needs to make equipment and material tests to determine the "true" speed of the film, and to learn precisely what alterations in the development process are needed to contract an extremely long tonal range so that it will fit on a piece of paper or film or to expand a limited brightness range

Table 3.3

Zone System Values and Their Physical Equivalents

Low Values

Zone 0: Maximum black. The blackest black that a print can be made to yield. Doorways and windows opening into unlit rooms.

Zone I: The first discernible tone above total black. When seen next to a high key zone it is sensed as total black. Twilight shadows.

Zone II: First discernible evidence of texture; deep tonalities that represent the darkest part of the picture in which a sense of space and volume is needed.

Zone III: Average dark materials and low values showing adequate texture. Black hair, fur, and clothes in which a sense of detail is needed.

Middle Values

Zone IV: Average dark foliage, dark stone, or open shadow in landscape. Normal shadow value for Caucasian skin portraits in sunlight. Also brown hair and new blue jeans.

Zone V: 18 percent gray neutral test card (inside the back cover of this book). Most black skin, dark skin, or sunburnt Caucasian skin, average weathered wood, grass in sunlight, gray stone.

Zone VI: Average Caucasian skin value in sunlight, diffuse skylight, or artificial light. Light stone, shadows on snow in sunlit landscapes.

High Values

Zone VII: Very light skin, light gray objects, average snow with acute side lighting.

Zone VIII: Whites with texture and delicate values, textured snow, highlights on Caucasian skin.

Zone IX: White without texture approaching pure white, similar to Zone I in its slight tonality, without a trace of texture.

Zone X: Pure white of the printing paper base, specular glare or light sources in the picture area.

subject to normal. Once this is done it is possible, based on the exposure given to the subject, to determine what changes in development are necessary to obtain the desired visual outcome.

The Zone System and Color

Using the Zone System for color photography is similar to using it for black-and-white work. The photographer has to learn the zones, be able to previsualize the scene, and place the exposures. The big difference is that there is much less flexibility in processing color because it is necessary to maintain the color balance between all the layers of the emulsion to avoid color shifts and crossovers. Another difference is that contrast is determined not only by light reflectance but also by the colors themselves.

Film-Speed Testing

The film-speed test is at the heart of the Zone System because the biggest technical obstacle most photographers encounter when working with color film is making the correct exposure. It is more critical than in black-and-white photography since the exposure determines not only the density but also the color saturation. Even with proper exposure techniques, if the film's speed does not agree with your working procedures the results will not be as expected. If you do not have exposure troubles, leave well enough alone. There is no reason to do a test when you could be out making photographs. If you have had problems with exposure, however, especially with underexposed negatives or overexposed slides, run a test and establish your personal film speed. If your exposures are still erratic, this indicates either a mechanical problem or the need to review your basic exposure methods.

The manufacturer's film speed is a starting point that is not engraved in stone. It is determined under laboratory conditions and does not take into consideration your personal lens, the camera body, exposure techniques, the subject,

Porter was a master of the dye-transfer process who became well known through his various publications, such as *The Place No One Knew: Glen Canyon on the Colorado* (1963). The Sierra Club used his "beautiful" color images to help awaken people to ecological issues and the dangers of uncontrolled technology and business, while having a side effect of helping color photography to become recognized as a legitimate art form.

© Eliot Porter. *Reuss Arch and Amphitheater, Davis Gulch, Escalante Basin, Utah,* 1965. Dye-transfer print. n/s. Courtesy of Eliot Porter Archives Amon Carter Museum, Fort Worth, TX.

and the quality of the light. You can customize your film speed to make it perform to your own style and taste. The film-speed test recommended here is based on the principles of the Zone System, but your results are determined visually, not through the use of a densitometer.

The Zone System and Transparency Materials

Exposure is everything with transparencies, since the film is the final product. If a mistake is made, such as overexposure or underexposure of the film, it cannot be readily corrected in the secondary process of printing. What is true for negatives is the opposite for positives (transparencies). The areas of greatest critical interest for judging proper exposure are those of minimal density. With negative material these are the shadow areas. With transparencies it is the highlight areas. When using the Zone System method of exposure control, meter off from the important previsualized highlight and then open up the lens to the required number of stops for proper zone placement. All other tones will then fall relative to the placed zone. The darker values will show up as long as the highlight is metered and placed correctly.

Finding Your Correct Film Speed with Transparencies

You will discover your personal film speed upon a correct rendering of the highlights. The zone used for this test is Zone VII. The characteristics of Zone VII (the lightest textured highlight) include blonde hair, cloudy bright skies, very light skin, white-painted textured wood, average snow, light gray concrete, and white or very bright clothes.

Zone VIII actually has less density, but it is so close to clear film that it can be difficult to visually distinguish it as a separate tone. It is the last zone with any detail in it. Zone VIII subjects include smooth, white-painted wood, a piece of white paper, a white sheet in sunlight, and snow entirely in shade or under overcast skies. Zone VIII contains extremely delicate values. It is easy to lose the sense of space and volume in very light objects. When seen beside Zone II or III it may seem to feel and be sensed as a pure white without texture.

Test Procedures

For this test, use a standard Zone VII value like a white-painted brick wall, a textured white fence, or a textured white sweater. Make the test with your most commonly used camera body and lens, and set the meter to the manufacturer's

suggested film speed. Take the meter reading only from the critical part of the subject and place it in Zone VII. This is done by opening up two f-stops or their shutter speed equivalents. Remember the meter is programmed to read at Zone V (18 percent reflectance value as with the gray card in the back of this book). "Correct" exposure is one that renders Zone V as Zone V (or any single-toned subject as Zone V, if the meter is working correctly). Then make a series of exposures, bracketing in ½ f-stops, three stops more and three stops less than the starting film speed. Next, develop the film following normal procedures. Mount and label all 13 exposures, then project them in the slide projector that you most commonly use. Look for the slide that shows the best Zone VII value—one that possesses the right amount of texture with correct color and is not too dark. This exposure indicates your correct film speed.

Transparency Film-Speed Observations

Transparency films generally seem to have a more accurate manufacturer's film-speed rating than do negative films. The slower films are usually very close, and you may even want to test them in 1/3 f-stop intervals, two full f-stops in both directions. Medium-speed transparency films tend to run from right on the manufacturer's recommendations to 1/3 to 1/2 f-stop too slow. High-speed films can be off by 1/2 to one full f-stop. Usually most photographers raise the transparency film speed from the given speed. This gives richer and fuller color saturation with a little underexposure. With slide film it is imperative that you meter with the utmost accuracy. When in doubt, give it less exposure rather than more. Do not be afraid to use some film. Bracket and be certain you have what you need and want.

Highlight Previsualization

Once you have determined your proper film speed, correct exposure entails pre-

visualizing the highlights only. Pick out the most important highlight area, meter it, and place it in the previsualized zone in which you want it to appear. You do not have to bother to meter the contrast range between the highlights and shadows. If you are in the same light as the subject being photographed, the correct exposure can be determined by metering an 18 percent gray card or, if you are Caucasian, simply metering the palm of your hand in the brightest light in the scene and then placing it in Zone VI by opening up one f-stop. The contrast of the image, just as with color negative film, will be largely a matter of the relationship of the colors that are in the scene being photographed.

Pre-Fogging Transparency Film

Photographer Fred Scruton has devised a method of pre-fogging 8 x 10 Kodak Ektachrome 64 for improved highlight and shadow density in direct, cloudless sunlight (figure 3.17) This method can be used on any nonsuper saturated positive or negative film.

Use two tungsten light sources (3200 K) to evenly illuminate a white, 32- x 40-inch piece of Fome-cor. Place your tripoded view camera about two feet in front of the Fome-cor. Focus on infinity (to avoid a bellows extension factor) and make sure the frame is fully filled with the out-of-focus Fome-cor.

Use 180 Y, 40 M CC filters and expose the film (one sheet at a time in the camera) to Zone II by underexposing from a reflective meter reading by 2 1/3 f-stops (taking into account the filter factors).

Opposite page
3.17 In his travels throughout the eastern half of the United States, Scruton found a reoccurrence of inner-city buildings that have been converted for religious use. His 8- x 10-inch view camera photographs see vernacular urban architecture as "artifacts adrift in cultural time." Scruton achieves the brilliant saturated colors by photographing under midday sun and controlling the contrast by prefogging his Ektachrome film and giving it minus normal development. Transparencies are scanned and further corrected in Photoshop before being printed.

© Fred Scruton. *River West Community Church, Milwaukee, WI, 1979.* 17 x 13 ⅓ inches. Inkjet print.

The Zone System is the traditional way for a photographer to gain greater mastery of materials. As skills are refined, confidence can be gained, thus reducing the time and energy spent on technique. This can free the imagemaker to devote more personal resources to the creation of new ideas and picture making. Of this photograph taken in the late morning, Strembicki says: "I was taken by the odd mix of carnival and religious quality of Mardi Gras parades and in particular the intimidating presence of the masked horseman or veiled prophet which often preceded each parade. I used a fill flash to heighten that sense of drama and cause the subject to pop out of the background on an otherwise flatly lit day. The negative film was intentionally over-processed by 20 percent to increase color saturation."

© Stan Strembicki. *Veiled Prophet, Rex Parade, Mardi Gras, New Orleans, LA*, 1990. 16 x 16 inches. Chromogenic color print.

The film is overexposed in the field through a 5 M CC filter (rated at ISO 20 instead of 64) by 1 2/3 f-stops and pull E-6 processed at minus 3/4. The film is "pulled" out of the developer early, at 4 1/2 minutes instead of the standard six minutes.

The heavy yellow/magenta filtration both neutralizes the strong blue cast normally seen in the shadows (except when they are on white) and compensates for the radical blue/cyanish color shift caused by the pull processing. The pre-fog density and the over-exposure provide significantly more shadow detail, at the expense of a slight loss of midtone highlight contrast. With this particular transparency film, the pull processing brings the highlight detail "back" to proper density, just as in classic black-and-white zone system processing. The film is drum-scanned, and inkjet and lambda prints are made.

Working with Negative Film

All the major color negative films can be processed in Kodak's C-41 process. This is not only convenient but also necessary. Attaining the correct balance of color dyes in the negative has not been an easy task. Standardization within the industry has made this less difficult. Even though it is possible to develop many different types of film in a common process, your results will vary widely. This is because each film has its own personality based on its response to different colors. You will need to try a variety of films and even different types of C-41 processes until you come up with a combination that matches your personal color sensibilities.

Exposing for the Shadows: Zone III

Color negatives, like black-and-white ones, are exposed for proper detail in the shadow areas. Adequate detail in a Zone III area is generally considered to indicate proper exposure. Zone III indicates "average dark materials." This includes black clothes and leather. In the print, proper exposure shows adequate detail in the creases and folds of these areas. Form and texture are revealed, and the feeling of darkness is retained.

Film-Speed Tests

A Simple Exposure Test

The simplest exposure test is one in which you find a Zone III value (subject) and then meter and place it using a variety of different film speeds (bracketing). The film is developed and examined with a loupe to determine which exposure gives the proper detail in Zone III. This provides the proper film speed.

A Controlled Test

Here is an easy and controlled method that provides more accurate results. On a clear day in direct sunlight, photograph a color chart and gray card (see back of this book). Make the test with the camera body and lens you use most often. Set the film speed according to the manufacturer's starting point. Take all meter readings from the gray card only. This way there is no need to change exposure for different zone placements. Make an exposure at this given speed. Then make a series of different exposures by bracketing in 1/2 f-stop increments two full f-stops in both directions.

As an example, say you set your film speed at 400 and determined that your exposure is f/8 at 1/250. You would make your exposure at this setting and then make four exposures in the minus direction and four in the plus direction. Leave your shutter speed at 1/250 for all exposures. Table 3.4 gives you the f-stops you would need to expose at and their corresponding film speeds.

Table 3.4
Film Speed Test Exposures
(ISO 400 with an exposure of f/8 at 1/250 second)

f-stop	Film Speed
f/16	1600
f/11 1/2	1200
f/11	800
f/8 1/2	600
f/8*	400*
f/5.6 1/2	300
f/5.6	200
f/4 1/2	150
f/4	100

*Starting exposure

Visually Determining the Correct Exposure

After making the exposures, process the film following normal procedures. Next place the film in slide mounts with each frame labeled according to its film speed, then project the frames in order, beginning with the highest film speed. Pay close attention to the black-and-white density scale on the page photographed.

Table 3.5
The "No Time" Modified Film Speed for Negative Materials

Starting Speed	Modified Speed
100	50–80
200	100–125
400	200–300

Table 3.6
The "No Time" Modified Film Speed for Slide Materials

Starting Speed	Modified Speed
50	64–80
100	125–150
400	500–600

As you look at the negatives, you should notice more of the steps becoming distinct as the speed of the film drops. Your correct exposure will show visible separation for all the steps in the scale.

What if you cannot decide? What often happens is that you can narrow your choice to two frames but then cannot decide which one is correct. If this occurs, choose the one that has more exposure. Color negatives do not suffer as much from overexposure as black-and-white negatives. Overexposing by even as much as two f-stops will not make a negative unprintable. Because the final print is made up of layers of dye and not silver particles, slight overexposure does not create additional grain. It builds contrast, but the only protection against loss of detail in the shadow areas is overexposure. Color saturation is controlled directly by exposure. Underexposure causes a loss of saturation that cannot be corrected during printing. Underexposure causes colors to look flat and washed out.

The "No Time" Approach

If you do not have the time to test a new film, use the guidelines offered in table

3.5 as starting film speeds for negative film. Table 3.6 recommends starting speeds for slide film.

When in doubt, give color negative film more exposure, but give color transparency film less exposure.

Contrast Control

In the case of color negative films there are two important considerations that determine the contrast. The first is that contrast is produced from the colors themselves in the original scene. Complementary colors (opposite each other on the color wheel) produce more contrast than harmonious colors (next to each other on the color wheel). This factor can only be controlled at the time of exposure. The addition of fill light when shooting and masking during printing are other methods to control contrast.

Brightness Range

The second factor in contrast control of color negatives is the overall range of light reflectance between the previsualized shadow and highlight areas. This is the same as with black-and-white negatives. It can be changed by modifying the development time. Unlike black-and-white film, the development time of color film cannot be changed as much because it will affect the color balance, which is finalized during development. It is possible to adjust the contrast by one zone of contraction or expansion without

Table 3.7 Suggested Starting Development Times in Kodak's C-41 at 100°F

Contrast of Scene	Development Time*
N – 1	2 minutes 40 seconds
Normal	3 minutes 15 seconds
N + 1	4 minutes

*All times based on first roll in fresh developer.

The Zone System was designed to help photographers think through and plan how they want the final image to look. This piece from a series called *Nature and the Western Landscape* was made at sunset and involved preplanning the point of view and time of day, and observance of what the clouds were doing. The exposure was made using a spot meter and placing the highlight of the rock face on Zone VI. This is an example of a situation in which an average reflected light reading would have produced an overexposed image. Dzerigian contends: "The tenous balance between change and stability in nature is a pivotal point in my photographic concern with the landscape. In its depth and complexity, order and chaos, the natural world can resonate in the human being an essential beauty, sense of awe, and harmony."

© Steve Dzerigian. *Spider Rock, Canyon de Chelly*, AZ, 1988. 9 ½ x 13 inches. Dye-destruction print.

serious color shifts or crossovers with most color negative films.

Table 3.7 suggests development times for Kodak's C-41 process in fresh developer for the first roll of film.

What Is "N"?

For those of you who are not acquainted with the Zone System, "N" stands for normal developing time. N minus 1 (N–1) is used when you have a higher than normal range of contrast and wish to reduce it. N plus 1 (N+1) is used when you have a scene with a lower than normal contrast and want to increase it.

Paper and Contrast Control

Unlike black-and-white printing, contrast control during color printing is very limited. It is possible to slightly increase the contrast of the final print by using a higher contrast paper. By combining the higher contrast paper with an N+1 development, you can increase the contrast to a true N+1 or to an N+1 1/2 and maybe even an N+2.

Chapter Four

FILTERING THE LIGHT

This image of four teenaged girls posing for the camera just before a seventh-grade social event is from the series *Girl Culture*, which explores the ways young American women use their bodies to express their individual identities. Greenfield used an 81A filter to reduce the appearance of blue light in this outdoor scene.

© Lauren Greenfield. *Alli, Annie, Hannah, and Berit, all 13, before First Big Party of the Seventh Grade, Dina MN,* 1998. Dimensions vary. Dye-Destruction print.

Our Sun: a Continuous Spectrum Source

Our sun radiates "white" light, which is a continuous spectrum of all the visible wavelengths that are produced by the elements burning on the sun's surface. As these wavelengths are separated out by absorption and reflection we see them as color. The shortest wavelengths appear as violet, the longest as red, and all the other colors fall somewhere in between these boundaries. The human eye can only detect a tiny portion of the electromagnetic spectrum, known as the visual

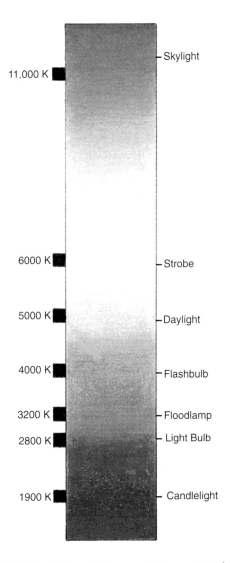

4.1 The Kelvin scale is how color temperature of light is measured. The bluer the light, the higher the Kelvin temperature. Table 4.1 gives common illumination sources and their approximate Kelvin temperature.

Table 4.1 Common Light Sources and Their Approximate Color Temperatures	
*Daylight Sources**	*Color Temperature (K)*
Skylight	12,000 to 18,000
Overcast sky	7000
Noon sun with clear sky (summer)	5000 to 7000
Noon sun with clear sky (winter)	5500 to 6000
Photographic daylight	5500
Noon sunlight (depends on time of year)	4900 to 5800
Average noon sunlight (Northern hemisphere)	5400
Sunlight at 30-degree altitude	4500
Sunlight at 20-degree altitude	4000
Sunlight at 10-degree altitude	3500
Sunrise and sunset	3000
Artificial Sources†	*Color Temperature (K)*
Electronic flash	5500 to 6500
Blue-coated flashbulbs	5500 to 6000
White flame carbon arc	5000
Zirconium-filled clear flashbulbs (AG-1 & M3)	4200
Warm white fluorescent tubes	4000
Aluminum-filled clear flashbulbs (M2, 5, & 25)	3800
500-watt 3400 K photolamp (photofloods)	3400
500-watt 3200 K tungsten lamp (photolamps)	3200
200-watt household lamp	2980
100-watt household lamp	2900
75-watt household lamp	2820
40-watt household lamp	2650
Gaslight	2000 to 2200
Candlelight (British Standard)	1930

*All daylight color temperatures depend on the time of day, season of the year, and latitude and altitude of the location.
†The age and the amount of use of bulb, lamp, or tube affect the color temperature.

spectrum. The ultraviolet (UV) wavelengths occupy the range just beyond the blue-violet end of the visual spectrum and are too small to be seen by the human eye. The infrared (IR) part of the electromagnetic spectrum begins just beyond the visible red wavelengths, which are too long to be seen with the human eye.

Color Temperature and the Kelvin Scale

The balance of the amount of colors that are contained in a continuous spectrum source of light, having all the visible wavelengths (red, orange, yellow, green, blue, and violet) in various amounts, is measured as color temperature. Color temperature is expressed on the absolute (Kelvin) scale. The Kelvin scale starts at absolute zero, minus 273.15°C on the centigrade scale (usually rounded off to minus 273°C). Absolute zero is the temperature at which all molecular motion theoretically stops. The degree symbol is not used when expressing the color temperature of a light source in Kelvins (K). The Kelvin temperature is determined by adding 273 to the number of degrees centigrade to which a black metal radiator would have to be heated to take on a certain color. A black body is used as a standard gauge since it does not reflect any light falling on it and only emits radiation when heat is applied to it. The Kelvin scale is to the color of light as the ISO scale is to the sensitivity of film (figure 4.1).

Color Temperature Meters

A color temperature meter can measure the photographic color temperature of a light source (figure 4.2). The most reliable and expensive meters compare the relative amounts of red, blue, and green energy in the light. They work well with sunlight and incandescent light sources, but are not as accurate for measuring fluorescent light. This is because light sources, such as fluorescent light, that do not radiate color continuously and evenly throughout the spectrum, cannot be given a color temperature. These discontinuous sources are assigned color temperatures on the basis of measurement with a color temperature meter and/or on the visual response of color film to these discontinuous light sources.

To operate a digital color meter, set the film type (daylight or tungsten), position the meter near the principal subject, point it at the camera and/or main light source, and read the temperature and filtration recommendations in the meter's display window. Its suggested filtration should work with negative film, but transparency film may require a test roll for accurate results due to fluctuations in the emulsion and processing (see section on testing for a critical neutral color match in this chapter, page 88).

The Color of Light

Although we think of daylight as being "white," it usually contains some color depending on the time of day, the time of year, and the weather. Artificial light is rarely white. Our brain remembers how things are supposed to look and makes us believe that the light is white even if it is not. It interprets the scene for us.

4.2 Shambroom's photographs from his book *Face to Face with the Bomb: Nuclear Reality after the Cold War* (2003) of bombers, missiles, submarines, warheads, and associated facilities throughout the United States are at once banal and evocative. With the distinct contrast in how the room is coolly lit, and the imposing presence of the looming warheads in this image, Shambroom seems to neither criticize nor glorify nuclear weapons. "My objective is to reveal the tangible reality of the huge nuclear arsenal, something that exists for most of us only as a powerful concept in our collective consciousness." To get sharp, color-balanced images in these industrial environments, he uses a color meter to determine what filter to use on the flash to match the ambient source.

© Paul Shambroom. *Untitled (W87/Mk21 Peacekeeper missile Warheads, F.E. Warren Air Force Base, WY)*, 1992. 48 x 61 inches. Chromogenic color print.

How Film Sees Color

Unfortunately, color film cannot do this and simply records what is present. Each color film is designed to accurately record the quality of light for a certain manufactured "normal" color temperature. If you use a film that does not match the color temperature of the light, the picture will have an unnatural color cast to it. Silver-based photographic materials have an inherent sensitivity to the blue wavelengths of the visual spectrum and to all the shorter wavelengths. Their sensitivity can be extended to green, yellow, and red visible wavelengths, as well as into part of the infrared portion of the spectrum.

Daylight Type Film

The most common color film is designed to give an accurate representation of a scene in daylight. At midday the Kelvin temperature of outdoor light is about 5500 K. Daylight films are designed to give faithful results between 5200 K and 5800 K. Daylight has predominately blue color content. If you make pictures at other times, such as early in the morning or at sunset, the light has less blue in it and the results will have a warmer than normal color balance. When the color temperature drops below 5200 K, daylight film begins to record the scene as warmer. The more you drop below 5200 K, the greater the color cast will be. In artificial tungsten light, daylight film produces a

With a large-format camera mounted on a tripod, an initial daylight exposure was made on daylight film, the shutter was closed, and the camera and film left in position until after dark. Then the shutter was opened and another series of exposures, using a small, battery-powered light with colored gels, was made on the same piece of film.

© William Lesch. *Red Mountain and Clouds*, 1989. Size varies: 16 x 20 through 30 x 40 inches. Dye-destruction print. Courtesy of Etherton Gallery, Tucson, AZ.

---

warm orange-reddish-yellow cast.

In winter light, everything appears slightly cooler or bluish. Light reflected off colored walls or passing through translucent objects creates a color cast that influences the entire scene. This is known as color contamination (see section on monochrome in chapter 13, page 242, for more information).

Tungsten and Type L Films

Tungsten Type B slide film and Type L negative film are color balanced at 3200 K to be used with 250- to 500-watt photolamps or spots. Using tungsten film in daylight produces a blue cast. If you use it with a light source of a lower (redder) color temperature, such as a household bulb, the result is yellower. If these shifts in color are not desired, they must be filtered out. The most critical results are generally obtained when filtering at the time of exposure, rather than attempting to correct the color shifts later.

Digital White Balance and Color Modes

Digital cameras have built-in white balance control, which compensates for variations in the color of common types of light so that white and gray objects appear neutral. Typically the white balance can be set to one of a variety of fixed values or can be measured manually. Also, high-end cameras have different color modes that can be selected to match a situation (see chapter 7, page

155, for details about both).

What Does a Filter Do?

A photographic filter is a transparent device that can alter the quality and quantity of light. It is placed in front of the camera or enlarging lens or in the path of the light falling on the subject. Filters that go in front of the lens must be of optical quality or they can degrade the image quality. Filters used in front of a light source or with a color enlarger do not have to be of optical quality, but they must be able to withstand high heat without becoming distorted or faded.

How Filters Work

Most filters are colored and work subtractively, absorbing the wavelengths of light of their complementary (opposite)

color while transmitting wavelengths of their own color. The color of a filter is the color of the light it transmits. For example, a red filter is red because it absorbs blue and green light while transmitting red light. Although a filter transmits its own color, it also passes all or parts of the colors next to it in the spectrum while absorbing part or most of all other colors. A red filter does not transmit yellow light, but it does allow some light from yellow objects to pass. This occurs because yellow is made up of green and red. The red filter passes the red portion of the yellow while blocking the green.

Filter Factor

Filters are normally uniform in color but may differ in density (color strength). The amount of light absorbed depends on the density of the filter. Since filters block some of the light, they generally require an increase in exposure to make up for the light lost due to absorption. This compensation is known as the filter factor and is indicated as a number, followed by an X sign, which tells how

4.3 Parker made use of Kodak Wratten filters numbers 24, 59, and 47 in producing this image. Parker comments: "I borrow ways of doing things in the darkroom from film, printmaking, and graphic design. I devise my way of thinking from fiction, poetry, philosophy, and painting. My sense of when it works comes from jazz. I use several enlargers and a large stereo system. The sheet of color paper and I walk around collecting projections. At the end of the exposure the sheet looks exactly as it did when I started. An odd thing the latent image is, in a visual art media. I do some small-time chemistry in a Jobo CPP2 processor and see what happened and go around again, retracing my spiral travels until I pull the cork from the bottle."

© Bart Parker. *Stone Daughters, Departed Sons*, No. 15, 1987. 20 x 16 inches. Chromogenic color print.

Table 4.2	
Filter Factor Adjustments	
Filter Factor	*Exposure Adjustment*
1.2X	+1/3 stop
1.5X	+2/3 stop
2X	+1 stop
2.5X	+1 1/3 stops
3X	+1 2/3 stops
4X	+2 stops
5X	+2 1/3 stops
6X	+2 2/3 stops
8X	+3 stops
10X	+3 1/3 stops
12X	+3 2/3 stops
16X	+4 stops
32X	+5 stops

Note: Cameras with thru-the-lens meters should automatically make the correct filter factor adjustment. When using a handheld meter, you'll have to manually make the adjustment. The aperture of a lens may be set in between the standard click stops to achieve accurate exposure adjustment.

much the exposure must be multiplied. A filter factor of 2X means that one additional f-stop of exposure is needed; 2.5X shows 1 1/3 additional f-stops are necessary; 3X means an extra 1 2/3 f-stops are needed; 4X indicates two additional f-stops of exposure. To simplify matters, many manufacturers indicate how many f-stops to increase the exposure. Table 4.2 shows the effect of filter factors on exposure.

Most thru-the-lens (TTL) camera metering systems give an accurate reading with a filter in place; otherwise the film speed can be adjusted to compensate. For example, if you are using a film with a speed of 100 and a filter with a 2X factor you change the film speed to 50. This provides the film with one additional f-stop to compensate for the filter factor. Some TTL meters can be fooled and give faulty readings with certain filters. Bracket your exposures when using a filter for the first time. Table 4.2 also shows the amount of additional exposure needed for many common filters when working with a handheld or non-TTL camera meter. Auto-focus systems may not operate properly with heavy filtration, diffusion, or certain special effects filters. If the system balks, switch to manual focus.

Dichroic Filters

Dichroic filters, such as those found in many color enlargers, act by interference. A thin coating on the surface of the filter

causes certain wavelengths to be reflected, and thus canceled out, while permitting other wavelengths to pass through it.

How Filters Are Identified

Filters are described and identified in a variety of systems. The most widely used is the Kodak Wratten number system in which filters are simply identified with a number, such as 85B (figure 4.3).

In color photography filters are employed to make changes in the color balance of the light that creates the image. The color of a light source is described in terms of its color temperature, measured in degrees Kelvin (K). If the color temperature of the light does not match that of the film, the final image will have a color cast to it. A color temperature meter can be used to provide a precise reading of the Kelvin temperature of the light source when extremely accu-

rate color correction is needed.

Match the Film to the Light

It is always best to match the light and the film with the correct filter at the time of exposure. Negative film allows for some correction when the print is made, but slide film leaves much less room for errors although new film technologies have made them more forgiving. Manufacturers supply slide film for daylight (5500 K), Type A (balanced for photo-flood lights at 3400 K), and Type B (balanced for studio lights at 3200 K). Type A and Type B film exposed in sunlight produce a strong blue cast, while daylight film exposed in artificial light has a distinct red-orange-yellow cast.

There are about a hundred different correction filters available to deal with the range of color temperature encountered. Of course, ignoring the rules and doing the opposite can produce startling visual results (figure 4.4).

Filter Categories Used with Color Films

The following are general categories of filters that are commonly employed with color films (figure 4.5).

Color Compensating Filters

Color compensating filters (CC) are used to make slight and precise corrections in one or two colors of the light. CC filters counteract small color shifts and correct minor color casts, and are usually used to control the primary colors. For example, a red CC filter reduces blue and green light. A filter of one of the secondary colors affects its primary complement. Thus a magenta filter reduces green light, a yellow filter reduces blue light, and a cyan filter reduces red light.

4.4 Varry lights her images of altered personal documents with incandescent light and shoots with daylight film. This intentional mismatch of light and film results in hues of dark amber and deep red, giving Varry's images an aged look that is key within her themes of nostalgia and time.

© Sandra Varry. *hand canceled*, 2002. 20 x 20 inches. Chromogenic color print.

The amount of light reduced depends on the filter's density. CC filters come in various densities of blue, cyan, green, magenta, red, and yellow. Their density is indicated by numbers like CC10R—the 10 represents a density of 0.10 and is commonly referred to as 10 units or points of red. CC filters are also employed to gain proper balance when color printing. CC filters can be used at the time of exposure to correct for a particular color cast that certain films produce.

Conversion Filters

Conversion filters are used to make large changes in color balance. Generally they correct a mismatch of film type and illumination, but they can be employed to create a deliberate color shift. They consist of 80 series (dark blue) and 85 series (amber/dark yellow) filters (see table 4.3). The common 80 series filters are used with daylight film to color correct it with tungsten light. For example, if you were photographing a person under a tungsten light source with daylight film, an 80A or 80B filter would render a more accurate color match. The 85 filters correct tungsten film when it is used in daylight. Also see table 4.3 to determine the correct combination of film and filter for common lighting situations. All these filters reduce the amount of light entering the camera lens and require an

4.5 Type L 4- x 5-inch negative film was chosen for its ability to deal with a mixed-light situation. Lauritzen made four separate exposures of this scene to combine natural and artificial light and to minimize contrast. First, a short exposure was made for the hills and the sky; second, an exposure was made for the entrance lights; third, an exposure was made for the neon; and fourth, an exposure was made for the street lights. Even with such exacting exposure controls, this print still required extensive dodging, burning, and localized color corrections.

© Erik Lauritzen. *The Gem*, 1989, 16 x 20 inches. Chromogenic color print.

Table 4.3 Table Conversion Filters for Color Films

Color Film Type	Designed for	Daylight (5500 K)	Lighting Conditions Photolamp (3400 K)	Tungsten (3200 K)
Daylight type (5500 K)	Daylight, blue flash, electronic flash	No filter	80B	80A
Type A (3400 K)	Photolamps (3400 K)	85	No filter	82A
Tungsten Type B (3200 K)	Tungsten (3200 K)	85B	81A	No filter

Table 4.4 Exposure Compensation with Conversion Filters

Filter	Changes Color Temperature From	To	Film	Exposure Increase In f-stops*
80A	3200 K	5500 K	Daylight	2
80B	3400 K	5500 K	Daylight	1 2/3
80C	3800 K	5500 K	Daylight	1
80D	4200 K	5500 K	Daylight	1/3
85	5500 K	3400 K	Tungsten (Type A)	2/3
85B	5500 K	3200 K	Tungsten	2/3
85C	4650 K	3400 K	Tungsten (Type A)	1/3

*These are suggested starting points. For critical work, especially with color slide film, a visual test should be conducted.

Table 4.5 Light Balancing Filters

Subject Conditions	Filtration for Daylight Films (5500 K)	Filtration for Tungsten Films (3200 K)
Sunrise, sunset	80B or 80C (blue)	82 (blue)
Two hours after sunrise or before sunset	80D (blue)	81 + 81EF (yellow)
Average noon sunlight	None	85B (orange)
Overcast	81A or 81B (amber)	85B + 81B
Open shade	81B or 81C (amber)	85B + 81A

Note: Sky conditions vary dramatically depending on the time of day, the weather, and the location. While these filters may not always fully correct the color, they should provide much better results than if no filter was used at all.

increase in exposure. They can also make focusing more difficult, reduce the depth of field, and extend shutter speeds to unacceptably long times. See table 4.4 for exposure corrections when working with common conversion filters.

Light Balancing Filters

Light balancing filters make smaller changes in the color balance than conversion filters. They are used to match an artificial light source more closely with a tungsten film (table 4.5). The 81 series filters, known as warming filters, have a yellowish or amber color to counteract excessive blue light and lower the color temperature. Use an 81A or 81B filter to reduce excessive blue in aerial, marine, and snow scenes. It is also effective on overcast and rainy days, in open shade, and directly after sunset. An 81C can be used in daylight conditions that have an inordinate amount of blue. Filters in the 82 series possess a bluish color to counteract excessive yellow and raise the color temperature of the light. An 82A filter is used to reduce the warm cast in early morning and late afternoon light.

Correcting Color Balance with Electronic Flash

Electronic flash has a color temperature equivalent to bright daylight, usually about 5600 K to 6000 K. Each unit is different; some tend to be cooler and bluer than others. Electronic flash also produces ultraviolet wavelengths that can appear as blue on color film. If your flash is putting out light that is too cool for your taste, a yellow CC or CP filter of slight color value can be cut and taped in front of the unit. Usually a filter with a value of 05 or 10 will make the correction. Filters can be intentionally used to provide creative lighting changes within a scene (figure 4.6). Flash can also be employed if you are shooting daylight film in tungsten light. The flash can help to offset the tungsten light and maintain a more natural color balance. Thoughtful use of flash can also be used to produce strongly contrasting effects of light

assignment

Make photographs under lighting conditions that do not match the type of light for which the film was designed or the white balance was set. Then, under the same mismatch of conditions, take corrective actions using filters, flash, or white balance. Compare your results. Discuss the emotional effect that is created when the film/white balance and light do not match. Might there be a situation when you would intentionally create a mismatch? Why? Observe problem situations that you keep encountering that a filter would help to solve. Base your purchases on your own shooting experiences and get the equipment that lets you make pictures you desire.

and shade known as chiaroscuro, which can set the psychological atmosphere of a scene (figure 4.7)

Neutral Density Filters

Neutral density (ND) filters are applied to reduce the intensity of the light by absorbing the same amount of all the wavelengths. ND filters will not affect the color balance or tonal range of the scene. They have an overall gray appearance and come in different densities (ND2, ND4, and ND8) that will cut the light by one, two, or four f-stops. An ND2 transmits 50 percent of the light, ND4 25 percent, and ND8 12.5 percent. Kodak's Wratten ND filters, available in dyed gelatin squares, come in 13 different densities, ranging from 0.1 (needing 1/3 f-stop more exposure) to 4.0 (needing 13 1/3 more f-stops of exposure). The Kodak density (logarithmic) values

are not the same as the ND filters labeled with simple filter factors.

An ND filter can also be employed anytime the light is too bright to use a slow shutter speed and/or large lens opening. An ND filter can also be used to reduce the depth of field. This can be effective in outdoor portraiture because it permits you to use a large aperture to put the background out of focus, thus giving more emphasis to the subject. ND filters can be employed in order to get a slower shutter speed and produce intentional blur action shots. For instance, a

4.8 It is the imagemaker's job to pay attention and control reflections. Bringing a virtual studio to the wilderness, Streetman superimposed a silver grid to make use of the reflection that shifts from silver to gray depending on the viewer's position. The clouds were painted on the underside of two large sheets of mylar. By placing the rocks under and over the mylar Streetman produces gestural marks with the reflections on the surface. Streetman says she designed visual invitations that cause the more curious observer to discover the deception and to be reminded of the traditional value of the artist as craftsperson.

© Evon Streetman. *Landscape and Systems*, 1984. 30 x 24 inches. Dye-destruction print with mixed media.

slow shutter speed would let the movement of cascading water be captured as a soft blur. Another example would be moving the zoom control of the lens during exposure, for which a shutter speed of 1/15 second or slower is necessary while the camera is on a tripod. ND filters can be useful in making pan shots or when you have to use a very high-speed film in extremely bright light. Center-weighted ND filters are used with certain panoramic cameras to correct for light fall-off that reduces the exposure at the corners of the image by up to one f-stop.

Reflections: Polarized and Unpolarized Light

Normally a light wave moves in one direction, but the light energy itself vibrates in all directions perpendicular to the direction of travel of the light wave. Such light is said to be unpolarized. Polarizers such as the naturally occurring mineral called Iceland spar transmit only the part of each light wave vibrating in a particular direction; the rest of the light wave is refracted away from its original direction. The portion of the light that is transmitted is called polarized light.

What a Polarizing Filter Can Do

A polarizing filter is made up of submicroscopic crystals that are lined up like a series of parallel slats. Light waves traveling parallel to these crystal slats pass unobstructed between them. The crystal slats block light waves vibrating at different angles. Because the polarized light is all at the same angle, a polarizing filter is designed to rotate so that it can block the polarized portion of the light.

The polarizing filter is a device used to polarize the light in photography. Modern polarizing materials such as Polaroid, first produced in 1932 by Dr. Edwin Land, have replaced the naturally occurring Iceland spar crystals. Polarizers are usually gray-brown in color.

Polarizers are used to eliminate reflections from smooth, nonmetallic, polished surfaces such as glass, tile, tabletops, and water, and they can improve color saturation by screening out the polarized part of the glare. This can make a clear blue sky appear deeper and richer and have more contrast without altering the overall color balance of the scene. The increase in saturation results from a decrease in surface glare. Since most semi-smooth objects, such as flowers, leaves, rocks, and water, have a surface sheen, they reflect light, thus masking some of the color beneath the sheen. By reducing these reflections, the polarizer intensifies the colors.

Inspired by roadside altars encountered in Japan, Tress incorporated his long-time themes of enlightenment, journey, and dreams into the series *Fish Tank Sonata*. He used a polarizing filter to control the reflections in the glass tanks. Tress often works with miniatures to approach "the hidden life of imagination and fantasy which is hungry for stimulation." His oeuvre consists of work ranging from documentation that is curiously fabricated, to creations of mythological scenarios that incorporate kitsch as a visual element and themes of daliy chaos and life and death.

© Arthur Tress. *Central Park*, from the *Fish Tank Sonata* series, 1987–1990. 15 x 15 inches. Dye-destruction print.

A polarizing filter can also be more effective than a haze filter for cutting through haze with color film because it reduces more of the scattered blue light and decreases reflections from dust and/or water particles (figure 4.8). The net effect is that the scene appears to be more distinct and sharp, while the visual sense of depth is increased and the vividness of the colors is added to. When copying original art and reproductions from books or photographing glossy-surfaced objects, maximum glare control can be obtained by using polarizers in front of the light sources as well as in front of the camera lens. Evaluate each situation before using a polarizer, as there are occasions where the purposeful inclusion of reflections strengthens the photographer's underlying concept.

Using a Polarizer

When using a polarizing filter, focus first; turn the filter mount until the glare decreases and the colors look richer; then make the exposure. The filter factor will remain the same, regardless of how much the filter is rotated. The filter factor varies from about 2X to 3X, depending on the type of polarizer used.

The amount of the effect is determined by how much polarized light is present in the scene and on the viewing angle of the scene. At an angle of about 35 degrees from the surface, the maximum reduction in reflections can be achieved when the polarizer is rotated to the correct position.

A polarizer may also be combined with other filters for special effects. There are polarizers with color available. These combine a gray and a single colored polarizing filter. Any color, from gray to the full color of the other filter, can be achieved by rotating the filter frame ring. There are also multicolored polarizers that combine a single gray polarizing filter and two colored polarizing filters. Rotating the filter frame ring alters the colors.

Linear and Circular Polarizers

There are two types of polarizer used in photography: the traditional linear kind and the newer circular model. If your camera has a semi-silvered mirror (this includes all current auto-focus SLR cameras), the linear filter will produce underexposed and out-of-focus pictures. Circular filters work on all SLR cameras without producing these undesirable side effects but are considerably more expensive. A linear model can be used with a semi-silvered mirror camera by (1) determining the exposure without the filter on the camera; (2) manually setting the exposure to compensate for the filter factor (give more exposure) before attaching the filter to the front of the camera's lens; or (3) manually focusing the camera. Do not rely on the auto-focus.

Special-Purpose Filters/Ultraviolet

Special-purpose filters include ultraviolet, haze, and skylight filters. All of these absorb ultraviolet (UV) radiation, reducing the effects of scattered light, which

4.9 To obtain an accurate color rendition, Moninger used a UV filter. The UV filter absorbs UV radiation and reduces the effects of light scattering that can produce a light-blue cast in the color dyes of the film. Moninger tells us about his *Nightflowers* series: "I am intrigued by the concept of 'obscuration' of the photographic subject. In these images, the metaphor is the limitation of human perception, the eternal barriers to aspiration. The flower forms are fractured by a veil of lens-like water beads. Extending the location work (New York City flower shop windows late at night) into a few studio setups, #21 was executed by placing cut flowers in a glass bell jar. The mist formed naturally."

© Jim Moninger. *Nightflowers* #21, 1987. 20 x 16 inches. Chromogenic color print.

adversely affects the color dyes (often giving a blue cast), producing a more accurate and natural rendition. Typically, a UV filter is effective with landscapes, especially photographs of mountains, seashores, or snow scenes, in which UV radiation is intense. UV filters can also help to ensure optimum quality when doing copy work, and close-ups of plants (figure 4.9) and objects with bright colors such as porcelain ware. UV filters are not effective in reducing the excess amount of blue light in scenes containing shade (81 series should be used). The UV filters have no filter factor, and many photographers leave one on their lenses to protect the lens surface from dirt, moisture, and scratches.

Special Effects Filters

Special effects filters produce unusual visual effects. Exercise care and thought before using one for they are overused and can be a visual crutch for unthinking photographers who lack genuine picture-making ideas. Most pictures made with them appear clichéd and overly predictable. Special effects filters include the following (see figure 4.10):

● **Center spot**: diffuses the entire area except the center.

● **Changeable color**: used in combination with a polarizing filter. Rotating the filter changes the color from one primary, through the midtones, to a different primary color. Available in yellow to red, yellow to green, green to red, blue to yellow, and red to blue.

● **Close-up**: fitted with a normal lens to permit you to focus closer than the minimum distance the lens was designed to accommodate (figure 4.11).

● **Color spot**: center portion of filter is clear with the surrounding area colored.

● **Color vignette**: filter with colored edges and clear center.

● **Cross screen**: exaggerates highlights into star shapes.

● **Diffraction**: takes strong highlights and splits them into spectral color beams.

	Type of Filter	Filter Factor	Typical Application
Correction Filters	Color Compensating	Yes	Slight Correction of Color
	Conversion	Yes	Large Changes in Color Balance
	Light Balancing	Yes	Smaller Changes in Color Balance
Standard Use Filters	Neutral Density	Yes	Reduces Intensity of All Wavelengths of Light
	Polarizing	Yes	Improves Color Contrast and Saturation; Reduces Glare on Nonmetal Objects
	Ultraviolet (UV)	Some-times	Cuts Haze and UV Light to Provide a More Accurate and Natural Rendition
Special Effects	Center Spot	No	Diffuses the Entire Area Except the Center
	Cross Screen	No	Exaggerates Highlights into Star Shapes
	Diffraction	No	Splits Strong Highlights into Spectral Colors
	Diffusion	No	Softens Focus; Mutes Color
	Double Exposure	No	Masks Half of the Frame
	Dual Color	Yes	Each Half of Frame Shows Different Color
	Framing	No	Masks Frame
	Multi-Image Prism	No	Repeats and Overlaps Image
	Prism (colored)	Yes	Makes Multiple Images in Spectral Colors
	Single Color	Yes	Changes Frame to Color of the Filter
	Split Field	No	Permits Differential Focus
	Underwater	Yes	Removes Cyan Cast at 10-Foot Depth or Deeper

4.10 Common filters and their typical applications in color photography.

● **Diffusion**: softens and mutes the image and color. Available in a variety of strengths that provide different degrees of softening effect.

● **Double exposure**: masks half the frame at a time.

● **Dual color**: each half of the frame receives a different color cast.

● **Fog**: delivers a soft glow in highlight areas while lowering contrast and sharpness. Available in several strengths. Effect varies depending on the aperture of the lens; stopping down reduces the effect.

● **Framing**: masks the frame to form a black or colored shape.

● **Graduated**: half the filter is colored and the other half is clear. The colored portion fades to colorless toward the center line of the filter.

● **Macro filter**: typically, when attached to a 50-mm lens on a 35-mm SLR camera, it permits 1:2 copying; when attached to a 100-mm lens, it enables 1:1 copying.

- **Prism/multi-image**: repeats and over-laps the image within the frame.
- **Prism/colored**: makes multiple images with spectrum-colored casts.
- **Split field**: allows differential focus within the frame.
- **Tricolor**: filter has three sections, red, green, and blue, in a single filter element.
- **Underwater**: removes the cyan cast that appears at a depth of 10 feet or more.

Note: Filter kits that utilize a universal holder and gelatin squares provide an economical way to work with a variety of filters.

Homemade Colored and Diffusion Filters

Making your own filters can save money and free you from using only manufac-tured materials. By using your ingenuity it is possible to create your own filters for artistic control of color. Although homemade filters may not match the quality of commercially manufactured fil-ters from optical grade materials, they can produce results that are not only acceptable but also even desirable. A uni-versal filter holder, attached in front of the lens, permits you to experiment with a variety of materials and can also hold gelatin squares of commercial filters.

All that is necessary to make a col-ored filter is some type of transparent material. Colored cellophane and theatri-cal gels provide simple starting places. The greatest versatility can be achieved by marking clear acetate with color felt-tipped pens. When held or taped in front of the camera, acetate filters are excellent at producing pastel-like colors. Photographing a light-colored subject against a bright background can heighten the pastel effect. There are endless possi-bilities, since you can make split-field fil-ters with numerous color combinations.

By photographing through transpar-ent objects such as stained glass or water,

it is also possible to transfer color(s) to a subject (figure 4.12).

Homemade diffusion filters can be made from any transparent material. Each material creates its own unique way of scattering the light and produces a dif-ferent visual effect. Although most pho-tographers use a diffusion filter at the time of camera exposure, it is also possi-ble to employ one in front of your

4.11 Finger constructs images that explore the ways in which we interact with nature as a natural resource, a symbolic object, and an aestheticized object. He shoots miniatures arranged on a table and lit by light filtered through a nearby window. To get the illusion he was after, Finger used a +4 diopter on a normal 50-mm lens, which enabled him to work extremely close and achieve very shallow depth of field with a handheld camera. Shining a yellow light at a round mirror created the moon.

© Bill Finger. *Full Moon*, 2003. 24 x 20 inches. Chromogenic color print.

enlarging lens when printing. Test some of the following materials and techniques to see which suit your needs:

- **Cellophane**: Crumple up a piece of cellophane, then smooth it out and attach it to the front of your lens with a rubber band.

- **Matt spray**: On an unwanted clear filter or plain piece of Plexiglas or glass, apply a fine mist of spray matt material.

- **Nail polish**: Brush some clear nail polish on a piece of clear glass or an unwanted UV filter. Allow it to dry and it's ready to use. Painting different patterns and/or using a stipple effect will deliver a variety of possibilities. Nail-polish remover can be used for cleanup.

- **Petroleum jelly**: Carefully apply petroleum jelly to a clear piece of glass or a UV filter with your finger, a lint-free towel, or a brush. Remove any that covers the sides or back of the support so it won't get on your lens. The direction of application and the thickness of the jelly will determine the amount of diffusion. Clean up with soap and warm water.

- **Stockings**: Stretch a piece of fine-meshed nylon stocking over the front of the lens and attach it with a rubber band. Use a beige or gray color unless you want the color of the stocking to influence the color balance of the final image. White stockings scatter a greater amount of light, so they considerably reduce the overall contrast of the scene.

- **Transparent tape**: Apply a crisscross pattern of transparent tape on a UV filter. The amount of diffusion is influenced by the width and thickness of the tape.

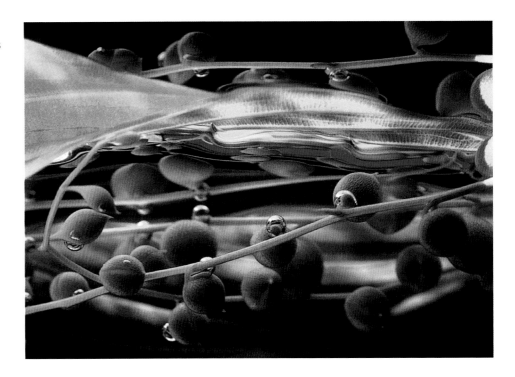

4.12 Camp tells us: "My work in color grew out of my beginnings as a poet who was writing imagist poems, but wanted to deal with color in a more tangible form than that expressed in words. ... I was influenced by Steichen's *Heavy Roses* into using dead and dying flowers as subject matter ... to escape the bounds of the traditional still life I made the transition from a vase to a bowl to an aquarium in which to float flowers in order to free them from the frozen specimen-looking appearance so many still lives possess. Water has many properties of its own, one of which is that it picks up colors that are in proximity to it. I discovered stained glass would act as a filter, transferring its color to the surface of the water as well as to the flowers themselves."

© Roger Camp. *Water Music* #24, 1995. 16 x 20 inches. Dye-destruction print.

Fluorescent and Other Gas-Filled Lights

A fluorescent light source consists of a gas discharge tube in which the discharge radiation causes a phosphor coating on the inside of the tube to fluoresce. Although fluorescent light may appear to look like light from another artificial source it is not. Fluorescent light possesses both a discontinuous and an unbalanced spectrum. The color of the light depends on the type of phosphor and gas used. It has peak outputs in the green and blue regions of the spectrum, valleys or deficiencies in red, and gaps of other wavelengths, and its intensity varies as the gas moves in the tube. This makes it a discontinuous source, lacking the full range of wavelengths that are present in the visible spectrum. Fluorescent light is generally unsuitable for naturalistic color photography. However, there are "full-spectrum" fluorescent lamps with a high CRI (Color Rendition Index) that have color temperatures of about 5000 K to 6000 K.

If you photograph using daylight film or with improper white balance under fluorescent light, the resulting image will have a green cast. This is not generally attractive, especially if you are making pictures of people; they will have a green cast to their skin. If this is not what you had in mind, corrective action is required.

Unnumbered filters are available to make general adjustments for the excessive blue-green cast of fluorescent lights. With daylight film there are three basic fluorescent filters to consider that will deliver good starting results: use an FL-D filter under daylight-type fluorescent lamps, and an FL-W filter with warm white or white-type fluorescent lamps. With Type B tungsten film, use an FL-B filter. For more accurate results, it is necessary to test with a variety of filters (see table 4.6). With a digital camera, experiment with different white balance settings.

The following are possible corrective actions that can be taken:

● Use a shutter speed of 1/60 second or slower to minimize the flickering effect of the fluorescent lamp.

● Replace the standard fluorescent lights with tungsten lights or with "full-spectrum" fluorescent lamps.

● Place plastic filters over the tubes that will make them closer to daylight.

● If possible, shoot a fast daylight negative film that has a speed of 400 or more. This provides two chances to make corrections, once at the time of exposure and again when making the print. The higher speed films have greater tolerances for this type of light.

● Experiment with the filter pack when making a print with a daylight negative film. Sometimes it is possible to get more naturalistic color with the use of only one filter, usually a yellow one. To color correct in printing, it may be necessary to set the magenta filter to zero in order to compensate for the excess of green cast. Results depend on the type of fluorescent tube, film, and enlarger.

● Use a fluorescent filter. They are available for both daylight and tungsten films and can be used with either slide or print film. These generally make a big improvement (figure 4.13). If critical results are needed, run tests using CC filters to determine the exact filtration. You will usually need magenta or a combination of magenta and blue filters. With daylight film, start with about CC30 magenta and add additional filtration if needed.

● Match tubes to films. Certain tubes photograph more naturally with specific films. For instance, daylight and color-matching tubes look more natural if you use a daylight-type film and filter. Warm

4.13 Concerns with exposing the myth of the document have led Jude to deal with the absurd placement of animals and objects in natural history museums. He wants to create "an awareness of the straight photograph's value not as a reliable formal document, but as a visual catalyst of thought." Public places, such as the museum in this picture, are often lighted by fluorescent lights that can be difficult to color correct. An FLD filter was used at the time of exposure. Jude states: "The flat lighting, along with a slight underdevelopment of the daylight transparency film, produced an acceptable level of contrast in the dye-destruction print. I find it best to somewhat compromise the quality of the transparency in order to avoid the usually harsh contrast of dye-destruction print."

© Ron Jude. `tural History Museum, 1990. 8 x 6 ¼inches. Dye-destruction print.

white tubes are more suitable with tungsten films and filters.

● Use an electronic flash as a fill light. This will help to offset some of the green cast and make the scene appear as our brain tells us it should.

● Use special films, such as Fujicolor

films, which have an additional fourth emulsion layer that responds to blue and green light (which forms a magenta dye image) and generates developer inhibitors that act on the red-sensitive emulsion layers to enhance the reproduction of blue-green colors. With proper printing filtration, people

Table 4.6 Filtering for Discontinuous Light Sources

Fluorescent Bulbs

	Film Type		
Lamp Type	Daylight	Tungsten	Type A
Daylight	50R	No. 85B + 30R + 10M	No. 85 + 40R
White	40M	50R + 10M	30R + 10M
Warm white	20B + 20M	40R + 10M	20R + 10M
Warm white deluxe	30C + 30B	10R	No filter needed
Cool white	30M + 10R	60R	50R
Cool white deluxe	10B + 10C	20R + 20Y	20Y + 10R
Unknown	30M	50R	40R

High-Intensity Discharge Lamps

	Film Type		
Lamp Type	Daylight	Tungsten	Type A
Lucalox	80B + 20C	30M + 20B	50B + 05M
Multivapor	20R + 20M	60R + 20Y	50R + 10Y
Deluxe white mercury	30R + 30M	70R + 10Y	50R + 10Y
Clear mercury	70R	90R + 40Y	90R + 40Y

Note: These general recommendations should only be used as starting points. For critical applications testing is necessary, as filter effect will vary from one kind of film to another.

photographed under cool-white fluorescents can have natural-looking skin tones.

High-Intensity Discharge Lamps/ Mercury and Sodium Vapor Sources

High-intensity discharge lamps, such as mercury vapor lights that are rated at about 4100 K to 4500 K and sodium vapor lights at proximity 2100 K to 2500 K, fit into the category of gas-filled lights. These bright lamps are generally used to light industrial and public spaces. They are extremely deficient in many of the wavelengths that make up white light, especially red, are difficult to impossible to correct for, and require extreme amounts of filtration (table 4.6).

Testing for a Neutral Color Match

Achieving a neutral color match with any discontinuous light source requires running tests with heavy filtration (this same test can be used in any situation requiring critical color balance). Shoot a test roll of transparency film, bracketing in 1/3 f-stops, with and without selected correction filters of the subject under the expected lighting conditions. Use a color temperature meter or see table 4.5 for suggested starting filters. Include a test target, such as the color reference guide at the back of this book, in the scene with the same light as the principal subject. Keep a record of each frame's exposure and filtration. Process and examine unmounted film on a correctly balanced 5000 K lightbox. Placing filters over the film lets you determine their effect. Putting a 20M filter over the film has the same effect as adding 20M in front of the camera lens when reshooting with film having the same emulsion batch number (printed on the side of the film box).

When using a digital camera, be sure it is set to the proper white balance.

Using the Color Reference Guide
Place the color reference guide next to the transparency on the lightbox. Look at the gray scale first, since it is usually easier to see which color is in excess. For example, if the gray scale has a slight blue cast, add a slightly yellow filter (05Y) over the transparency. Scan rapidly back and forth between the color reference guide and the image to see if it looks correct. If it does, this indicates that a 05C filter should be used to achieve a neutral color balance with the same film emulsion batch and processing chemicals. This same procedure can be used with negative film, bracketing in 1/2 f-stops and producing test prints to be compared with the color reference guide.

Why a Color May Not Reproduce Correctly

The dye layers of color film are designed to replicate what the designers believe is an agreeable rendering for most subjects in a variety of situations. There can be times when it is impossible to recreate a specific color, even when the film has been properly manufactured, stored, exposed, and processed. Film designers concentrate on trying to reproduce flesh tones, neutrals (whites, grays, and blacks), and common "memory" colors such as sky blue and grass green well under a variety of imagemaking situations. This results in other colors, such as yellow and orange, not reproducing as

---

a s s i g n m e n t

Photograph a subject under fluorescent light with no color correction. Next, under the same fluorescent conditions, try one or more of the suggested corrective actions. Compare the two. Which do you prefer, and why?

The gas-filled lights in this scene of a gas station at night could cause the appearance of a green cast in the image as it was shot using daylight film. In this case, Gelles made all color corrections digitally using Photoshop after the film was processed.

© Judy Gelles. *Gas Station, Melbourne Beach, Florida,* 2002. 15 x 15 inches. Inkjet print.

well. Color films are not sensitive to colors in precisely the same way as the human eye is. For example, color film is sensitive to ultraviolet radiation. A fabric that reflects ultraviolet energy appears bluer in a color photograph than it does to the human eye. This is why a neutral garment, such as a black tuxedo made of a synthetic material, may appear blue in a color print. Using an ultraviolet filter can reduce this effect.

Other fabrics absorb ultraviolet radiation and re-emit it in the blue portion of the visible spectrum. Since the human eye is not exceptionally sensitive to the shortest (blue) wavelengths of the spectrum, this effect, known as ultraviolet fluorescence, is often not noticed until viewing a color print. White fabrics, for instance a wedding dress that has had

brighteners added during manufacture or laundering to give it a whiter appearance, are the most likely candidates to appear with a blue cast in a color photograph. Unfortunately a filter over the lens will not completely correct the problem. An ultraviolet absorber such as a Kodak Wratten Filter No. 2B is needed over the light source of an electronic flash for accurate correction.

Another trouble spot is anomalous reflectance, which results from high reflectance at the far-red and infrared end of the spectrum, where the human eye has almost no sensitivity. This is commonly observed in color photographs of certain flowers, such as blue morning glories and gentians, which reproduce badly because color films are more sensitive to the far-red portion of

the spectrum than is the human eye.

Also, some organic dyes used to color fabrics, especially synthetic materials, often have high reflectance in the far-red portion of the spectrum. The effect is most frequent in medium- to dark-green fabrics, which may reproduce as neutrals or warm colors. There is no effective correction.

Color Crossover

A color crossover occurs when the highlight and shadow areas of a color transparency or negative are of different color balances. This condition is almost impossible to correct without physical or digital retouching. Crossovers can be produced by using an incorrect film under a specific light source, longer or shorter

exposure times than the film was designed for, improper storage, and/or outdated film. While often unwanted, color crossovers can produce unexpected visual excitement by creating an unreal color palette.

Taking a Chance

Do not be afraid to make pictures even if your film or white balance does not match the color temperature of the light. Sometimes you can get an evocative color mood piece when this mismatch occurs. Often the combination of different light sources enlivens and creates

surprise in your picture (figure 4.14). When in doubt, make it and see what it looks like. At worst you will learn what does not work for you. At best, you may have interacted with the unexpected and come away from the situation with something artist Jean Cocteau would have referred to as "astonishing." If you are going to be a photographer, you have to make pictures. Make many exposures as they provide you with a springboard for not only your current work but future ideas as well. "Art is about taking chances. Danger and chaos—those are the real muses an artist must court," said Robert Rauschenberg. Be a visual explorer and see what you can discover.

4.14 Try making photographs even if the film does not match the exact lighting conditions. The mismatch can create a lively interchange of unexpected color combinations, thus producing images with striking color balances and a heightened sense of mystery. Graham exposed 4- x 5-inch Type S negative film at about 9.00 p.m. and supplemented it with multiple pops from a portable flash unit.

© David Graham. *The Sea Missile Motel, Cocoa Beach, FL*, 1989. 30 x 40 inches. Chromogenic color print. Courtesy of Black Star and Laurence Miller Gallery, New York, NY.

Chapter Five
COLOR FILMS' COLOR

Parker's enigmatic work mingles pictorial clarity with thematic ambiguity. Through a process of recontextualization, Parker bestows "human implications" upon her constructions. By placing prosaic materials in unfamiliar situations and surprising juxtapositions, Parker allows viewers to infuse them with their own inventive meaning.

© Olivia Parker. *Exit*, 1991. 24 x 20 inches. Diffusion transfer process. Courtesy of the Polaroid Collection, Cambridge, MA.

Transparency Film

Characteristic Advantages

Color transparencies, also known as color slides, are positives that are made on reversal film. Each image you look at on transparency film is the original piece of film that was exposed in the camera. What you see is what you get. Prints, on the other hand, are second-generation images, made by enlarging a negative onto color printing paper. The old rule that says the fewer generations we have to go through for a final image the better the quality holds true. Slides are what Marshall McLuhan referred to as a "light through" medium, viewed by transmitted light that passes through the image only once. Prints are a "light on" medium seen by light that is reflected from them. The light bounces off the base support of the print and passes through the image in the emulsion twice, coming and going. This effect doubles the density, which in turn reduces what can be seen within the print itself. Due to this "double-density effect," slides have certain advantages over prints made from negatives, including the sharpest grain structure, maximum color separation, the best color saturation (intensity), and more subtlety in color and detail.

The viewer can distinguish a wider tonal range because the slides are viewed by transmitted light. A high-contrast slide image can have a "readable" tonal range, from the whitest white to blackest black, of about 400:1 when projected, and even more when viewed directly. This ratio is an indicator of how well the detail and color saturation are clearly separated in the key highlight and key shadow areas. A color print viewed in normal room light can have a tonal range of about 100:1. It is usually closer to 85:1 due to light scattering by the surface of the print. It is said that an "average" daylight scene has a brightness range of 160:1 or higher. This means that slide film can do a superior job of capturing a fuller range of tones in many situations. Also, since transparency film provides greater luminosity, the percep-

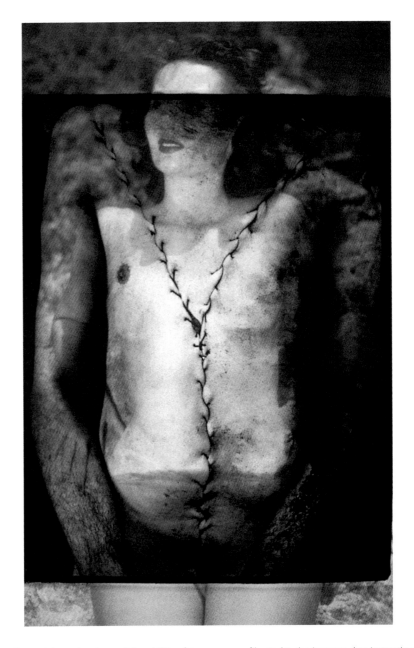

Silverthorne takes advantage of the ability of transparency film to let the imagemaker instantly see what happens when two pieces of film are sandwiched together. Working on the theme of death and the body, Silverthorne examines the thin line that separates Eros and Thanatos. His work often simultaneously juxtaposes attraction and beauty with the forbidden and the repulsive. In this dialogue between life and death, Silverthorne has stated: "I wanted to show that there was no way around this incident of death."

© Jeffrey Silverthorne. *Mother and Father*, 1988. 24 x 20 inches. Dye-destruction print.

tion of a subject's brightness can make it look more luminous, evoking a visual response that is more intense than the original. This can be an effective aesthetic device that utilizes the subjective nature of color to give an impression that the subject is emitting light.

Transparency film's wider tonal range translates into higher contrast. This contrast gives the slide film increased color saturation, most noticeable in the slower films, and helps its ability to differentiate details in the highlight areas. This is most observable in the difference between diffuse and specular highlights, the classic example being a white flower with water droplets. The white petals reflect light in all directions (diffused highlights), while the water droplets directly reflect light as a bright catchlight (specular highlights). Slide film clearly shows the difference between the two; in a print the subtlety of the separation can be lost.

Generally, transparency film is exposed to produce acceptable detail in the key highlight areas of a scene. Both color saturation (vividness) and density increase proportionately with less exposure. For this reason many photographers intentionally underexpose their slide film by changing the manufacturer's standard ISO (International Standards Organization) rating. For example, a film rated at ISO 64 could be modified in the range of ISO 80 to 120. Experimentation by bracketing in 1/3 or 1/2 f-stops is desired.

The processing of slide film provides the user with a finished product without any additional steps, and because no printing is involved in producing the final image, slide film can be processed at home without a great deal of specialized equipment. Their small size makes transparencies easier to edit, index, and store. The cost per final image is between 20 and 30 percent less than that of negative film images. Transparencies are the choice for photographic reproduction, because printers can make color separations directly from them. They are also ideal for direct digital translation via a film scanner.

Disadvantages of Transparencies

Despite their good points, slides do have their disadvantages. They are small and difficult to see; generally a projector and a screen are required for proper viewing. Since the final image is contained on the film base itself, each slide is unique and must be handled with care to prevent damage when being viewed. Both of these characteristics can make slides less convenient to use than prints.

Unlike negative film, transparencies can only be manipulated slightly through development to effectively alter the range of contrast. This is because the color balance of the film is directly affected by development. The biggest disadvantage to someone who is learning to work in color is that there is no second chance to make corrections with slides as there is when making a print. Transparency film has a much narrower exposure latitude than negative film. An exposure error of even a 1/2 f-stop can ruin the picture since both the color and the density of the completed picture are determined by exposure. Overexposed highlights become chalky white with no detail. Underexposed shadows are bulletproof black. Nor is slide film as versatile as negative film in mixed-light situations. It is possible to make some corrections by recopying the slide, but this adds contrast and takes away the initial advantages of slide film. Fast slide film (ISO 400 and above) tends to be much grainier than equivalent speed print films.

If a print is made from a slide via an internegative, there are twice as many color and tonal distortions to deal with as when working with negative film. Prints made through a direct-positive process such as Ilfochrome Classic can suffer from color distortion due to the lack of a corrective mask on the slide film. These prints also tend to be more contrasty than normal and may require a contrast reduction mask to print correctly (see chapter 6, page 139).

How Transparency Film Works

Transparency film makes a positive, rather than a negative, image. Most films use the "tripack" structure (a few now have a "quadpack" design), a sandwich of three gelatin layers that contain light-sensitive silver halides. During exposure, each layer records one of the primary

Images made on transparency film can be directly translated into digital form on a scanner. Weintraub developed an approach of layering image fragments for a series dealing with artificial light and vernacular elements of urban architecture. "For me, digital imaging is a means to control image processing, so that the image can be made totally mutable and plastic. The process I use for repeated layering and dissolves is directly connected to my intent to develop an image that evokes a complex architectural space, and which conveys the ambiguous and sometimes paradoxical multiplicity of messages of the urban environment. ... The unnatural and artificial color spectrum, while 'cheerful' and engaging, underlines a troubling separation from nature and accentuates the desolation of the made environment."

© Annette Weintraub. *Night Sight*, 1993. 31 x 47 inches. Tiled phase-change prints.

colors of light. White light, which is a mixture of blue, green, and red, creates a latent image on all three layers. Other colors formed by mixing the light make latent images only in those areas that are sensitive to those colors. For instance, yellow, which is a mixture of green and red, makes a latent image only in the green and red layers. The blue layer does not record it. Imagine a large red ball. In the final picture, it appears red because the dyes of the colors complementary to blue and green were formed in two layers of the film during development. When the slide is viewed in white light, the blue and green are subtracted from the light, which leaves only red to be seen. Slide film, unlike negative film, has no color mask to correct inherent imperfections of the green-sensitive and red-sensitive layers of the film.

Recent technical advances in color negative films are being applied to slide materials. For example, Fuji's Provia 100 Professional film contains at least three sublayers in each of its three color-sensitive emulsion layers having different sizes and shapes of silver halide crystals to enhance color quality and improve gradation and tonal rendition. Provia is also the first slide film to use developer inhibitor releasing couplers (DIRs). These compounds work during first development to boost saturation, control contrast, and improve sharpness. Also, the film's granularity value is even lower than that of other current ISO 25 films, and its grain is very consistent in size, which makes it appear even finer.

E-6 Processing

All the major color transparency film manufacturers use a standard chromogenic development process (E-6) to produce the cyan, magenta, and yellow dyes in their three-layer emulsion structure. There are other manufacturers, such as Beseler and Unicolor, and each has variations in their version of the E-6 process. The label on the film box or cassette will state if it can be developed by this method.

In E-6 chromogenic development the first step is similar to black-and-white processing (table 5.1). A silver-grain negative image is developed in each of the layers of the emulsion. The silver appears where the film has been struck by light. White light affects all three layers, while red, for example, forms silver only in the red-sensitive layer. No colored dye is formed during this stage of the process.

Next, the first development is halted and the film is "fogged" through either chemical action or exposure to light, so that the silver grains can be formed throughout all layers of the emulsion.

During color development the remaining silver is developed and the subtractive primary dyes are produced in the emulsion layers in proportion to the amount of silver that is formed. These dyes make up the final image. At this stage the film looks black because it has metallic silver in all the emulsion layers and color dyes in many places.

To be able to see the dye-positive image, the film has to be bleached. The prebleach has agents that enhance image stability and contains only trace amounts of formaldehyde, thus reducing the possibility of user contact with free formaldehyde. The bleach changes all silver into silver halide crystals. The fixer then removes all the silver halides from the film, leaving only the dye-positive image. Some processes combine the bleach and the fix into one step.

Table 5.1	**Kodak E-6 Process**	
Step	*Time in Minutes**	*Temperature (°F)†*
The first three steps must be carried out in total darkness		
First developer	6‡ (1) and (2)	100.4 +/−0.5
Wash	2	92 to 102
Reversal bath	2	92 to 102
The remaining steps can be carried out in room light		
Color developer	6	100.4 +/−2
PreBleach	2	92 to 102
Bleach	7	92 to 102
Fixer	4	92 to 102
Wash	6	92 to 102
Final Rinse	1	92 to 102
Dry	as needed	up to 140

Note: Before beginning to process film, read and follow all the manufacturer's warning, mixing, and disposal instructions to ensure your health and that of the environment.
*All steps include a 10-second drain time.
†For the best results, keep all the temperatures as close to 100°F as possible.
‡Development time changes depending on the number of rolls that have been processed. Check the capacity of the solutions with the instructions. Mixed solutions have a limited life span. Follow the manufacturer's recommendations for storage and useful time limits of all solutions. Times will also change when film is processed in a rotary processor.
(1) Initial agitation: For all solutions, tap the tank on a 45-degree angle to dislodge any air bubbles. No further agitation is needed in the reversal bath, prebleach, or final rinse.
(2) Additional agitation: Subsequent agitation is required in all other solutions. After tapping the tank, agitate by slowly turning the tank upside down and then right side up for the first 15 seconds. For the remaining time of each step, let the tank rest for 25 seconds, then agitate for five seconds. Keep the tank in a water-tempering bath to maintain the temperatures for both first and color developers.
With noninvertible tanks, which cannot be turned upside down, tap the tank on a 45-degree angle to remove air bubbles, and rotate the reels at the indicated times to achieve proper agitation.

The wash takes away the remaining fixer. The final rinse is the last step, which is mainly a wetting agent used to reduce water spotting and prompt even film drying. Its concentration can be varied to accommodate various drying conditions.

Temperature Control

All color processes are extremely sensitive to time, temperature, and agitation. New technical advances, such as multi-layered coating, mean the latest generation of slide films is even more "process sensitive" than its predecessors. Time and temperature are critical to obtain correct color balance and density. For optimum results, you must maintain the correct range of temperatures throughout the process. If this is not possible, have a professional lab develop the film.

In the Kodak E-6 process, the developing steps are the most sensitive. Tolerances for consistent results follow:

FIRST DEVELOPER
Time: plus/minus 5 seconds
Temperature: plus/minus 0.5°F (0.3°C)

COLOR DEVELOPER
Time: plus/minus 15 seconds
Temperature: plus/minus 1.1°F (0.6°C)

Water Bath
To maintain these critical temperatures, a water bath is recommended. Fill a deep tray or pail with water so that it is equal to the depth of the solution in the storage containers. Bring the water temperature slightly above the actual processing temperature (100.5°F, or 38°C) to allow for cooling due to ambient room temperature. Allow the containers and loaded film tank to stand in the water until they reach operating levels. Measure the temperature inside the solution containers without allowing the thermometer to touch the container wall. Be certain the thermometer is accurate. When not agitating, keep the processing tank in the water bath. Keep the wash temperature the same as that of the bleach and fixer.

Handling and Agitation

Load film in total darkness. Handle the film only by its edges and ends. Use a light-tight processing tank so that processing can be done under room light.

Proper agitation is crucial with all color processing. Too little or too much agitation causes uneven or unusual color balance and/or density effects in the processing of the film. Proper agitation in the developer is a must. It is done by inverting the tank, rotating the tank, or rotating the reels. Follow agitation instructions based on the type of tank used. If only one roll of film is being processed in a multireel tank, place the loaded reel in the bottom and fill the tank with empty reels.

Stainless steel tanks and reels are recommended because they can be inverted, offer a clean and even agitation pattern, do not absorb chemicals, are easy to clean, and are durable. However, they are more expensive, initially harder to load, and require practice to correctly get the film put onto the reel.

Allow film to hang and naturally air dry, undisturbed, in a dust-free environment. The final rinse can be mixed with distilled water. Shake the loaded film reel over the sink to break the surface tension. This will permit the final rinse to flow freely and run to the lower end of the hanging film. A lint-free, disposable paper towel, such as a Photo-Wipe, can be gently used on the nonemulsion side of the film.

Table 5.2 **Starting Points for First Developer Time Compensation**	
Camera Exposure Time*	First Developer in Minutes†
One stop overexposed	4
Normal exposure	6
One stop underexposed	8
Two stops underexposed	11½
Three stops underexposed	16

*Color slide film that is more than one f-stop overexposed or more than two f-stops underexposed will not deliver normal color balance or density.
† Time based on first roll in fresh solutions.

Most color slide films can be push processed one f-stop and still deliver acceptable results. Wanting to handhold the camera in a very low light situation, Lincoln pushed 1600 speed slide film to 3200. Her film was given additional time in the first developer to compensate (see table 7.3 on page 151).
© M.L. Lincoln. *Waiting For the Subway*, 1990. 16 x 20 inches. Dye-destruction print.

E-6 Processing Adjustments

Most E-6 process films can be exposed at different speeds and still produce acceptable results if the first developer time is adjusted to compensate (table 5.2). Use the standard times for all other solutions. Adjustments in processing can allow certain films to be successfully push processed or can save film that has been exposed at the wrong ISO rating. However, when regular film is push processed it can suffer a color balance shift, a change in contrast, and a decrease in exposure latitude. Highest quality is achieved when normal speed rating(s) and processing are observed.

Special Processing

Generally transparency material can be identified if it carries the suffix "chrome." The majority of transparency films, such as Agfachrome, Ektachrome, and Fujichrome, can be processed at most laboratories or by yourself. Custom labs will do push processing. The quality of these laboratories varies tremendously. Check them out before giving them any important work to do.

E-6 Troubleshooting

Table 5.3 lists some common E-6 processing problems, their probable causes, and possible corrective actions. Follow all safety recommendations when handling chemicals.

Diversity of Materials

Brands

Transparency film is available in many brands and in different speed ranges. Each manufacturer uses its own dyes, yielding noticeable variations in the colors produced. Certain brands emphasize distinctive colors; others may have an overall cool (blue) or warm (red and yel-

---

Table 5.3 **E-6 Troubleshooting Guide**

Problem	Cause and Correction
Improper color balance	Solution contamination. Clean all equipment thoroughly. Organize and label solutions to ensure proper sequencing.
Overall blue color cast	Improper color developer mixing or incorrect color developer alkalinity (pH). Use reverse-osmosis treated water or add 1 Ml/L of sodium hydroxide per five units more yellow wanted in color balance (equivalent to about a CC05Y filter). Be sure to adhere to safety rules for working with sodium hydroxide.
Green shadows	Exhausted reversal bath. Replace with fresh solution.
Overall green color cast	Reversal bath omitted.
Red specks	Improper bleaching. Rebleach in fresh solution.
Overall red color cast	Insufficient bleach aeration. Rebleach with vigorous agitation.
Overall yellow color cast	Improper color developer mixing or incorrect color developer alkalinity (pH). Use reverse-osmosis treated water or add 1 Ml/L of sulfuric acid per each five units more blue wanted in color balance (equivalent to a CC05B filter). Follow all safety rules when handling sulfuric acid.
Yellow or muddy highlights	Exhausted fixer. Refix in fresh solution and repeat wash and final rinse steps.
Images appear both negative and positive or very light color	Developer exhausted. Replace with fresh solution. Color developer temperature too low. Check thermometer. Process at correct temperature.
Images too dark	Underexposed film. Check camera meter and review exposure methods. Or first developer time too short, temperature too low, or lack of proper agitation.
Images too light	Overexposed film. Check camera meter and review exposure methods. First developer time too long, temperature too high, overagitation. Color developer temperature too low.
Dirt, dust, and spots	Mix final rinse with distilled water. Hang in dust-free area and allow to air dry undisturbed. Gently wipe nonemulsion side of film with a soft, disposable, lint-free paper towel (such as Photo-Wipes).
Light crescents	Kinked film. Practice loading developing reels with unwanted film. Don't force film onto reels.
Streaks or blotches	Make sure film is properly loaded on reel. Poor agitation. Follow correct agitation methods for each step.
Dyes fade after short time	Prebleach step skipped.

Table 5.4
Major Manufacturers of Color Products

Agfa
100 Challenger Road
Ridgefield, NJ 07660
201-440-2500
www.agfahome.com

Eastman Kodak
343 State Street
Rochester, NY 14650
800-242-2424
www.kodak.com

Fuji Photo Film USA
200 Summit Lake Drive, 2nd Floor
Valhalla, NY 10595
800-755-3854
www.fujifilm.com

ILFORD Imaging USA Inc
West 70 Century Road
Paramus, NJ 07652
201-265-6000
www.ilford.com

Konica USA
725 Darlington Avenue
Mahwah, NJ 07430
800-285-6422
www.konica.com

Jobo Fototechnic
P.O. Box 3721
Ann Arbor, MI 48106
734-677-6989
www.jobo.com

Polaroid
1265 Main Street
Waltham, MA 02451
800-225-1618
www.polaroid.com

Unicolor Photo Systems, Inc.
7200 Huron River Drive
Dexter, MI 48130
800-521-4042
www.photosys.com

low) bias, which allows a choice of color palette. Brands also differ in their contrast, grain structure, saturation, and overall sharpness. Some films are designed for specific applications, such as portraits, which allows you to match films to your purposes. Be aware that different lenses, especially older lenses, deliver distinct color rendering. New multilayer coating techniques allow modern lenses to provide a greater standardized color response. Since these characteristics cannot be compensated for during a secondary step like printing, it is important that the photographer choose a transparency film whose bias fits both the aesthetic and the technical concerns of the situation. If you plan to scan your film, choose an emulsion that has been optimized for scanning.

Manufacturers have been busy making changes in almost every film currently on the market. For this reason, it is futile to attempt to describe the characteristics of each film; this information becomes rapidly outdated. Visit the major film manufacturers' websites (table 5.4) for information on their current products. The only way to keep up is to use the different films and evaluate the results for yourself. You can read test reports and talk with other photographers (especially online), but choosing a film is a highly personal matter. Experience is the best guide. Try different films in noncritical situations to learn their strong and weak points. After some experimentation you will most likely discover that there is one type of film you prefer. It is worth the time to work with one film and learn its characteristics and personality, because this will be helpful in obtaining consistent and pleasing results.

Film Speed

Each brand offers a selection of different film speeds. The speed, or light sensitivity, of a film is determined from a set of procedures established by the International Standards Organization (ISO). Films can be divided into four basic categories based on their speed: slow films have an ISO below 100, general-use films possess an ISO of between 100 and 200, fast films have an ISO of 200 to 400, and ultrafast films have an ISO of 400 or more and are often designed for push processing.

In general, the slower the film the greater the color saturation, the tighter the grain structure, and the better the color contrast, all of which make the image appear sharper. Slower films also have less tolerance for exposure error. Faster films look grainier and do not have as much color contrast or saturation. They have a greater ability to handle small exposure errors and limited mixed lighting conditions. In low light conditions faster films are able to capture a greater variation in hue and tone than print film, by sacrificing grain and sharpness. (For a more detailed discussion of grain see section on brands, grain, and speed in chapter 5 page 96). Choice of film should fit the situation and personal color preference. For instance, a slow enhanced saturation slide film may make the reds and blues in a scene pop out, but its overly warm and contrasty nature may not be suitable for traditional portraiture.

As the speed of a film increases there is a drop-off in quality (color rendition, grain, sharpness). These effects are more noticeable in slide film than in print film. At ISO 400, print film remains superior. In the ISO 1000 to 1600 range, print films have a decided edge. This is because print films use ingredients such as developer inhibitor releasing (DIR) couplers to prevent overdevelopment and grain buildup. The DIR technology is now in use with some of the slow slide films. Print film also uses integral masks, which are dyes that help to improve color saturation and cancel out unwanted color shifts.

Technical innovations are producing film improvements on an on-going basis, so it can be useful to try new films as they are released. Choose film with care so that it will work for your situation. Try not to get into the position of making the circumstances fit the film.

Reciprocity can be used to a photographer's advantage. In this case, the color shifts that normally occur when a negative is exposed for too long resulted in vivid colors not present in the original scene. This carefully framed night scene of a corporate office building is representative of Fournier's work which draws attention to repetitive visual patterns found in manmade objects and in nature.

© Nicole Fournier. *Corner of High-Rise Building*, 2003. 20 x 24 inches. Chromogenic color print.

Amateur and Professional Films Compared

Both amateur and professional films have similar color quality, grain characteristics, image stability, and sharpness. The main difference is in the color balance of the films. As all color film ages, the characteristics of its color balance change.

An amateur photographer typically buys a few rolls of film at a time. The film might remain in the camera at various temperatures for long periods of time before it is processed. Allowances for this type of use are built into the film during manufacturing. For example, if a film's color balance shifts toward yellow as it ages, the color balance of the emulsion is made in the complementary direction, blue, to compensate. This allows time for the film to be shipped and stocked, and to sit in the camera. By the time the film is finally shot and processed its color balance should still be close to optimum.

Professional films are manufactured at their optimum point for accurate color balance and consistent speed. These films are designed for refrigerated storage by both the dealer and the user. They should be processed immediately after exposure.

Daylight, Tungsten, and Type A Films

The color performance of a film varies depending on the lighting conditions in which it is used. Slide materials work best when properly matched to the type of light under which they are exposed (see chapter 4, page 73). Daylight films work best in daylight and with electronic flash. Tungsten slide film is balanced with photo floodlights. Type A film is balanced for 3400 K bulbs. Type B film is balanced for 3200 K bulbs.

Make certain the film used matches the light under which it is going to be exposed, because any mismatch between film type and light source will be dramatically evident. Daylight slide film exposed under floods or household bulbs comes out an orange-yellow-red; tungsten slide film shot in daylight comes out blue. This can be corrected at the time of exposure through the use of the proper filter over the lens (see chapter 4, page 75).

Under mixed-light conditions, situations illuminated by daylight and artificial light or scenes with both tungsten and fluorescents, there is no way to simply color correct the scene if the slide is the finished product. Even if a print is made or the film is scanned, corrections will probably be limited in scope.

In open or deep shade, or in overcast daylight, the film may record the scene with a cool, bluish cast. A warming filter, such as an 81A, can be used to correct this.

In contrasty lighting, slide film can produce bleached-out highlights and dark, inky shadows.

Transparencies

Transparency Duplication

Once transparency film has been exposed and processed, the major method to make corrections and/or modifications is by slide duplication (dupes). It is possible to change colors and combine images for effect but at the expense of an increase in contrast and loss of subtle detail. Most 35-mm cameras accept a rigid-tube copying accessory that replaces the lens. The slide is placed in front of a light diffuser in the copying tube and is lighted either by daylight or by electronic flash. Thin plastic CC filters are used to adjust or modify the color balance. This is an excellent tool for experimentation, especially when naturalistic color rendition is not a priority. Making your own color-accurate dupes can be difficult and requires a number of test rolls to determine correct exposure and filtration. Unless you make dupes frequently and in large quantities, you are better off having them made by a professional lab.

Commercial duplication makes use of a specialized copying stand with diffused electronic flash and built-in color filters. Commercial labs should use special low-contrast duplicating films. When accurate copy slides are required, use only a first-class professional lab because the quality of dupes can vary greatly (see also the section on copy work in chapter 9, page 196).

Viewing Transparencies

In order to critically judge the quality of a color transparency it is necessary to have

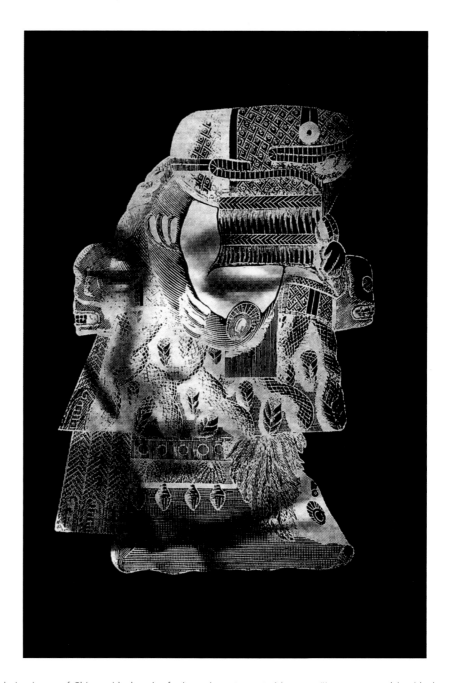

Exploring issues of Chicana ideology is of primary importance to Montoya. "In my own evolving ideology I question my identity as a Chicana in occupied America, and articulate the experience of a minority woman in the West. I work to understand the depth of my spiritual, political, emotional, and cultural icons, realizing that in exploring the topography of my conceptual homeland, Aztlan, I am searching for configurations of my own vision." For this image Montoya sandwiched a Kodalith and 4- x 5-inch transparency, producing a moiré pattern, and rephotographed the resulting sandwich on a slide duplicator.

© Delilah Montoya. *Sapagonia*, 1995. 36 x 24 cm. Chromogenic color transparency.

a viewing light source (illuminator) that possesses specific characteristics, that is, a correlated color temperature of 5000 K (see chapter 4, page 72). Light sources that range in color temperature from 3800 K to 5000 K are satisfactory for general viewing by the public if they emit adequate amounts of light in the blue, green, and red portions of the spectrum. If a transparency is viewed with a tungsten light source it will have a red-yellow color bias. If it is viewed against a

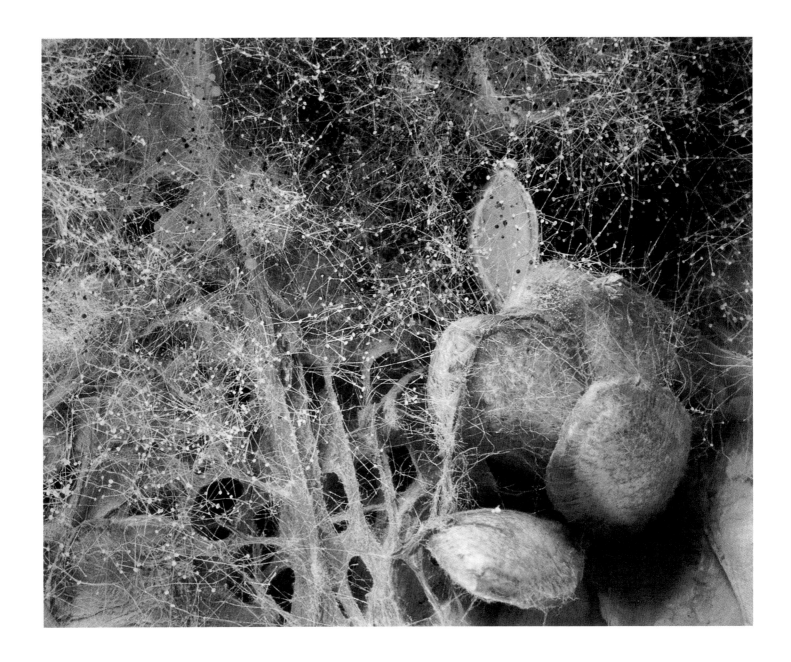

Using a 4 x 5 monorail camera with a 90-mm lens set at f /32, Schneider chose daylight film and strobes to bring out the intense detail and color of fruit in its various stages of decay over a five-week period. "The images are an exploration into looking and how photography can show the unseen of the every day. My art making is compelled by a desire to blend the beautiful and the repulsive." Her photographs are printed four times larger than the subject, which monumentalizes the contrast between the fruit in its bright early stages and the "desiccated black mass" it becomes at the end of five weeks.

© Betsy Schneider. *Apricot.2* from *Ripeness is All*, [4], 1997. 16 x 20 inches. Chromogenic color print.

---

blue sky it will likely be biased in the blue direction.

Ideally transparencies should be shown in a projector with a high-intensity color-corrected lamp. The most popular projectors use the round, slotted Kodak Carousel trays that hold 80 or 140 slides. The 80-slide trays are less vulnerable to jamming and can accommodate thicker cardboard, plastic, or glass mounts. For correct viewing, hold the slide in its proper orientation (how the scene looked in reality), turn it upside down, and drop it in the slot in the tray. The emulsion side of the film should be facing the lens and screen.

Color Negative Film

Color Negative Film Characteristics

Color negative film is the first part of a flexible two-stage process for making prints on paper. The method is similar to that used for transparency production, except that the film is processed into a negative instead of a positive. This means that areas in the original that were dark appear as light and colors show as their complement (opposite) on the film. Color negative film possesses an orange integral mask (a color mask) to correct for deficiencies in the green- and red-

Leppman photographs the insides of garages just after dark to conjure the hyper-familiar feeling of just having arrived home. The scenario for these scenes necessitates long exposures and makes the tungsten and fluorescent lights in the space her only light source. Leppman's use of daylight film makes color balance challenging when printing, but successful results can be achieved because of the versatility of color negative film, which is good for mixed-light situations and long exposures.

© Erika Leppmann. *Arriving Home: 468 Fir Avenue*, 2002. 16 x 20 inches. Chromogenic color print.

sensitive layers of the film.

Color negative film is easier and quicker to process than transparencies. It is convenient because unlimited prints can be produced, once the additional printing equipment is acquired. Prints are easy to store, send, and display without the need for such additional equipment as a slide projector and screen, and a darkened room. Prints allow intimate contact with the work, giving the viewer time to become involved with the image.

Negative films are versatile, offering greater exposure latitude than slide films, and they give the photographer another opportunity to interact with the work.

Exposure latitude is a film's ability to provide acceptable results when less than optimum exposure was made. Both the color saturation (degree of color intensity) and density increase with more exposure, which is the opposite of transparency film. Negative film should be exposed to produce acceptable detail in the key shadow areas. When in doubt about the proper exposure, it is usually best to slightly overexpose the film. Many photographers intentionally overexpose their negative film by decreasing the manufacturer's ISO film speed rating. For example, a film with an ISO of 100 might be rated at 80, while an ISO 400

This image is the result of negative manipulation in which Murphy mimicked the method used to make a normal color negative; 4- x 5-inch black-and-white film was shot, processed, and then hand-colored with color markers. The final colors are complements of the color applied to the negative; thus orange becomes blue, and cyan becomes red. The background of the skull is a crumpled photocopy, and the black lines are scratch marks made directly on the negative. This series evolved when Murphy learned that a close friend was terminally ill. The work reflects upon the complexities of hope, desideration, and desire in the rational and spiritual questioning of death. For Murphy the skull (bones) has developed a renewed spiritual quality in an attempt to suspend the finality of extinction.

© Jeff Murphy. *Rabbit Skull*, 1990. 24 x 30 inches. Chromogenic color print.

film could be shot at 200. Bracket in 1/2 f-stops to discover what works best for your situation. Slight overexposure can also produce a tighter grain pattern. This is because the final image is made up of color dyes rather than silver.

Negative film has a wide latitude for overexposure, often up to four f-stops, which can be corrected when the print is made. If the film is greatly under-exposed, more than two f-stops, the result is a weak, thin negative that produces a flat print lacking in detail and color saturation/richness. Changing the color balance, contrast, density, and saturation is possible during the printing process, which can produce a final piece that is a more accurate reflection of the

photographer's concerns. For these reasons, negative film tends to work better in contrasty and mixed-light conditions, and for people pictures where wide varieties of skin tones can be adjusted during the printing process. For available light shooting, high-speed color negative film (ISO 800) delivers a tighter speed-to-grain ratio than comparable slide film. Beware of using a film with a higher speed than necessary for the conditions; this can result in the loss of highlight detail in the final print.

Negative film can record a tremendous amount of information, which can be digitally reworked. At the time of processing, professional labs can also scan the negative film to provide both an ana-

log and a digital version of your images. In addition, you can have small, inexpensive prints made that provide more information than a contact sheet, and these prints may also be scanned for use.

The major disadvantages of color negative film are that more time and equipment are required to get the final image, and the quality of the obtainable color is not as high as that of transparency film. If a normal print and a slide of the same scene are compared, the transparency will have more brilliance, greater detail, deeper saturation, and more subtle color because the transparency film itself is the final product and it is viewed by transmitted light. The negative requires a second step, printing, to get to the final image, resulting in a loss of quality because the print paper is viewed by reflected light. The paper absorbs some of the light, known as the double-density effect, causing a loss of color and detail. If a print is the desired end product, the negative/positive process offers the most accurate color rendition. This is because the negative film contains an integral mask (a color mask) that corrects deficiencies in the green- and red-sensitive layers of the film.

Negative Film Construction

Think of color negative and reversal film as a sandwich that is constructed on a single piece of bread. The bread in this case is called the base. Three different silver halide emulsions that are sensitive to blue, green, and red light form what is called the tripack on this base (see figure 1.6, page 15).

Each emulsion layer is coupled to the potential dyes, magenta, yellow, and cyan, which are used to form the color image. These dyes are the complements of the green, blue, and red hues that made up the original scene. When the film is exposed, a latent image is created in each layer. As an example, red light is recorded in the red-sensitive layer of the tripack, but it will not affect the other two layers.

Colors that are made up from more than one primary color are recorded on several of the layers of the tripack. Black does not expose any of the emulsion, but white light is recorded on all three layers (see figure 1.7, page 15).

Type S and Type L Films

Some manufacturers design films specifically for different exposure situations. For example, Kodak's "Professional" color negative films come in two versions. Type S, for short exposures, is balanced for daylight and designed for an exposure time of 1/10 to 1/10,000 of a second. Type L, for long exposures, is balanced for tungsten light (3200 K) and for exposure times of 1/50 to 60 seconds. Tungsten negative film is now also available in 35 mm and 120 formats. If exposure time and/or the color temperature of the light do not match the film, filters are necessary to correct the color temperature. Small mismatches can be corrected when making the print.

C-41 Process: Chromogenic Development of Negative Film

During the chromogenic development process both the full-black silver image and the color dye image are formed simultaneously in the tripack. Next the film is bleached, which removes the unwanted black silver image. This leaves the three layers of dye showing the scene in superimposed magenta, yellow, and cyan, each one being a complement and a negative of the green, blue, and red from the original scene. Now the film is fixed, during which the unexposed areas of the emulsions are made permanent. Washing then removes all the remaining unwanted chemicals. Last, it is stabilized for maximum dye life and then dried (see figure 1.8, page 16). The final color negative has an overall orange mask. The orange color is due to colored couplers that are used to improve color reproduction by reducing contrast and maintain-

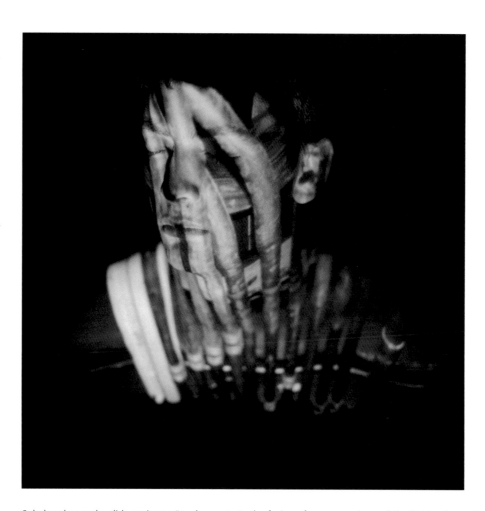

Sokolowska used a slide projector "to demonstrate the fusion of our memories and the hidden forces that shape us into who we are." Sokolowska chose 120 tungsten film to take advantage of a larger film format and match the color temperature of her light source, which saved time in the darkroom because she did not have to make drastic color corrections. Sokolowska also bracketed to ensure precise exposure.

© Ursula Sokolowska. *Automaton #10, The Automata series*, 2002. 40 x 40 inches. Chromogenic color print.

ing accurate color during the printing of the negative.

Most current negative films can be developed in the C-41 process (table 5.5). To be sure that the film you are using is compatible with C-41, check the box or cassette. Many of the latest films are extremely process sensitive and require very accurate temperature control to avoid color shifts, lack of color saturation, changes in contrast, and increase in grain. Read and follow the sections in this chapter on temperature control and handling and agitation (see page 95). Read and follow all the manufacturer's safety warnings, mixing, and disposal instructions to ensure a safe and healthy working environment. C-41 negative

films are stored and handled in the same manner as E-6 slide films (see chapter 5, page 94). Major manufacturers such as Kodak provide Material Safety Data Sheets on their websites.

C-41 Troubleshooting

Table 5.6 identifies some of the basic C-41 processing problems, their probable causes, and their possible corrections.

How the Chromogenic Color Print Process Works

A chromogenic color print is made when light is projected through a color negative onto color printing paper. The light

Table 5.5 Kodak C-41 Process

Step	Time in Minutes*	Temperature (°F)†
The first two steps must be carried out in total darkness		
Developer	3 ¼‡ (1) and (2)	100 +/– 0.25
Bleach	6 ½	100 +/– 5
The remaining steps can be carried out in room light		
Wash	3 ¼	75 to 105
Fixer	6 ½	100 +/– 5
Wash	3 ¼	75 to 105
Stabilizer (3)	1 ½	75 to 105
Dry	As Needed	Up to 140

Note: All times and temperatures are for small tanks—not more than four reels. If using a rotary-type processor such as the Jobo, changes in time will be necessary.

*All steps include a 10-second drain time.

†For the best results, keep all temperatures as close to 100°F as possible. When not agitating the solution, keep the processing tank in a water bath. Before processing, warm the tank in the water bath for about five minutes (see water bath section on page 85).

‡Development time changes depending on the number of rolls that have been processed. Mark the number of rolls processed on the developer storage container. Check the capacity of the solutions with the instructions. Mark the mixing date on the storage bottle. All solutions have a limited storage life. Check the instructions to determine how long solutions will last under your storage conditions.

(1) Initial agitation: For all solutions, tap the tank on a 45-degree angle to dislodge any air bubbles. No further agitation is needed in the stabilizer.
(2) Additional agitation: Subsequent agitation is required in all other solutions. After tapping the tank, agitate by slowly turning the tank upside down and then right side up for the first 30 seconds. For the remaining time in the developer, let the tank rest for 13 seconds and agitate for two seconds. Since the time in the developer is short, proper agitation is a must or uneven development results. For the remaining time in the bleach and fixer, let the tank rest for 25 seconds and agitate for five seconds. When using noninvertible tanks, which cannot be turned upside down, tap the tank on a 45-degree angle to remove air bubbles, and rotate the reels at the indicated times to achieve proper agitation.
(3) The stabilizer may be mixed with distilled water. Shake your loaded film reel over the sink to break the surface tension. This allows the stabilizer to flow freely and run to the lower end of the hanging film. A lint-free, disposable paper towel, such as a Photo-Wipe, can be gently used on the nonemulsion side of the film to remove excess stabilizer, dust, and processing debris. Allow the film to hang undisturbed and naturally air dry in a dust-free environment.

is filtered at some point before it reaches the paper. The paper, like the film, has a three-layered tripack emulsion composed of silver and dyes that are used to form the image. Each layer is sensitive to only one color of light, which is complementary to the dyes found in the negative. When the print is made, the colors from the negative are reversed. For instance, a red ball would be recorded in the cyan layer of the negative. When light passes through the negative, only green and blue light are transmitted. This exposes only the layers in the paper emulsion that are sensitive to green and blue light,

releasing the complementary magenta and yellow dyes in the paper. The magenta and yellow dyes recreate the red ball from the original scene. Where there is clear film in all the emulsion layers, white light produces a latent image in each of the layers of the print emulsion. This produces black when the print is processed.

Developing the Print

When the print is developed, each of the three layers of the exposed emulsion develops into a positive black-and-white silver image that represents the third of

the spectrum it recorded (red, green, and blue). Wherever the silver is deposited, dyes that correspond to that color are formed. For example, where blue light strikes the paper, only the yellow layer of the tripack, which is complementary to blue, is affected. The blue light forms a positive silver image and a directly corresponding yellow dye. After development, the paper contains the exposed tripack of positive silver and dyed images. Next the print is bleached. This converts the silver to silver halides, which the fix then removes. Usually the bleach and fix are combined so that this process takes place more or less at the same time. This leaves only a positive dyed image that is washed and then dried. Since the image is formed by dyes, these prints are called dye coupler prints.

The colors in the resulting image are those that are reflected back to the eye from the light falling on the print. An object that is red looks red because the yellow and magenta dyes in the print emulsion absorb the blue and green wavelengths from the light falling on it, reflecting back only the red.

C-Print Misnomer

Prints made from negatives in the C-41 process use chromogenic development to produce the cyan, magenta, and yellow dyes in their emulsions and are known as chromogenic or dye coupler color prints. The term chromogenic was coined by Rudolph Fisher, who patented the use of color couplers in 1912 and 1914 (see section on subtractive film and

Opposite page
"A common impulse in my projects is to understand and illuminate seemingly overwhelming and abstract power systems. Although town council and community meetings are open to the public, the process of governance can seem somewhat invisible and separate from the lives of ordinary people," says Shambroom of his series *Meetings*. Not wanting to interfere with the character of the meetings, he chose to use the available light and take advantage of the versatility of high-speed negative film.

© Paul Shambroom. *Wadley, Georgia (population 2,468) City Council, August 13, 2001*, 2001. 33 x 66 inches. Inkjet print.

Table 5.6 C-41 Troubleshooting Guide

Problem	Cause and Correction
Negatives too dark	Overexposure. Check camera and meter. Review exposure methods. Overdevelopment. Time too long or temperature too high. Check thermometer for accuracy. Review temperature, time, and agitation procedures. Contaminated or incorrectly mixed developer.
Negatives too light	Underexposure. Check camera and meter. Review exposure techniques. Underdevelopment. Time too short or temperature too low. Check accuracy of thermometer. Review temperature, time, and agitation procedures. Developer exhausted, incorrectly mixed, or contaminated. Check mix date, number of rolls processed, and storage conditions. Out-of-date film.
Dense with high contrast	Bleach time too short. Unaerated bleach. Bleach temperature too low. Bleach incorrectly mixed or overdiluted.
Clear film with no edge marks	Bleached before development. Film was not a C-41 process film.
Clear film with edge marks	Unexposed film.
Dark crescent-shaped marks	Kinked film. Practice loading unwanted film on reels. Only handle the edges and ends of the film. Do not force film onto reel.
Unusual color balance and contrast	Solution contamination. Dump and remix contaminated solutions. Clean all processing equipment after each use. Mix and store all solutions in clean containers. Clearly label all containers. Return chemicals to proper containers.
Dust, dirt, and spots	Mix stabilizer in distilled water. If water is extremely hard, follow stabilizer bath with Kodak PhotoFlo 200 Solution mixed in distilled water. Allow film to dry naturally in an undisturbed, dust-free environment. To facilitate the free flow of the stabilizer, shake your loaded film reel over the sink to break the surface tension. A lint-free, disposable paper towel (such as Photo-Wipes) may be used to gently wipe the nonemulsion side of the film.

chromogenic development in chapter 2, see page 40). Prints from these processes are commonly called chromogenic color prints (because there is a black-and-white process; see later section on chromogenic black-and-white film, in next column) or dye coupler prints. Color prints may also be referred to by the specific paper they were made on, such as Ektacolor. The opposite method for making color prints is the dye-destruction process, or silver dye-bleach method, in which all the color dyes are built into the emulsion and selectively removed during processing (see sections on dye-destruction process and Ilfochrome Classic in chapter 6, pages 133 and 137).

Many people and organizations still call modern color prints Type C. This widely used misnomer is not an accurate description for the current materials. Some people think the "C" is shorthand for chromogenic or color coupler print, but Type C was actually a specific product, Kodak Color Print Material, Type C, that was introduced in 1955. In 1958 Kodak introduced Ektacolor Paper, Type 1384 to replace Type C in photofinishing applications. Type C continued to be available for professional use for some time but has not been made for decades. Today "C-print" is a slang term that refers to just about any color print made from a color negative, thereby distinguishing it from a print made from a slide.

Film Speed, Format, and Grain

The look of a final print is linked to the film speed and format size of the negative. Slower films appear sharper, possess greater color saturation, and have a fuller tonal range and less apparent graininess. Faster films appear less sharp, with less color saturation and more apparent graininess. The larger the film format, the less apparent the visible grain.

Processed black-and-white film is made up of particles of metallic silver called grain. Graininess is the subjective perception of a mottled random pattern. The viewer sees small, local-density vari-

ations in an area of overall uniform density. Although color negatives and transparencies contain no silver, they do exhibit graininess. This is because undeveloped color films contain silver compounds, which are removed by the bleach and fix, that help form the color dyes as they are developed. As the color dyes are created, dye clouds form around the silver particles and remain even after the silver is removed, retaining the silver grain pattern. These clouds of dyes form the grain in a color negative or transparency. Kodak's print grain index is a method used to subjectively evaluate the perceived print graininess from color negative films by using a uniform perceptual scale based on a diffusion enlarger. For details about this assessment, visit the Kodak website, www.kodak.com, and download their publication E-58.

Many photographers intentionally overexpose color negative film by 1/3 to one full f-stop to improve shadow detail and saturation and to reduce graininess (see chapter 14, page 267). Others take advantage of the two-step process and purposely slightly overexpose and overdevelop in order to heighten contrast for dramatic effect. Slight to moderate overexposure of color negative film, unlike overexposure of black-and-white film, creates larger dye clouds in each of the emulsion layers. As the dye clouds expand, they overlap and fill in from layer to layer, lending the appearance of less graininess.

Chromogenic Black-and-White Film

Ilford XP2 Super is an ISO 400 film, available in 35-mm and 120 rolls and is the latest generation of monochromatic negative material to make use of new chromogenic color coupler technology. Special DIR (developer inhibitor releasing) couplers yield ultra-fine grain, high-acutance images. Ilford XP2 Super, like regular color negative materials, produces finer grain when overexposed. This film has wide exposure latitude

(ISO 50 to 800), which allows it to record subjects with a broad brightness range while producing excellent highlight detail with no grain.

Ilford XP2 Super is processed in standard C-41 chemistry alongside all other color negative films. No special handling is required because times and temperatures remain the same and the film will not contaminate the chemicals in any way. After processing, the negative is composed solely of stable dyes and is completely silver-free. This means that this film may be processed and printed by any lab offering C-41 service. XP2 Super can be printed on either color or black-and-white paper. If prints show a slight color cast on regular color paper, have the printer use an unexposed strip of processed color film to provide the orange mask to correct this situation.

There are other chromogenic black-and-white films, such as Kodak's Porta 400 and Professional T400CN. The Porta 400 is a multipurpose film intended to be printed on color paper, including machine prints, and has been optimized for scanning. The T400CN can be printed on either black-and-white or color paper. T400CN film is for printing on silver-halide photographic papers and may be preferable for those who use manual enlargers for printing on conventional black-and-white papers, as it provides a brighter image on the enlarger easel. Both are pushable and have ample exposure latitude.

Polaroid Materials

Modern instant photography began in 1948 with the marketing of Edwin Land's Polaroid process. Polaroid's first full-color instant film, Polacolor, capable of producing a color print in 60 seconds, was introduced in 1963.

Most people associate instant films with family snapshots, but it is possible to make beautiful, intimate, and unique color photographs with these films. They are convenient and provide immediate feedback in any shooting situation.

Professional photographers routinely use Polaroid film to check composition, lighting, reciprocity, and the working order of their equipment. The information gained from a Polaroid test shot can help the photographer make corrections and create a stronger image. Commercial photographers also use Polaroid film—instant pictures are wonderful icebreakers to give away when photographing people and it is always a thrill watching the image come up. The artistic use of the material has helped it gain acceptance as a valid medium.

Late in his life, Walker Evans became very rhapsodic about the SX-70 camera and in an interview with *Yale Alumni Magazine* said:

> *I've now taken up that little SX-70 camera for fun and become very interested in it. I'm feeling wildly with it. But a year ago I would have said that color is vulgar and should not be tried under any circumstances. … [I use it to] extend my vision and let that open up new stylistic paths I haven't been down yet...A practical photographer has an entirely new extension in that camera. You photograph things that you would not think of photographing before. I don't even yet know why, but I find that I'm quite rejuvenated by it.*[1]

Evans went on to comment that the SX-70 process put all the responsibility on the photographer's mind and eye, leaving nothing to be added by technique.

Palma recreates the look of old black-and-white photographs to give his images a sense of history. He uses chromogenic black-and-white film because it is a convenient way to get black-and-white negatives (and prints) through color processing. Palma then prints and sepia tones the photographs and paints them with bitume (tar).

© Luis Gonzalez Palma. *Esperanza*, 2001. 20 x 20 inches. Gelatin silver print with paint. Courtesy of the Schneider Gallery, Chicago, IL.

Polaroid SX-70 and Spectra System

The Polaroid SX-70 system was introduced in 1972 and although it was discontinued in 1981, Time-Zero color-positive film is still made and can be exposed in a Polaroid SX-70 camera, under an enlarger, or with a special film back. It has an ISO of 150, develops in five minutes at 70°F (21°C) and has an image area of 3.1 x 3.1 inches (7.9 x 7.9 cm).

The Spectra System, introduced in 1986, is a group of automatic handheld cameras with a few manual overrides.

The Spectra film has an ISO of 640, takes three minutes to develop at 70°F (21°C), and produces an image area of 3.6 x 2.9 inches (9.2 x 7.3 cm). Polaroid also makes a variety of cameras that use the 600-type film.

Diffusion-Transfer: the Polaroid Process

The Polaroid SX-70 and Spectra development processes use the diffusion-transfer method, which is self-developing in natural light and is the basis for self-processing instant photography materials.

After the shutter is pressed, the motor drive, which is powered by a battery in each film pack, automatically ejects the film through a set of rollers that break a pod of reagent located at the bottom of each piece of film. Development is then automatic and requires no timing. The best results are obtained at about 75°F (24°C). If it is colder, the color balance can shift to the cool direction. This can be compensated by putting the film inside your shirt to keep it warm while it is developing. Development can take place in daylight because the light-sensitive negative is protected by opaque dyes

This Polaroid SX-70 photograph is part of a 10-year project documenting nightlife in New York City as seen by a "camera girl" who was simultaneously earning a living selling Polaroid pictures to clubgoers. Smith tells us: "Using a Polaroid SX-70 camera with a sonar focusing device enabled me to simultaneously image and project onto film the important information in a dark and densely populated space. Working quickly and intuitively, I could grab and materialize fleeting impressions of people who came to experience the 1980s version of mass modern electronic entertainment and decor in the nightspots of the most hyped-up city in the world during that time."

© Sharon Smith. *Cigarette Girl, The Ritz, New York*, 1980. 3 ¼ x 3 ¼ inches. Diffusion-transfer print.

in the reagent. Both the positive and negative images are contained within each sheet of film.

As the picture forms, a number of things occur at once. First the silver halides are reduced to metallic silver in the exposed areas of each of the three additive primary light-sensitive layers. As this happens, the complementary subtractive primary dye developers move through the layers of the negative and the opaque reagent to form a white background for the picture. Now the dye developers are prevented from moving up to the positive image area by the

developing silver. This layer will now only pass certain colors through. For example, the blue layer blocks the yellow dyes but not the cyan and magenta dyes. Within a few minutes all the dyes that have not been blocked travel through the white opaque layer and become visible. The process automatically completes and stabilizes itself, resulting in a completed dry print.

These films are balanced for daylight and electronic flash, but they can be exposed under any light source by placing CC filters in front of the lens of the camera, or the exposure sensor in the

case of automatic cameras. It is also possible to correct for differences in color balance from one pack of film to another with the CC filters.

Exposure is automatically determined by the Polaroid camera. This can be controlled to a limited degree by adjusting the exposure wheel on the camera to either the darker or lighter setting.

Changes in time and/or temperature alter the outcome of the final print. An increase in temperature makes the colors appear warmer, while decreasing the temperature produces cooler hues. Extending the development time can increase color saturation and overall contrast. A drop in development time can flatten or mute the colors while reducing contrast.

Store the film in its sealed box. Keep it cool and dry. For prolonged life, this film can be refrigerated above 34°F (1°C), but do not freeze it. Let the film warm to room temperature before use.

See Chapter 16, page 306, for Polaroid manipulations and transfers.

Instant Film and the View Camera

Polaroid makes color materials for larger format cameras. Polacolor is a family of color print materials, available in 3 ¼- x 4 ¼-inch and 4- x 5-inch sizes for both daylight and tungsten. They are designed to be exposed in special Polaroid film holders. A variety of custom backs for everything from a Hasselblad to a Holga is available from other sources.

Polaroid also makes a print film for use with an 8- x 10-inch view camera that requires its own special Polaroid film holder and processor for development. Color materials are available for other special uses, such as Polaroid's 20- x 24-inch cameras, which can be rented from Polaroid.

Since 1992 Fuji has also been making a 4- x 5-inch instant film, but it is only available on the gray market in the United States.

Additional Information
Polaroid provides telephone technical assistance at 800-225-1618, Monday through Friday, 8

a.m. to 8 p.m. (eastern time).

BAKER, ROBERT and BARBARA. *Instant Projects Instant Projects: A Hand-book of Demonstrations & Assignments for Photography Classes*. London, Polaroid 1986.

Creative Techniques Brochure. Polaroid 2002 (call 800-662-8337, ext. PO21).

Four Designs Company (www.fourdesigns.com) specialize in Polaroid equipment. They sell, restore, repair, and upgrade Polaroid Pack Film and SX-70 cameras and convert select Polaroid roll film cameras, for use with contemporary 3- x 4-inch pack films.

Storage and Handling of Color Films

All color films should be stored in a cool, dry place in their original packing, away from color-processing chemicals and substances that contain formaldehyde. New and simulated leather and cellular foam products can release small amounts of formaldehyde and should not be used as film bags. All color films should be exposed before the expiration date indicated on the film package and processed as soon as possible.

Do not leave film in strong sunlight or in a hot location, for example near a heating duct or in the glove compartment of a car. Load and unload the camera in subdued light.

When processing film, especially sheet film, avoid touching the emulsion surface. Handle film by its edges. If necessary, wear clean, lint-free cotton gloves.

Protect film against cleaners, industrial gases, motor-exhaust fumes, mildew and fungus preventatives, paints, processing chemicals, and solvents.

For consistency, store film in the refrigerator at less than 55°F (13°C). When film is taken out of the refrigerator, allow it ½ to 1 ½ hours to warm up to room temperature before removing it from its original packing. This prevents condensation from forming on the film surface. With the exception of Polaroid materials, film can be placed in a freezer for long-term storage.

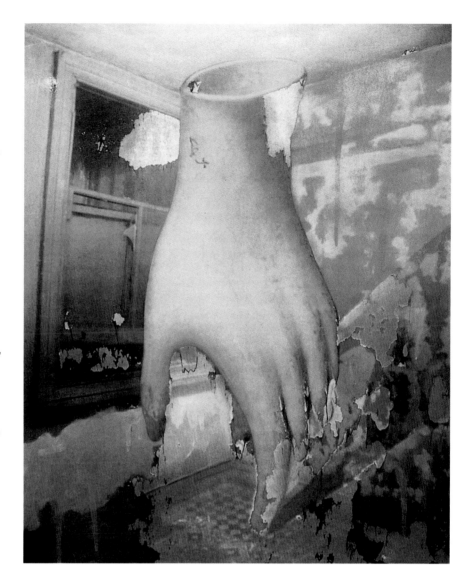

For this image, a homage to René Magritte, Reuter outputted the image to a 4- x 5-inch film recorder and printed it as an image transfer using a 20- x 24-inch Polaroid studio camera. Reuter says the image-transfer process "can alter, transform, and move the image to a level of image artifact ... a physical object that has interest beyond the image it carries. The elements of color, texture, and scale contribute to the power of the piece as it is perceived as the viewer stands in front of it. ... Reworking is the final step and I use it to enchance the emotional elements of the image that I experienced in its original creations."

© John Reuter. *Balance*, 1995. 20 x 24 inches. Diffusion image transfer with dry pigment and pastel.

Exposed film should be processed as quickly as possible. If a delay is unavoidable, put the film in a resealable food-storage bag and place it in the refrigerator. Allow it to reach room temperature before processing.

Processed color film is subject to color fading from light (especially UV), high temperatures, and humidity. To avoid the adverse effects of heat, light, and moisture, processed film should be kept in mounts or archival sleeves and stored in a cool, dark, and dry location with good ventilation. The temperature should be kept below 77°F (25°C) with a relative humidity of 30 to 60 percent. For long-term storage, a temperature below 50°F (10°C) with a relative humidity of 30 to 50 percent is recommended.

For more information on storage of color materials, especially prints, see chapter 9 page 194.

This image of Kudzu, a weed that grows out of control in places in the South, was made using a 4- x 5-inch camera and reversal printing. In this case, out of concern for the high cost of film, Fogel used film that was almost out of date. By making sure to keep the film frozen while in storage before use, he was able to achieve excellent results.

© Harris Fogel. *Kudzu Near the Great Park, Atlanta, Georgia*, 1989. 8 x 10 inches. Dye-destruction print.

Opposite page

In a time of increased airport security, Bacon uses X-Ray technology to question the startling contrast between ordinary objects found inside common traveling bags and the heavy scrutiny they undergo through advanced surveillance technology. By placing images of war, violence, and power in place of the mundane objects typically found inside a woman's handbag, Bacon calls attention to the false sense of comfort she suggests America has fallen into as a result of technologies we take for granted.

© Pat Bacon. *Pink Handbag*, 2003. 13 x 17 inches. Inkjet print.

X-Ray Equipment at Airport Security

X-ray equipment such as that used in airport security systems can fog unexposed film. Film fogging can occur around any radiation source, including doctor's offices, medical labs, hospitals, and factories. The effect is increased with the intensity of the X-ray, the cumulative number of inspection exposures, and the sensitivity of the film. Films having an ISO film speed rating of 800 or higher are more susceptible than slower films. Ask for a hand inspection of your camera equipment. Carry film in a special lead shield pouch designed to protect film against low-dose X-ray inspection units. Visual inspection is the only protection against high-dose X-ray machines. Pack film without its packing canister in a clear plastic zip-lock type bag for quicker hand inspection. Screening equipment will not affect digital camera images or film that has already been processed, slides, videos, or picture CDs. As long as airport security remains in flux, it is best to check websites such as the Federal Aviation Administration (www.faa.gov) for the latest information and advice on getting photographic equipment safely through airport and other security networks. Be aware that non-United States airports have their own rules.

Endnotes

[1] *Walker Evans at Work.* New York: Harper & Row Publishers, 1982, 234–35.

a s s i g n m e n t

DIFFERENCES IN FILMS

Research films online, then select and shoot a different brand of film from film that you have used before and answer the following questions. What differences do you notice when you compare this film with what you had previously used? Look at the color balance. Is it warmer or cooler? Is the color saturation similar? What about the contrast? Is it higher or lower? Are the grain patterns and structures the same? Compare flesh, neutral, and white tones to see how they differ. Which film do you prefer? Why? Is there a time when you would prefer to use one of these films instead of the other? Why? Post your finding online in one of the photo product review sections.

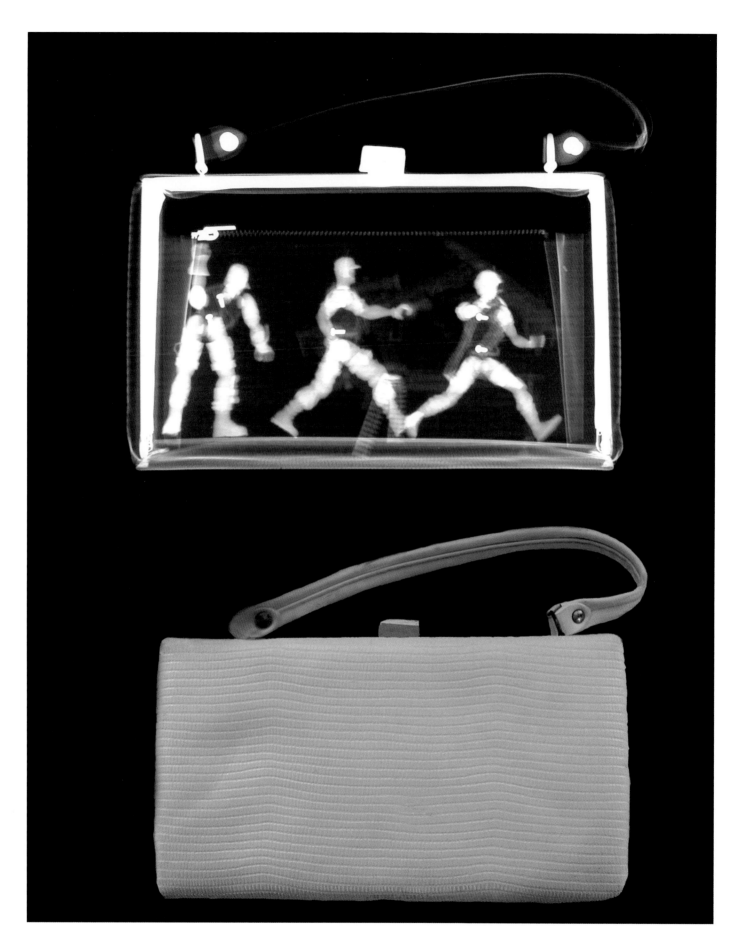

Chapter Six

COLOR PRINTING

Campbell hand painted a gelatin silver print, rephotographed it as a 4- x 5-inch transparency, and used this to produce a large color transparency. Campbell created the look of a stained-glass window by cutting the transparency material into five parts, with each piece being placed between Plexiglas onto multiple modular lightboxes fastened together to form one image. The work alludes to the Western spiritual tradition in art to critique our contemporary "worship" of rationalistic values and its destructive effects. Campbell comments: "Our hubris pervades contemporary life, from capitalist disdain for the ecosystem to the destructive effects of technological weaponry to the increasing attempts by biotechnology to play God. These 'stained-glass windows' are part of a 'chapel' dedicated tongue-in-cheek to this 'Modern Theology.' Here, the *Angel of Earth* refers to environmental pollution as she lies in dirt, surrounded by tin-can lids, bottle caps and banana peels in the shape of fleur-de-lis."

© Kathleen Campbell. *Angel of Earth*, from *Angel Series or Photographs of Widely-Known Non-Existent Beings*, 1996. 28 x 32 inches. Duratrans.

In this series, Sultan relies on the versatility of color negative film to handle a wide variety of lighting situations as he photographs on porn film sites in the San Fernando Valley, CA. He deals with the theme of loss and desire by focusing on how ordinary objects and activities associated with mundane domestic life can be transformed when viewed in the context of the highly sexualized film sets.

© Larry Sultan. *Boxer Dogs, Mission Hills*, from *The Valley*, 2000. 30 x 40 inches. Chromogenic color print. Courtesy of Janet Borden Inc., New York, NY.

Basic Equipment and Ideas for Color Printing

Some photographers believe that color printing is difficult, but if you can make a successful black-and-white print, you can make a successful color print as well. The methods presented here are designed to teach the basic concepts and techniques needed to make a chemical-based color print with a minimum of equipment. There are always new methods appearing on the market, but once you learn these basic principles, you will be ready to adapt to future changes without difficulty. There are some differences between working in color and black-and-white that you need to know about.

The Enlarger

Three basic types of enlarger are used to make chemical color prints: condenser, diffusion, and digital.

Condenser Enlarger

A condenser enlarger uses one or more condenser lenses to direct the light from the lamphouse into parallel rays as it goes through the negative. This type is widely used in black-and-white printing because of its ability to produce greater apparent sharpness and because it matches the standard black-and-white contrast grades of paper extremely well. Condenser enlargers are easily adapted to make color prints using color printing filters.

Diffusion Enlarger

In a diffusion enlarger, which is commonly employed in making color prints, the light is mixed in a diffusing chamber. With this type of enlarger the light is traveling in many directions (diffused) as it reaches the negative. The diffusion process ensures the proper mixing of the filtered light, offers a suitable contrast for color printing, makes defects in the negative less noticeable, and softens the final print. There are black-and-white and color diffusion enlarger light sources.

Both condenser and diffusion heads offer advantages and disadvantages. When the opportunity presents itself, try each type, compare, and see which characteristics you favor.

Digital Enlarger

A digital enlarger relies on a "digitized" negative that can be sized, exposed, and processed on conventional color chromogenic paper. Negatives and slides are scanned by the enlarger before they are corrected for color, density, contrast, sharpness, and over- and underexposure. Dust and scratches can also be corrected using imaging software. Images are then digitally sized and exposed onto photographic paper using red, green, and blue lasers. Images can also be entered into the enlarger via a disk, CD, or camera flash card. Due to equipment cost, training, and maintenance these enlargers are generally only available at professional labs. They provide a bridge between the chemical and digital processes and are excellent in terms of repeatability and for making large-scale prints.

Dichroic Systems for Printing Color

The best color enlarging system is the dichroic colorhead, which is a self-contained unit with filters, a color-corrected, high-intensity light source balanced for color papers, a UV (ultraviolet) filter, heat-absorbing glass, and a white-light switch (figure 6.1). Collectively, the filters are known as the color pack. They are used to adjust the color of the white light during printing in order to properly color balance the print. This colorhead normally contains three filters (cyan,

magenta, and yellow) made with metalized dyes. These enable the printer to work more accurately. The dichroic head also enables you to make moderate changes in the filter pack without affecting the printing time. Most modern dichroic systems are in diffusion-type enlargers. Black-and-white printing can be done on any color enlarger by dialing the filter setting to zero.

Converting Black-and-White Enlargers

Many black-and-white enlargers can be converted to color by replacing the black-and-white head with a dichroic head. A less expensive method is to use CP and CC filters.

The Filter

CP Filters

CP (color print) filters can be used with an enlarger that contains a filter drawer. The CP filters change the color of the light before it reaches the negative. They are only available in the subtractive primary colors and are not as optically pure as the CC filters, but they do cost less. The major advantage of the CP filters is that they go above the lens, eliminating the focus and distortion problems associated with CC filters, which are located below the lens. A UV filter and heat-absorbing glass are needed with both CC and CP filters to protect the film and shield the paper from UV exposure. Both filters can be used with either condenser- or diffusion-type enlargers, but not with

6.1 A composite dichroic diffusion color enlarger is a self-contained system that features separate colored filter controls, a color-corrected high-intensity light source, a UV filter, heat-absorbing glass, and a white-light switch.

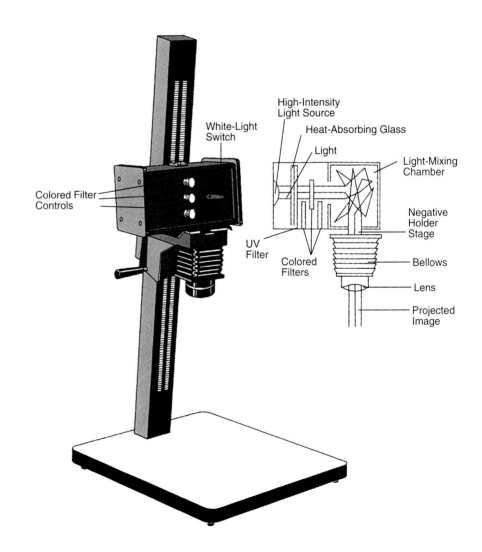

White-Light Switch

Colored Filter Controls

High-Intensity Light Source

Heat-Absorbing Glass

Light

Light-Mixing Chamber

Negative Holder Stage

UV Filter

Colored Filters

Bellows

Lens

Projected Image

a cold-light enlarging head. The cold-light system uses coils or grids of glass gas-filled tubing that produce a colored light that is not suitable for color printing.

CC Filters

CC (color correction) filters are optically pure gelatin acetate filters that are placed in a filter holder under the enlarging lens. CC filters are available in both additive and subtractive colors and in a wide range of densities. CC filters change the light after the image has been focused, which can cause problems in loss of image contrast, distortion of the picture, and a reduction in overall sharpness. Economic use of filters (i.e. one CC20 filter, not four CC05 filters) helps to alleviate these problems. Wear thin cotton gloves when handling these filters in order to prevent the filters from getting dirty and scratched. Avoid leaving the enlarger light on when it is not needed, because prolonged exposure to light causes the filters to fade. The use of CP filters under the lens is not recommended because they will likely overly diffuse the image.

The disadvantages of using nondichroic filters include the need to recalculate your exposure after changing filters and their susceptibility to scratching and fading.

The Voltage Stablizer

Regardless of the type of enlarger or filter system, a voltage stabilizer (figure 6.2) is needed. Some of the dichroic systems have a voltage stabilizer built in. Any changes in the voltage to the enlarger during exposure produce changes in the color balance. To prevent this from occurring and to have consistent results, a voltage stabilizer is connected between the timer and the power outlet.

The Enlarging Lens

Use the best enlarging lens you can afford. Inexpensive lenses, with four or fewer elements, may not produce a flat field of focus, thus making it impossible

to get both the center and edges of the image sharp. They also may not be accurately color corrected. Poorly made lenses can produce spherical aberrations, which lower image definition and cause focus shift. This causes a loss of image sharpness when the lens f-stop is changed from wide open (during focus-

A properly produced image from a color negative enables the viewer to fully participate in the photographer's presentation of a particular moment in time and space and reflect how its meaning can shift as the photograph ages.

© Len Jenshel. *World Trade Center*, 1971. 16 x 20 inches. Chromogenic color print. Courtesy of Laurence Miller Gallery, New York, NY.

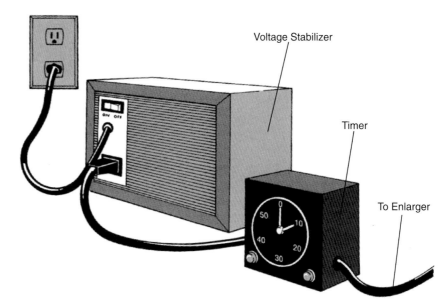

6.2 A voltage stabilizer is needed when making color prints because power fluctuations during exposure may produce changes in the color of the light source. This may cause changes in the color balance of the print, making corrections and consistency difficult to achieve.

ing) to its stopped-down position (for exposure). High-quality lenses have six or more elements and are better corrected for color. The best are labeled APO (apochromatic). Make sure the lens is clean and there is no light flare from light leaks around the enlarger. Most enlarging lenses provide optimum sharpness when stopped down two to three f-stops from their maximum aperture (f/8 or f/11).

The Easel

Most easels are painted yellow by the manufacturer, which works well for black-and-white printing because the yellow color reflected onto the paper during exposure does not affect it. This is not the case with some color papers, which can be sensitive to the reflected yellow light; the papers can be fogged by it. However, papers with opaque backings, such as Ilfochrome Classic, are not affected by reflected color. The problem of paper being fogged by a yellow easel can be solved by spray painting the easel baseboard with a flat-black enamel or covering it with opaque paper.

The Safelight

The standard OC black-and-white safelight fogs chromogenic color paper, so a #13 filter is used in the safelight when printing from negatives (slides are printed in total darkness without a safelight). The #13 filter can be used with any type of safelight that has a screw- or slide-in filter slot. The latest LED (light-emitting diode) color safelights provide even more light. Since color paper is sensitive to all colors of light, safelight handling should be kept to a minimum; it is possible to fog your paper even under a #13 filter. Safelight fog first appears as a cyan stain in the white borders and highlight areas of the print.

A small pocket flashlight with an opaque paper shade is a great help in getting about and setting things up at your work station (figure 6.3). For a modest investment, there are mini-battery-powered safelights that can be worn around the neck.

Multiple station darkrooms are places of collective activity and require responsible behavior to protect the efforts of all concerned. As color materials are extremely sensitive to light, it is necessary to exercise care when pointing a flashlight or turning on any white-light source in the darkroom. Do not turn on the enlarger light if the head is raised. If an individual darkroom is available, printing can be done in total darkness when a #13 filter is not available and the paper can be processed in a drum under full illumination.

Ambient Light

Color paper has a broader spectral sensitivity than black-and-white paper, so it is more prone to fogging and color shifts caused by ambient light. Ideally, the walls and ceiling around the color enlarger should be a matt black. Ambient light may come from such sources as light leaks in the enlarger negative stage, illuminated timers having both digital

#13 Amber Safelight

Opaque piece of paper that acts as an aperture control device for the penlight.

6.3 Because color paper is sensitive to a wider range of wavelengths of light than black-and-white paper, it requires a different safelight in order not to fog the paper. A small, pocket-style flashlight, with an opaque piece of paper wrapped around it to act as an aperture control, can provide additional light for setting up at the enlarging station.

and luminous readouts, electrical devices with red "on" lights and/or illuminated dials, and reflections from shiny apparel and/or other darkroom equipment including burning and dodging tools.

Mask all potential ambient light sources with black felt, black tape, or opaque weather stripping. Make sure certain timers are safe or cover them or turn them away from the easel area. Make all darkroom tools out of opaque materials.

The Drum Processor

A drum processor (figure 6.4) rotates with the appropriate chemicals inside the drum and is the best alternative to an automatic color print processor. Processing can be carried out in room light with a minimal amount of chemistry. When using a processing drum, be sure it is clean and dry. When loading the drum, place the base of the exposed paper against the wall of the drum, with the emulsion side curling inward upon itself. Be certain the lid is secure before turning on the white light. Process on a flat, even surface covered with a towel for good traction as the drum rotates with the chemicals inside. There are many types and styles of drum and base available. Check them out and see which you prefer. Use a drum such as the Jobo that has no feet or big edges to get in the way, and rolls easily on a level surface. A motor base can aid in attaining proper agitation and consistency, which in turn will make printing easier, simpler, less costly, and more enjoyable. Drums are available in sizes from 8 x 10 inches to 16 x 20 inches. More than one print can be processed at a time in a drum. For instance, the 16- x 20-inch model can do up to four 8- x 10-inch prints. Read the manufacturer's suggestions for use, processing times, and amounts of chemicals. Kodak publications usually refer to the drum as a "tube."

Temperature Control

Temperature control is necessary for most color processes. Being off by as little as .5°F can cause a change in the

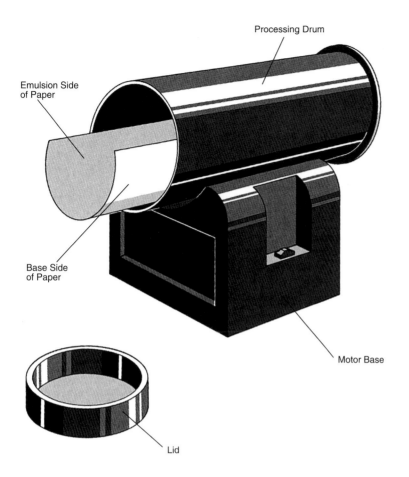

Processing Drum

Emulsion Side
of Paper

Base Side
of Paper

Motor Base

Lid

6.4 A processing drum mounted on a motor base is a convenient and inexpensive tool for making color prints. The base of the paper is placed in contact with the interior wall of the drum, with the emulsion side of the paper curling inward.

color balance. Check your thermometer against one known to be accurate. The Kodak process thermometer is an excellent standard of comparison. Corrections can be made if yours is off. If the standard reads 100°F and yours says 101°F, simply process at 101°F instead of 100°F based on your thermometer's reading.

The least expensive method of temperature control is the water bath (see chapter 5, page 95). Chemicals are put into cold or hot water until they reach operating temperature. The temperature must be maintained, which requires constant monitoring. This method makes accuracy and consistency difficult to maintain.

If you can afford it, buy a temperature control storage tank, or make your own using a fish tank heater and a soda pop cooler. The consistency of

the results, plus their convenience, offsets the cost. If you are fortunate enough to work in a lab with an automatic print processor, it takes care of temperature control, replenishment rate, and processing.

Bring the chemicals to their operating temperatures in their sealed bottles in a water bath before exposing the paper. Small, clean glass jars make good one-shot chemical containers when using a tabletop drum. Put tape on the side and label a separate jar for each step. Make a mark on the side of the jar to indicate the proper amount of chemical needed for each step. Avoid contamination by always using the same bottles for the same solutions. Have a container ready for proper disposal of chemicals. Check and maintain proper temperature or your results will be chaotic and will not be repeatable.

Color Printing Notebook

Regardless of the process or method used, keep a notebook to record final print information. This establishes a basic starting point that will make it easier to produce a print when a similar situation occurs with a certain type of film. It also makes reprinting quicker. Commonly recorded information is provided in table 6.1. Copying this table, punching it with a three-hole paper punch, and inserting the copies into a loose-leaf binder can establish a color printing notebook.

Each color enlarger has its own time and filtration differences, but the information in your notebook will help you to arrive at a final print with more ease. In a group darkroom, find an enlarger that you like and stick with it. Learn its quirks and characteristics so that you are comfortable working with it.

Safety

Follow the manufacturer's instructions and the guidelines found in the safety addendum (see page 344). Wear Neoprene gloves, which repel acids and bleach, when handling chemicals. Obtain Material Safety Data Sheets (MSDS) from each manufacturer. Work in a well-ventilated area, and avoid breathing in any chemical fumes. If you are sensitive to fumes, wear a protective organic vapor mask.

Principles of Subtractive Printing: the Qualities of White Light

White light is made up of blue, green, and red wavelengths, known as the additive primary colors. The three colors that are produced by mixtures of the paired additive primaries are cyan (blue-green), magenta, and yellow, called the subtractive primary colors. We will work with the subtractive method because it is the most widely used. Each subtractive primary represents white light minus one of

Table 6.1	**Color Printing Notebook**

Date: _____

Subject or title of print: _____

Type of paper used: _____

Enlarger lens: _____

Lens f-stop: _____

Yellow filtration: _____

Cyan filtration: _____

Type of film used: _____

Negative number: _____

Enlarger used: _____

Enlarger height or print size: _____

Exposure time: _____

Magenta filtration: _____

Burning and dodging instructions: _____

Date: _____

Subject or title of print: _____

Type of paper used: _____

Enlarger lens: _____

Lens f-stop: _____

Yellow filtration: _____

Cyan filtration: _____

Type of film used: _____

Negative number: _____

Enlarger used: _____

Enlarger height or print size: _____

Exposure time: _____

Magenta filtration: _____

Burning and dodging instructions: _____

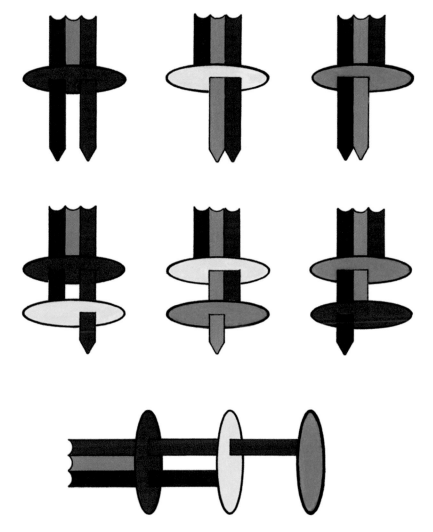

6.5 A graphic presentation of how white light is affected as it passes through the subtractive primary color filters, illustrating the basic principles of subtractive color printing.

three would be eliminated. This also builds extra density (gray), which requires extended printing time. The effect is known as neutral density. The same color changes can usually be achieved without affecting the print density by using only two of the subtractive filters.

The general rule for printing color negatives is to use only the magenta and yellow filters, and leave the cyan set at zero. This eliminates one-third of the filter calculations and makes printing faster and easier. Whenever possible subtract colors from your filter pack rather than add them. Most printing materials deliver the optimum response with a minimum of filtration.

Figure 6.5 shows what happens as white light is passed through the different subtractive filters.

Color Paper Selection

There are fewer choices of color printing papers than there are of black-and-white printing papers. There are no fiber-based papers. All the regular materials are resin-coated (RC), with a thin, water-resistant plastic coating that facilitates rapid processing and drying. Some special-use materials have a heavier polyester base. You will want to experiment, since each manufacturer's paper delivers differences in contrast, color balance, and surface texture. Papers come in matt, semimatt (also known as luster or pearl), glossy, and textured finishes. The glossy surface reflects light and gives the impression of highest color saturation, contrast, detail, and sharpness. It also reveals any surface defects, especially fingerprints, and is highly reflective.

Color papers are generally available in only a limited range of contrasts. Typically there is an all-purpose version for general use, a lower contrast paper for portrait work, and a slightly higher contrast version. The difference in contrast is only equal to about half a grade of black-and-white paper contrast. No variable-contrast papers are available, so contrast is most easily controlled by the initial exposure of the film and the film's devel-

the additive primaries (cyan equals white light minus red, magenta equals white light minus green, and yellow equals white light minus blue).

Subtractive primaries are the complements (opposites) of the additive primaries. Thus cyan is complementary to red, magenta is complementary to green, and yellow is complementary to blue. When you determine your filter combinations for printing, think of all the filters in terms of the subtractive colors. This means blue equals magenta plus cyan, green equals yellow plus cyan, and red equals yellow plus magenta.

Additive colors are converted to their subtractive equivalents in the following manner:

10 Red = 10 Magenta + 10 Yellow
20 Red = 20 Magenta + 20 Yellow

Filters of the same color are added and subtracted normally:

10 Magenta + 10 Magenta = 20 Magenta
30 Magenta − 10 Magenta = 20 Magenta

Neutral Density

Whether you work with the dichroic, CC, or CP filters, they all contain cyan, magenta, and yellow. Each of the three subtractive filters blocks out one of the three components of white light—blue, green, and red. If all three filters were used at once, not only would the color balance be changed, but also some of all

opment time. Papers are compatible with both optical and digital printing devices.

Paper Handling

Handle paper by its corners and from the base side with clean, dry hands. Touching the emulsion will leave a fingerprint good enough for the authorities to identify you. If problems continue with fingerprints, get a pair of thin cotton gloves to wear when handling the paper. Be sure to wash the gloves periodically.

Determining the Emulsion Side
It can be difficult to determine which is the emulsion side of the paper in total darkness. Here are some ways to distinguish the emulsion side from the base side of the paper.

● The emulsion side of the paper looks dark bluish-gray under the safelight.
● The paper generally curls in the direction of the emulsion.
● Most paper is packed emulsion side up in the box. It is often packaged with only one piece of cardboard, which is facing the emulsion side of the paper.
● Use the glow from a luminous timer dial or a strip of luminous tape on the darkroom wall. The paper reflects light on the nonemulsion side. This will not fog the paper.
● Slightly moisten your thumb and index fingers, then grip one small corner of the paper. The side that sticks to your fingers is the emulsion side.
● If all else fails, cut an edge from a piece of the paper and look at it under white light to determine the emulsion side.
● If the paper looks white under the enlarging light, you have probably printed on the wrong side; throw it away and start again. Printing and processing through the wrong side of the paper results in a fuzzy reversed image with an overall cyan cast.

Changes in Paper Emulsion
Each batch of color paper has different characteristics that affect the exposure and filtration. Because of this the paper is given an emulsion number that is sometimes printed on the package. Each time the emulsion number is changed it is usually necessary to correct the exposure and filter information. In order to avoid these

problems, buy paper in as large a quantity as is affordable. It is better to purchase a 100-sheet box of paper than four 25-sheet packages that may have been made at four different times. As the manufacture of color papers has improved, there is a less noticeable difference in color balance from emulsion to emulsion.

Storage
Color paper keeps better if refrigerated. It can be frozen if you do not expect to use it for some time. Allow enough time for the paper to reach room temperature before printing or inconsistency will result. It takes a 100-sheet box of 8- x 10-inch paper about three hours to warm up.

Check the expiration date on the paper box before buying. Purchase paper from a source that regularly turns over its stock. With a permanent marker, write on the box the date you acquired your paper. Most properly stored paper lasts at least 12 to 18 months after opening. Keep paper away from high temperature and humidity. Chromogenic color paper that has started to deteriorate will deliver ivory borders instead of white.

General Printing Procedures

1 Select a properly composed and exposed negative.
2 Clean the negative carefully. Use film cleaner and soft, lint-free paper products such as Photo-Wipes. If there are problems with dust or static, use an antistatic device. If you want to avoid the radiation contained in a static brush, get a static gun such as a Zerostat, which is sold in music stores. The static gun and a good sable brush will get the job done and eliminate unnecessary spotting of the print later. Using canned air can create more problems than it solves. The propellant can come flying out onto the negative, making a bigger mess

than was already there. If you do use canned air, carefully follow the manufacturer's working guidelines. Use a product that is environmentally safe, containing no chlorofluoro-carbons.

If the film has been improperly processed or handled and is noticeably scratched, apply a liquid no-scratch substance such as Edwal's No-Scratch. Clean the negative and paint No-Scratch on the entire nonemulsion side. If the negative is badly scratched, paint it on both sides. This treatment diffuses the image slightly. After printing, be sure to remove all the No-Scratch with film cleaner and Photo-Wipes. If you lose the little brushes that come with the No-Scratch, cotton swabs are an excellent substitute.

3 Turn on the power to the enlarger.
4 Remove all filters from the light path. Many dichroic enlargers have a white light switch that will do this automatically.
5 Open the enlarging lens to its maximum aperture. Having as much white light as possible makes composing and focusing easier because this has to be done through the orange mask of the negative film.
6 Set the enlarger height, insert the negative carrier, and focus using a focusing aid. Have a piece of scrap printing paper at least the same size and thickness as the print in the easel to focus on. This makes composing possible on a black easel and ensures the print will have maximum sharpness.
7 Place the starting filter pack, based on past experience or the manufacturer's suggestion, into the enlarger. If you forget to put the filters back into the enlarger after focusing and then print with white light, the print will have an overall reddish-orange cast.
8 Set the aperture at f/5.6.
9 Set the timer for 10 seconds.

10 Place the unexposed paper emulsion side up in the easel.

Take your time. Do not worry about making a mistake. That is part of the learning process.

11 Have on hand an opaque sheet of cardboard that is at least the same size as the printing paper. Cut away one-quarter of it. It should look like a fat L (figure 6.6). Place it firmly on top of your printing paper. This one-quarter is now ready to be exposed.

12 Expose this first quadrant at f/5.6 for 10 seconds.

13 Move the cardboard L to uncover a different quadrant while covering the one that was just exposed. Stop the lens down to f/8 and expose for 10 seconds.

14 Repeat this process two more times until you have exposed each of the four quadrants one time at a different aperture for 10 seconds. Upon finishing this process there will be four different exposures. They will be at f/5.6, f/8, f/11, and f/16, all at 10 seconds, which is the ideal exposure time for a color negative.

Any setting within the eight- to 20-second range is fine. Color paper can suffer reciprocity failure during extremely short or long exposure times. Whenever possible, adjust the aperture so that the exposure time is as close to 10 seconds as possible to avoid color shifts due to reciprocity failure. Changes in the number of seconds used for the exposure are more likely to produce shifts in color than changes made by using the aperture. Some timers are inaccurate at brief exposures. If there appear to be inconsistent exposures, check the timer against one that is known to be true.

15 Follow the instructions for whichever process you are working with. The current standard is Kodak's RA-4.

16 Dry and evaluate. When drum processing, a handheld blow dryer speeds drying of test prints but can leave drying marks. If this is a prob-

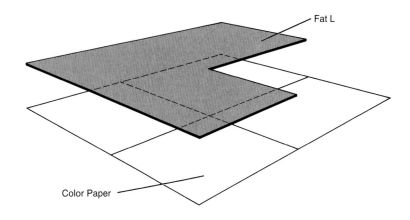

Fat L is moved so that each quarter of the paper is uncovered for its own separate exposure.

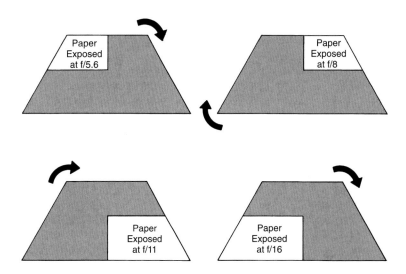

6.6 The fat L is used to find the proper exposure of color paper. Each quarter of the paper is exposed using a different f-stop with the same exposure time for all four exposures. Changes in the amount of exposure time may cause changes in the color balance.

lem, air dry the final print by hanging it from one corner on a wire line in a clean, dust-free area. Color balance is not correct while a print is wet. It usually has an overall blue cast and the density appears darker until after it has dried. There are a number of common problems that occur in the processing of prints. The troubleshooting guide (table 6.2) and the manufacturer's instructions can help solve these difficulties.

The Kodak RA-4 process (table 6.3) provides a standard by which

you can compare the other negative-to-print processes in a drum processor. Many institutions have small print processors that may operate with different chemicals, times, and temperatures. The automatic print processors offer ease and reliability by providing constant processing times, temperatures, and replenishment rates. Whatever the process, be consistent so that repeatable results are achieved. It is necessary to have clean working conditions or you run the risk of contaminating the chemistry.

Table 6.2 Troubleshooting/Prints from Negatives

Problem	Possible Cause
Unrealistic color	Incorrect filter pack
Overall red/orange cast	Exposure with white light
Reddish fingerprints	Emulsion touched prior to processing
Light crescents	Paper kinked during handling
Very light print	Emulsion facing wrong way in drum
Light and dark streaks	Prewet not used Not enough agitation in developer Drum not on level surface Paper stuck in machine rollers
Light streaks or stains in paper feed direction	Paper feed tray damp
Blue or magenta streaks	Stop bath is not working
Pink streaks	Water on print prior to processing
Red streaks	Lack of prewet
Bluish appearing blacks	Developer is too diluted Developer time is too short Not enough drain time after prewet
Black specks and marks	Tar buildup in developer
Cyan stain	Developer contaminated by bleach-fix Paper fogged by safelight
Overall reddish cast	Developer heavily contaminated by bleach-fix
Pinkish highlights	Developer temperature too high
Yellow-greenish highlights	Presoak too hot
Dark specks or spots	Rust in the water supply
Lack of contrast	Developer temperature is too low Developer is too diluted Development time is too short Lack of agitation Not enough developer solution Developer is exhausted Chemicals outdated
Cream-colored borders	Too high developer temperature Too long development time Improper mixing of developer
Bluish magenta stain	Stop bath exhausted Wash rate is too slow
Grayish purple metallic haze	Bleach-fix exhausted
Scratches to print emulsion	Paper put into processor emulsion side up
Ivory-colored print borders	Paper has expired

Making a Contact Print

Making a contact print is recommended because the orange mask of color negative film makes "reading" color negatives difficult. The contact print provides the opportunity to see the negative in a print form. You can see what was done right and wrong in the coverage of the subject, both aesthetically and technically; you can see things that may have been missed in the examination of the negative; and it can point the direction toward the pursuit of an idea or improvement of a technique.

Photographer Richard Avedon said: "I learned from [Alexey] Brodovitch to learn from myself, from my accidents and dreams. Your next step is most often in your false step: Never throw away your contacts. The photographs you took when you were not thinking about taking photographs—let them be your guide."[1]

Contact Print Steps

1 Place a neatly trimmed strip of paper emulsion side up under the enlarger. Make sure the enlarger is high enough that the beam of light will completely and evenly cover the paper of the full contact print. If you are using a color print processor, be sure the paper is big enough to go through the machine's rollers without jamming. When making an 8- x 10-inch contact print set the enlarger to the proper height used to make an 8- x 10-inch print. This will give a closer idea of the actual enlarging time for the finished print.

2 Place the film emulsion side down on top of the paper. Cover with a clean, scratch-free piece of glass, or use a contact printing frame. If safelight conditions are dim or nonexistent, leave the negatives in their protective sleeves. Check the protective sleeves to make certain they do not affect the clarity and color balance of the contact print or the filter information from the contact may not be correct when it is applied to making the final print.

3 Set the starting filter pack (based on filtration determined from previous experience, manufacturer's guidelines, or standard test negative). If you have no previous information, use 40M and 50Y as a starting point.

4 The fat L can be used to determine correct exposure, following the method previously outlined in making the print (see page 110. Some people do not like using the fat L for contact prints. Instead, a piece of cardboard is used to block the light and move it across the paper to create six separate exposure increments as in black-and-white printing (figure 6.7). Try exposing at f/8 in three-second increments (three, six, nine, 12, 15, and 18 seconds). If the entire test is too light, open the lens to f/5.6. If it is too dark, stop the lens down to f/11 and repeat the procedure.

5 Process, dry, and evaluate.

6 Pick the area that has the best overall density. Recalibrate the time so it is in the 10-second exposure range. For example, if the best time was f/8 at six seconds, adjust the exposure so that the new exposure is f/11 at 12 seconds. Make any changes in the filter pack based on the information obtained in the area of best density. To avoid reciprocity failure, which produces color shifts, try to maintain exposure times in the eight- to 20-second range.

7 Make a new contact print of the entire roll based on these changes.

8 Process, dry, and evaluate.

Reading the Contact Sheet/Determining Correct Exposure

The information from the contact print will make it easier to choose the best negative to print. The guiding mantra is

Table 6.3	**Kodak Ektacolor RA-4 Drum Processing Steps at 95°F**	
Processing Step	*Time* min:sec*	*Temperature (°F)*
Prewet	0:30 +/–0:05	95 +/– 2
Developer	0:45†	95 +/– 0.5
Stop	0:30 +/– 0:05	95 +/– 2
Wash	0:30 +/– 0:05	95 +/– 2
Bleach-Fix‡	0:45†	95 +/– 2
Wash*	1:30**	95 +/– 2
Dry	As needed	Not over 205

*Each step includes a 10-second drain time.
†Changes in time of one second less or five seconds more than normal may produce color shifts.
‡After bleach-fix, paper can be handled under room light.
*When possible, remove print from drum and wash in a tray or print washer with a continuous water flow that provides a complete change of water at least every 30 seconds.
**Longer wash times are acceptable and even desirable to remove unwanted chemicals.

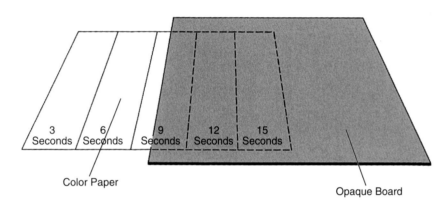

6.7 Some people do not like the fat L method for determining exposure for a contact print and instead use an opaque piece of board to block the light. In this method, like in black-and-white printing, the exposure time is varied while the f-stop remains unchanged. Once the exposure is calculated, it is adjusted to be in the 10-second range, with any additional exposure changes being made by adjusting the f-stop.

whatever color you see is the color you add. If the selection looks too magenta on the contact print, add more magenta to the filter pack before making the first test. This step begins the process of making that perfect print even more rapidly. In general, the information obtained from an 8- x 10-inch contact print (exposure and filtration) can be transferred as a starting place for the creation of the 8- x 10-inch enlargement. If you decide the ideal exposure is f/8 at 10 seconds with a filter pack of 40M and 50Y, then apply that to make your print. Standardizing film and processing will keep printing variations to a minimum,

often within five units.

Print Evaluation

People often ask about the correct type of light for evaluating prints. The answer is that it depends. A print may be deemed color correct in normal daylight conditions, but when displayed under artificial light, the color balance may not appear acceptable. For the most accurate results the print should be examined under lighting conditions similar to those under which the finished print will be viewed, which are often mixed-light conditions. For prints to be viewed under average daylight conditions, a print viewing area can be constructed that has two four-foot 5500 K full-spectrum fluorescent lamps about four to five feet from the viewing surface.

Evaluating a Print

1 Make sure the paper is completely dry. Is the exposure correct? First determine the best overall density because changes in it will affect the final color balance. It is troublesome to determine correct color balance in a print that is over- or underexposed. The ideal exposure is determined by being able to distinctly discern the edge of the film from the black of the paper. Also, look carefully at sensitive areas such as facial and neutral tones. This helps to determine which exposure will give the proper treatment for what you have in mind. Disregard extreme highlights and shadow areas; they will need burning in or dodging. Underexposure makes areas of light tones lose detail and appear white. Overexposure of light tones produces unwanted density, a loss of color separation, and an overall grayish look.

2 After deciding on the best density, determine which color is in excess. It is easiest to see the incorrect color in a middle-tone area. If there is a face in the picture, the whites of the eyes are often a key spot to make this determination. Avoid basing the color balance on shadow areas, extreme highlights, and highly saturated colors.

3 The most effective way to tell which color is in excess is by using a color print viewing filter kit such as the one made by Lee Filters (figure 6.8). One side of the filter set is designed for negative printing, the other side for positive (slide) printing. Use the appropriate side.

Methods for Using Viewing Filters

There are a number of different ways to use viewing filters. One or a combination of the following methods should be helpful in determining the color balance of the print.

Filters Next to the Print
Under lighting conditions similar to those under which the final print will be seen, place a piece of white paper next to the area of the print to be examined. The filters are available in six colors: magenta, red, and yellow (the warm colors) and blue, cyan, and green (the cool colors). Deciding if the print is too warm or too cool can immediately eliminate half of these filters. Then glance rapidly back and forth between the key area and the white piece of paper to see if the color that is in excess can be determined.

The white paper is a constant to avoid color memory (see section on color memory in chapter 1, page 20). If this does not work, take the green filter and place it on the white paper at a 45-degree angle so that the light passes through the green filter and strikes the white paper, giving it a green cast.

Glance rapidly back and forth between the color that the filter casts onto the white paper and the key area being examined in the print in order to see if the color cast matches. If it does, the excess color is green. If it does not, follow the same procedure with the blue filter. If the blue does not match, try the cyan. If there is a problem deciding between green and blue, it is probably neither. It is most likely cyan, the combination of blue and green light. Printing experience has shown that cyan is in excess more often than either blue or green. Notice if one color appears regularly in excess in your printing, and be on the lookout for it.

Now use the viewing filter to determine the amount of excess color by judging which of the three filter strengths the color cast comes closest to. Is the excess slight (a five-unit viewing filter), moderate (10 units), or considerable (20 units)? If the change is moderate, requiring a 10-unit viewing filter, make a 10-point correction in the filter pack.

The dichroic head makes it possible to fine-tune a print with small changes in the filtration of two or three points. Moderate changes in filtration, of 10 to

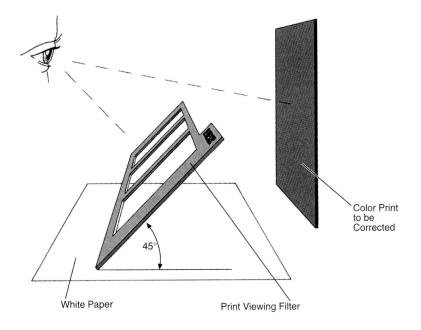

White Paper   Print Viewing Filter

Color Print to be Corrected

45°

6.8 Colored print viewing filters are effective for learning how to recognize all the basic colors used in color printing and may be employed to make visual corrections of color prints. The correction method shown here demonstrates one technique for determining which color is in excess. Be certain the light striking the correction filter and the print is of equal intensity and quality.

20 units, generally will not affect the print density with the dichroic head. When working with CC and CP filters changes in filtration must be compensated for by adjusting the exposure time. An increase in filtration requires an increase in exposure to maintain proper print density. Use the manufacturer's suggestions until experience is gained.

Filters over the Print

Another method of making filter corrections with color print viewing filters involves looking at the print through the filter that is the complement (opposite) of the color that is in excess. To use this method, flick the filter over the print and look through it at the key examination area. Keep the filter about six inches from the print surface. Do not put your eye directly against the filter because it will adapt to that color. Do not let the light that is illuminating the print pass through the filter on its way to the print. Whichever filter and density combination neutralizes the excess color and makes the print appear normal is the combination on which to base the corrections. If the print looks too blue, it should appear correct through a yellow filter. Make the determination as rapidly as possible. Do not stare too long, because the brain's color memory takes over and fools you into thinking the scene is correct (an example of color adaptation). The brain knows how the scene is supposed to look and will attempt to make it look that way, even if it does not. When in doubt, go with your first judgment.

The Color Ring-Around

The color ring-around is a traditional method of color evaluation in which a neutral print is compared with a series of standard selections (figure 6.9). Its purpose is to promote an understanding of the thought process that goes into making properly exposed and balanced prints and learning to recognize the additive and subtractive primary colors. The typical ring includes a "correct" print along with a series of "incorrect" prints made from the same negative. This includes a perfectly neutral print and one print with each of the six colors printed in varying degrees of excess. The ring should be made from your own standard negative and printed on your standard paper choice.

Color Ring-Around Procedure

The key to this assignment is to make your "perfect" print and then carefully follow through, applying a high degree of craft to the remaining prints. Set the enlarger height to make a small enlargement (about 3 x 2 ½ inches) and stop the lens down to about f/11. Determine and record your perfect exposure (which will remain constant for each image) and color balance. Copy table 6.4. Write your exposure and color balance information in the top two lines (for example: f/11 at five seconds with 40 Magenta, 35 Yellow, and 0 Cyan) and then calculate and write the filter changes onto your chart and use that data to expose the ring (exposure time remains the same for all prints). Also make one print with the white light setting so that you will know what that looks like too. Then trim the 14 prints and attach them to a black, gray, or white matt board. Assemble the

---

Table 6.4   Color Ring-Around Calculations

Exposure Time	f/____	____ seconds	
Perfect Color Balance	____ Y	____ M	____ C
White Light Setting. Leave the setting the same and expose using white light.			
Perfect + 10 Red (-10 Y –10 M)	____ Y	____ M	____ C
Perfect + 20 Red (-20 Y –20 M)	____ Y	____ M	____ C
Perfect + 10 Green (+ 10 M)	____ Y	____ M	____ C
Perfect + 20 Green (+ 20 M)	____ Y	____ M	____ C
Perfect + 10 Blue (+ 10 Y)	____ Y	____ M	____ C
Perfect + 20 Blue (+ 20 Y)	____ Y	____ M	____ C
Perfect + 10 Cyan (+ 10 Y +10 M)	____ Y	____ M	____ C
Perfect + 20 Cyan (+ 20 Y +20 M)	____ Y	____ M	____ C
Perfect + 10 Magenta (-10 M)	____ Y	____ M	____ C
Perfect + 20 Magenta (-20 M)	____ Y	____ M	____ C
Perfect + 10 Yellow (-10 Y)	____ Y	____ M	____ C
Perfect + 20 Yellow (-20 Y)	____ Y	____ M	____ C

White Light

+ 20 Yellow

+ 20 Red

+ 20 Magenta

+ 10 Yellow

+ 10 Red

+ 10 Magenta

Perfect

+ 10 Green

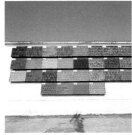

+ 10 Cyan

+ 10 Blue

+ 20 Green

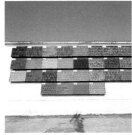

+ 20 Cyan

+ 20 Blue

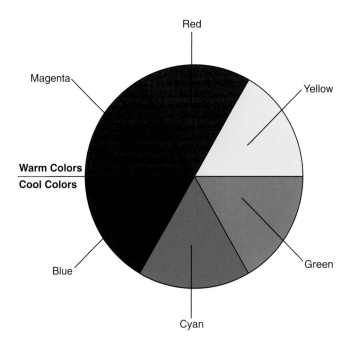

Red

Magenta

Yellow

Warm Colors
Cool Colors

Blue

Green

Cyan

	Slight Correction	Moderate Correction	Considerable Correction
Too Red	Add 05M + 05Y	Add 10M + 10Y	Add 20M + 20Y
Too Green	Subtract 05M or Add 05C + 05Y	Subtract 10M or Add 10C + 10Y	Subtract 20M or Add 20C + 20Y
Too Blue	Subtract 05Y or Add 05C + 05M	Subtract 10Y or Add 10C + 10M	Subtract 20Y or Add 20C + 20M
Too Cyan	Subtract 05M + 05Y or Add 05C	Subtract 10M +10Y or Add 10C	Subtract 20M +20Y or Add 20C
Too Magenta	Add 05M	Add 10M	Add 20M
Too Yellow	Add 05Y	Add 10Y	Add 20Y

Opposite page

6.9 Johnson reflects: "Making a color ring-around helps teach the relationships of color and the effect of changing filtration, but more importantly, it emphasizes the craft of color printing and presentation. Displaying the completed ring-around in a working area can be useful for students to refer to when color printing for it enables one to see warmer or cooler prints and be able to make informed decisions."

© Keith Johnson. *Avon, NY*, 2000. 7 x 7 inches. Chromogenic color prints.

6.10 The basic rules for making changes in the filter pack. (a) First it is determined from the color wheel if the print is a cool or warm color, then it is decided which color it is. Using the colored print-viewing filters, it is decided how much correction is needed. (b) The chart is a reference to determine how much and which filters must be used to make the desired correction.

Table 6.5	Basic Subtractive Filtering Rules

- To reduce magenta in the print, add magenta filtration.
- To reduce yellow in the print, add yellow filtration.
- To reduce red in the print, add magenta and yellow filtration.
- To reduce cyan in the print, subtract magenta and yellow.
- To reduce green in the print, subtract magenta.
- To reduce blue in the print, subtract yellow.

wheel in the manner of figure 6.9 with the complementary colors opposite each other; cool colors on one side and warm colors on the opposite side. Attach them to the board and label each one.

Discover the Method That Works for You
Traditionally, the ring has been used because it seemed to provide an empirical way to learn how to tell the differences in color balance. The problem that arises is due to the psychological and subjective components of color classification, which mean that we do not necessarily learn to recognize color differences in a logical manner. Regardless of the method, the way to overcome the color learning curve and clarify this process of recognition is to make and evaluate prints. Most of us can learn just as rapidly by diving in and our ability to absorb new information remains high when we continue to print from new and stimulating negatives. Ultimately, it makes no difference which method is used. Seeing is a slippery business and we see things in our own way and in our own time. Experiment with one of these methods; if it does not work, try another. Discover which method does the job for you. You may even come up with a better way.

Françoise Gilot, the French painter and printmaker who dared to love and then leave Picasso, said:

I had to find my own path toward artistic freedom. This did not mean having less regard for the gods and demigods atop Mount Olympus, but simply recognizing that, each human experience being unique, each artist has the burden and the privilege to bear witness, thus adding something to the wealth of human culture. Since for generations women have been notoriously silent, it was incumbent upon me and my female contemporaries to reveal an as-yet-unfathomed side of the planet—the emergence of a sunken continent of thoughts, emotions, and wisdom.

In color printing, each one of us must find our own way.

Changing the Filter Pack
When modifying the filter pack (figure 6.10) a filter of the same color can be added, although it is more desirable to subtract a complementary filter. This is because the paper responds better with a minimum of filters and also because it is best to keep the exposure time in the 10-second range. In most cases use only the magenta and yellow filters. Leave the cyan set on zero. Do not have all three in the pack together because doing so produces unwanted neutral density (gray). Avoid extremes of exposure to prevent reciprocity failure.

Memorizing table 6.5 is helpful because this information is needed every time a change in the filter pack takes place. It provides the answers to the six most commonly asked questions in color printing.

Burning and Dodging

Just as in black-and-white printing, burning in, giving the print more exposure, makes it darker, and dodging, giving the print less exposure, makes it lighter. In color printing it is possible to change not only the density of a print but also the color balance of selected areas by burning and dodging. If you burn in an area with more yellow light, you reduce the amount of yellow in that area. Waving a CC or CP filter below the enlarger lens during exposure is another

way to change the color balance for a specific area. For instance, a yellow filter can be waved across the projected sky area to make the sky bluer or a blue filter can be waved across the color shadow areas of a projected image to make it warmer (more yellow). Start with 10 units of whatever color you want to work with. Be prepared to add exposure time to compensate for denser

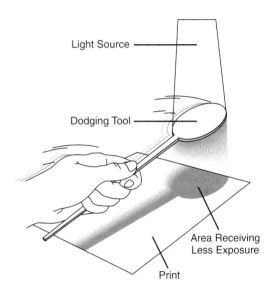

6.11 A "dodger" is employed to give an area of a print less exposure. It is necessary to keep the dodger in motion during exposure to avoid creating an outline of the tool.

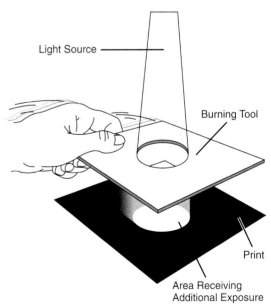

6.12 A "burning" tool is used to give an area of a print more exposure. It must be kept in motion during exposure or a dark halo effect will be visible around the edges of the area receiving more light.

Dodging and burning tools may be made in a variety of forms. Flynt made his own "dodging mats" in order to emphasize various areas of the composition and surface integrity of the print. During this process the print received a number of exposures, each with a different filter pack. This idea is clarified by Flynt's statement: "I work primarily with dancers and performers who are equally interested in the movement possibilities afforded underwater. The additional elements superimposed in the darkroom further distance the viewer from the traditional perception of the photographed figure in space. The overlays provide an ironic element of place or structure that the original underwater setting lacked. The pool provides the neutrality of the studio, combined with the spontaneity of the street."

© Robert Flynt. *Untitled*, 1989. 11 x 14 inches. Chromogenic color print.

filters. Too much burning and/or dodging can cause a color shift to take place in those areas.

A "dodger" can be made by cutting a piece of opaque cardboard in the shape of the area that will be given less exposure and attaching it to a dowel, pencil, or wire with a piece of tape (figure 6.11). Keep the dodger moving during the exposure or an outline will appear on the print. A ballpark range for dodging is about 10 to 20 percent of the initial exposure. An area being dodged can seldom tolerate more than a 30 percent dodge before the differences between the overall exposure and the area being dodged become apparent. For example, a black area will turn gray with a color cast.

A "burning" tool can be produced by taking a piece of opaque cardboard that is big enough to cover the entire print and cutting a hole in it to match the shape of the area to be given more exposure

Scales prefers working with 400-speed negative film in the 6- x 6-centimeter format because of the latitude and flexibility it gives him when printing his scenes of everyday life in New York City. "I try to make images that allude to the reality of being black in America. The photographs are descriptions of my perceptions of ordinary places and people—in the complexities of living. I do not pretend to understand them, each person. In fact, the discoveries are most often within myself, observing these documents of my own sights."

© Jeffrey Henson Scales. *Grant's Tomb*, 1993. 19 x 19 inches. Chromogenic color print.

(figure 6.12). Keep it in constant motion during exposure to avoid the outline effect. Generally, burning in requires more time than dodging. Bright highlight areas, such as skies, often require 100 to 200 percent of the initial exposure time. Reciprocity failure can occur while burning in, producing color shifts that may require a change in the filter pack for the area being given the extra time.

Save These Tools

After a while your collection of opaque burning and dodging tools will meet most printing needs, saving construction time and speeding up darkroom work. Some photographers do most of their burning and dodging with their fingers and hands. Others prefer to purchase commercially prepared tools. Do whatever works best for you.

Final Decisions and Cropping

Once the correct filter pack and exposure are determined, check the print for exact cropping. A handy way to determine whether the print has been cropped properly is to cut out a pair of Ls from a piece of white board. These Ls can be overlayed with one another on the print to determine the exact cropping of the final picture.

Also, reconsider standard notions of what makes a good photograph by enlarging a portion of your original negative and/or experimenting with different planes of focus.

Look at the Print in a Mirror

If the print still does not look the way you wish, try an old painter's method for

De Marris is involved in constructing sets, much like stage setting for plays, in which all items are precisely chosen and arranged. Long exposures, lasting minutes, give her the chance to enter the scene during the actual taking of the photograph to light very specific areas. Flood lamps and/or light bulbs of various colors, mixed with flashlights, modeling lights, and strobes with colored gels, provide a surreal color scheme. Duraflex printing materials allow De Marris to make very large and rugged prints, with the presence of a painting on a wall, which reveals the importance highly saturated color plays in her imagery.

© Pamela De Marris. *Renunciation # 4*, 1990. 50 x 50 inches. Chromogenic color print.

seeing the work in a different fashion: look at the print in a mirror. Reversing the image allows you to momentarily forget your original idea and see the work as a viewer might or in a totally different manner than before. This could provide the clue to the direction you need to take to let the picture deliver its message to its future audience.

Internegatives

A color print can be made directly from a slide using a separate positive printing process or with a regular color negative print processing method by first making what is called an internegative. An internegative is a negative made from a transparency, usually by projecting the image onto sheet film. Many labs will make standard internegatives at a modest cost that deliver acceptable results for most general daylight situations. For critical work, a custom internegative is probably necessary. However, since internegatives are a generation removed from the original they tend to produce prints that do not match the color accuracy and/or sharpness of a print made

YOUR FIRST COLOR PRINT

Begin with a simple composition, shot on daylight-type negative film with an ISO of about 100 in normal daylight outside conditions. Do not shoot under any type of artificial light, including flash. Be sure to include a human flesh tone by shooting someone with whom you are familiar and can reference if needed. Many photographers also include a gray card (such as the one in the back of this book) and a color chart for reference (on the reverse side of the gray card). Others like to incorporate a black and a white object as well to get the correct color balance. Include any colored objects that you think will be helpful in your learning process.

Photographing color references is not necessary, but it can be helpful for making impartial decisions. It is necessary to remain objective, but keep in mind that color photography is highly interpretive and therefore subjective as well. There are no standard formulas for color balance that can be applied to every situation. It is either the color that you want and like or it isn't. It makes no difference how accurately you can render the gray card if the colors do not do what you have in mind.

It is not a math problem you must solve, but a visual one. There is more than one correct answer, but do not use this as an excuse for ignorance. You must learn technique and be able to control it in order to be proficient in the craft of imagemaking. Likewise, do not let equipment or technique get in the way of making photographs. Keep in mind there are things to look at and things to photograph. Sometimes things we look at are worth photographing and sometimes they are not. Just because something is worth looking at does not mean it will translate well into a photograph.

Other things that may be problematic to look at can make exciting pictures. How do you know the difference? By photographing and determining for yourself. In 1974 Garry Winogrand wrote an essay about his work entitled "Understanding Still Photographs," in which he said: "I photograph to see what things look like photographed."

Using a 4- x 5-inch camera and straight negative printing methods, Whaley blends the languages of photography and painting to evoke a theatrical state between the imaginary and the real. Under the guise of the still-life genre, Whaley's *Natura Morta* (Dead Nature) series reflects the conflicts that exist between our civilization and the natural world. Whaley states: "Through Western art historical references and the juxtaposition of the beautiful and the unexpectedly morbid, or the serious and the whimsical, the work explores the ironic tensions between these two worlds and the time-bomb inherent in that conflict."

© Jo Whaley. *Communication Theory*, 1994. 20 x 24 inches. Chromogenic color print. Courtesy of the Robert Koch Gallery, San Francisco, CA.

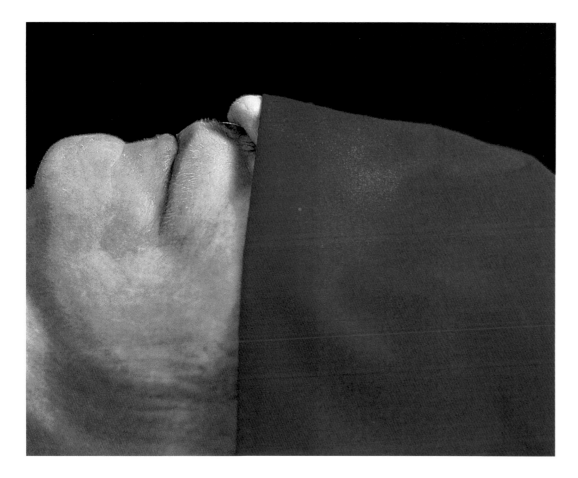

Working in the straightforward fashion of a studio photographer, Serrano looks closely at subjects most people would prefer to ignore. Serrano confronts our anxiety concerning scopophobia, the fear of looking and the fear of being seen. Serrano is not interested in transcending his literal subject matter; his images are about what they are of, and any allegorical capacity hinges on the significance of what is before the lens. Serrano favors the dye-destruction process because it is "particularly well suited for such colors as reds and yellows which coincidentally have figured prominently in my work."

© Andres Serrano. *The Morgue* (*Infectious Pneumonia*, 1992). 49 1/2 x 60 inches. Dye-destruction print with silicone, plexi-glass, and wood frame. Courtesy of Paula Cooper Gallery, New York, NY.

directly from an original camera negative. Also, if you are not satisfied with the way that a slide has printed (see next section), try making an internegative from the slide and see if it will deliver more desirable results.

Display and Print Materials

Kodak Professional Endura Transparency Digital Display Material is made for digital film and paper recorders for the production of large-scale color transparencies directly from digital files, color negatives, and internegatives. It is sturdy and translucent, making it ideal for backlit transparencies on illuminators without diffusers. Ilford makes a similar product called Ilfocolor Translucent Display Film. Kodak Professional Endura Transparency Optical Display Material is a clear-based transparency material for use on illuminators with built-in diffusers. A comparable

product is Ilfocolor Clear Display Film.

Ilfocolor Deluxe is a color negative or digital file print material on a polyester base that is useful when a durable image base is required. It has an extremely high-gloss surface with Ilfochrome Classic-like color saturation. It is available for the RA-4 process and does not require any changes in processing times. Ilfocolor Century E (ICE) is an RA-4 RC paper designed for digitally controlled laser and electronic enlarging systems. Kodak also makes plastic-based Duraflex Plus Digital Display Material for reflection prints. Typically these materials are used for commercial applications, but artists favor them for making large prints because of their sturdiness.

All of the above-mentioned display materials are processed in a regular RA-4 setup, but some may require longer processing times than normal RA-4 papers (see specific product instructions, available online). These materials should be handled in total darkness and may be

intermixed in the same chemistry as other color print materials without any ill effects.

Making Prints from Color Transparencies

The Dye-Destruction Process

When a high-quality print is wanted directly from a color transparency, the current standard is the dye-destruction or silver dye-bleach process (see chapter 2, page 41). In this method all the dyes are present in the emulsion and processing destroys the dyes that are not needed to make the final image. Many color printers believe the the dye-destruction process offers superior color, resolution and sharpness; greater dye stability; fewer processing steps; and easier to maintain processing temperatures than other methods and it is the only process discussed. The most widely used and

rior results. This means a slide that has been slightly underexposed by 1/3 to 1/2 of an f-stop. A contrasty slide is difficult to print, because the process itself adds contrast to the finished print. A slide that might normally be considered a little flat often prints surprisingly well.

Since slides do not have the orange mask to compensate for inadequacies in the negative/positive system, expect to lose a certain amount of detail and subtlety in the tone and color of the reversal print.

The sensitivity of these materials is such that safelights cannot be used. The paper must be handled in total darkness until it is loaded in a drum or processor.

Making a Print

To make a print, remove the slide from its mount and clean it carefully, because dust spots will appear as black spots on the final print, making spotting difficult. Insert the slide into the negative carrier. Tape may be applied along the sprocket holes to keep the piece of film in place. Now follow the above-listed procedures (see page 120) for making a print from a negative.

Determining the Emulsion Side of the Paper

It can be difficult to determine which is the emulsion side of the paper in total darkness. Here are four ways to tell which is the emulsion side and which is the base side of the paper:

● The paper has a tendency to curl; the emulsion will be on the outside of the curve.
● Use the glow from a luminous timer dial or a strip of luminous tape on the darkroom wall. The paper will reflect light on the nonemulsion side. This will not fog the paper.
● Ilford suggests rubbing both sides of the paper while holding it up to your ear. The emulsion side makes a different sound than the base side. If this method is used, be careful not to damage the paper and have clean hands to avoid

Casebere does not work in direct response to an actual subject (such as a real prison) but by contemplating it through images, texts, and popular beliefs and then constructing a visual interpretation of his finding. Casebere's model of the panopticon, the ideal prison of the nineteenth century, elicits an unsettling sense of edgy mystery. This emotional response is provoked by how Casebere directs his studio lights to produce deep shadows. His camera placement does not reveal the real size of his model. The shiny surface of the dye-destruction print calls attention to the lone light in the window and makes the viewer speculate on what is going on inside.

© James Casebere. *Panopticon #2*, 1992. 40 x 30 inches. Dye-destruction print. Courtesy of Michael Klein Gallery, New York, NY.

supported process is Ilfochrome Classic P-30P, formerly known as Cibachrome, which can be processed in a drum or table-top processor.

Basic Reversal Printing Guidelines and Procedures

Making a color print from a transparency is very similar to making a color print from a negative, but there are some key differences to bear in mind.

The most important step in reversal printmaking is selecting an "ideal" transparency since all the results are based on it. Generally, a slide with a greater than normal color saturation produces supe-

leaving fingerprints. With Ilfochrome papers, the emulsion comes facing the label on the inner light-tight package.

● If all else fails, cut an edge from a piece of the paper and look at it under white light to determine the emulsion side.

Drum Processing Procedures

Check and maintain proper temperature or your results will be chaotic and will not be repeatable.

Presoak the paper for 60 seconds in a water bath to ensure even development. Drain times are considered to be part of the normal processing times. If the presoak is 60 seconds and it takes 10 seconds to drain the drum or tray, start to drain at 50 seconds.

When rolling the drum on a flat surface, make the pattern of agitation uneven during the first 30 seconds. Lift the drum up slightly on one side, roll it, and then lift it up on the other side. Note that Ilford does not recommend tray processing for Ilfochrome materials.

Exercise care in handling a wet print because the emulsion is very soft and easy to damage. After processing, dry the

It is important to be able to make a print directly from a slide. The image can then be viewed in a wider variety of surroundings. It also affords the photographer the opportunity to interact with the picture and to make changes and corrections. Here Troeller combined a monochrome palette, limited depth of field, and dye destruction's naturally high contrast to make a vibrant illusion in space. She adds: "Photographing nudity at healing sites and spas required using a fast slide film because much of the work was in non-window interiors where flash was invasive. I found the discontinued Kodachrome 200 very sensitive to reds and skin tones in this light."

© Linda Troeller. *Contrexeulle Spa*, 1989. 16 x 20 inches. Dye-destruction print.

"During the later part of the 1980s," Simmons says, "I was dealing [often using dollhouse-size figures] with the superficiality, with the exterior mode we inhabit, with the confusion between ourselves and our possessions: a self-image based on what we do and where we live and how we function and certain kinds of cold disappointments in terms of truth and lies. One of the things I'm working on in my new work is imagining the daydreams and the night dreams and the fantasies of the characters that I've created. Now I'm concerned about what's going on inside … it's important for me to address their inner lives."

© Laurie Simmons. *Cafe of the Inner Mind: Dark Cafe*, 1994. 35 x 53 inches. Dye-destruction print. Courtesy of Metro Pictures, New York, NY.

print with a handheld hair dryer or in an RC paper print dryer. Do not dry it in a regular dryer that was designed for fiber-based papers because this will melt the plastic coating on the print and leave a mess on the dryer. To avoid hair dryer marks, air dry the final print by hanging it on a wire line from one corner in a warm, dust-free area.

Evaluating a Print

For the best results compare the test strip with the original slide or a similar slide of the same subject. Look at it in the same type of light that you expect to view your finished print. Pick the exposure that you like the best and check for color balance in key areas. If possible, look at a white or neutral area when deciding which color is in excess. Use the Color Print Viewing Filters kit on the side that is labeled: "prints from slides" as a guide as previously discussed (see page 124).

The guideline for determining proper density is to print for your key highlight area, thus ensuring the retention of highlight detail. If there is more than about a six f-stop difference between the key highlight and the key shadow (a brightness range of 1:64), burning in the shadow areas is usually a necessity. Another point

Table 6.6 **Essential Reversal Printing Rules**
● More exposure gives you a lighter print, not a darker one.
● When looking at your test strip, keep in mind that the darkest strip has actually had the least amount of exposure.
● To darken an area, give it less exposure.
● To lighten an area, give it more exposure.
● To make a print darker, give it less exposure.
● To make a print lighter, give it more exposure.

to consider is that slide films were designed for projection and not for print-making. No reversal paper is capable of retaining the total range of density and color that was in the original slide.

The main thing to remember when printing from slides is that all the rules of negative printing must be turned around (table 6.6). This could prove to be a bit confusing if you have been negative printing. Take a little extra time and think before you act. It could save time, money, and a great deal of anger. They don't call it reversal for nothing.

Color Correction Procedures

To remove the excess color cast from a print, you remove that color from the filter pack. All the negative printing filter rules also apply in reverse. Depending on the process, cyan filters may be employed. Be sure to have only two colored filters in the pack at once or unwanted neutral density will be produced. Refer to table 6.7 to avoid confusion.

Work in units of about five to 10 for a slight change in color, 10 to 20 for a moderate change, and 20 to 40 for a considerable effect. Generally, changes of five units or fewer are hardly noticeable in reversal printing, except when trying to match subtle color tones in a final print. Be bolder with corrections than in negative printing. A general rule is to double the corrections in reversal printing, based

Table 6.7 **Reversal Filter Pack Changes**			
Print Is Too	**Add**	*or*	**Subtract**
Blue	Yellow		Cyan and magenta
Yellow	Magenta and cyan		Yellow
Green	Magenta		Cyan and yellow
Magenta	Cyan and yellow		Magenta
Cyan	Magenta and yellow		Cyan
Red	Cyan		Magenta and yellow

on your negative printing experience. Leaps of 10, 15, or even 20 units at a time are not unusual. Starting test strip times could be five, 10, 20, and 40 seconds at about f/8 or f/11. Unlike printing from color negatives, it is possible to make prints with white light and all the filter settings on zero.

Having determined the correct number of seconds required for exposure, make future exposure changes, whenever possible, using the aperture of the enlarging lens (table 6.8). Changing the amount of seconds can affect the established color balance. This procedure can reduce the need for making additional corrections to the color pack.

After making the appropriate changes, make a new test print and re-evaluate following the same procedures.

Table 6.8 **Using the Aperture of the Enlarging Lens to Control Exposure**
● If the print is slightly dark, open the enlarging lens about 1/2 f-stop.
● If the print is dark, open the aperture of the enlarging lens about one f-stop.
● If the print is slightly light, close the enlarging lens about 1/2 f-stop.
● If the print is light, close the aperture of the enlarging lens about one f-stop.

6.14 This piece is part of a series of dye-destruction prints made from color negatives instead of color slides. It was made in the studio using broken glass and mirrors. According to Dzerigian: "Using the negative image and its subsequent reversal of values and hues established the abstraction and light from within qualities I was looking for in this symbolic still life."

© Steve Dzerigian. *Union*, 1984. 8 ¾ x 13 inches. Dye-destruction print.

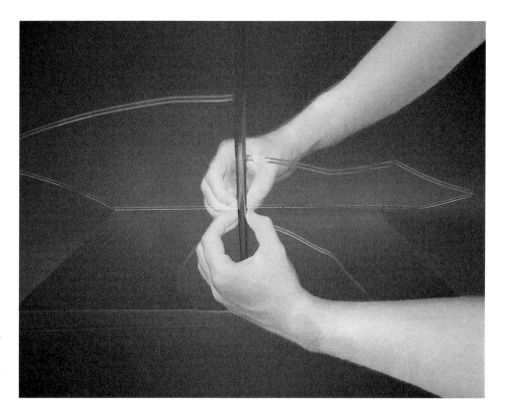

Local Color Correction

It is possible to selectively add colors to a print during exposure. Hold a color printing (CP) filter under the lens so that it covers the area you wish to alter. A CP filter can be cut into smaller pieces and attached to a support wire to filter smaller areas of a print. The amount of filtration depends on the effect desired. With reversal papers, filter densities up to 50 units may be used for dramatic effects.

Variations

Ilfochrome Classic material can be exposed directly in a camera, resulting in a direct-positive color image. Filters can be placed in front of the lens at the time of exposure to make color corrections and changes. Another possibility is to print color negatives instead of slides. The outcome is a negative color print instead of a positive color print (figure 6.14).

The Ilfochrome Classic Process P-30P

Since its introduction in 1963 as Cibachrome, Ilfochrome Classic has become the standard for the other slide-to-print processes to be compared with and matched against. For this reason, the Ilfochrome Classic Process P-30P is offered as the starting process for making prints from slides. Ilfochrome Classic is noted for its vivid color intensity, with exaggerated red sensitivity. It is not the only process. If you try it and find it is not to your satisfaction, use another process.

The Ilfochrome Classic Process P-30P (table 6.9) is carried out at 75°F (24°C) plus or minus 2°F. Follow all safety procedures recommended by Ilford and this text. Avoid getting chemicals on your skin; when mixing and using the processing solutions, wear protective eye gear and gloves; work in a well-ventilated area. Process P-30P developer and fixer contain chemical ingredients common to typical black-and-white developer and fixer formulations. The bleach, however, is unique and contains p-toluene sulfonic acid, which is very acidic in solution and is a strong irritant to the skin and eyes. The acidity is easily neutralized when the bleach waste is added in equal quantities to developer waste during the processing sequence. After neutralization the mixture is easily biodegraded in a properly operating secondary sewage treatment plant. The P-30P waste fixer solution contains photographic silver, which must be removed before disposal in most municipal sewage treatment facilities. The silver can be recovered by metallic replacement or electrolytic methods.

To make an 8- x 10-inch print with an Ilfochrome Classic-style drum, pour 2.5 ounces (75 ml) of each solution into a separate clean container and place the containers in a tray of water at 78°F

Table 6.9
Review of Ilfochrome Classic Process P-30P

For making an 8- x 10-inch print at 75°F with 2.5 ounces of chemical per step

Step	Time
1. Presoak	30 to 60 seconds
2. Develop	3 minutes
3. Rinse	30 seconds
4. Bleach	3 minutes
5. Rinse	15 to 30 seconds
6. Fix	3 minutes
7. Wash	3 minutes minimum
8. Dry	As needed

House explores various legends of sea goddesses by constructing a special tank, 4 feet x 6 feet x 18 inches deep, in order to shoot figures in water in the studio. The tank is Plexiglas, so backdrops of different colors can be placed underneath and lights with gels can be illuminated from the sides as well as through the water. The brilliant red glow of "water on fire" was created by wrapping the strobes with red cellophane. Salome's veils were replaced by sea anemones whose fluorescent colors were enhanced by leaving the shutter open, turning off the strobe's modeling lights, and exposing the image to black light for about 45 seconds at f /32. Ilfochrome, with its exaggerated red, provides the vehicle to deliver a startling large-scale exhibition print.

© Suda House. *Salome from the Aqueous Myths*, 1986. 40 x 30 inches. Dye-destruction print.

1. In total darkness, place exposed paper in a clean and dry drum. Be certain the ends of the drum are securely attached. Now processing can take place in white light.

2 Presoak. Stand the drum on end and pour water (75°F) into the funnel opening. The water will flow into the cap, but it will not come into contact with the paper until the drum is tipped over on its side. Set the timer for one minute and start it going. On a level surface immediately lay the drum on its side and begin rolling it rapidly back and forth, making more than one complete revolution each way. At the end of the minute, drain the water into a nonmetal container that will be used to dispose of all used chemicals.

3 Developer. Following the same steps as for the presoak, pour the developer into the top of the drum. Set the timer for three minutes and begin to process. During the first 15 seconds agitation should be rapid, vigorous, and somewhat irregular to avoid creating a uniform pattern that can produce staining. At the end of the development time drain the used solution into a clean container for partial reuse.

4 Rinse. Pour three ounces (90 ml) of water into the top of the drum. Agitate the water rinse for 30 seconds and drain into the disposal bucket.

5 Bleach. Pour bleach into the top of the drum. Set the timer for a minimum of three minutes and begin agitating the bleach in the same manner as the developer. The bleaching time may be increased by up to five minutes if highlights do not look clear. When bleaching is completed, drain the used solution into a clean container for partial reuse.

6 Rinse. Pour three ounces (90 ml) of water into the top of the drum. Agitate the water for 15 to 30 seconds and drain into the disposal bucket.

(25.5°C). This will maintain a proper average processing temperature because temperature drifts in a downward direction under normal room conditions. Process P-30P can be replenished one time by adding 1.25 ounces (37 ml) of fresh chemical to an equal amount of

used chemical. The temperature must be adjusted to maintain 75°F. Be careful to avoid contaminating the chemicals.

Follow these steps when using the Ilfochrome Classic process:

7 Fix. Pour fixer into the top of the drum. Set the timer for three minutes and begin agitating the fixer in a gentle and uniform manner. At the completion of fixing drain the used solution into a clean container for partial reuse.

8 Wash. Carefully remove the print from the drum; it is easy to damage the wet emulsion. Wash the print in a tray for at least three minutes in rapidly running clean water at 75°F.

9 Dry. Remove surface water with a squeegee or clean chamois cloth. Drying can be accomplished in a number of ways: the print can be hung up, laid flat (emulsion side up) on a blotter or drying rack, dried in a print dryer designed for resin-coated papers, or dried with a blow dryer. Prints must be completely dry before they are evaluated for proper color balance and exposure.

10 Cleaning the drum. After processing is complete, take the drum apart and thoroughly wash and dry all its components, inside and out, before processing the next print.

11 Replenishment. To reuse the chemicals one more time, save 1.25 ounces (37 ml) of each solution. Pour the remainder, which will be disposed of (see following step), into a plastic, not metal, container. All the chemicals must be mixed together so that they can neutralize one another before they are discarded.

12 Chemical disposal. When the printing session is complete, put all the chemicals together in the plastic container in the following order to neutralize them: developer, bleach, and fix. Do not dispose of the chemicals individually. Adding the chemicals in a different order produces sulfur dioxide fumes. Then pour the neutralized mixture down the drain with running water. For additional information call the Ilford Emergency Hotline at (866) 446-1103.

Table 6.10 Troubleshooting Ilfochrome Classic

Print Problem	Possible Cause
Light flare	Paper fogged
White, yellow, or bluish streaks across print	Loose drum end cap
	Processor not properly closed
Overall reddish cast	Light fog from stray (red) light
Dark with red-orange cast	Exposed through back of print (luster)
Black with no image	Exposed through back of print (glossy)
Irregular color streaks	Wet drum
Blue border/gray highlights	Developer contaminated
Orange cast/blacks bluish	Developer contaminated with fixer
Uneven tones/gray areas	Not enough chemicals used
Flat contrast and dark	Development time too short
No blacks and light	Development time too long
Print is black	Development step skipped
	Developer exhausted
Dull and milky	Bleach time too short
Gray highlights	Bleach exhausted
	Bleach too cold
	Bleach time too short
Black with faint image	Bleach defective
	Bleach step omitted
Brown-red borders	Bleach carried over into fixer
	Not fixed long enough
Dark, dull fogged	Print fixed before it was bleached
Flat and yellow	Print not fixed
Yellow edges	Lack of agitation
Pink-magenta borders	Overagitation
Greenish borders	Outdated paper
	Paper improperly stored
Reticulation	Inconsistent temperatures
Cyan stain	Drum not properly cleaned

Processing Problems

There are a number of common mistakes that occur when working with Ilfochrome Classic materials. The troubleshooting guide in table 6.10 and the manufacturer's instructions should help you to get back on the right track.

Masking for Contrast Reduction

Due to the lack of graded papers and various developer formulas that can be used in black-and-white printing, controlling the contrast of a color print can be problematic. You will probably encounter a slide that turns out to be difficult to print and cannot be corrected by burning and/or dodging. You may want to try a contrast mask when subtle detail

Dunitz concentrates on the spectral qualities that can be created on sheets of stainless steel and titanium. Changes in the surface are effected by using a torch, a wire brush, and/or an electric grinder. Alternations are also made by wiring an insulated paintbrush to a DC converter and voltage regulator. The image is rendered with water and baking soda as controlled changes in the voltage alter the colors. The dye-destruction process provides a direct and dramatic translation of the results.

© Jay Dunitz. *Pacific Light # 28*, 1985. 48 x 64 inches. Dye-destruction print. Courtesy of the National Museum of American Art, Smithsonian Institution, Washington, DC.

must be retained. To make a mask the original slide is contact-printed, along with diffusion material to keep it slightly out of focus, onto panchromatic black-and-white film. This film is processed and then placed in register with the original slide, then a print is made in the usual manner. The higher densities of the mask "fill" the lower densities of the original slide to reduce the overall density range.

The effect of the mask is generally most evident in the reduction of excessive contrast in the highlight areas. An increase in detail should be visible in the key shadow areas as well. The purpose of a mask is to make a good print better and not to "save" a badly exposed slide.

A Web search will yield detailed information about specific masking methods.

Endnotes

[1] RICHARD AVEDON, *American Photography* 2, no. 4, July/August 1991, 60.

[2] JOHN RUSKIN, *The Works of John Ruskin*, vol. X. Edited by E.T. Cook and Alexander Wedderburn. London: George Allen, 1903–12, 201.

Chapter Seven
DIGITAL INPUT

Nakagawa tell us: "Ma means a temporal as well as spatial gap. I see this gap in my own memory. This work bridges the gap and brings it to the present." Nakagawa digitally combined an image from his grandfather's archives dating from 1928 and his father's 8-mm Kodachrome movies from 1960, in order to reconsider his family history through his bi-cultural heritage of United States and Japan.

© Osamu James Nakagawa. *Rain*, from the series *Ma*, 2003. 30 x 40 inches. Inkjet print. Courtesy of the McMurtrey Gallery, Houston, TX, and Sepia International, New York, NY.

The author gratefully acknowledges Greg Erf with the assistance of John Valentino in the preparation of the digital chapters.

Digital Photography: An Introduction

The public embrace of digital photography has produced a new type of photographic image. This evolutionary process is akin to the advent of the first mechanical reproductions of photographs in the late nineteenth century. These early mechanical processes, such as halftone photoengraving and photogravure, began shifting photography away from its native means of reproduction. They were nonphotographic developments that were deployed in newspapers and magazines due to a strong desire for inexpensive, mass-produced images and text. In the late twentieth century, this same aspiration drove the development of digital images.

The digital revolution got into full swing during the later 1990s and has challenged the fundamental aesthetics, meaning, and vocabulary of the photographic image. Digitization has dramatically changed our image-reproduction processes as the photographic image has been extended to the Internet, CDs, and DVDs. The cross-pollination of film and digital cameras, still and moving images, gelatin silver, and digital prints has created a new awareness about what photography once was, now is, and is becoming. Digital imaging can eliminate the darkroom experience by transferring the chemical and physical creative experience to the computer screen. Consumer and professional image-editing software facilitates photo enhancing, photo retouching, and photo-collage that alter the original camera-based reality. Now, as digitalization is rapidly replacing silver-based photography as our primary source of camera-generated imagery, it is a good time to stop, evaluate, and explore some of the key artistic, conceptual, and social issues affecting digital imagemaking in the context of photographic history. The digital revolution is not only about the increasing ease of digital capture and output, but also about its accessibility to the general public and the proliferation of vernacular imagery that will ultimately affect the role of the professional photographer and how images are used and understood in our society. It is the realization of William

Henry Fox Talbot's dream of everyone becoming his or her own publisher.

Truth and Illusion

The word photography has Greek roots; it derives from *photos* (light) and *graphos* (drawing), which establishes the notion of "light drawing" that was first attributed to the camera obscura around the 1500s. The premise of photography has not changed since Talbot invented the negative/positive photographic process in the 1830s. Its purpose remains to provide a means to capture and make permanent what one sees with light in a manner similar and acceptable to that of human vision. A camera and lens focuses light on to a flat, light-sensitive material that is processed or electronically stored, permanently capturing the various densities for later reproduction. Ultimately, it makes no conceptual difference whether images are captured on glass, paper, film, or electronic sensors.

Traditionally photographic film is a chemical-based emulsion made up of light-sensitive, silver-halide grains applied to a support base. These grains become the individual receptors for light, which are later processed to create a permanent image. Although it may first appear that these silver-halide grains are the same size and evenly distributed, on the microscopic level you can see that they are of various sizes and randomly dispersed. The emulsions for both film and paper contain the same microscopic, various-sized and randomly distributed silver halide crystals that when used together to produce photographic images have a distinctive physical look that we have come to embrace as photographic "realism" or "truth." It has been said that

Connell uses the same model to highlight issues related to multiplicity of the self to the new authenticity and truth that have been created in the digital age. Connell explains: "These images were created by scanning and manipulating two or more negatives in Photoshop. Using the computer as a tool to create a believable image is not that different from accepting any photograph, or any story about two people, as an object of truth. The events portrayed in these images look believable and are based on real-life situations I have witnessed; yet they have never occurred. This is comparable to the multilayered psyches of the self. By digitally creating a photograph that is a composite of the same model, the self is exposed not as a solidified being in reality, but as a representation of social and interior investigations that happen within the mind."

© Kelli Connell. *The Space Between*, 2002. 36 x 46 inches.Chromogenic color print. Courtesy of Barry Whistler Gallery, Dallas, TX.

the nineteenth century began with people believing what was rational to be true and ended with people believing what was in a photograph to be true. Now people don't know what to believe.

Digital photography has a different makeup that is based on a complex microchip composed of electrical receptors, known as pixels. A pixel or picture element is one of the tiny points of light that make up the image on a computer screen. When these receptors are exposed to light an individual charge is generated. This charge is then transferred to a microprocessor, where it is converted and saved into a binary code (a series of zeros and ones). The code operates like a light switch in two states, "on" and "off," and allows the digital image to

be easily manipulated, stored, and displayed. Each switch, usually a tiny silicon transistor, represents a binary digit or "bit." The more switches there are the bigger the numbers that can be represented. Groups of these "bits" are combined to create pixels. The more bits that make up a pixel (8, 16, 24, and 48) the more image information they contain. Typically a photographic image is made up of millions of pixels, each receiving a different amount of charge from an exposure. The camera's microprocessor converts these charges to a digital file in a fraction of a second. The electrical receptors or pixels are laid out like an industrial grid of small squares or hexagons, which defines the structure and look of a digital image in different ways from that

This series of images is based on post-Gutenberg allegorical compositions from the sixteenth through the eighteenth centuries that incorporate a variety of social iconographies. Grizzell Larson says that "because I appreciate the physicality of the materials and the challenge in managing detail in a tactile way, I first produced a master collage by cutting and pasting, which was scanned and manipulated to produce detailed and richly saturated colors that were more effective than the original. What interests me is the confluence of the old with the new in making records that reflect and document some of our own present-day quandaries, including those of a subjective nature and those regarding our place in, and commitment to, an ever-evolving and—unpredictable—scientific culture."

© Sally Grizzell Larson. *Untitled from the series Emblems, Book I*, 1996–2003. 20 x 16 inches. Inkjet print.

of film images.

As the technology has improved, the visual disparity between film and digital imagery has grown smaller, but critics still contemplate their underlying psychological differences. Silver-based photography has been predicated on its real time and space connection because of the negative. The negative is the physical object from which a photographic print is made and it possesses a direct historical link to the time and place of its recording. It is precisely this specific corporeal witnessing that has allowed people to embrace photographic truth. Photographers wanting to maintain this real time and space connection only use digital methods to enhance rather than alter the content of their images in the manner that Ansel Adams used the chemical darkroom to bring forth the underlying meaning in his photographs. For them the digital darkroom is more evolutionary than revolutionary. On the other hand, an original digital recording cannot offer any such bodily proof that people can grab onto and hold. The ease with which its binary codes can be manipulated to transform an image into something it was not originally makes the digital image psychologically more effective for building illusion.

In addition, silver-based paper photographic processes, from calotypes to chromogenic color prints, possess a subtle yet distinguishing visual depth that allows you to "look into" the print's surface that is difficult to duplicate. This is because the silver image is embedded on the underside of the top gelatin layer, positioning itself in between the top surface and the paper base. This transparency visually contains the image and objectifies the views, helping to promote the notion that believability is built in to photography. In contrast, digital imagery, with its reliance on inks and resolution, is more akin to the mechanical reproduction processes of relief printing, engraving, and etching. The key difference has been that images made from these processes reside on the top of the surface and therefore remove a sophisticated marker that made silver-based photography a surrogate for truth.

Now, even this distinction is fading as new digital output materials become available. In the past, digital printers could only produce images on a limited number of paper stocks. Today there are papers, canvas, cloth, film, and vinyl materials that can draw the ink into the surface, not only giving these materials the transparency that was only possible in a gelatin silver print, but also allowing the print the ability to survive outdoors

Abe tells us "During the nineteenth century the Japanese wood block print, UKIYOE, influenced Western art and functionally existed as photography in its time." Abe's series *Digital Art: Chapter One* utilizes current photographic technology to question the meaning of the photograph in culture. It explores cultural disparities and the value of originality.

© Koya Abe. *Digital Art: Chapter One—The Naked Lunch (triptych)*, 2000. 40 x 30 inches (each panel). Chromogenic color prints.

for months without fading.

As these remaining differences between the mediums disappear, digital technology reflects our society's search for a definitive surrogate of truth as well as a source of meaning of art. Digital technologies simultaneously make it easier and faster for some photographers to continue to act as surrogate keepers of the truth, while encouraging others to expand the boundaries of the medium.

The Comparative and the Cultural Eye

In the Newtonian sense of forming principles that can be broadly applied, the comparative eye and the cultural eye offer imagemakers two ways of thinking about chemical and digital methods and their relation to the desired outcomes. The comparative eye encourages an imagemaker to compare, contrast, and evaluate film and digital ways of making photographs. Its purpose is to establish the "value" of a photograph based on its native attributes, such as color saturation, grain, and sharpness. This procedure allows photographers to discover the medium's inherent advantages and limitations, and how to work within

those parameters. In his seminal work *Art in the Age of Mechanical Reproduction* (1936), writer/philosopher Walter Benjamin discussed how the means of production of a piece of art changes the reaction of the audience toward that artwork. When a work of art is produced by mechanical means the "aura" of the art, which is tied to the mystique of the artist, is changed (some say lost). In this way the comparative eye emphasizes the craft and skill that photographers bring to their work.

In digital imaging, traditional craft operations are assumed by the machine, making these operations a computer's greatest asset as well as a source of criticism that can separate digital work from the traditional art discourse. Modern media has caused the aura of the unique mark of the artist to fade and be replaced with the anonymous mass-hand of technology. Some people still imagine that a computer can magically make them creative imagemakers. Reliance on the computer's preprogrammed solutions only removes the human fingerprint from the decisions that artists customarily want to control. Computer art is no different from other art forms in that meaningful work requires human guidance and an investment of time, effort, and thought. The computer is a power-

ful and transformative tool and as with any other tool you have to learn how to use it effectively.

The cultural eye determines "significance" based on the expressive aesthetic, historical, and social qualities that give a photograph its context or cultural content. The camera and the computer are mediated ways of seeing. Customarily the camera has had a covenant with society as an automatic, objective observer that makes no subjective assertions. The digital image does not make this pledge. Informed viewers understand that the digital image is about fabrication. A computer can provide a junction between photography, illustration, music, painting, and video in ways that change a viewer's response to each separate media. The digital transformation allows a photographic image to resemble an oil painting, a watercolor, or almost anything, which requires a different interpretation. Previously, surrealistic artists distorted perspective and scale while juxtaposing commonplace objects in unusual contexts. Such images ask viewers to make connections they would not normally make. The computer artist, by changing the context or content of images, can also ask viewers to make associations that are normally not possible or that are difficult to produce with conventional photographic methods. The net effect of this convergence is that cultural value can no longer be easily determined through surface distinctions or quick overall impressions.

While the paths between chemical and digital arts continue to blur, overlap, and vanish, they often ask fundamentally different questions about how reality is constructed and interpreted. It is up to imagemakers to learn what approach possesses the attributes that are most suitable for conveying their intentions and how to utilize them.

Immateriality and the Digital Image

Since camera-based images were being made centuries before the invention of photography, photography itself can be viewed as a progression in the evolution

of camera images. Although the digital image shares many of the characteristics of the silver-based photograph, the technology that forms the digital image is intrinsically different because the digital image exists as numerical data and never has to be represented as a physical entity. This lack of immateriality places the digital image in a state of constant flux, a

condition of never knowing if it is truly itself or if it is just waiting to be changed into something else. Even a print from a digital file can only be considered a representation of that image at a particular moment in time.

A Digital Conundrum

Before the invention of photography, the aura or value of an artwork was tied to its uniqueness; the distinctive talents of the artist who made the piece, and the fact that there was only one original image. When a digital file is duplicated the specific binary code that describes the image is exactly copied, allowing the digital image to be infinitely and perfectly reproduced. This can produce a conundrum. Since there is no physical difference between copies of digital images, every image can be considered an original. If every image is an original then every digital image is also a repro-

duction since there is no way to determine which version came first, resulting in a renewed questioning of the meaning and value of the original. This impressive contradiction grants digital imaging an authoritative way of being paradoxical by acknowledging the pleasure of the doppelganger (the twin), even when we are unable to apprehend it.

What Constitutes Reality?

Since the invention of the daguerreotype, people have been altering photo-based images. Every day we are bombarded with modified images in newspapers and magazines, and on television. Knowledgeable observers know that the way a photographer selects their subject matter and then frames and crops the images shapes the "reality" of a photograph. A photographer's decision about these matters can change an image and therefore its meaning. A typical viewer

This screen shot shows the original images Meyer used to digitally construct his final representation. "Today more than ever the artists should re-establish the role of a demiurge and show doubts, destroy certainties, annihilate convictions so that, at the other end of confusion, a new sense and sensibility can be created."
Joan Fontcuberta, introduction to the print version of *Truth & Fictions*.

©Pedro Meyer. *Truths & Fictions, A Journey from Documentary to Digital Photography*, 1994. CD-ROM.

has been taught to trust photographs, especially ones in the media, as accurate representations of reality, but digitalization has lead viewers to become less naive and question the truthfulness of images. The first public outcry occurred when *National Geographic* digitally moved the Egyptian Pyramids closer together to accommodate the vertical cover on its February 1982 issue. The print media has reacted to such digital manipulation with internal rules and proposed ethics codes, but despite ongoing tales of photographic deception, many people continue to believe in the authority and veracity of photographs.

Digital images, which look like traditional photographs, can betray that trust because of the ease with which the separation between media and art has been removed. For example, in 1994 *Time* magazine darkened the face of O.J. Simpson before his murder trial to make him appear more menacing, and during

the 2003 US-led invasion of Iraq, a photographer for the *LA Times* was fired for combining two of his own photographs to form a new composite view. This chameleon-like nature of the digital image ignores the rules established by our culture to identify different types of reality, which can foster a sense of digital anxiety and doubt in regard to the truth. The degree of post-camera control offered by digital editing (compositing) has also been critiqued as a threat to our notion of photographic identity as it has been established through a fragile social contract between the subject and the imagemaker.

Digital Differences

An early criticism of the digital image was that it was made by the actions of a program writer and not an imagemaker. This phenomenon was not without historical precedent. The camera has shaped

our system of photographic representation. Its monocular vision, seeing the world from a single linear viewpoint, is a construct at the heart of classical systematic Aristotelian thinking. The development of the handheld camera and flexible roll film defined an entire way of seeing and it leaves a highly identifiable footprint.

An issue new computer users encounter is their inability to apply real-world intuition to the machine. Although computer programmers attempt to simulate a tactile experience with tools that replicate an airbrush, paintbrush, or pencil, they are still imitations that respond differently from traditional tools. When working with any new tool, users must develop a set of intuitive actions based on their experience of the machine. Many of the existing digital tools were created to suit someone else's needs or designed for general use. Nevertheless, imagemakers always find ways to make

Georgiou uses the computer to make images that cannot be photographed to speculate how future civilizations might perceive our present culture. This faux-documentary presents recurring forms of the "power-glyphs" found in monolithic ruins and petroglyphs across North America. Georgiou created this image using a combination of digitized photographic images and live capture video images that have been manipulated together in digital form.

© Tyrone Georgiou. *Plug Ruins, Utah from Unexplained Archaeology of North America,* 1991. Variable size. Digital file.

tools and materials fit their personal vision. Programs are available that give digital imagemakers the ability to author software and customize imagemaking tools, giving them the same flexibility as their analog cousins.

Just as with a film negative, you must be aware that the digital data displayed on a computer screen often carries more information than can be outputted, making an understanding of the final product essential for deciding when an image is finished. Knowing why you started making the image is another indicator of comprehending when it is finished. The adage less is more can also be applied to digital images, as there comes a point when further alterations become confusing. Since many viewers will be looking for the digital changes, those alterations should have a purpose that furthers the image's content / context.

Finally, we have been culturally conditioned to accept the wall on which an image is displayed as neutral space. Under this paradigm the wall should not affect how the viewer reads the content / context of a piece. Work that exists on a computer screen does not operate under this assumption. The physical apparatus of the machine has an entirely different set of connotations that include all of the other uses of a computer (word processor, telephone, and checkbook). Work that exists on a computer's screen has to overcome this limitation. Digital images

To show the intertwined relationship among humanity, nature, and technology, Lee creates hybrid images of human and natural forms by scanning her own body and then manipulating the images in Photoshop. Lee says: "I am interested in stretching identity and creating virtual bodies that deliver a sense of perplexity and paradox by finding a balance between revelation and deception. I want to make the images visually convincing while maintaining their formal integrity. Therefore, finding the initial visual likeness by observation and examinations comes first and is far more important and effective than relying on the technical capability of the software."

© Bovey Lee. *Body Garden—Peaches,* 2001. 8 x 10 inches. Inkjet print. Courtesy of Jellybean Photo, New York, NY.

that are printed out as photographs or lithographs begin to take on the skin, the characteristics, and the connotations of those mediums.

Appropriation, Stock Images and Copyright Issues

Since ancient times people have "borrowed" from other sources to produce new work. As in any recorded medium, art is based on knowing and building from itself. The current artistic environment, which actively promotes the mining of pre-existing materials, along with the ease with which digital data can be copied and pasted, has brought the issue of appropriation to the forefront. The use of source material should be examined on an individual basis, taking into account the concepts of fairness, originality, content, and the motivation of the artist. When appropriating images ask the question, does the appropriation create significant new meaning and/or context for people to ponder? Legally an idea cannot be copyrighted; only the expression of an idea may be protected. Generally, in the educational and artistic arenas, we can assume that if an appropriated image is contextually removed from the original, is unrecognizable or has been substantially altered, then a new image has been created.

Appropriation can also be a political/social act. Artists such as Richard Prince, Sherrie Levine, and Barbara Kruger have used it to challenge the notion of authorship, originality, power, and sexism. In these cases the original was directly referenced, but the ideas expressed through the appropriation differed from the originals. This validates and legitimizes the work in a postmodern art world.

When images are made for commercial purposes, copyright becomes a more complicated and thorny issue. Photographers who make their living by making and selling photographs for their livelihood have fought to define the legal

Drawing on the methods and strategies of advertising, Kruger reuses studio-type images and text to deal with capitalism, patriarchal oppression, and consumption. Kruger attempts to deconstruct consumerism, the power of the media, and stereotypes of women by showing how images and words can manipulate and obscure meaning. About her work, Kruger states: "The thing that's happening with photography today vis-a-vis computer imaging, vis-a-vis alteration, is that it no longer needs to be based on the real at all. ... Photography to me no longer pertains to the rhetoric of realism; it pertains more to the rhetoric of the unreal rather than the real or of course the hyperreal."

© Barbara Kruger. *Untitled*, 1990. 143 x 103 inches. Photographic silk-screen on vinyl. Courtesy of Mary Boone Gallery, New York, NY.

status of the photographic image. In the United States, copyright usually belongs to the person who presses the shutter. This includes copyright of stock images that are available on photo CD-ROMs or downloadable from the Web. Many stock image packages include reproduction and alteration rights in the cost of the CD; others require usage fees and may not allow image alterations. In other situations, such as with many photojournalists, the image may belong to the news-

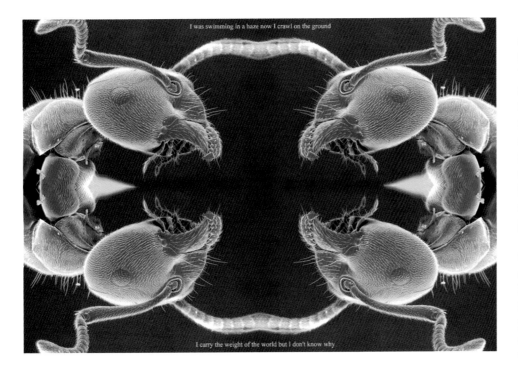

I was swimming in a haze now I crawl on the ground

I carry the weight of the world but I don't know why

Essington appropriates black-and-white scientific and medical images and manipulates and colorizes them in Photoshop. Essington says: "I prefer this method because I can choose the desired color and high saturation of all, or part of, an image that is not possible with conventional materials. In this case I chose the red orange for its earthen quality. I picked the ant for its ability to lift several times its body weight and the text refers to carrying a burden. I often have a hard time letting things go and consequently feel like I carry the weight of my troubles."

© Mark Lewis Essington. *Untitled*, 2002. 7 x 10 inches. Inkjet print. Text reads "I carry the weight of the world but I don't know why."

A big question is, how many pixels are needed for a digital camera to match the microscopic silver crystals in film? Technically speaking, there are the equivalent of approximately 20 million pixels in a typical high-quality 35-mm color negative. The difference of opinion is over how small and how close pixels and dots have to be for our eyes to recognize continuous tone. Some say that as few as 9 million pixels can look as good to the eye as a 35-mm film print, except when greatly enlarged, while others insist that 14 million pixels are necessary. This is an update of the old bogus photographic dispute of whether you need a small- or large-format camera to make good pictures. The real question is not whether you need a 2-megapixel or 14-megapixel camera to make good photographs, but what the aesthetic and technical requirements are for the final image. Just as the size and quality of a film negative determine the character of a gelatin silver print, so the quality and size of your electronic sensor (input), regardless of its source, is the critical factor in influencing the look of the final output.

paper or client who paid for its production (known as work for hire). Bear in mind that the use of copyrighted images without permission is illegal. Also, celebrities such as the Rolling Stones own the rights to their images and you are legally obligated to pay them a royalty to use their likeness for any commercial purposes

For additional information see US Copyright Office, Library of Congress, www.loc.gov/copyright, or contact an intellectual property rights attorney.

Pixels and Silver Crystals

Since its invention, film has provided inexpensive, easily retrievable, sharp, continuous tone pictures. In contrast, digital film (electronic sensors) uses pixels, at a variety of resolutions, to create

the illusion of continuous tone (see figure 7.1). The image produced by a camera lens is in analog form, as in a continuously variable scale like the volume control on your CD player that can be changed in a smooth progression from soft to loud. Likewise, a film image has a continuous scale of tones from light to dark.

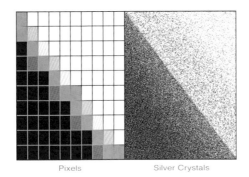

Pixels   Silver Crystals

7.1 How pixels and silver crystals optically capture light

Digital Cameras

Digital cameras have an image sensor, positioned where the film would normally be in a conventional camera, which transmits electronic pulses to the camera's on-board computer for processing. CCD (Charged Coupled Device) and CMOS (Complementary Metal Oxide Sensor) are the most common types of light-sensitive chips used for image gathering. CCD sensors are devoted to light capture only and rely on the onboard camera computer to complete the imaging process into bits. CMOS sensors include light sensors with digitization circuits so that the chip directly outputs digital bits to the camera computer, requiring less camera circuitry.

An image sensor has millions of light-sensitive cells arranged in a grid. When an exposure is made the lens focuses light on the sensor and each cell, which

has a red, green, or blue filter in front of it, measures the intensity of the light that falls on it. Every position on the grid is recorded as a solid-toned pixel with its color, brightness, and position given as a series of numbers. Once the image is recorded (digitized), imaging software can be used to select and alter the color, brightness, and position of any pixels.

Although digital cameras resemble film-based cameras, there are major differences that can significantly affect the image. The human eye can accurately record detail in light intensities within a camera range equivalent of about 15 to 30 f-stops in a scene. By comparison, color slide film captures a range of light intensities of about five f-stops. Digital cameras capture a range of light intensities of about eight to nine f-stops—not as good as the human eye, but almost twice as much as color film. This increased range makes it possible for digital cameras to photograph in extremely low light without a tripod or additional artificial light. Many digital image sensors can also capture blues, dark greens, and fluorescent colors more accurately than film.

Digital cameras do away with the darkroom, using professional quality imaging software to create pictures. Digital and film cameras are fundamentally alike; it will be the choice of optics, format, cost, and features that determine which will work best for you. Once you have mastered the proper camera setting, digital cameras can match the quality of film cameras, bearing in mind that quality is a relative term. With pixels and silver halide crystals on equal footing, it is critical for imagemakers to gain a personal understanding of the differences digital and film cameras offer in their recording and output capabilities. Quality is not intrinsic, but determined by individual aesthetic choices and reproduction needs. This chapter and the next one discuss the aesthetic and technical differences imposed by your digital choices.

Visual Acuity and 300 DPI

Visual acuity is the capability of the human eye to resolve detail, but this power of human vision to recognize fine detail has limits. When it comes to digital imaging, the point where dots, lines, and spaces are seen as continuous tone to the human eye is approximately 300 dots per inch (dpi). This is why photographic printers, known for high-quality output, have resolutions of 300 dpi and higher. There are many variables, such as individual differences in visual acuity, lighting conditions, and viewing distance, but generally 300 dpi is considered acceptable for mimicking continuous tone. An 8- x 10-inch digital print viewed at 12 inches (30 cm) easily allows the dots to be seen as a continuous tone to the average eye. As prints are made larger the viewing distance increases, which theoretically means the dpi could be reduced.

Modern printers create images in a variety of ways. Depending on the way a printer lays down its dots on a page, a print made at 200 dpi on one printer can look finer than a print made at 400 dpi on another. Regardless of what printer you use, 300 dpi has become the standard for amateur photographers wishing to display personal snapshots. The more demanding critical eye, such as professionals intending to greatly enlarge their digital files and still maintain continuous tone quality at close viewing distances, will require 600 to 8000 dpi output (see figure 7.2)

7.2 Continuous line appears as dots become too small for the eye to differentiate between the spaces and the dots

Table 7.1 Screen Resolutions and Printed Image Size

Digital Image		Screen Image (FIRST VIEW)	Printed Image
Image Resolution	=	Screen size at 72 ppi (pixels per inch)	Image size printed at (300 dpi dots per inch)
640 x 480	=	22.58 cm x 16.93 cm (8.889 in x 6.667 in)	5.42 cm x 4.06 cm (2.133 in x 1.6 in)
800 x 600	=	28.22 cm x 21.17 cm (11.111 in x 8.333 in)	6.77 cm x 5.08 cm (2.667 in. x 2 in)
1024 x 768	=	36.12cm x 27.09 cm (14.222 in x 10.667 in)	8.67 cm x 6.5 cm (3.413 in x 2.56 in)
1280 x 960 (1.3 megapixel)	=	45.16 cm x 33.87 cm (17.778 in x 13.333 in)	10.84 cm x 8.13 cm (4.267 in x 3.2 in)
1600 x 1200 (2.1 megapixel)	=	56.44 cm x 42.33 cm (22.22 in x 16.665 in)	13.55 cm x 10.16 cm (5.333 in x 4 in)
1800 x 1200 (2.3 megapixel)	=	63.5 cm x 42.33 cm (25 in x 16.665 in)	15.24 cm x 10.16 cm 6 in x 4 in)
2048 x 1536 (3 megapixel)	=	72.25 cm x 54.19 cm (28.444 in x 21.333 in)	17.34 cm x 13 cm (6.827 in x 5.12 in)
2400 x 1600 (4 megapixel)	=	84.67cm x 56.44 cm (33.333 in x 22.22 in)	20.32 cm x 13.55 cm (8 in x 5.33 in)
3032 x 2008 (6 megapixel)	=	106.96 cm x 70.84 cm (42.111 in x 27.889 in)	25.67 cm x 17cm (10.107 in x 6.693 in)
4560 x 3048 (13.89 megapixel)	=	160.87 cm x 107.53 cm (63.333 in x 42.333 in)	38.61 cm x 25.81 cm (15.2 in x 10.16 in)

Digital Camera Features

Resolution

When choosing a digital camera the key feature to consider, after optical quality, is the resolution. This is measured in millions of pixels, known as megapixels. Generally, 1-megapixel digital cameras can create 2- x 1-inch prints at 300 dpi, without cropping, that are almost indistinguishable from 100 ISO 35-mm film (see chapter 8, page 169). 3- and 4-megapixel digital cameras can make indistinguishable prints up to 5 x 7 or even 8 x 10 inches. 5-megapixel cameras and higher have no problem producing 8- x 10-inch prints that are almost indistinguishable from film prints. The main advantage of choosing a digital camera with more megapixels is that it allows you to crop more freely to produce high-quality 8- x 10-inch prints from selected areas of your image file. The camera only records resolution. When the image file is first opened, it is the imaging software program that calculates the dpi and corresponding print dimension. Generally, by default, images are displayed at 72 dpi (Web quality) with their corresponding print dimensions. This can be a problem as the standard for photo-quality images is an output of 300 dpi and not 72 dpi. Achieving photo-quality output requires converting the default 72 dpi to 300 dpi, which will reduce the default print dimensions (see table 7.1). Being able to make the proper conversion from 72 to 300 dpi is essential for photo-quality printing. Figure 7.3 illustrates this relationship between megapixels, pixel dimensions, and print size. Notice that the image must be doubled

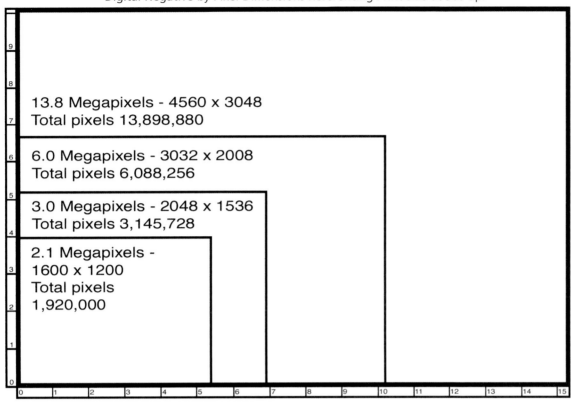

13.8 Megapixels - 4560 x 3048
Total pixels 13,898,880

6.0 Megapixels - 3032 x 2008
Total pixels 6,088,256

3.0 Megapixels - 2048 x 1536
Total pixels 3,145,728

2.1 Megapixels -
1600 x 1200
Total pixels
1,920,000

7.3 Digital negative by pixel dimensions

Baker used a digital camera to ground her *Collisions* series within the traditional photographic record, yet it still allowed her the leeway to explore altered color and spatial relationships. Baker informs us that the source images for this image (reading left to right) are: "a white top of a truck in green foliage, the bed of a blue truck with a tail light, and a piece of rusted metal. The balance between the identifiable and abstract qualities of the wreckage relies on the puzzle-like transitions of prominent edges and the decreased color saturation on the right side of the image."

© Jennifer Baker. *Truck Bed*, from the *Collisions* series, 1999. 6 ¼ x 9 inches. Inkjet print.

Hallman uses the computer, with its fluid technology of pixels, as a stage for critical examination of his own experience as a man in this culture. By using himself as principal actor, Hallman neutralizes the issues surrounding the representation of individuals and focuses attention on ideas. "Partly because of the tableau methodology, and the flexible range of computer color, I feel more responsible for the meaning and expression carried by color in this work. It is a pleasureful and powerful seduction, requiring a new and constant mindful attention."

© Gary Hallman. *Cul de Sac Pas de Deux #3*, 1995. 24 x 36 inches. Inkjet print.

in megapixels to significantly increase picture size at 300 dpi.

The resolution of digital cameras is comparable to edge sharpness or detail in a film image. Digital resolution is determined by the number of light-sensitive pixels that convert light into electrons in the camera's image sensor. On a computer screen a pixel is one of the tiny points of light that make up the image, and the greater the number of pixels the higher the resolution. On a digital camera, a pixel is a photodiode that records the color and brightness of the light that hits it. For instance, a resolution of 1600 x 1200 indicates that the digital camera produces images at a maximum of 1600 horizontal pixels by 1200 vertical pixels or 2.1 megapixels, compared with 20 million pixels for 35-mm color transparency film.

LCD Monitor

The best digital cameras have an LCD (liquid crystal display) monitor on the back of the camera, which shows the image that the lens focuses on. This allows you to compose the image without using the optical viewfinder and lets you see previously recorded images in the camera's memory card so you can review your work as you make it. LCDs can be difficult to see in bright light or at particular angles, they use a great amount of battery power, and are not an accurate guide to color or focus.

Lens Coverage and Depth of Field

Unless the image sensor is the exact size of a comparable film format, the image area covered by your lens will be different for a digital camera than for a 35-mm film camera. Generally manufacturers list their conversion equivalencies, based on the size of their sensor chip. Most pocket digital cameras have image sensors smaller than 35-mm film, which decreases the area of coverage, or field of view, in a scene. A 10-mm lens on a digital camera might show the same field of view as a 50-mm lens on a 35-mm camera, enhancing the telephoto capabilities of the lens

at the expense of reducing wide-angle coverage. These cameras often require an auxiliary wide-angle lens attachment to achieve wide-angle capabilities.

The smaller image sensors and smaller lenses of digital cameras tend to create a much smaller circle of light formed by a lens known as "circle of confusion" (see chapter 16, page 320). This smaller circle of confusion is therefore sharper with a smaller digital sensor than those formed by 35-mm film cameras. This can make obtaining a shallow depth of field, the range of distance between the nearest and farthest points from the camera that is rendered acceptably sharp, very problematic. For instance, many digital cameras make it extremely difficult, if not impossible, to create the soft-focus background that is accepted practice in portraiture and nature photographs. To attempt a shallow depth of field, use the longest focal length and the largest f-stop possible. Even then, the results will be less dramatic than with a 35-mm film camera. The smaller image sensors and lenses of inexpensive and pro-consumer digital cameras will dramatically increase the depth of field, which can make a digital f/4 the equivalent of f/22 on a 35-mm film camera.

Digital ISO

Digital cameras, like their film counterparts, allow the user to adjust for different lighting conditions by changing the aperture and the shutter speed. In addition, film camera users can change the type of film in the camera. The ISO (International Standards Organization) of a film refers to its sensitivity to light. Film-based and digital cameras both use the ISO designation to describe sensitivity to light and the resulting effect on an image. The higher the ISO number the more sensitive it is to light but the grainier the picture becomes with film and the more noise increases with digital sensors.

A digital camera cannot change the size of its photodiodes (the digital equivalent to a grain of silver halide) in its

7.4A ISO 200 & **7.4B** ISO 1200 Erf uses a flash to photograph people at close range during the late evening hours. This dramatizes the individual in the foreground while de-emphasizing the background as the light from the flash does not travel much beyond 12 feet. The initial digital picture was taken at ISO 200. The second example has been enhanced to better illustrate what the digital noise would look like had the scene been photographed at ISO 1200.

© Greg Erf. *Main Street*, 2000. 8 x 10 inches. Inkjet.

imaging sensor. To compensate for varying light levels, digital cameras adjust the electrical gain of the signal from the sensor. Increasing the gain amplifies the power of the signal *after* it has been captured on the image sensor. This is the digital equivalent of "push processing" film in low-light situations. The major advantage of digital ISO is that the user can change the ISO of any individual frame. For example, frame 9 can be exposed outside at ISO 100 while frame 10 may be exposed indoors at ISO 800. Digital camera manufacturers have made an effort to align the digital ISO settings with film ISO ratings, but while they may be close, the digital ISO numbers should be used only for reference.

Digital Aberrations: Noise, Banding, and Blooming

Although changing the ISO in a digital camera is more effective than push processing film, it has its side effects. The higher the ISO setting the more likely it will be that pictures contain "noise" in the form of randomly spaced, brightly colored pixels. Digital noise occurs most often in brightly lit or dark scenes where some pixels function incorrectly, resulting in "dead" or "hot" pixels. Hot pixels are bright white and dead pixels don't

show any color. Using ISO 400 and higher or working in dim light may degrade the image quality with noise. Noise is a factor with all digital cameras, but it is reduced with higher megapixel cameras (see figure 7.4). Many digital camera manufacturers suggest turning off "image-sharpening" features as these will exacerbate the noise problem. Imaging software programs usually have a noise filter that can help reduce noise by discarding pixels that are too different from adjacent pixels.

Banding, unpredicted bands that appear in areas with no detail, is also more likely to occur at a higher ISO. Blown-out highlights that do not possess detail and have spread or "bloomed" into adjacent image areas are caused by overexposure and are known as blooming. Bracketing and exposure compensation is recommended to keep blooming in check.

White Balance

Film cameras have only two options for color balance, daylight and tungsten film. All other corrections must be made with filters in front of the lens at the time of exposure or during printing. Digital cameras can automatically or manually adjust the color balance of each frame

electronically according to the color temperature of the light coming through the lens. The better cameras have a larger variety of settings for different lighting sources that can include any of the following: daylight, cloudy, shade, incandescent, and fluorescent (see table 7.2). High-end digital cameras also offer white balance bracketing for mixed lighting sources. Learning how to adjust and control the white balance can mean the difference between capturing that spectacular sunset or having the camera automatically "correct" it down to gray sky.

Digital Camera Color Modes

Digital cameras have image-processing algorithms designed to achieve accurate

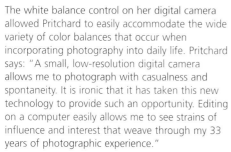

The white balance control on her digital camera allowed Pritchard to easily accommodate the wide variety of color balances that occur when incorporating photography into daily life. Pritchard says: "A small, low-resolution digital camera allows me to photograph with casualness and spontaneity. It is ironic that it has taken this new technology to provide such an opportunity. Editing on a computer easily allows me to see strains of influence and interest that weave through my 33 years of photographic experience."

© Janet L. Pritchard. *Page 1, Year 1*, from *Views from the Interior: Family and Photography*, 2002. 24 x 30 inches. Inkjet print.

color, but there are variables within these programs and within the scene that may produce distinct color variations. Professional cameras offer a range of application modes. For instance, one mode might be optimized to set the hue and chroma values for skin tones in por-

traits. A second mode could be Adobe RGB gamut based, which gives a wider range of color for output on six- or eight-color printers (see color management in chapter 8, page 176). A third mode could be optimized for outdoor landscape or nature work.

Optical and Digital Zoom

Digital cameras are equipped with optical zoom, digital zoom, or both. Optical zoom physically magnifies the subject by moving the lens elements to the desired magnification. Digital zoom magnifies the image by increasing the number of pixels until the desired magnification occurs using a process called interpolation. Interpolation is a set of mathematical logarithms automatically applied when the original pixel dimensions are

changed for resizing (see interpolation in chapter 8, page 166). Digital zoom constructs, or interpolates, pixels to zoom in on a subject, which degrades the overall image quality because the program makes up information that was not in the original.

Memory Buffer

Higher end digital cameras have a memory buffer for the temporary storage of images during shooting. The camera will hold a number of these files in the buffer depending on the quality (size) of the file. Once this buffer is filled, these images are written onto the memory card in the camera. The recording time can be as short as a few seconds or as long as many minutes, and exposures cannot be made during this time.

Removable Camera Memory Storage

Digital cameras provide limited amounts of internal storage capacity and use removable memory cards to store images. When the removable memory becomes full the data can be transferred to a computer or to a printer for output. There are numerous reusable types and sizes of removable memory and the selection is primarily based on the latest technology and your working equipment.

Common Digital Camera File Formats

The digital file uses a binary code to electronically record data such as an image or text, and allows it to be stored, processed, and manipulated in a computer. Although all images are written in binary code, there is a variety of file formats for saving and for images. Each format has a unique method of translating the resolution, sharpness, value, and color of a digital image and each has its uses, advantages, and limitations.

Most digital cameras provide several file format options, such as TIFF, RAW, and JPEG, plus a range of quality settings that can be set to meet the needs of a particular situation. When creating digital image files, think of these files in a manner similar to film. Consider the file format options, such as TIFF, RAW, and JPEG, as the film type (grain). Think of the quality settings, such as low, medium, and high, as the film format, such as 35 mm, 2 1/4 x 2 1/4 or 4 x 5 inches, and the look one gets when these are contact printed. To get predictable results from your digital photography you must know the differences between various file formats and quality settings along with the final print size to get the desired results.

Compression Algorithms: Lossless and Lossy

It is essential to know how to store digital information to obtain the desired image. Digital cameras can "compress" images to save file space on the memory card. There are numerous file compression types and they all fit into two basic categories, lossless and lossy. Lossless compression indicates a compressed file's ability to recover all the original data when the file is uncompressed. Compression algorithms, a set of mathematical program instructions, are designed to reduce the original file size to create extra storage space or to speed up file transfer over a network. Lossy compression permanently reduces a file by eliminating redundant data or data not visible to the average eye; this data cannot be recovered. This results in a loss of image quality that is proportional to the amount of compression. Most lossy file types give options to determine how much compression is desired. Different file types are best for different applications (see box 7.1).

TIFF

This is an acronym for Tag Image File Format. TIFF files are currently the standard in the graphics and printing field. TIFF files are used to exchange files between applications and computer platforms, and for high-quality printing. Compression options can be used, but generally are not because of a loss in image quality and because many high-quality output devices will only accept uncompressed TIFF files. Even if compressed, TIFF files will be much larger than inherently compressed GIF or JPEG files. TIFF is known as an interchange format, easily opened on any platform, and is considered one of the most universally accepted high-resolution file formats.

JPEG

JPEG, Joint Photographic Experts Group, is the default file format used on most dig-

---

Box 7.1 **Other Major Digital File Types**

GIF stands for Graphics Interchange Format and is a lossy format primarily used for the Web. GIF is excellent for flat color graphics, but not ideal for photographs.

PNG, Portable Network Graphics, format was designed to supplant the older GIF format and can substitute many common uses of the TIFF format. PNG is a lossless file format with good compression whose two major uses are the World Wide Web and image editing.

EPS is short for encapsulated postscript. EPS files were designed for saving high-resolution documents, illustrations, and photographs for electronic prepress for page layout software in the printing industry.

PICT is encoded in Macintosh's native graphics language. PICT files are lossless, and can be opened on the Windows platform and saved in most software applications.

BMP is the standard Windows image format. It is lossless and designed for pictures or graphics.

Program-specific file types such as Photoshop (.psd) or Illustrator (.ai) are native file formats that contain the maximum amount of information about an image for use in its own native program. Sometimes these native files are much larger than similar common file formats because program-specific features are only saved in native file formats. When saving the image to a common file format, which is sometimes called a non-native file format, the image's layers may have to be combined, and certain formatting information may be eliminated.

ital cameras because it allows for the maximum number of pictures per megabyte of memory. JPEG is a compression format with great control over file sizes using the Basic, Normal, and Fine settings on your camera to manage final output quality. JPEG is an excellent file format, but images cannot be restored to their original file size because information has been permanently eliminated. The JPEG image file format uses a lossy compression scheme and is commonly used for low-resolution continuous tone images on the Web. JPEG compression also allows the creator to decide between file size and image quality; higher quality means larger file size and smaller file size means lower image quality. JPEG files should not be opened and resaved multiple times because the images will slowly deteriorate (due to the lossy compression scheme) and become soft and pixilated. Compression has been likened to crushing an eggshell and gluing it back together. During the rebuilding process tiny pieces are lost, the glue smears, and the shape is not quite smooth. The more you crush, the more noticeable the defects, such as abrupt color highlights graduations, loss of sharpness, jagged lines, and swirling patterns known as artifacts. It is always best to go back and work from your original file format (RAW, TIFF, PSD) when remaking JPEG files.

RAW and Post-Processing

The RAW file format is a type of import/export format rather than a storage format. The RAW file format can be considered a pure "digital negative" because it contains straight binary files with information pertaining only to individual pixels from the image sensor. When a RAW image format is saved (shutter released) only the sensor data is saved without post-processing such as color balance, color palette compression, size, white balancing, or some sharpening that is required with other file formats. The data is not formatted for a specific application and the main advantage to these files is that they are uncompressed and smaller than TIFF files. RAW files

can be difficult to work with because they must be imported using plug-in modules that require all of the image parameters to be set prior to importing, which can destroy some data if not set correctly. It is therefore best to rely on the built-in post-processing controls and postpone using RAW files until image management is thoroughly understood. When experimenting with RAW files, be sure to work from a duplicate image file.

Opening Files

Regardless of the type of file you are working with, all computer files have what are called "file headers," which is the portion of the file that tells the computer what the file is, what program created it, the date it was created, and so on. Although the files themselves can easily go back and forth between various computer systems, the file headers do not always work properly. When you double click on a file, the computer reads the header and attempts to guess what to do with the file. Sometimes it guesses wrongly. If you have trouble opening a file, open it within the application.

Storage Mediums for Final Image Files

Besides hard drives, there are many expandable and portable devices that can aid in the storage and transportation of information. From the 1970s to the early 1990s, the 5 ¼-inch floppy disk and later the smaller 3 ½-inch floppy disk were the standard for storing files. Each disk held respectively 400 to 800 kilobytes (KB) and 1.4 megabytes (MB), or 1,433 KB, of information. Then a typical word-processing file might require 8 KB, but today an image file can easily exceed 100 MB (100,000,000 KB), requiring gigabytes of storage space. Storage devices are continually being developed and improved. The following are some that have made a major impact on the digital medium.

Compact Disk (CD) and Digital Versatile Disk (DVD)

These inexpensive metallic disks, coated with a clear resin, use laser technology to optically record data and are standards for reliably distributing large quantities of information, including text, images, sound, and video. CDs hold approximately 700 MB of information and DVDs can hold from 4.7 GB up to 9 GB, depending on the type. CDs and DVDs can be written on once (CD-R, DVD-R) or be rewritable (CD-RW, DVD-RW). There are competing formats for DVDs so do the research to select the format most suitable for your needs.

Mechanical Storage

Mechanical storage is the most common and least expensive type of storage device. Hard disk drives are metal disks coated with iron oxide that spin and rely on a synchronizing head to read/write digital information. The head floats just above the surface and magnetically charges the oxide particles to store the digital data.

Internal Hard Disk Drives

Hard drives are where a computer's programs and files are stored. When the computer is turned off, all saved data remains on the hard drive. Hard disk drives come in a variety of sizes measured in gigabytes and terabytes.

External Hard Disk Drives

Small and portable, these hard disk drives connect directly to the computer through various external ports. They are an ideal solution for transferring large digital files and backup of valuable data. Many of these drives are hot swappable, allowing them to be connected or disconnected without turning off the power.

Solid State Storage: Hard Drives, USB Drives, and Flash Memory Media

Solid-state storage is neither magnetic, like hard disk drives, nor optical, like

CDs or DVDs, but is electrically erasable, RAM-like memory that is available for both internal and external applications. Access time is faster than with a disk because the data can be randomly accessed and does not rely on a read/write head searching for data on a rotating disk. In addition, this type of storage uses less power and is shock resistant, but has a higher cost per megabyte of storage than mechanical storage.

The most common solid-state storage devices are the flash memory cards used to record images in digital cameras and USB drives. They all come in a wide variety of storage capabilities, physical shapes, and names. Flash memory cards require special adapters, known as card readers, which plug into standard computer ports. USB drives only require a USB port and are about the size of a pack of chewing gum.

Scanners

Scanners are input devices that digitize information directly from printed or photographic materials in a method similar to photocopiers. Aside from a digital camera, scanners are the most common type of equipment for getting images into a computer. Light is reflected off or through an image or object and interpreted by light sensors. Color scanners use RGB filters to read an image in single or multiple passes. After the scan is complete, software is typically used to make color and contrast corrections and to

Flax states that upon being introduced to the computer, it became clear that she could bring information examining the roles of parents and children into her work. Woven throughout the examination of family and society is the ever-present knowledge that these new technologies have an awesome potential to change the way we communicate and understand the world. Flax says: "I try to maintain an awareness of their power, never simply thinking of them as painting tools, but always as communication devices." Working with this technology has caused Flax to rethink the confines of two-dimensional picture space and to produce work that appears as an artist's book on paper and CD-ROM, and on the Internet. This image is part of a series of four Iris prints and also a plate in an artist's book by the same title.

© Carol Flax. *Some (M)other Stories: A Parent(hetic)al Tale, Page 2*, 1994. 26 x 34 inches. Inkjet print.

Taylor used the scanner as a camera to capture two antique tintypes of brothers (who were in her family) on a scanner and brought them into her computer. Then she scanned a second tintype for background texture and cracks. Taylor used a digital camera to capture the horizon landscape, and scanned a black-and-white image of grease spots on a floor to make the foreground holes. Everything was layered together in Photoshop. Colors were adjusted to create a mood fitting this haunting and strange fictional landscape.

© Maggie Taylor. *Life Goes On*, 2002. 15 x 15 inches. Inkjet print.

Babbitt's romantic portrait began as a black-and-white print; he scanned it and added color and details from other prints. Babbitt reflects: "Making images with digital technology allows me to take my vision to a place where virtually anything I can imagine is possible. Digital technology does not replace traditional chemical photography, it enhances it. It is a matter of evolution."

© Steve Babbitt. *Nancy*, 1998. 6 x 9 inches. Dye sublimation print.

Drum Scanners

Drum scanners generally produce the most accurate way of digitizing flat media. An image is read on a glass drum while being spun at several thousand revolutions per minute. Scans of both prints and transparencies made on these comparatively expensive devices are more precise and translate images with greater detail than do traditional

---

crop and adjust image size. Although manufacturers use their own software, there are some basic scanning features and procedures (see table 7.4).

Flatbed and Film Scanners

Flatbed scanners, capable of digitizing images in a variety of resolutions, are the most common tools for digitizing documents. These devices allow the user to preview the image and make minor corrections before scanning. Although designed to digitize prints, some flatbed scanners can handle transparencies.

Film scanners are specifically designed to capture the minute details of small negatives and transparencies by transmitting light through an image, making them more expensive than flatbed scanners.

Digital Camera Backs

Digital camera backs designed for commercial applications are available for 120 and 4- x 5-inch film cameras and their sensors offer unparalleled digital image capture. Adaptation of a digital back is akin to using a Polaroid back, with the exception of the need for digital storage.

a s s i g n m e n t

SCAN-O-GRAM—SCALE AND SPATIAL EFFECTS

Utilize a scanner to create an image made from found objects. Practice scaling the composition by following the formula in box 7.2 to make the found objects larger than life. Start by collecting a variety of two-dimensional and three-dimensional objects that will fit comfortably on your scanner to create a 4- x 5-inch composition. Next, create a background using a piece of any colored material cut to 4 x 5 inches or a photograph approximately that size. First arrange the found objects face down in the middle of the scanning bed, then place the 4- x 5-inch background material on top of the objects. Close the scanner top, preview the scanning bed, and select a scanning area that includes the 4- x 5-inch cut material that has been used for the background. Once you are satisfied with the composition, set the scale at 200 percent to produce a final image that will be enlarged and printed to 8 x 10 inches. Now determine the printer resolution, calculate the input resolution needed, and set it before final scan. Finally make a series of prints increasing both the scale and the input resolution (see box 7.2), and compare the differences in the various prints. Look specifically for how scale changes the spatial relationship between the viewer and objects because they are now much larger than life.

flatbed scanners. However, some high-end flatbed scanners are capable of scanning prints, 8- x 10-inch transparencies, or film at a quality that can rival drum scans.

Scanning Guidelines

Although there are numerous types of scanner, some basic principles are applicable in most scanning situations. Scaling and resolution must be set at the time the image is scanned. The input settings draw reference from the original image, producing the best-quality scan. A common mistake is to allow the photoimaging software to automatically set the final size (scaling) and resolution, which may force interpolation to occur and degrade the final image. Select the appropriate resolution based on the intended use (table 7.3).

Determining the best resolution for continuous tone prints is based on the maximum dpi of the printer being used. Good scanning software will allow a user to input a scaling factor into a dialog box and then do the file size math automatically. If your software does not do this, use the simple formula in box 7.2 to calculate input resolution based on printer resolution and the scaling of the image. For example, if you are using a 300 dpi printer you will need to scale a 4- x 5-inch print at 400 percent to make a 16- x 20-inch digital print, requiring an input resolution of 1200 dpi.

Box 7.2   Formula For Determining Input Resolution

PRINTER RESOLUTION   X   SCALING   =   INPUT RESOLUTION

300 dpi   X   400%   =   1200 dpi

Table 7.4   Scanning Steps

1   Open the scanning software. Often this can be done through imaging software, under File>Import>Name of the scanning software. Many scanners use an independent software application to drive the scanner. In this case, open the independent application and proceed to the next step.

2   Set the scanner for positive or negative. Many scanners are dual use, with the ability to scan photographic positives (reflective) and negatives or slides (transparent). Make sure the scanner is properly physically configured for reflective or transparent materials and set to the proper media before scanning.

3   Grayscale or color. Even though scanning in grayscale is possible, scanning in color often provides superior results because the scan is occurring in three channels (red, green, and blue) instead of one. If black and white is desired, simply change the image to grayscale in the imaging software after it is acquired.

4   Place the image/negative or object facing the correct direction in the scanning bed. For flat artwork, be sure to place the image squarely on the scanning bed as this will reduce the amount of post-scanning scaling and rotating.

5   Perform a preview scan of the entire scanning bed. This will allow you to see the entire scanning area and the image to be scanned. Use the Marquee Tool to select the target area as closely as possible, eliminating all unwanted data.

6   Make tonal adjustments. Most good scanning software will create a preview of the image based on the area you selected with the Marquee Tool. All scanning software has settings to control the contrast, brightness, and color balance of images. Change these settings to get the previewed image color balanced as closely as possible before scanning. The most important adjustment to make is contrast. An image that has excess contrast contains less information about tonal values. Slightly flat contrast images contain more information in the highlight and shadows and generally provide better results in post-scan processing. After scanning use your photo-editing software to make final color and contrast adjustments to an image.

7   Set file size. Before scanning, decide what size your final print is going to be. Scanners display and define size in two ways, image size and resolution. Most scanning software will display the size of the area being scanned, multiplied by a scaling factor. Increasing the scale of the image will increase the dimensions of the final scanned image. Increasing the resolution of the scan will increase the potential quality of the image. Both operations will increase the file size. As a general rule the larger the file size, the more options you have in working with the finished scanned image.

8   Scan image.

9   Save file. Once your image is scanned immediately save the file. Keep these scans safe and work only with copies of these images.

Table 7.3
Scanning Resolution

Use	Scan Resolution
Internet	72 dpi
Newspaper	150 dpi
Glossy magazine	300 dpi
Photo-quality print	300 dpi
Large fine-art print	4000 dpi and higher

Chapter Eight

DIGITAL OUTPUT

In *Video Portraits* people gaze at the camera for one hour and, by extension, at us. After their initial self-consciousness passes, the subjects sink into a meditative state and the camera reveals barely perceptible changes in mood and emotion. Struth's restrained use of the medium combines the stasis of painting with photography's embrace of the fleeting. The final 59th minute of each *Video Portrait* hovers over the endless movement of Times Square, reducing the vocabulary of art to its simplest premise—to look, to see, and to reflect—the videos invite discernment, receptivity, and calm consideration.

© Thomas Struth. *Video Portrait: Raphael Hartmann*, from Thomas Struth's *The 59th Minute: Video Art on the Times Square Astrovision*, 2/4–6/30/2003. Dimensions vary. Time projection. Presented by Creative Time, New York, NY. Photo © www.charliesamuels.com, 2003.

Digital Printing Technology

Pixels and crystals are now on equal footing as affordable digital cameras allow us to produce photographic files equal or superior to the conventional film images of the twentieth century. However, every step forward in digital camera resolution must be matched by advancements in printing technology. As the capacity of digital cameras increases their ability to capture and store more pixels, so must the abilities of the printers that are used to output these images.

Conventional color photographic printing by means of a chemical darkroom produces continuous tone analog images that are made up of random dots of color dye that form around microscopic pieces of silver. Unlike their analog counterparts, digital prints can be made on a variety of papers with wax or with pigmented inks, with laser light on conventional photographic papers, or with pigments that are sublimated into a gas and blended to form images, or they can be etched into a metal plate and printed with lithographers' inks. What most of these methods share is the initial conversion of the image by a computer into a series of dots. The limiting and differentiating factor in all digital means of printing images is the way these dots are mechanically placed on a surface and the size of the smallest dot the device is able to produce. There are many printer choices, from low to high resolution, capable of simulating continuous tone photographs. Some can make digital prints that are indistinguishable from

Marc observes: "It is different making stand-alone photographs as opposed to cataloging elements for montage possibilities. One must juggle physical scale and meaning plus determine the degree to which believable relationships between elements are maintained. This Mississippi montage merges a wrought-iron fence and houses (possibly an extension of the slave quarters) in Vicksburg near the Cedar Grove Plantation, a cotton field, a plow, and a male torso with Phi Beta sigma fraternity brands and text from a slave owner's letter defending his decision not to emancipate his slaves."

© Stephen Marc. *Untitled from Passage on the Underground Railroad*, 2002. 9 x 26 inches. Inkjet print.

chemically made prints, while others can produce images with a color or smoothness not possible with traditional photographic processes. Figure 8.1 shows the differences in how a continuous tone image is formed from film, digitally on a screen, and by ink.

Displaying the Image

Screen Resolution (PPI) and Dot Pitch

Screen resolution, pixels per inch (ppi), and print resolution, dots per inch (dpi), are two different measurements and are often incorrectly used interchangeably. They must be clearly understood to properly scan, scale (image size), and to prepare images for the Web or to print. Screen resolution (ppi) is the maximum number of pixels per inch a monitor can display at any one time. Ppi is determined by the manufacturer and cannot be changed. It is usually between 72 and 95 ppi, but varies slightly from monitor to monitor. The dot pitch (figure 8.2) rating of any screen only determines the quality of the display monitor. Dot pitch is measured in millimeters (mm) and theoretically the lower the number the sharper the image. Although cathode ray tube (CRT) and liquid crystal display (LCD) screens are mechanically different, the dot pitch rating is still the same and ultimately only slightly affects image size on a screen, but *not* print size.

Print Resolution (DPI)

Print resolution, (dpi) or dots per square inch, refers to the number of dots a printer can apply within one physical inch on paper. Dpi is variable and many inexpensive printers average 1200 dots per square inch.

Image quality is increased when more and smaller dots are contained within the same inch of physical space on the paper or material. The most common color printer for photographs is an inkjet printer, which sprays tiny dots of color to create an image from a digital file. The

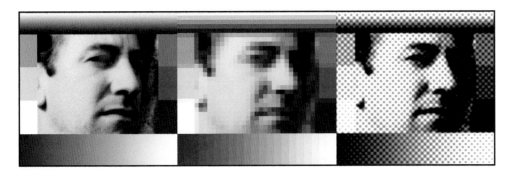

8.1 Forming a continuous tone image from film (grain), digital (pixels), and ink (halftone).

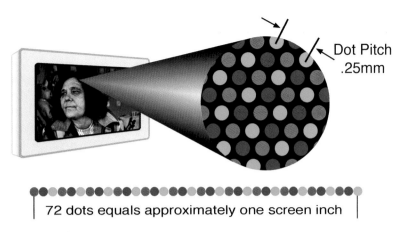

Dot Pitch
.25mm

72 dots equals approximately one screen inch

8.2 Screen dot pitch

higher than the screen resolution of 72–95 ppi and viewed on the screen at 100 percent. The screen image will appear larger than you anticipated, requiring scrolling of the screen image.

Figure 8.3 was scanned at 300 dpi with a print dimension of 3 ⅝ x 2 ⅞ inches. Notice that the screen rulers now exceed one inch of actual length and width when viewed at 100 percent. The computer correlates each printer dot (dpi) as one screen dot (ppi), making the initial image appear much larger on screen because of the physical limitations

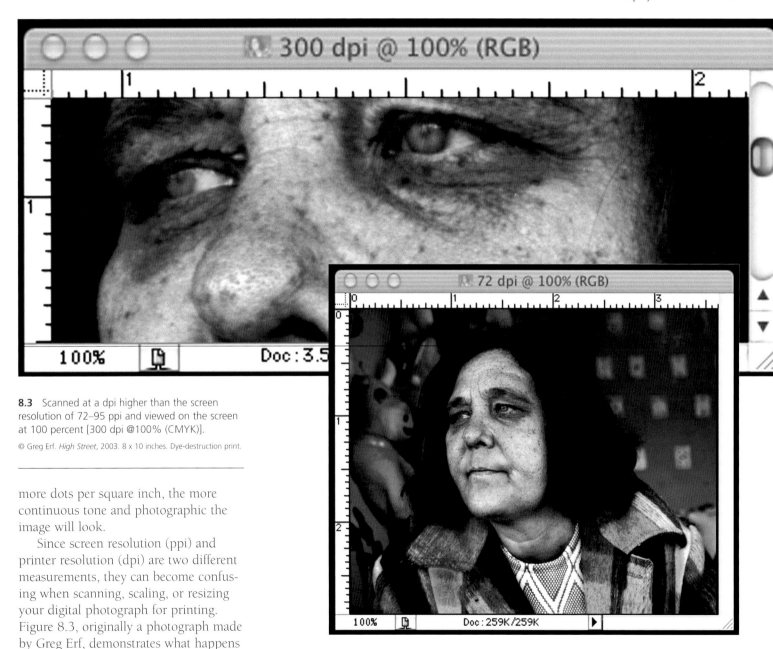

8.3 Scanned at a dpi higher than the screen resolution of 72–95 ppi and viewed on the screen at 100 percent [300 dpi @100% (CMYK)].

© Greg Erf. *High Street*, 2003. 8 x 10 inches. Dye-destruction print.

more dots per square inch, the more continuous tone and photographic the image will look.

Since screen resolution (ppi) and printer resolution (dpi) are two different measurements, they can become confusing when scanning, scaling, or resizing your digital photograph for printing. Figure 8.3, originally a photograph made by Greg Erf, demonstrates what happens to an image that is scanned at a dpi

8.4 72 dpi @100% (CMYK)

of dot pitch. Now it requires 300 screen pixels (ppi) to represent the 300 printer dots (dpi) on screen. This would be considered a 4:1 ratio in regard to the image's scale on screen when compared to the actual print size. The image will still print 3 ⅝ x 2 ⅞ inches, but at higher resolution.

In figure 8.4 the same photograph was rescanned at 72 dpi at the same dimensions, 3 ⅝ x 2 ⅞ inches. Notice the picture and rulers now closely approximate one inch of actual length and width when viewed at 100 percent in the photo-imaging software. With this 72 dpi scan the screen size and print size will be similar because the screen dot pitch (ppi) closely resembles the true physical inch when output to paper. This would be considered a 1:1 ratio in regard to scale when viewing at 100 percent on screen when compared to the print size (see figure 8.4 again).

The Image Window

To help keep track of all the variables in a digital file, software programs display many key pieces of information about the image. Figure 8.5 identifies this data that surrounds the working image and describes their meaning.

Sizing a Digital File

As previously discussed, file size in megabytes (MB), screen resolution (ppi), and print resolution (dpi) are three different measurements that need to be understood to be able to properly scale, scan, and prepare images for printing or the Web. Although closely related, MB, ppi, and dpi are not a true measure of the actual image size when outputted to paper or viewed on the screen.

The size and quality of the final print is first determined by how many pixels were originally exposed by the camera or scanner. The original exposure or scan is absolutely crucial toward determining levels of quality for the final print. Digital cameras capture images based on the common settings of High, Fine,

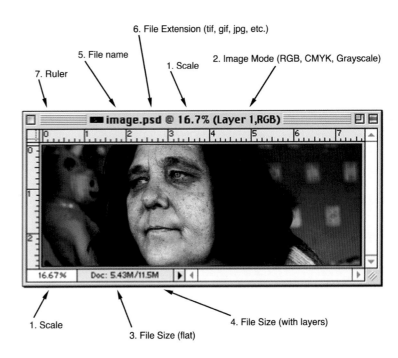

8.5 Image Window, [image psd @ 16.7% (Layer 1, RGB)]

Box 8.1 Definitions of Information Displayed with a Digital Image File in Figure 8.5

Scale: Since a monitor can only display about 72 ppi, your image program scales the image to show the difference between the screen display (ppi) and the targeted print resolution (dpi) of the actual image. Figure 8.5 above shows an image with a bit depth of 300 ppi. In this case the software has scaled the display of the image to only show 16.7 percent of the actual pixels contained in the image.

Image Mode: Imaging programs allow you to work in a variety of color modes including RGB, CMYK, grayscale, bitmapped, duotone, or LAB. Some filters and operations can only be performed in RGB mode.

File Size: This area shows the size of the file when it contains only one working layer.

File Size (with layers): Layers are transparent surfaces that can be individually placed on top of the original image, adding to the file size. You can move, scale, draw, edit, and paste on to any layer without disturbing the other layers or the original image. Adding layers while working allows you to work separately on the various parts of your image, which helps to organize and manage the workflow. Flattening an image converts all the layers back into one, reducing the file size. Images that are sent to high-quality printers often have to be flattened before printing.

File Name: Most imaging software will display the name of the file somewhere along the top of the image window.

Extension: Extensions describe the file format to the computer's operating system. PCs and Web browsers require the three-letter file extension, such as .doc or .jpg, to be included in a file's name in order for it to be opened or displayed.

Ruler: Most imaging software includes an option for displaying a ruler alongside an image. You can usually define the particular units a ruler uses in the program's preferences.

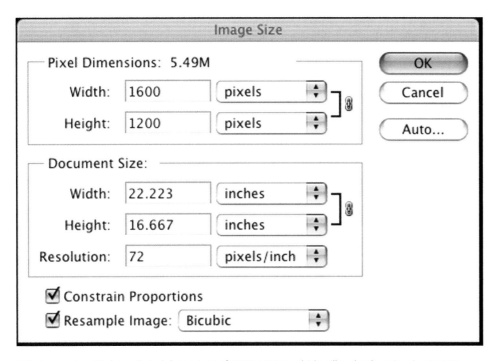

8.6 Image size, 72 dpi and pixel dimensions of 1600 x 1200, which will make the print size 22.222 x 16.667 inches at 72 dpi.

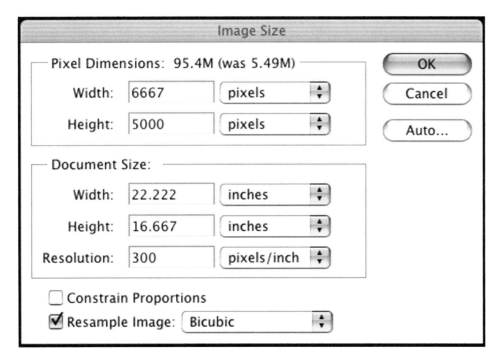

8.7 Image size, resolution box to 300 dpi

Normal, and Basic. Low-resolution settings, such as Basic for the camera or 72 dpi for scanning, will produce a file usually of under one megabyte that is only suitable for images appearing on the computer screen or on a Web page.

Once the file is captured/scanned, changing the resolution will affect the file in different ways, depending on how the change is made. For example, a digital camera using the Fine setting might produce an image file of 1600 x 1200 pix-

els. Depending on the camera and software, this image may import into your software program at a default resolution of 72 dpi and pixel dimensions of 1600 x 1200, which will make the print size 22.222 x 16.667 inches at 72 dpi (see figure 8.6).

The print size is very large at 72 dpi and when outputted to paper would produce a pixilated image with only 72 dots per square inch for an image to be printed 16.66 by 22.22 inches. In this image, changing the default 72 dpi up to 300 dpi, for seemingly better visual acuity, will result in adding 31 million more pixels to the image because width and height dimensions were left unchanged and not scaled down proportionately! The computer has to resample, also known as interpolation (see below), by placing extra pixels into the image. To do this the computer looks at adjacent pixels and places new pixels between them that are based on an average of the original two, making the image look soft and out of focus.

To change the resolution (dpi) to an existing file, simply change the number in the resolution box to 300 dpi (see figure 8.7). This change will not affect the print size or improve the print quality because resampling/interpolation will occur. Only the file size (5.59 MB to 95.4 MB) will change with no increase in detail. The original uninterpolated 72-dpi image file and its new 300-dpi interpolated counterpart will print very similarly. There is no gain in the detail of the interpolated image file. Reshooting at a higher pixel dimension is the only way to truly get the necessary fine detail required at larger print sizes.

Interpolation or Resampling

Interpolation is a set of mathematical logarithms automatically applied when the original pixel dimensions are changed for resizing. Interpolation cannot add or subtract detail; it only randomly adds or subtracts pixels, making a "best effort" when resizing the original pixel dimensions. There are many interpolating logarithms that perform slightly

HAROLD, SENIOR GREETER AT THE WAL-MART VISITOR CENTER: BENTONVILLE, ARKANSAS

different mathematical computations, but the end result is still degradation of the original image file that will affect image quality as the computer is literally making up the information.

The three most common modes of resampling, which appear when the Resample Image box is checked, are Bicubic, Nearest Neighbor, and Bilinear. Always use Bicubic interpolation because it gives the smoothest results. Although Bicubic takes longer to compute, the speeds of today's computers make the time difference negligible. Nearest Neighbor is the fastest interpolation method, producing the most jagged results, and Bilinear splits the difference between the two.

Equivalent Image Size

When first learning to control camera exposure with film you come to understand the concept of equivalent exposure. This model states that when you change from a slow shutter speed (1/60 of a second at f /11) to a faster shutter speed, you must compensate by using a larger aperture (1 /125 of a second at f /8) to maintain the same exposure. The reverse is also true. A similar equivalent concept holds true for changing the sizes of digital images. Figure 8.8 shows two Image Size windows for the same image, which can be found under Image in the top Main Menu categories. By linking the document sizes by checking the Constrain Proportions box (default on) and unchecking the Resample Image box, you can change the resolution of an image without interpolation occurring to it, thereby maintaining the original pixel dimensions.

By unchecking the Resample Image box the proportions of the height, width, and resolution become linked. The value of one variable can then be altered and the program automatically compensates by increasing or reducing the other two, which is similar to the light meter model that automatically adjusts f-stops to maintain equal exposure when the shutter speed is changed. Before and after pictures (figure 8.8) show equivalency because when we increased the resolution the software program automatically subtracts from the height and width to maintain the same file size. Notice that in the Pixel Dimensions box the number of pixels referencing height and width has not changed and neither has file size.

The Real Size of a "Digital Negative"

A good way to understand the relationship between picture size, pixel dimen-

Before changes (default view)   File size

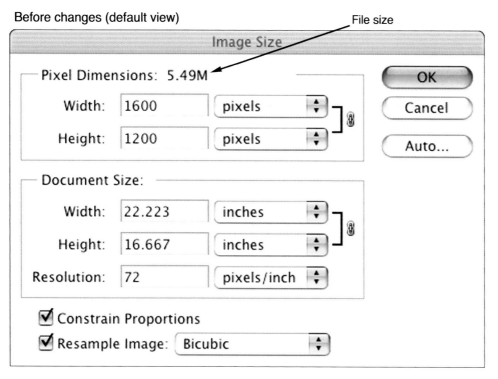

After changes (default view)   File size remains the same

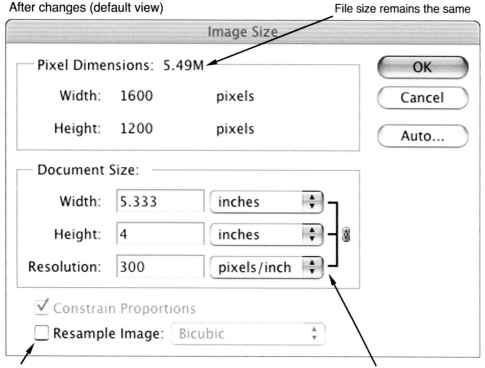

Click in the check box next to Resample Image and this turns linking to Resolution on and off. When Height, Width and Resolution are linked (Resample Image un-checked) the image stays in proportion when any changes are made to Height, Width and Resolution, avoiding Resample Image or interpolation.

8.8 Image resampling, before and after [Resample Image, Linking File Size, Width, Height and Resolution].

sions, and dpi is to think of pixel dimensions as representing the real size of the "digital negative." The digital negative is the total number of pixels from which there are a limited number of uninterpolated print dimensions available to produce the sharpest images regardless of dpi. Print size or print resolution (dpi) is not as significant as minimizing the effects of interpolation by only resizing proportionally to pixel dimensions. A 2.1-megapixel digital camera or a 300-dpi scan at 4 x 5 inches are both capable of producing a digital negative of 1,920,000 pixels. Figure 8.9 illustrates the relationship between dpi, interpolation, and print size. Note: as the print resolution increases from 72 dpi to 1200 dpi, the print size is proportionately decreased to maintain the original number of pixels to the digital negative. Also notice two exceptions, the interpolated files will print less than optimal because pixels were randomly added or subtracted to compensate for altered dpi or print dimensions, which did not remain proportional to the original 1,920,000 pixels.

Table 8.1 shows how to make sure that the original pixel dimensions (ppi) correlate exactly to the final output size (dpi) in regard to length and width. The pixel dimensions should always remain constant as the digital negative is enlarged or reduced. For example, when using a 2-megapixel camera on the Fine setting, an image file of 1600 (W) x 1200 (L) pixels equaling 1,920,000 total pixels is made. These 1,920,000 pixels now represent the physical size of the image and become the limiting factor when resizing the image for optimum results. Since 300 dpi is considered the acceptable printing resolution to create digital pictures similar to film photographs, you divide 300 into the original pixel dimensions to determine the optimum output print dimensions, which is 5.33 x 4.00 inches for this example (table 8.1). To avoid pixelization related to interpolation it is best to adjust the print size by changing the target dpi. Increasing the target dpi will make the printed image smaller and decreasing the target dpi will make the printed image larger. This method will assure that the pixel dimensions will remain constant, avoiding any interpolation.

Keep in mind that interpolated images are created when changes occur to the original pixel dimensions. These interpolated images can be acceptable and can be used in many applications. Note: pixellation or loss of sharpness sometimes attributed to interpolation can also be a result of improper scaling or sizing.

The versatility of digital capture allowed Jurus to transform the proportions of this image to fit in with a portfolio made with a Hasselblad X-Pan panoramic format camera. The color was created to reflect a favorite drink called *Swamp Water*.

© Richard E. Jurus, II. *Big Fish*, 2003. 24 x 60 inches. Inkjet print.

Table 8.1 **Calculating Optimum Print Dimensions**

Pixel Resolution	÷	Target dpi	=	Optimum Print Dimension
(W) 1600	÷	300	=	5.33 inches
(L) 1200	÷	300	=	4.00 inches

Achieving Photographic Quality

Inkjet Printers: Dpi to Dots to More Dots

Photographic-quality inkjet printers are needed to produce prints that have the look of continuous tone. Their print-head design allows them to spray minute amounts of ink onto the receiver material at resolutions of 1440 x 720 dpi and higher. They can also deliver subtle detail with more accurate and saturated colors and print on a wider variety of materials than their less expensive office counterparts. These quality printers can use more permanent inks and include additional colors, greatly increasing the range of colors (color gamut) beyond traditional color photography.

All inkjet printers use different amounts and methods of applying inks to create photo-realistic images. General-purpose quality inkjet printers use four inks, cyan, magenta, yellow, and black, while higher end photo-quality inkjet printers can easily exceed four colors by

The Digital Negative and Interpolation

8.9

Target Resolution (dpi)	Digital Negative	Pixel Dimension	Total Pixels	Print Size
72	Uninterpolated	1200 x 1600	1,920,000	16.6 x 22.2 inches
150	Uninterpolated	1200 x 1600	1,920,000	8 x 10.6 inches
150*	Interpolated	600 x 800	480,000	4 x 5.3 inches
300	Uninterpolated	1200 x 1600	1,920,000	4 x 5.3 inches
300*	Interpolated	2400 x 3200	7,680,000	8 x 10.6 inches
600	Uninterpolated	1200 x 1600	1,920,000	2 x 2.6 inches
1200	Uninterpolated	1200 x 1600	1,920,000	1 x 1.3 inches

*Both these interpolated files will show some pixellation, but the file with less than the total original pixels will show less pixellation.

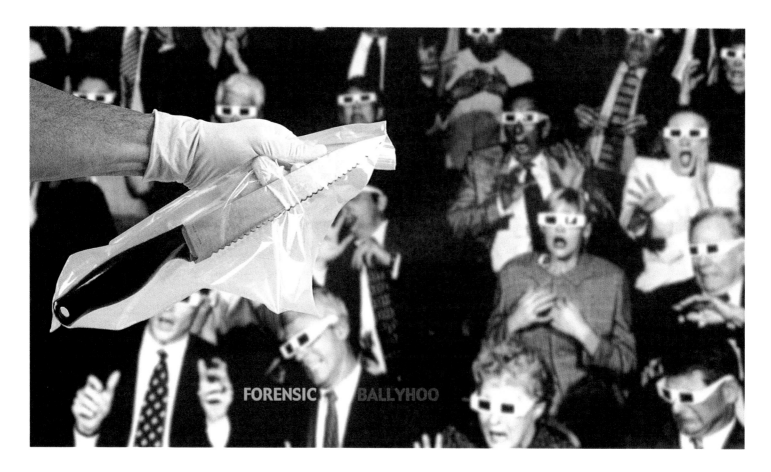

Keown uses the fluidity of digital data to explore the social and technological dilemmas of contemporary society. Keown inputted images from both a digital camera and scanner that he manipulated in Photoshop and printed, mural-size, on vinyl media. Keown says: "I print on water-fast matt vinyl for its flexibility of presentation. With an adhesive backing, the work can be exhibited in a frame, adhered directly to a gallery wall in an installation context, or placed in an outdoor environment (with its three–four month light-safe life)."

© Gary Keown. *Forensic Ballyhoo*, 2003. 31 ½ x 60 inches. Inkjet print.

Box 8.2
Good Computer Habits

Save Often: Problems with the power supply or misread data can cause the computer to malfunction. Frtequently saving data is often the only way to avoid problems. Once every 15 minutes is not too much. When working on large, important projects make copies on a reliable removable medium for safekeeping.

Delete Old Files: A drive filled with old, no longer used files can become a liability by preventing you from having an adequate scratch disk.

Back Up: Make periodic backups on an external storage device. Although uncommon, files can be corrupted by everyday use or by a computer virus (a devious program designed to infect computers and destroy or interrupt data.)

adding orange, green, and lighter versions of cyan, magenta, and gray. Creating photo-quality photographs is dependent not only upon how many droplets fit within an inch (dpi) of space, but also on the size and pattern of the ink droplets. When a photo-quality inkjet printer creates an image from a 300-dpi file it is not just creating one droplet of ink for each pixel (ppi) or dot (dpi), but rather it places four or more droplets of ink to represent each pixel. Currently eight-color inkjet printers use hundreds and hundreds of nozzles to apply varying degrees of color and value.

Inkjet printers are rather complicated printing devices that must control all those nozzles accurately to create droplets of ink that can convince the eye of continuous tone. The best inkjet printers are capable of delivering excellent photo quality between the ranges of 150 and 360 dpi. Although these printers are capable of resolutions up to 2880 dpi, it is generally not worth the printing time and storage space to produce image files greater than the visual acuity of the human eye.

Paper: Uncoated and Coated

Uncoated (porous) printing papers are the most readily available papers and are best identified as the inexpensive xerographic, inkjet or laser-jet papers used primarily for text. Structurally, these

Kennedy's pieces were inspired by the idea of creating a metaphoric icon that celebrated the here and now of nature. She collects materials on local walks that she places on a scanner, which has had its heavy lid replaced with a lightweight tent of black felt. Kennedy then creates a simple palette by manipulating the color from RGB to grayscale and finally to Quad tone that is printed onto Crane's Museo paper, an archival paper.

© Marie Kennedy. *Strength*, 2000. 11 x 11 inches. Inkjet print.

Inks: Dye and Pigment Based

There are also two groups of inks: water-soluble, dye-based and pigment-based. Inexpensive inkjet printers employ water-soluble dye inks and should only be used when permanence is not a concern, for example for color proofing and short-term use. Photo-quality inkjet printers can use pigment-based inks, which contain pigments that make the inks more fade resistant.

Print Permanence

There has not been enough independent empirical testing to accurately predict the permanence of inkjet prints, and the equipment and materials have been in flux. To maximize longevity, use coated (micro-porous) papers and the best-quality pigment-based inks currently available. When permanence is a major concern, it is best to evaluate the current array of inks and papers before buying a printer to make sure everything is compatible and capable of producing the desired results. Using papers and inks from different manufacturers is not recommended because manufacturers only test, rate, and guarantee permanence based upon their own system of papers, inks, and printers. Choosing papers and inks from different manufacturers may produce the visual results you are looking for, but be sure the combination has been tested for maximum longevity (see chapter 9, page 193, for factors affecting permanence).

Printing Methods and Output Issues

Thermal Printing

Dye-sublimation printers work with RGB, CMYK, and grayscale images. In this process the pigments, contained in thin plastic sheets, are turned into a gas and transferred onto a piece of specially coated paper. The colors are not laid side by side as in a halftone process, but are

papers are raw cellulose wood fibers bleached and processed into the standard letter- and legal-sized formats. These papers are less uniform in their brightness, surface texture, absorbency, and pH level than coated papers. Because they are uncoated, they absorb more ink, allowing them to print and dry fast to the touch. The downside of these materials is that they are susceptible to fading due to environmental factors and exposure to light.

Coated papers (micro-porous) have special coatings that either modify or completely cover the cellulose fiber, making the paper achieve superior print results and archival qualities. These papers are designed to resist fading although drying times can be somewhat longer. Coated papers are available in a variety of traditional photographic surfaces including high gloss, semi gloss, flat matt, and luster, as well as in many canvas-like textured surfaces. Nonporous materials are polymer or vinyl-based printing materials for banners or decals. The smart advice is to check the kind of coating or surface that exists with the printing material to be used and choose the appropriate type of ink, making sure the printer you use can handle the combination.

Bronstein digitally captures spontaneous moments from her life, then paints and tones them in Photoshop before making LightJet prints. Bronstein says: "working in the negative reveals qualities and details that are unseen in the positive, and takes me back to the source of photography: Light. The negative is a beautiful and mysterious thing, a direct recording of reflected light, it holds all the details that often get lost in the journey to become a positive print."

© Marcie Jan Bronstein. *Ben, Thanksgiving Lunch*, 2001. 25 x 25 inches. Chromogenic color print.

blended to create a continuous tone print. Depending on the support material (paper base) and storage conditions, these prints can be expected to last up to 10 years before fading is noticeable.

Thermal-wax printers are similar to dye-sublimation printers, melting thin coatings of pigmented wax onto paper. Some can print on a variety of papers, but the life span of these prints is shorter than that of dye-sublimation prints.

Desktop Inkjet Printers

Desktop inkjet printers are inexpensive and use water-soluble inks and plain paper to make color prints. Better quality paper will yield higher quality images. Some dye-based inkjet printers produce prints that are impermanent and can, without protection, fade within six months.

Iris Print

The Iris printer was the first printer used in digital fine-art reproduction. Iris prints are a type of inkjet print produced by spraying millions of fine dots of ink per second onto paper. Created on a

spinning drum, these gallery-quality prints can be made on virtually any material that will accept ink. The Iris printer uses dye-based inks that produce some of the most vibrant and widest tonal values available. Depending on the type of ink, paper, and coating, such prints could have a life span ranging from as little as six months, but generally Iris prints are made to last decades. Once the standard for high-quality fine-art reproductions, Iris prints have become a special purpose niche process. Nevertheless, Iris prints continue to be the standard measure for digital prints.

LightJet

LightJet or Lambda are brand names for printers that expose a digital image directly to color or black-and-white photographic paper using red, green, and blue laser beams. The resulting images are processed in regular photographic chemistry and therefore possess the same surface and permanence properties as traditional photographic prints. LightJet prints are extremely sharp and very close to continuous tone because the LightJet's resolution would exceed 4000 dpi when compared to conventional half-tone printing.

Giclée Printing

Giclée, French for spray or spit, is a chic phrase for inkjet printing. Technically, even an inexpensive inkjet printer produces giclée prints. Giclée was first associated with Iris printers, which initially defined the digital fine-art print market. It was used to appeal to print connoisseurs who expected state-of-the-art inkjet printing with a certain level of permanence, but the term is not regulated and hence carries no warranties of any sort.

Mural Size Prints

Creating photographic high-quality digital images is a reality for both the consumer and the professional, and can be seen in the art world's embrace of mural-size prints. Even though digital cameras

Goodine is "interested in the politics of representation and wanted to bridge the gap between 'high' and 'low' art audiences by creating a super-real, mural-size rendering of bunnies and children." Goodine had high-quality scans made at a service bureau to get the most textural and modeled rendering on the surfaces of the fur and skin.

© Linda Adele Goodine. *Standard Bred* from the series *Standard of Perfection*, 2002. 120 x 96 inches. Chromogenic color prints.

can exceed the sharpness of 35-mm film cameras, the enlarging limitations remain constant. Digital photography is not a magic bullet for making large prints from small cameras. A blow-up from any type of 35-mm equivalent media will show a loss of sharpness due to the increase in grain or pixelization in proportion to the size of the enlargement.

Once affordable digital image sensors become available in medium and large formats, film will eventually become obsolete. Until this occurs, the best practice for making big fine-art digital

imagery is to record the image on a large-format film and scan the film at the highest possible resolution. Such prints require film scans in excess of 4000 dpi and up to 8000 dpi, along with professional scanners and printers. Making digital prints exceeding the capabilities of desktop printers, 13 inches in height, widths up to 40 inches, requires floor-model photo-quality inkjet printers. Many of these printers are capable of producing prints up to 64 inches in height, and in widths as long as the roll of papers will allow, which can exceed 100 feet.

Labate considers the camera, the studio, and the computer as his private laboratory. "I use tape, wire, screws, and nails to set up the objects for photographing with a digital camera in the studio using White Lightning Monolights. From the studio, I upload the images from the digital film into my computer. With imaging software tools, I use virtual tape, wire, nails, and screws to complete the constructions that began in the studio. I'm left with a body of work where the 'REAL' collides with the 'MADE-UP.'"

© Joseph Labate. *Prototype*, 2003. 29 x 22 inches. Inkjet print.

Mixed Digital Media

With the availability of high-quality, large-format printers and a wide variety of printing materials, the possibilities of digital mixed media have just begun to be explored. Photographers have always experimented with the surface of the print, some by applying pigment to the surface, others by collaging different photographic images and materials together. All of these methods can be brought together using the digital print as well. In addition to traditional glossy paper, manufacturers have developed materials such as artist canvas that can be run through a digital printer and then painted on with acrylic or oil paints like a conventional canvas. Materials such as Polysilk cloth can be printed on and then become waterproof, which allows them to be exposed to the elements or even washed. Other materials include translucent and transparent films that can be used as backlit prints, as photographic negatives, or in muti-layered images.

Preparing the Digital Print for Mixed Media

New developments in digital media are currently being driven by the advertising industry. Most of the store displays, such as ads found in supermarkets, are now being produced on large-format printers. Artists have to be aware of the demands of the advertising industry when using these new materials. Advertisers want their materials to be sturdy enough to be walked on or displayed outdoors, but they are not necessarily interested in images that will last for more than a few months or a few years. Luckily many of the same qualities that make an image last for 25 months outdoors will allow those same prints to last years or decades when they are properly displayed indoors (see chapter 9, page 194).

One thing that imagemakers can do to protect their images from damaging UV or when preparing images for mixed media applications, such as acrylic or oil paint, is to seal the surface with a spray or liquid coatings. These coatings are water or solvent based and can be used with water-sensitive inks. Since many of the coatings can yellow or crack over time, researching and testing a particular combination before use is recommended.

Film Recorders

Although you may have digitized an image and manipulated it on computer, you can convert that image back into the traditional photographic realm. A film recorder transfers a digital image onto ordinary color or black-and-white film that you can view, project, print, and store as traditional silver materials. For color imaging, the device exposes regular photographic film through red, green, and blue filters to provide image data in raster or bitmap form. The dominant use for film recorders is making 35-mm slides for presentations.

Service Bureaus

The hardware necessary for many output options is expensive; using service bureaus with knowledgeable technical support is a viable option for photographers not expecting to do high-volume work. Service bureaus, commercial printers, copy centers, and professional photography labs can scan and print images to your specific needs. Many specialize in high-quality and large-scale digital reproductions with the latest technology. The quality of the output always depends on the skill of the operators and the maintenance of the equipment, but as a general rule if it's not done to your satisfaction a service bureau will repeat a job until it is.

Working with a Computer

As a camera condenses a three-dimensional scene into a two-dimensional representation, the computer seamlessly combines different media into a virtual representation, retaining the qualities of some and eliminating the qualities of others. Anything that can be done with a camera, paintbrush, or drafting set can be simulated on a computer.

Large, high-resolution images require extra processing time and plenty of available hard-drive space to operate efficiently. A 100 MB file should have at least five times that amount (500 MB) of free hard drive space to make use of the imaging software tools and the filters.

The computer is a powerful tool for experimenting with ideas and design, but it is not always best for producing an image. Images stored on silver-based film provide a tremendous amount of permanent information that is easy to access and economic to store. If you are not planning to significantly manipulate an image, a wise choice still could be silver-based photography.

The Color Monitor

All monitors use an additive RGB color system (see Chapter 1, page 13). Any combination of these light primaries always produces a lighter result. Since light is transmitted from the image, the colors tend to be more saturated and luminous. The printed image uses a CMYK subtractive system to form an image on a sheet of paper. Any increase in pigment density subtracts the initial amount of light, producing a darker result.

There is an inherent visual difference between images seen on your monitor, other monitors, and output devices. Sophisticated monitors allow for color correction as well as contrast and brightness adjustments, but these only affect how the image appears on your monitor and not on other monitors and/or paper output. Color-management hardware and software is available to help control the color balance between monitors and output.

How Monitors Show Color

Depending on the monitor size and the amount of video memory (VRAM), it is possible to see and manipulate millions of colors with image-processing programs. All video monitors represent color by displaying minute RGB dots, which are displayed on the monitor as pure color. All other colors shown on-screen are a mixture of pixels used to approximate the color needed. In addition to full color images, grayscale images can be produced, with 256 shades of gray, as can bitmap images, which are purely black and white.

What Is Bit Color?
Bit depth describes the number of bits (the smallest unit of information on a computer) assigned to each pixel and refers to the number of shades of gray or the number of colors that can be represented by a single pixel. The greater the number of bits (2, 4, 8, 16, 24, 32, or 64), the greater the number of colors and tones each pixel can simulate (see box 8.3). The bit depth of your computer's display is the number of different colors it can show at any given time. The size of the display and the amount of video RAM you have on the graphics card controls bit depth. 64-bit color is the highest level of color a computer can produce, while 24 bits and above create color variations well beyond the range of human perception. Even though human perception is limited to 24 bits and below, 32- and 64-bit color can improve color accuracy and correction on screen.

In imaging software such as

Box 8.3 **Bit Color**
2 bit = black and white
4 bit = 16 colors
8 bit = 256 colors
16 bit = 32,0000 colors
32 bit = millions of colors (16.8 million)
64 bit = billions of colors (4.2 billion)

Photoshop, images contain either 8 or 16 bits of data per color channel. In an RGB file an 8-bit/channel image has an overall bit depth of 24 bits (8 bits x 3 channels = 24 bits); a similar CMYK file has a bit depth of 32 bits (8 bits x 4 channels = 32 bits). Images that have 16 bits of data per color channel have a much greater color depth, translating to greater distinctions in color. In this mode RGB files have a bit depth of 48 bits (16 bits x 3 channels = 48 bits) and CMYK images have a bit depth of 64 bits (16 bits x 4 channels = 64 bits). Currently working in 16-bit/channel mode severely limits the software's and the imagemaker's ability to manipulate an image. In 16-bit/channel mode images can only contain one layer and many image filters and image adjustment functions are unavailable.

Color Management (ICC Profiles)

In 1993 a group of eight software and digital output device manufacturers formed the International Color Consortium (ICC) to establish and maintain a set of international color standards. The group introduced a standard device profile format, known simply as ICC, to define how different color devices, often made by different manufacturers, produce color images. An ICC profile is a file that describes how a particular device reproduces color (printers or monitors). These profiles map onto an image file the characteristics of different output devices with their limited color ranges, making the output of images from varying devices predictable and observable.

Profiles, Profiles, and More Profiles
In the digital environment every workstation has a unique color range or "printable color space" sometimes known as "color gamut." ICC profiles are small digital files that help the computer determine the actual viewable and printable color space of the device. These files are sometimes preloaded in an image or software program, but many need to be loaded based on the device or the media being printed on. Color space is determined by everything that goes into making the image, including the camera or scanner (input), the type monitor (viewable color space), and the printer along with its specific combination of inks and paper (output). The ICC profiles "remap" or reassign a new color value to a digital image when color values are detected outside the viewable or printable color space. Sometimes the shift is not severe or even detectable. The standard ICC profiles, called "generic profiles," are designed as a "best guess" method of normalizing many variables over the widest variety of possible environments and can do a good job. Factory ICC profiles are best and can reduce time and

effort when color correcting, but not always.

Anyone with conventional color darkroom printing experience will see the same functionality between determining the correct filter pack and using ICC profiles. In conventional color printing a series of cyan, magenta, and yellow filters is used to correct color balance based on the type of film, light source, paper, temperature, and chemicals. The ICC profiles are the digital equivalent. In a controlled working environment with well-maintained equipment, a good understanding of ICC color management can minimize the color correction process with digital images. Just as in conventional color printing, "tweaking" the color balance is a continuous process. ICC profiles are based on the monitor settings, such as contrast, brightness, color temperature, tint, and RGB, and have their place in making critical work. In a controlled working environment with the proper software and color calibration equipment, the color calibration of the monitor to the printer can be done very precisely. In a group lab environment where the monitor controls and room lighting are inconsistent, it is usually easier and quicker to first print a digital image file that contains both a grayscale and color scale chart. This print is compared directly to the monitor and the necessary adjustments are made to the monitor to match the print. Although this color-management style is not empirical, it works well to compensate for the numerous unexpected changes that constantly occur in a group work environment. Also, regardless of what a calibration program states, color response is subjective and it is our eyes that ultimately determine whether a color print achieves its desired results.

Other Digital Colors
Many software applications allow for the manipulation of color according to its hue, saturation, or luminosity (HSL), or through a licensed color system such as Truetone or Pantone. These last two systems allow for the most understandable color manipulation on the computer.

Process color, or CMYK, is the traditional printing method of lithographic printers. This set of subtractive primary colors is the system used by most color printers. Many output devices cannot print all the colors a computer is capable of processing. Some software packages will warn you if a particular device cannot print a selected color. Computer users can make color separations for printing using the CMYK mode. When switching from RGB to CMYK the computer dulls the screen colors to simulate a subtractive print. High-end multicolor printers rely on RGB to manage all their possible color options. Duo-tone effects, applying a second accenting color, are also possible.

Digital Memory

RAM

When a program begins, its contents are loaded into random access memory (RAM). Instructions the computer needs to perform its tasks are stored and processed in RAM chips, sometimes called memory chips, which come in a variety of sizes, pin configurations, types, and formats. The amount of RAM a computer has directly affects its performance and capabilities and is easily expanded. Most software applications include minimum memory requirements on their printed material. However, to effectively run the program you may need much more RAM so it is prudent to research programs before purchasing them.

ROM

Permanently installed in the computer, read only memory (ROM) contains the basic instructions the computer needs to start up and to draw objects on a screen. Unlike RAM, ROM is unalterable.

Hard Disk

The hard disk, usually installed inside the computer, is where applications and files are stored. Since image files are often larger than the available RAM,

some software applications use the hard disk to temporarily store information. The program shuffles information from the hard disk (the scratch disk) into RAM, where it is processed. This enables the program to complete complex operations and functions, such as "undo" and "preview." The scratch disk can take more than five times as much space as the original image because it stores several different versions of the image. The

computer's hard disk must have enough free space to accommodate these temporary files.

Software and Imaging Applications

While the computer is a potent tool, it is an empty vessel, dependent on the instructions contained in software appli-

McCormack blends opposites by using an oatmeal box pinhole camera to produce 8- x 10-inch black-and-white negatives that he scans and colorizes by ignoring standard color-management profiles, and pulls curves in each of the color channels "to make an image rooted in sixteenth-century optics juxtaposed with twenty-first-century digital technology."

© Dan McCormack. *Bridget + Kelly 11-28-01-1CC*, 2001. 7 ½ x 7 ½ inches. Inkjet print.

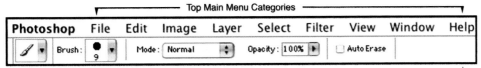

| Photoshop | File | Edit | Image | Layer | Select | Filter | View | Window | Help |

Brush: 9 | Mode: Normal | Opacity: 100% | ☐ Auto Erase

⌐ The Editable Options Bar that appears here is different with each active tool, Brush tool shown here ⌐

8.10 The top Main Menu categories and editable tools options

cations. Images created on a computer need not be solely photo based. The program's own internal tools, coupled with devices such as pressure-sensitive graphic tablets, let the user simulate the effects of other media as well as create unique digital images.

Different software packages may be used at different stages in the image-making process A single application can provide adequate tools for an imaging project, but it is often necessary to combine the strengths and tools of other software to create desired effects.

Raster/Bitmapped Software

Most programs that process photo-based pictures operate with raster (bitmapped) images. The advantage of the bitmapped image is its ability to be edited pixel by pixel. Photo-based or raster image programs such as Photoshop do not keep individual objects as separate entities. Items must be applied to a background / layer, at which time any alteration will affect surrounding areas, replacing data or leaving holes. Increasing the size of an image increases the number of pixels, spreading out data. Reducing the size of an image eliminates pixels and reduces image quality.

Raster/Bitmapped Software

Vector graphics (object-oriented) programs offer a wide range of options for manipulating lines and polygons. Vector graphics programs treat objects as separate entities that can be colored, stacked, reshaped, or moved without affecting the background or any other object. Designed for drafting and illustration purposes, vector software is not ideally suited for photo-realistic images.

Basic Digital Imaging Categories and Tools

Top Main Menu Options

Regardless of the imaging program, there are common and unique categories located in the top Main Menu that offer access to many functions for editing images. The most common categories are File, Edit, View, Insert, Layer, and Filter (see figure 8.10). Within these categories there are hundreds of selections that, when used in combination with the toolbar, can create several thousand ways to manipulate an image.

Cut and Paste Function

Located in the Edit category in the top Main Menu, Copy and Paste give the ability to replicate and move information. Both are essential and powerful functions of the computer. Cutting and pasting is possible between files made on different pieces of software as well as between documents made on the same software. Sometimes the data structure of the information is not always compatible. Most well-developed software applications have a set of procedures, usually located under File or Edit in the top Main Menu, for converting and opening files produced by different applications.

Scale and Distort Function

Located in the Edit Category, in the top Main Menu under Transform, Scale and Distort are the primary clues to depth perception that are manipulated to change the context or to create an image that challenges the viewer's assumptions.

An entire image or parts of an image can be foreshortened to simulate perspective, or stretched vertically or horizontally to fit into a defined area.

Overall print-sizing controls are usually located in the Image category in the top Main Menu under Image Size or Canvas Size. Both these functions make the image larger or smaller when outputted. Altering the canvas size allows for the creation of blank drawing space around the image (or crops the image) while altering the image size affects the overall dimensions of the image.

Digital Filter Function

An image can also be manipulated through a wide variety of functions called filter effects located in the top Main Menu category called Filters. All programs offer a wide variety of built-in common filter effects, such as pixelate, blur, mosaic, distort, sharpen, reticulation, chalk, charcoal, and many other artistic effects. In the nineteenth century, photographers turned to the aesthetic strategies of painting for guidance. Today, third-party software manufacturers have done the same, producing filter effects known as plug-ins that further transform the common digital tools used to simulate drawing and painting. As image-makers continue to discover an original digital aesthetic, there will be less of a reliance on older mediums and filters that simulate them, allowing an authentic digital syntax to emerge and grow.

Toolbar Icons for Additional Photo Editing

Many of the common editing tools began in Photoshop and have since migrated to other programs. The various tools are located in a floating toolbar that defaults to the right or left side of your screen. Refer to the manufacturer's manual or the application's Help Menu for complete and detailed descriptions of all tools. Many of the visible tools on the toolbar have hidden options that are revealed by simply using Click-Hold or Option-Click on the visible icon, depending on the program. Also, each tool has editable options that are usually displayed in an Options Bar underneath the top Main Menu on the screen when the tool is active. The Options Bar is useful for changing many options related to the active tool, such as brush size, type of gradient, font size, transparency, and colors.

Common Toolbar Icons from Photoshop

 When a black arrow appears in the lower right-hand corner of a tool icon there are more similar tools to be found by clicking and holding the mouse button on the icon.

Select and Move Tools

 **Marquee Tools**
The Marquee Tools are used for creating simple geometric selections in your images (rectangle, elliptical, and single-row selections are all similar options). Since a computer cannot read your mind, use the Marquee Tools to indicate the area you want to work with. Once an area is selected, any adjustments, tools, or filters will only be applied to the selected area.

 Move Tool
One of the most useful innovations in the development of Photoshop was the inclusion of layers found under Window in the top Menu. Using layers image-makers can move or copy pixels on one layer to another layer. Layers can then be altered independently. The Move Tool allows you to move selections or the entire contents of a layer to another layer for unlimited image control.

 Lasso Tools
The Lasso is a freeform selection tool. Unlike the Marquee Tool the Lasso allows you to draw both straight-edged and irregular selections. The Lasso Tools

have three similar modes: Freeform Lasso, which draws complex irregular selections like a drawing pen, Polygon Lasso, which draws simple straight segments, and Magnetic Lasso, which follows the closest edge in an image.

 Magic Wand Tool
The Magic Wand selects all pixels of a similar color or tone to the pixel clicked. The tool selects pixels within a certain tolerance that ranges between 0 and 255 tones. A tolerance of one (1) will select only pixels of that same color. A tolerance of 100 will pick all pixels that are 50 tones lighter and 50 tones darker than the pixel selected.

 Crop Tool
The Crop Tool is used to draw a rectangle around a portion of an image and discard all image information outside that area. The size of the rectangle can be adjusted before cropping and can also be tilted, rotated, and distorted by using control points on the edges of the selected object.

Drawing Tools

 Brush and Pencil Tools
The Brush Tool allows you to paint with a selected color. The size, shape of the brush, and edge sharpness can be changed in the options palette. The blending mode, opacity, and flow of the brush can also be changed. The Pencil Tool allows you to draw a line in a specified pixel size. The Pencil Tool creates sharper edges than the Brush Tool because it leaves out the anti-aliasing (softening of edges) that the Brush Tool employs.

Retouching Tools

 Healing Brush and Patch Tools
The Healing Brush Tool is used to sample an area of an image and copy that sample to another area. The tool is useful

for removing imperfections from images because the tool matches the colors of the sampled pixels with the area around the target imperfection. In addition to matching the color of pixels, the Patch Tool matches the lighting, texture, and shading of the sampled pixels to the target receiving area.

 **Stamp Tool**
Like the Healing Brush, the Clone Stamp Tool is used to sample pixels in one part of an image and clone (copy) them to another part of an image. As in the case of the Brush Tool the size, blending mode, opacity, and flow can be tailored to suit the task. The Clone, Healing and Patch Tools are excellent for removing dust spots and repairing damaged photographs.

 Eraser Tools
The Eraser Tools delete or alter pixels. When working on the background layer or with the layer transparency locked, the pixels will be changed to the background color. In other situations the pixels are erased and become transparent. The Background Eraser samples the color in the center of the brush (indicated by a brush shape with a cross hair) and deletes that color in the target area. The Magic Eraser changes or erases all similar pixels within a certain tolerance (tonal range).

 Fill Tools
The Paint Bucket Tool fills an area with the foreground color. Like other tools with a tolerance, setting the Paint Bucket will replace all of the adjacent pixels that fall within the specified tolerance range. The Gradient Tool works with the foreground and background colors to create a gradient between the two colors.

Dodge and Burn Tools
As in the darkroom, the Dodge Tool and the Burn Tool are used to lighten or darken areas of the image. The size of the tool, the range (highlights, midtones, or shadows), and the exposure can be defined.

Type Tools

The Type Tool is used to create horizontal or vertical type anywhere in an image, or to make a Type Mask in the shape of type. Any font that is properly installed and available to your operating system can be created. The font size, color, leading, kerning, and justification can be set in the tool's control panel.

 Dropper (Color Picker) Tool

The Eyedropper Tool samples the color of selected pixels to designate a new foreground or background color.

Zoom Tool

The Zoom Tool increases or decreases the screen magnification of images. Changing the size of the image on the screen allows the imagemaker to see the image in greater or lesser detail, but does not change the printed size of the image.

Changing Mouse Pointer

When tools are selected, the mouse pointer matches the tool icon. Many of the drawing and painting tools are circles, which represent the selected width. Each cursor has a hot spot where the effect begins, for example the tail of the lasso's loop for the Lasso Tool is where the selection begins.

Option/Shift/Command Keys

Knowing when to the use the option, shift, or command keys in conjunction with the active tool is necessary to use many of the tools and their functions. For example, using the Option (Mac) or Alt (PC) key with the Zoom Tool changes the mouse pointer to a plus or minus, allowing you to zoom in or zoom out of the image on screen. Also, using the Shift key with the Magic Wand allows you to add to your previous selection so that you can group many selections.

Damsels in Armor reflects the brutality of the war experience. Original photography was done at various museums and the women's faces were selected from 1950s glamour photography. Typically 20 sources are combined into 30 to 40 transparent layers; these are manipulated in Photoshop to create surreal yet believable compositions that "bear witness to the inevitable price of engagement; no suit of armor can shield them from the acid scars of battle and triumph's glory is transient."

© Viktor Koen. *Damsel No. 7* from the series *Damsels in Armor*, 2002. 24 x 35 inches. Inkjet print.

The Computer as Multimedia Platform

Moving images, or video, address time in a different way than a still image. With video the viewer tends to be involved within the flow of events, while the still image is an abstract entity that calls for a more concentrated viewing and interpretation. The assembling and editing of video images on a computer is known as nonlinear video. Software packages edit video by creating fragments called clips.

A clip of video can be combined with sound, previewed, and altered.

Cell-animation programs, many of which are vector-drawing programs, manipulate discrete objects and create the illusion of movement by showing sequential frames with incremental motion. The cell elements can be independently controlled, allowing the background to remain stationary while objects in the foreground display motion.

QuickTime movies incorporate a series of compression PICTS and allow moving images and sound to be created, stored, and viewed. QuickTime movies compensate for the speed of your computer, keeping the sound properly synchronized with the picture.

Three-dimensional modeling programs are vector-drawing programs that have the capability to render an object and simulate the effects of light. The completed object can be viewed from any angle and direction. Three-dimensional modeling programs are often coupled with an animation component that allows the piece to be presented as a movie.

MANUAL reflects: "One interpretation of this image raises questions regarding the ecological health of the foggy landscape. A second sees it as homage to Nature in the age of electronic information. The image is a composite of several sources. The dead bird's head and background are from separate digital files made from a digital camera and the table and laptop computer have been rendered in a 3D modeling program."

© MANUAL (Ed Hill/Suzanne Bloom). *Omen*, 2002. 18 x 33 inches. Inkjet print. Courtesy of Moody Gallery, Houston, TX.

The Internet and the World Wide Web as a Virtual Gallery

The Internet is a series of networks developed in the early 1970s as a decentralized Cold War communication system between government, academic, and private research labs. Today through a modem, any computer user can send digital data via the Internet or can directly send data to any other user who has a modem. Online services allow the user to download an image file and electronically mail it to other users. The advantages of this method are that both users can receive and send material, even if the other person's computer is turned off. The downside of the Internet continues to be the time it takes to transmit data, and compatibility issues, especially with image files.

The World Wide Web (WWW) and other virtual spaces offer a unique environment for sharing information, images, and other media. Digital galleries on the Internet have become major presentation venues for displaying images. Some of these virtual spaces even mimic the conventions of the traditional gallery by creating virtual frames and walls.

Viewing images in a gallery setting is a separate experience from looking at images on a computer monitor or in a book. A 4- x 5-foot image carries a distinctly different message from one that is 8 x 10 inches in size. The computer screen changes these circumstances by making all images roughly the same size, and having them viewed by transmitted light. The aura of a gallery setting is replaced by the appearance of the desktop. Efforts by major art auction houses, such as Sothebys, to have online art auctions failed because converting Web browsers into collectors has been a task intrinsically unsuited to the screen of the Internet—a medium that severely limits the opportunity to experience works of art. In other cases, work made specifically for the Web has been embraced by major museums and galleries, such as the Guggenheim Museum, which has begun commissioning and collecting online art for its permanent collection alongside painting and sculpture. As more serious imagemakers utilize the Internet, the presentation, selection, and quality of the images continues to expand and evolve.

The Chemical, the Dry, and the Hybrid Darkroom

The reasons for working with any process should be embedded in the context of the imagery. Camera-based imagery has evolved into three distinct categories: silver, digital, and hybrid. The silver process offers the familiarity associated with the chemical darkroom that dates to the origins of photography. Digital methods allow speedy and precise image creation within the convenient environment of a dry darkroom. The hybrid approach combines the desired characteristics from both worlds to obtain unprecedented image control.

The problems associated with both dry and hybrid print technology are the overall expense and the constantly changing base of knowledge. The cost of high-end scanners and printers needed to maximize the quality of digital prints far exceeds the cost of the best-equipped chemical darkroom. Inkjet printing technology for black-and-white or color prints is affordable, but still problematic, with a great deal of debate about what method is best or even acceptable. The hybrid printing approach using LightJet or Lambda technology, which uses photographic paper for final output, is not

available for home use because of the high cost of the printers. The hybrid approach requires you to send files to a high-end professional lab for final output, and with that comes a loss of artistic control.

It is not possible, without becoming academic and esoteric, to aesthetically compare digital prints with conventional silver prints because visually they are now equal. Only in extreme cases will a viewer need to be aware of the technological differences between a digital and silver print to appreciate the image. Ultimately it is the artistic powers of the imagemakers and their use of subject matter that really counts, although from an artist's point of view as a maker of art, digital technology is still far from being considered a mature visual medium.

Digital artists working with digital files from cameras or scans continue to spend enormous amounts of time dealing with the technical and computer issues: transferring, backing up, converting files, tweaking printer profiles, replacing ink cartridges, making test prints, sharpening, cleaning, curve-adjusting files, dealing with driver issues, and calibrating scanners, to mention only a few complex issues. What digital imagemakers need to remember is that these same issues and arguments were made about color photography a generation ago. During the first few decades of chromogenic color photography the materials and equipment were out of the reach of most photographers, making them dependent upon technicians in commercial labs to print their images. Major art museums questioned the permanence and artistic merit of color photographs. The Museum of Modern Art in New York, for example, refused to add color images to its collection until as late as 1976, when it granted its first solo color photography exhibition to William Eggleston (see chapter 2, pages 43 and 44). At that time many in the art establishment considered color photography to be the tacky realm of advertising and

family snapshots. Photographers themselves were some of the harshest critics of color photography. Walker Evans called color photography "vulgar" and Robert Frank insisted that "black and white are the colors of photography."

In the coming years, artistic, economic, and environmental pressures, along with changing audience expectations, will contribute to the diminishing use of silver-based photography. Digital tools are advancing, helping photographers to return to the essence of photography by providing them with new and simpler tools for "correcting," as opposed to altering, the content of their vision. As the quality and variety of digital images expand, photographers will find new applications in art, business, and science, creating new pathways for the digital image to travel and making it a ubiquitous part of daily life.

References

DiNUCCI, DARCY, et al. *The Macintosh Bible*, 8th ed. Berkeley, CA: Peachpit Press, 2001.

FREEMAN, MICHAEL. *The Complete Guide to Digital Photography*. London: Sterling Publications, 2002.

GROTTA, DANIEL, and WEINER, SALLY. *Digital Imaging for Visual Artists*. New York: Windcrest/McGraw Hill, 1994.

LONG, BEN. *Complete Digital Photography*, 2nd ed. Hingham, MA: Charles River Media, 2002.

MITCHELL, WILLIAM J. *The Reconfigured Eye: Visual Truth in the Post-Photographic Era*. Cambridge, MA, and London: MIT Press, 1992.

RITCHIN, FRED. In *Our Own Image: The Coming Revolution in Photography*. New York: Aperture Foundation, 1990.

SPALTER, ANNE MORGAN. *The Computer in the Visual Arts*. Reading, MA: Addison-Wesley Pub Co., 1999.

Chapter Nine

PRESENTATION AND PRESERVATION

DeSouza excavates and decrypts embedded socio-political and cultural codes to dispel the notion that landscape is a neutral entity. DeSouza uses photography and digital imaging to capture and manipulate his meticulously sculptured landscapes that are made of societal refuse, which blur the nature of his disciplines and accentuate our questioning and experience. The title plays off of the White City, which was built for the 1893 Chicago World Fair to herald the arrival of America as a new world power. The mural-size print is mounted on aluminum for support.

© Allan deSouza. *Everything West of Here is Indian Country*, 2003. 20 x 50 inches. Chromogenic color print. Courtesy of Talwar Gallery, New York, NY.

Once a color photograph has been made, it is necessary to prepare it for presentation and to be able to properly store it for future use. Finished prints may have visual defects such as dust marks or scratches that can be corrected by spotting them with a fine-point brush and dye. Digital prints should be electronically spotted before printing as the variety of output materials can present numerous technical problems. Special thought needs to be devoted to unconventional formats, such as artists' books and installation pieces, which often require custom presentation solutions.

Spotting Chromogenic Prints

Spotting is generally carried out before the photograph is matted or mounted. Good working techniques should keep spotting to a minimum. Although spotting is usually done to correct minor print blemishes, there are other expressive avenues of manipulation that can be investigated. For instance, a very light area in one corner of the print can have density added to lower its luminance (light reflected from the surface) so it does not draw the viewer's attention away from the subject. In color both the density and color balance of the area that is being spotted must be matched. To make this task as easy as possible, the following materials are needed:

● Premixed color-spotting dyes, such as Kodak Liquid Retouching Colors and Retouch Methods liquid colors, are recommended. These dyes are designed to go directly into the emulsion, blend to a

color similar to it, and leave no residue on the surface. Spotone black-and-white materials can also be useful. Some people use watercolors, oils, and other types of dye, but the problem with these materials is that they fade at a different rate from the dyes that make up the print. Over time the area that has been spotted with nonstandard materials can become distinctly visible from the rest of the photograph.
● Sable brush with a good point, size number O or smaller.
● Mixing palette. Enamel or plastic watercolor palettes work well. Some people prefer to mix on a piece of paper, clear acetate, or glass.
● Container of clean distilled water.
● A couple of sheets of white paper or white processed photographic paper (whatever you use).
● Paper towels.
● Clean cotton glove.
● Good light source (5000 K lamp, north light, or combination of cool and daylight lamps).

How to Spot Color

Follow these procedures when spotting a color chromogenic print:

1 Put the print on a smooth, clean, and well-lit surface. Place a clean sheet of white paper over the print, leaving the area to be spotted visible. A window can be cut in the paper to spot through, offering additional protection to the print. Put the cotton glove on the nonspotting hand. This prevents the print from getting fingerprints and hand oil on it. Our bodies also contain and give off sulphur,

Long used a Hulcherama 120 rotating panoramic camera to make 360-degree photographs for his *Pre-Law Wastelands: Abandoned Mine Lands of Southern Illinois* series. Long constructed a circular presentation enclosure to surround viewers and allow them to become part of the landscape, reminding us of the importance of environmental protection laws.

© Jonathan Long. *Untitled (Acid Mine Drainage #2)*, 2002. 48 x 552 inches. Installation size: circular 8 x 14 foot wall. Chromogenic color print.

which can stain the print. The paper provides a neutral viewing surface, which helps act as a visual guide in matching the color balance.
2 Place small amounts of the color dyes that will be used onto the palette.
3 Wet the brush in the water. Draw a line with it on a paper towel to get rid of the excess water and to make a fine point.
4 Dab the brush in the dye. Draw a line on the white processed photographic paper or a separate sheet of white paper to see if the color matches. Compare the line with the area to be spotted. Blend with other colors, including black and white, until the color matches.
5 Once the correct color balance has been achieved, horizontally draw a line with the mixed dye on the paper towel to remove any excess dye and water. The brush should appear dry, but inside it will remain wet and hold a small amount of dye. To apply the color to the print, gently touch the tip of the brush with a small stroke to the surface. Practice on the processed white paper before working on the final print.

6 For very small spots, create a series of dots. This helps to match the grain structure that forms the image. Do not paint it in, because this will be noticeable since the print is made from points, not lines (figure 9.1). Make one pass using this dot method. There should be some areas of white still visible in between the dots. Let it dry for a minute. Make another pass with the dot technique, filling in some more of the spot. Let it dry and see if it matches. Repeat if necessary, but do not apply too much dye. Different movements will deliver different effects. For small areas and fine white lines, start the tip of the brush at the beginning of the line and make tiny side strokes, which blend the line into the surrounding area much easier. For wider spots, slightly bend the brush. For wide lines or for a dye wash, fan the brush (figure 9.2).

7 When you have finished spotting, wash the brush with warm water and soap. Rinse completely, and carefully repoint the brush between the thumb and index finger.

A blob, a line, or an area that is too dark draws as much attention to the eye as a spot. Take time and be subtle. Do not overdo it. This is not like painting a brick wall with a roller.

Scratches

You can repair surface scratches that have removed one or more dye layers of the paper emulsion by applying liquid dyes. For the best results, make sure that the dilution of the dye is correct. Do not add neutral dye to the colored dye; added density is not necessary. A cross-section of color negative paper would reveal a top down sandwich of cyan dye, magenta dye, yellow dye, resin coating, and paper base. A scratch that removes the top (cyan) dye layer appears red; to correct it, add cyan dye of the proper concentration to neutralize the red and match the adjacent area. A scratch that goes through the top two (cyan and magenta) dye layers appears yellow. To correct it, first add magenta dye, and then cyan dye, in the proper concentrations to match the adjacent area. After you apply the correct concentration of dye, use a finishing lacquer to restore an even surface.

Dealing with Mistakes

If there is too much dye on the print, quickly remove it by letting a piece of paper towel absorb it. Do not rub or smear it.

If the color does not come out

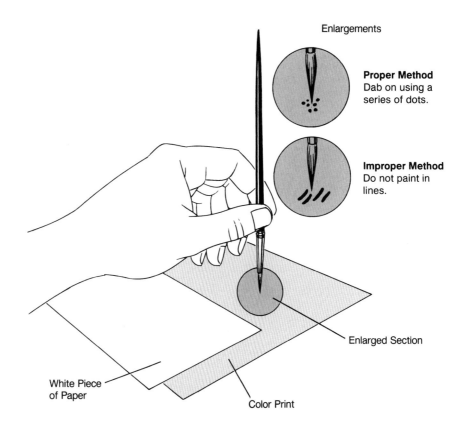

Enlargements

Proper Method
Dab on using a series of dots.

Improper Method
Do not paint in lines.

Enlarged Section

White Piece of Paper

Color Print

9.1 The method for properly spotting a print: A well-pointed brush containing the properly matched color dye is dabbed onto the print. A white piece of paper reveals the area to be spotted while protecting the remainder of the photograph. It also acts as a visual reference point, letting you see if the spotting dye is making the desired match with the surrounding area.

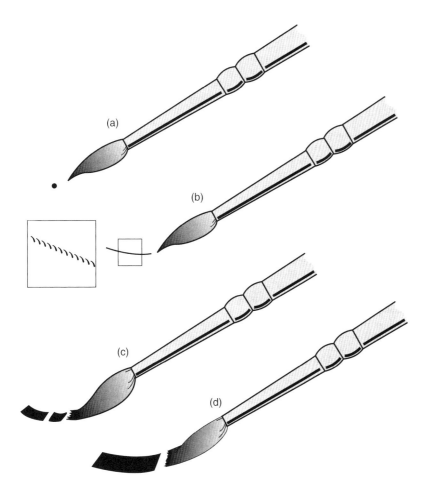

9.2 Sketch (a) For very small spots, just touch the brush to the photograph with a small stroke. Only the tip of the brush should touch the print, releasing the dye onto the emulsion. It is important to work with the tip of the brush in fine or small areas. The dye in the brush flows from the ferrule to the very tip of the brush, which is a single hair. (b) For white lines and small spots, prepare the brush with the correct color and make sure you have a good point. Place the very tip of the brush at the beginning of the line and make little side strokes instead of trying to fill it in with a single stroke. The short side strokes will blend the line into the surrounding area more readily than a single stroke. (c) To cover a wider spot or to blend, slightly bend the brush. (d) To retouch wide lines or to make a dye wash, fan the brush.

correctly or if too much dye is absorbed, attempt to remove the spot with a drop of 5 percent solution of ammonia and water. Apply it with a clean brush. Let it sit on the spot for about 60 seconds, then absorb it with a piece of paper towel. Let it dry before attempting to start spotting there again. If this does not work, let the spot dry, cover it with white dye, and start over.

If you are unhappy with the overall results, wash the print with room-temperature water for five minutes, dry, and start over. If the dye does not come out, try putting a tiny amount of ammonia on the print, gently rub, and rewash. Drying can be done with a handheld hair dryer. Excess water can be removed by lightly patting the print with a lint-free towel.

Digital Retouching

The computer is an extremely powerful tool for retouching and repairing images (see figures 9.3 and 9.4). A moderately to severely damaged image or negative can be scanned, repaired, or spot toned and then be output using an inkjet printer or a digital enlarger, or be returned to a negative or slide using a film recorder. One of the most important advantages of repairing an image digitally is that after the image is scanned the original image is not touched and cannot be accidentally damaged any further during the repair or retouching process. Some of the tools in the software program Photoshop that are most useful for repair or retouching images are described in chapter 8, page 178.

Spray Lacquers

After the dyes have dried, there may be a

9.3 In preparation for repairing this damaged photograph made by F.W. Deahna of the *Buffalo Press Cycling Club*, June 19, 1920, Valentino scanned both halves of the torn image and then brought the scans together into a single file in Photoshop.

© John Valentino, 2003.

9.4 Using the Healing Brush, Patch Tool, and Cloning Stamp, Valentino copied the missing visual information along the tear from the areas immediately next to it. The contrast was adjusted using Levels, the color was adjusted, and the image was sharpened. The man's eye was repaired by selecting and copying the eye on the right, duplicating it, flipping it, and placing it on the left side. The new eye was then blended in to match the background.

© John Valentino, 2003.

difference in reflectance between the spotted areas and the rest of the print, especially with glossy paper. If this is noticeable, some photographers spray the picture with a print lacquer, which creates even reflectance over the entire photograph. Print lacquers are available in glossy and matt finishes. There is considerable debate about the long-term stability of prints treated with spray lacquer. There are reports that lacquers can crack, flake off, and discolor the print surface. For these reasons lacquers should not be used on fine-art prints or photographs in museum collections. If a lacquer must be used, Lacquer-Mat lacquers and Sureguard McDonald Pro-Tecta-Cote 900-series noncellulose nitrate lacquers are recommended. For the best results, read the manufacturer's instructions for proper application and handling of these materials. Work only in well-ventilated areas, and follow all safety guidelines.

To ensure an even spray follow these guidelines in a clean spray booth environment:

1 Shake the spray can for a few seconds before each use.
2 Remove any lacquer from the nozzle opening.
3 Begin spraying with the spray directed off the print surface.
4 Spray in even, overlapping strokes.
5 Keep the nozzle perpendicular to the print surface for even coverage.

Spotting Prints from Slides

When spotting prints from slides, the major difference is that the dust spots appear as black, not white. These black

spots have to be covered with white before spotting them. Small black spots can be removed by etching the surface of the print with a sharp, pointed blade, such as a #11 X-Acto, until the speck is gone. This must be done with great care so that the surface of the print does not become too rough and visually objectionable. Color should be applied with an extremely dry brush only. Lacquer spray will probably be needed in both cases to eliminate the differences in reflectance between the spotted and nonspotted areas of the picture.

Ilfochrome Classic materials often will not respond to conventional retouching methods due to the way the product is manufactured and processed. Special retouching kits, such as those from Photographers' Formulary, can be used to correct color casts, reduce color densities, and bleach colored or black specks. The correct color can then be

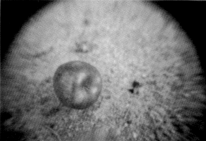

Tümer relates: "My neighbor Mr. Martinez was obsessed with finding gold. Purchasing his magnifier at a yard sale intensified my own obsession for finding what I seek and value, and the triptych illustrates the inspection process of looking for a visual treasure. With this series I felt the almost miniature prints had their greatest impact when placed on a page. I tipped each photograph into an area on 16- x 11 ½-inch Arches 140 lb watercolor paper that I embossed with an etching press. I mounted each print with Gudy, an archival adhesive. This archival presentation contributes to the feeling of a small jewel nestled in a coffer. Ultimately, I designed a portfolio cover with handmade earth-toned and textured paper that housed these loose pages and made an edition of 10 Planted portfolio books, each containing 23 images."

© Laurie Tümer. *Planted: Under Mr. Martinez' Magnifier, Española*, 2002. 1 ½ x 7 inches. Chromogenic color print tipped into embossed watercolor paper.

applied on the white spot. Large area color reductions, and even total bleaching, can be carried out. Special bleaching agents and solvents can be used to dissolve the cyan, magenta, or yellow emulsion layers.

Archival Presentation

Although manufacturers readily use the term "archival," there is no accepted definition of what archival means. What we do know is that every color image has a natural and limited life span and that the length of the life span depends on the individual process used and how the image is cared for. The goal of archival presentation is to protect the image from physical harm and to guard against things that accelerate the aging process (see the section on print preservation later in this chapter, page 193). This ensures that the work lasts as long as it is physically feasible. A capable presentation job can enhance the visual appeal of a work, protect it, and send the message that it is something worth taking care of.

Mat Board Selection

To select the proper type of mat board you should become more informed about how various products affect color materials. Consider the following factors:

1   **Composition board** is the most widely available and has the least longevity. Typically, composition board is made up of three layers: a thin top paper sheet, usually colored; a middle core layer, made of chemically processed wood pulp; and a bottom paper backing. The core layer is the troublemaker because it contains a collection of acids and chemical compounds that break down and produce even more acid. These acids are transported in microscopic amounts of airborne water vapor onto the surface of your work. They start attacking the image, often within a year or two, causing discoloration and fading. UV radiation from the sun and/or fluorescent lights can accelerate this chemical reaction.

The same thing can happen when a work is backed with corrugated cardboard or kraft paper. The acids in these materials invade the work from behind, and by the time this makes itself known, irreversible damage has taken place.

2   **Conservation-grade board** consists of thin layers, all of the same color, called plies. One type of board is made from purified wood pulp and is simply known as conservation board. The other type is made from 100 percent cotton fiber and is called rag board. Plain conservation board can be used for most archival operations, since it costs less, has equal longevity, and is easier to cut when making window mats. Most board is available in two, four, six, or eight plies. Four-ply board is good for most presentations.

3   **Acid-free board** is known as the board of choice. Unfortunately, this description has proved to be very misleading. The term "acid free" is no longer considered to be the supreme test of a board's permanence. Some manufacturers have only put a piece of acid-free paper behind the wood pulp of traditional composition board. Others have added regular wood pulp heavily treated with alkaline calcium carbonate. With the passage of time the impurities in the board deteriorate and form acids and peroxides, thus producing or returning to a highly acidic board. When selecting acid-free board, be certain all the materials in the board are 100 percent acid free. Also, as paper ages it tends to shift toward the acid end of the pH scale. Buffering with calcium carbonate, which is added to many conservation-grade boards, can counteract this effect. The "acid-free" label is still an important criterion, but it is not the only thing you need to consider when making a selection.

4 Buffered and nonbuffered board is being debated in the conservation community. Since our physical surroundings are slightly acidic, and because paper tends to become more acidic with age, manufacturers of premium mat board have been adding calcium carbonate to offset this tendency. Current research indicates that color materials may be affected by the presence of this alkali buffer and that for longest life; they should be mounted only on nonbuffered, acid-free board. This recommendation applies to all chromogenic prints processed in RA-4, as well as to dye-transfer prints. Cyanotype prints are also reported to have discolored in the proximity of buffered materials. At this time, there is no published research indicating a problem with using buffered board with gelatin-silver, black-and-white materials.

The Window Mat

The window mat, now considered the standard enclosure for photographic prints, is made up of two boards, larger in all dimensions than the print. The top board, known as the overmat, has a window with beveled edges cut into it. This is attached with a tape hinge along one side of the backing board. The print is positioned and attached to the backing board so it can be seen through the window (figure 9.5). The mat gives the maximum protection to the print while it is being shown and also when it is stored.

It provides a raised border to contain the work and when the work is framed, it keeps the glass from directly touching the print surface. If the window mat is damaged or soiled for any reason, it can always be replaced without damaging the print. A mat can be cut with a hand mat cutter, such as a Dexter or Logan, which requires some practice using. Almost anyone can cut a mat with a machine such as the C & H mat cutter. For those who have only an occasional need of a mat, have a local frame shop make one for you.

Keep in mind the type of light the print will be viewed under when selecting mat board. Daylight tends to have a blue cast, incandescent light is orange, and fluorescent light is generally greenish.

To make a window mat follow these 12 steps:

1 Have clean hands and a clean working surface.

2 Work under light similar to that under which the print will be seen.

3 Protect the cutting surface with an unwanted piece of board that can be disposed of after it gets too many cut marks.

4 Using a good cork-backed steel ruler, measure the picture exactly. Decide on precise cropping. If the picture is not going to be cropped, measure about $\frac{1}{16}$ to $\frac{1}{8}$ of an inch into the picture area on all sides if you do not want the border to be seen.

5 Decide on the overall mat size. Leave enough space. Do not crowd the print on the board. Give it some neutral room so that the viewer can take it in without feeling cramped. Box 9.1 provides a general guide for the minimum-size board with various standard picture sizes.

Many photographers try to standardize their sizes. This avoids the common hodgepodge effect that can be created if there are 20 pictures to display and each one is a slightly different size. When the proper size has

been decided, cut two boards, one for the overmat and the other for the backing board. Some people cut the backing board slightly smaller ($\frac{1}{8}$ inch) than the front. This way there is no danger of it sticking out under the overmat.

6 In figuring the window opening it is helpful to make a diagram (figure 9.6) with all the information on it. To calculate the side border measurement, subtract the horizontal image measurement from the horizontal mat dimension, and divide by two. This gives even side borders. To obtain the top and bottom borders, subtract the vertical picture measurement from the vertical mat dimension and divide by two. Then, to prevent the print from visually sinking, subtract about 15 to 20 percent of the top dimension and add it to the bottom figure.

7 Using a hard lead pencil (3H or harder to avoid smearing), carefully transfer the measurements to the back of the mat board. Use a T-square to make sure the lines are straight. Check all the figures once the lines have been laid out in pencil.

8 Put a new blade in the mat cutter. The C & H cutter uses a single-edge razor blade with a crimp in the top. Slide the blade into the slot and adjust it so that it extends far enough to cut through the board. Hand tighten only, using the threaded knob at the end of the bolt.

9 Line up the markings with the mat cutter so that it cuts inside the line. Be sure to check that the angle of the blade is cutting at 45 degrees in the "out" direction for all the cuts, in order to avoid having one cut with the bevel going in and the other with it going out. It helps to practice on some scrap board before doing the real thing. When ready, line up the top left corner and make a smooth, nonstop straight cut. Make all the cuts in the same direction. Cut one side of the board and then turn it around and cut the opposite side until all four cuts are made. With the C & H mat cutter, start the cut a little ahead of where your measurement lines intersect and proceed to cut a little beyond where they end. With some practice, the window will come right out with no ragged edges. If you continue to make overcuts, simply stop short of the corners. Then go back with a single-edge razor blade and finish the cut. Be sure to angle the blade to agree with the angle of the cut. Sand any rough spots with very fine sandpaper. Erase the guidelines with an art gum eraser so that the pencil marks do not get on the print.

10 Hinge the overmat to the backing board with a piece of gummed linen tape (figure 9.5). The mat will now open and close like a book, with the tape acting as a hinge.

11 Place the print on the backing board and adjust it until it appears properly in the window. Hold it in place with print-positioning clips or a clean, smooth weight with felt on the bottom.

12 Use photo corners to hold the print to the backing board. They will be hidden by the overmat and make it easy to slip the print in and out of the mat if you need to do so for any reason (figure 9.5).

Dry and Wet Mounting

Dry mounting used to be the most common way to present a finished print for display. It is a fast and neat method to obtain print flatness, which reduces surface reflections and gives a work more apparent depth. Prints can also be wet mounted with glues and liquid adhesives, which can be useful when working with certain non-traditional materials. There are a number of problems resulting from dry mounting:

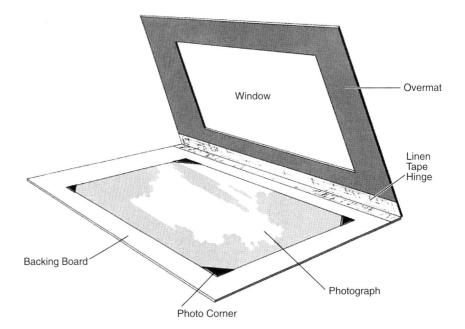

9.5 The construction of a typical hinged window mat. The use of photo corners facilitates removing the photograph from the mat without harming it.

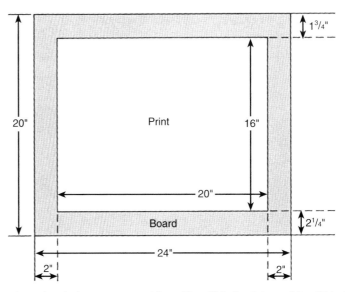

9.6 The dimensions of a window-type overmat for a 16- x 20-inch print on a 20- x 24-inch board. More space is usually left on the bottom of the mat than at the top to keep the print from appearing to visually sink on the board. The side borders are generally of equal dimensions.

● The possibility of ruining a finished print with dry mounting through accident and equipment or material failure exists.

● After a print has been dry mounted, changes in heat and humidity, especially if the print is shipped, can cause it to wrinkle or come unstuck from the board. This happens because the print and the board do not expand and contract at the same rate. Since they are attached and the board is stronger, the print suffers the consequences.

● The adhesives in the tissue are not considered to be archival and can have adverse effects on the print, causing it to deteriorate.

● If the print is dropped face down it is offered no protection and the print surface can be damaged.

Box 9.1 Minimum-size Mat Board

Image Size	Mat Board Size
(all dimensions in inches)	
5 X 7	8 X 10
8 X 10	11 X 14
11 X 14	16 X 20
16 X 20	20 X 24

Taylor was searching for "a strategy to create a visual dialog between my own images and historic images that I appropriate. I wanted to figure out how to address scale and proximity, which I had identified as the central themes of my project. I did this by engineering a wet-mounting technique using PVA glue for both gelatin silver and inkjet prints on handmade forms that are fabricated from birch plywood and Masonite. The resulting sculptural form heightens the object quality of the images at the intersection between history and mythology."

© David Taylor. *Pivot Irrigation/Burning House*, 2000. 19 ½ x 33 x 2 inches. Mixed media.

• If the board is damaged in any way there is a problem. Dry mounting is not water soluble, so it is almost impossible to get the print released undamaged from the dry mount. This makes replacement of a damaged board extremely difficult.

• Many resin-coated (RC) color papers react negatively to heat. High temperatures can produce color shifts and mottling and, in the case of Ilfochrome Classic, can cause it to lose some of its glossy finish.

• Other methods of dry mounting with spray mounts and glues are not recommended because the chemical makeup of these materials can have an adverse effect on all color materials over time.

Curators and collectors no longer dry mount work that is received unmounted. It is also not advisable to dry mount unless you made the print yourself or there is a duplicate available. If you still want to dry mount after considering these problems, follow the guidelines in the next section.

The Dry-Mounting Process

Dry-mounting tissue is coated with adhesive that becomes sticky when it is heated. This molten adhesive penetrates into the fibers of the print and mounting board and forms a bond. It is best to use a tacking iron and a dry-mount press to successfully carry out the operation. A home iron is not recommended because it can create a series of unnecessary complications.

When mounting an RC print be certain that the dry-mounting tissue has been designed for use with RC paper or the print may blister and melt. Use four-ply mounting board so that the print does not bend. Keep the color selection simple. Use an off-white or a very light gray-colored board. The board should not call attention to itself or compete with the picture. To obtain maximum print life, use a nonbuffered, acid-free board. Regular board contains impurities that in time can interact with and damage the print.

Dry mounting onto rigid material, such as aluminum, is often used to maintain the integrity of large-scale prints.

Use these steps in the dry-mounting process (necessary materials are shown in figure 9.7):

1 Turn on the tacking iron and dry-mount press. Let them reach operating temperature. Check the dry-mount tissue package for the exact temperature because it varies from product to product. The temperature for RC color material will be lower than that for fiber-based black-and-white paper. Using a temperature that is higher than recommended will damage the resin coating of the print.

2 Make sure all materials and working surfaces are clean and level. Wipe all materials with a smooth cloth. Any dirt will create a raised mark between the print and the board.

3 Predry the board and non-RC prints (do not redry Ilfochrome Classic prints). Place a clean piece of paper on top of the board (Kraft paper is all right but should be replaced after each mounting operation) and the prints to be predried. Place this sandwich in the press for about 30 to 60 seconds (depending on the thickness of the board and the relative humidity). About halfway through this procedure, momentarily open the press to allow water vapor to escape and then close it for the remaining time. This should remove any excess moisture.

4 Place the print face down with a sheet of mounting tissue at least the same size as the print on top of it. Take the preheated tacking iron and touch it against a clean piece of paper that has been placed over the tissue in the center of the print. This one spot should be enough to just keep the print and the tissue together. Do not tack at the corners.

5 Trim the print and tissue together to the desired size. Use a rotary trimmer, a sharp paper cutter, an X-Acto knife, or a mat knife with a cork-

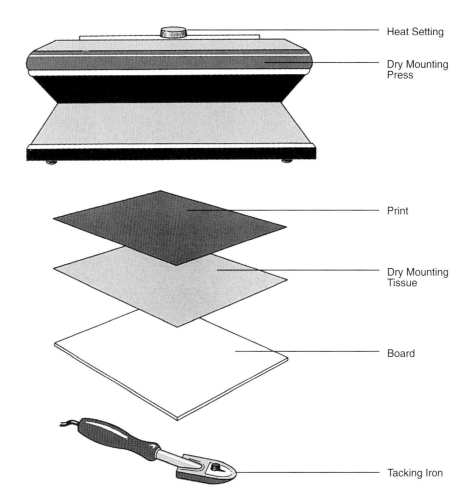

Heat Setting

Dry Mounting Press

Print

Dry Mounting Tissue

Board

Tacking Iron

9.7 The basic materials for dry mounting a photograph. Make certain the temperature setting on the dry-mounting press matches that of the materials being used to avoid damaging the photograph during the dry-mounting process.

backed steel ruler. If you flush mount, the corners and edges of the print are susceptible to damage and it cannot be overmatted unless you crop into the image area.

6 Position the print on the board. The standard print position has equal distance on both sides and about 15 to 20 percent more space at the bottom than at the top. If there is not more space at the bottom, the print appears to visually sink at look bottom heavy when displayed on a wall. Carefully make the measurements using a good metal ruler, and mark the board in pencil to get a perfect alignment.

7 Align the print and tissue face up on the board according to the pencil marks. Raise one corner of the print

and with the iron, tack that corner of the tissue to the board. Next, tack the opposite corner. Now do the remaining two. The tissue must be flat or it will wrinkle.

8 Put this sandwich of print, tissue, and board with a cover sheet of clean paper on top into the press. Make sure it is at the proper operating temperature for the materials. Use tissue that does not have a release point of more than 205°F (96°C) and watch for any changes in color on the print surface. Close and lock the press and heat for about 30 to 45 seconds. Check the product for exact times.

9 Remove the sandwich and place it on a level surface under a weight to cool. Seal makes a special metal cooling weight for this purpose.

Floating a Print

Some prints do not look good matted or mounted. The board interferes with the workings of the space within the picture. In cases like this, "float" the picture as described in the guidelines below.

There are the steps to follow, which should be carried out on a clean, level surface.

1 Decide on the final picture size.
2 Trim the print to these dimensions.
3 Cut a nonbuffered, acid-free backing board or a piece of acid-free Fome-Cor to the same size as the print. Acid-free Fome-Cor will not chemically
interact with the picture and is cheaper than archival board.
4 Have a piece of Plexiglas cut to size.
5 Put the sandwich of Plexiglas, print, and board together with a frameless device such as Swiss Corner Clips and it is ready.
6 Clean the surface only with Plexiglas cleaner as regular glass cleaner can damage the Plexiglas.

Print Preservation

Materials That Damage a Print

There are other methods of displaying finished prints. Whichever method you select, avoid having any of the following materials in contact with the print, because they are harmful to photographs and can cause damage over a period of time: animal glue, brown envelopes or wrapping paper, cellophane tape, cardboard, glassine, masking tape, rubber cement, spray adhesives, white glues, and adhesive-coated pages and plastic covers in "magnetic" pressure-sensitive albums. Avoid contact with wood, shellac, varnish, and any material made with PVCs (polyvinyl coatings). Do not write on the backs of prints with a ballpoint pen because the ink can bleed through and stain the prints.

Selecting the correct medium is crucial to reaching your audience. In the 1970s Wegman began incorporating his dog, Man Ray, into his real-time videos. In 1978 Wegman started condensing these spare studio video performances onto large-format Polaroid material, resulting in the publication of *Man's Best Friend* (1982). Wegman's switch to a still, reproducible format enabled his work to reach a broader public market.

© William Wegman. *Dusted*, 1982. 20 x 24 inches. Diffusion transfer print. Courtesy of Holly Solomon Gallery, New York, NY.

Factors Affecting Color Stability

All the widely used color processes are made from dyes. All color dyes are fugitive, meaning they fade over time. There are three major factors that affect the stability of the dyes. The greatest enemy is known as light fading and is produced by all types of ambient light and UV radiation. The duration, intensity, and quality of the light dictate the rate of change. The second is called dark fading and it begins as soon as the image is made. It is caused by ambient relative humidity and temperature and would occur even if the image were sealed in a light-tight box. Both these processes affect the cyan, magenta, and yellow dye layers, but not at the same rate, causing the image to change color over time. The last process, called staining, is caused by color couplers that remain in the emulsion after processing. It typically produces a yellow stain in the border and highlight areas. The stain forms gradually, and there is no way to remove it.

Staining is still a problem with most chromogenic papers, including all current RA-4 papers.

Choosing the correct material for different situations ensures a better outcome. For example, chromogenic papers are not intended to be displayed in direct sunlight in a showroom or studio window. In this case, color display materials should be used. Color stability is a factor photographers need to consider when selecting color materials. However, the combination of film and paper that delivers the color attributes and handling characteristics the imagemaker desires remains the driving force behind most photographers' decisions.

Regardless of which process or material you use, your images can achieve their maximum natural life span if a few precautions are exercised.

Color Material Life Span

In the past color print dyes commonly faded within 10 years. Kodak claims that the images on its latest color paper will still be "acceptable" to most people after more than 100 years in a photo album, without extended exposure to light and more than 60 years under normal ambient light conditions at home. Inkjet prints can last for a few months or as long as ordinary color photographs, depending on the printer, ink, and paper, but they are often more vulnerable to degradation than conventional prints, especially in terms of moisture. Claims have been made that pigment-based color prints will last 500 years without fading.

Many people want to know how long their color pictures will last. The answer is we don't know. Information in this area remains highly volatile and there is still no reliable set of standards or a database to give definite responses. Henry Wilhelm, an independent researcher in the field of photographic preservation, provides published tests, but it should be noted that his findings have not been substantiated by other independent research. For his reports about older films and papers, see:
Wilhelm, Henry. in Brower, Carol. *The*

Permanence and Care of Color Photographs: Traditional and Digital Color Prints, Color Negatives, Slides, and Motion Pictures. Grinnell, IA: Preservation Publishing Company, 1993. For his latest test information, including digital, see: www.wilhelm-research.com

Keeping What You Have

Print Display and Storage Conditions

Avoid displaying prints for extended periods under bright lights. Some people have tried to protect prints with UV-filter glazing on the glass. However, Wilhelm says this will offer little or no additional protection for most types of color print. Tungsten spots offer a minimum of harmful UV. Fluorescent lights can be covered with UV-absorbing sleeves. Keep display temperatures below 80°F/27°C. Protect the print surface from physical contact from fingers, smudges, or anything that might produce a scratch or stain, and be careful how the prints are stacked in storage.

Make new prints of old images on newer, more archival material. Have two prints of important images made on stable material, one for display and the other for dark storage. Make copy prints of all one-of-a-kind pictures, including Polaroids.

Ideally, color prints should be stored in a clean, cool (50 to 60°F; 10 to 15°C), dark, dry, dust-free area with a relative humidity of about 25 to 40 percent. Avoid exposure to any UV source, including sunlight and fluorescent lights, because UV rays cause the dyes to fade faster. Archival storage boxes, with a nonbuffered paper interior, offer the best protection for color prints. Use desiccants (a substance that absorbs moisture) if you live in an area of high humidity. Keep photographs away from all types of atmospheric pollutant, adhesive, and paint, and any source of ozone. Check the storage area periodically to make sure there has been no infestation of bugs or micro-organisms.

Film Storage

Color negative film should be properly stored in the dark, except when being used to make prints. Keep projection of original slides to a minimum. Duplicate important originals, and project only the dupes. Don't leave slides on light tables or lying about any longer than necessary. Promptly duplicate older slides that show signs of fading. Store slides in archival boxes or in polypropylene pages. Protect negatives in polyester or high-density polyethylene inside conservation paper boxes, metal boxes of baked enamel finished on steel, or safe plastic boxes. See chapter 5, page 109 for information on storing unexposed color film.

Digital imagemaking software often makes the restoration of faded color negatives and slides possible.

Cold Storage

Freezing offers the greatest stability for negatives and prints. Light Impressions (see box 9.3, page 198) sells cold storage envelopes designed for freezing processed film. Zip-Lock seal bags can also be used. With billions of pictures now made every year, photographers should give some thought to what is worth saving. The US National Archives and Records Administration offers "Cold Storage Handling Guidelines for Photographs" online.

Digital Archives

Another way to archive images is to transfer them to a digital format. Digital data is a good candidate for long-term image storage because it can be exactly duplicated and is not made from organic dyes that will fade over time. However, it has several substantial drawbacks.

Transferring Images to a Digital Format

One problem with transferring analog images into a digital format is the transfer process itself. Negatives and prints must be scanned before they can be stored. If a digital archive is to be useful the original scan must accurately capture color and detail. Many consumer film scanners do not have the resolution necessary to capture all the information in a negative or print, especially highlights and shadow detail. It may be worth the extra expense to obtain a top scanner or get high-end scans done at a service bureau. Always remember to back up your files.

Long-Term Storage and Migrating Digital Archives

While the easiest way to move and save digital information is on magnetic media such as ZIP disks, it is not the best way to store images in the long run. Magnetic media will fade over time and can be damaged by heat, humidity, and magnetic and electrical fields. Currently the most archival way to store electronic data is on CD-ROM. Kodak claims their CD-R Gold Ultima, which uses a pure gold reflective layer, has a life expectancy of 200 years. But will there be a device to read that CD in 199 years? It is unlikely that current CDs and DVDs will be widely used 10 or 20 years from now, or that current file formats will be compatible with software in the future. This is not a justification to avoid digital storage, since color negatives will also begin to fade in 10 years. The ease with which digital information can be copied gives you a viable future option to migrate (copy) these images to newer and more archival hardware/software as it becomes available. See Box 9.2.

Digital Prints

Since the early days of digital imaging the inkjet printer has been the mainstay of electronic output. When these printers became available to the artist market imagemakers were impressed with the image quality, but disappointed with image stability. In the 1990s a cottage industry sprang up to develop different inks and media; each type has its advantages and disadvantages.

Box 9.2 Guidelines for Handling Digital Media

1. Keep magnetic media away from strong magnetic or electrical fields.

2. Do not touch magnetic recording surfaces.

3. Avoid bending or flexing a disk or CD.

4. Always handle CDs by the edge or center and avoid touching the non-printed side.

5. Use a felt-tip pen to write on a CD as the recording layer is very close to the labeling surface of a CD-ROM. Write in the clear area around the center of a disk to avoid the possibility of the ink affecting the recorded data. Do not use a ballpoint pen to label a CD or allow the label or underside to be scratched.

6. Keep food and drink away from the storage media.

7. Store disks and tapes in a dust-free environment in a vertical position (do not lay flat).

8. Store disks away from direct sunlight between 60 and 70° F with a relative humidity of between 35 and 45 percent.

9. Annually read a sampling of the digital information to check for degradation.

10. Copy the information to another disk every four to five years to refresh the data and migrate to newer, more archival hardware/software/materials.

11. Remove light dust by brushing from the center out. Never wipe in a circular pattern. If a CD must be cleaned use mild soap and water. Blot it dry with an absorbent cloth to avoid rubbing the surface. Never use chemical solvents.

Dyes
Dye-based inks were the first to be developed by printer manufacturers and are the standard inks supplied by office supply and computer stores. Generally these inks have excellent color and saturation but fade rapidly. Dyes can bleed, feather, or spot upon contact with liquids, or soften and bleed in conditions of high humidity.

Pigmented Inks
Pigments have a greater resistance to light-fading than dyes, but generally have substantially lower color saturation and are not as readily absorbed into paper, which makes them prone to fingerprints, smears, and smudges. Pigmented inks combine the light-fastness of pigments with the brightness of dyes, thereby providing a good compromise. While the images tend to last longer and have good color saturation, they can appear mottled because of the uneven absorption of the dye and pigment inks. Because dyes and pigments can absorb and reflect light differently (they have different spectral reflectance characteristics), they can look like a match in daylight, but be differently colored when viewed under tungsten or fluorescent light, a phenomenon known as metamerism.

Pigment Inks
Pigment ink and acid-free paper combinations have received archival ratings of upwards of 200 years by independent testing laboratories. These labs perform accelerated fading tests using high doses of light and varying humidity to make predictions on how long an image will last before fading becomes substantially noticeable. These predictions have recently been questioned because many of the labs did not take gas fading, pigments' ability to withstand fading due to prolonged exposure to air-born contaminants such as ozone, into account. Ozone is created by a variety of sources, including cars, solvents, and household cleaners, and can fade pigment inks in months.

Media
Contemporary printers can print on a variety of different media including gloss

Ressler used a special macro lens and a copy stand to photograph her collages dealing with the "(re)presentation of female stereotypes. Here a woman is operating a camera, suggesting an alternative to the 'male gaze' that has prevailed in Western culture." The constraints of working from existing materials led Ressler to turn to digital collage.

© Susan Ressler. *Missed Representations* (series), *Colours*, 1984. 11 x 14 inches. Dye-destruction print.

and matt paper, acid-free rag, canvas, cloth, and vinyl among others. The material a digital print is made on often has a greater effect on its longevity and color reproduction than the inks. While acid-free papers are considered the best for image longevity, print life expectancy predictions are frequently based solely on specific ink and paper combinations. Coated papers are available that can improve the color gamut of inkjet prints, make them dry faster, and make them water resistant, but these coatings can destroy an ink's ability to withstand fading. Also a number of pigment and pigmented inks are not compatible with gloss papers because of ink-absorption problems. Media and ink formulations are changing rapidly. Research the latest information on specific inks and media before beginning your digital project and consider reprinting images as improvements are made in materials.

Protecting Digital Prints
With the present selection of inks and media the best way to protect images is to keep prints made with pigments out of direct sunlight and present them under glass using only acid-free papers and matting materials. The frame and glass can reduce the amount of harmful atmospheric contaminants the prints are exposed to.

Copying Work

Making slides or digital files of your prints or of pictures in books for a presentation or for appropriation purposes is relatively simple. The pictures to be copied can be positioned vertically on a wall or laid on any convenient flat surface. The camera can be tripod mounted or handheld, depending on the light source and film sensitivity. Camera movement must be avoided to produce sharp results. Be sure the camera back is parallel to the print surface and the lighting is uniform. Avoid shadows falling across the picture. Use a slow film or digital ISO setting for most accurate color rendition and grain structure/noise.

Lens Selection

The choice of lens affects the outcome. Use an apochromatic lens that has been color corrected for three primary spectra colors and that has the flattest field possible along with the best edge-to-edge definition. This will deliver uniform sharpness at the same distance from the center and the edge of the lens. For 35-mm copying a normal-length macro lens, such as the 60-mm Nikkor Macro, is best. Zoom lenses, with a macro mode, tend to produce soft (not sharp) results. Bellows attachments or auxiliary lenses, such as Proxar lens sets of varying degrees of magnification, can convert a normal focal-length lens into a useful copy lens.

With a large-format camera use an apochromatic lens, which is designed for reproduction and often used on a process camera for graphic arts work. It corrects chromatic aberration that produces red-green-blue fringing around the edges of color images, and gives maximum sharpness and flatness of field.

Type of Light

Good results can be obtained most easily by using a daylight color slide film or digital color-balance setting and shooting the pictures outside, on a clear day, in direct sunlight, between the hours of about 10 a.m. and 2 p.m., to avoid shadows, which can create an unwanted color cast. Use a UV filter to eliminate unwanted UV radiation.

If copying is done indoors, a tungsten film or color-balance setting should be used with artificial lighting. Be certain the film or digital color-balance setting matches the Kelvin temperature of the lights. Two lights should be placed at equal distances on either side of the tripod-mounted camera at a 45-degree angle to the picture being copied to produce even, glare-free light (figure 9.8).

Exposure

Indoors or out, take a meter reading from a standard neutral gray card such as the one inside the back cover of this book for the most accurate results. Metering off the picture itself produces inconsistent exposures. Let the gray card fill the frame, but do not focus on it. For close-up work, the exposure should be determined with the gray card at the correct focus distance. Try to let the image fill as much of the frame as possible, without chopping off any of it. If you haven't done much copying or are using a new film, bracket using 1/3 to 1/2 f-stops in the direction of underexposure.

Only those slides that have been accurately exposed should be used. Generally, it is important to choose images that form a cohesive group when viewed together and that reflect the visual concerns of the photographer.

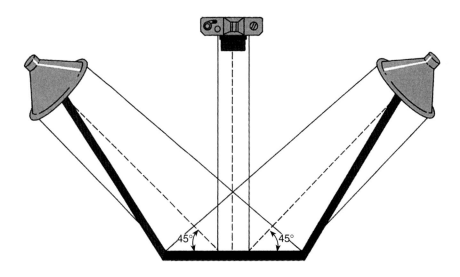

9.8 When copying work, two lights should be set up at equal distances on each side of the camera at 45-degree angles to the work being copied. Meter from a gray card, not off the surface of the work being copied. Make sure the film and the light sources have the same color temperature. Polarizing filters can be attached to the lights and/or the camera to allow the photographer to control reflections and to increase color contrast and saturation.

Slide and Disk Presentation

Slides must be well presented. This means the photographer's name, the slide title and size (with height before width), the date the image was made, and the type of process should be clearly printed on each slide mount with the top (the correct way to view the slide) of the image indicated (figure 9.9).

When sending digital images, make it easy for your work to be seen. Prepare files that open quickly on any platform. Set images to run in a slide show program. Often when your work is being reviewed a number of people will be involved in the process and they still prefer to have non-virtual, concrete references. Don't expect reviewers to print your files. With this in mind, include thumbnail printouts of what is on the disk and provide hard copy of any text documents.

Finding the "Top"

A colored dot is often used on a slide mount to indicate the top position. There are two competing schools of thought as to where the colored dot should be placed. The first group puts the dot on the upper right-hand corner of the mount. This way a viewer has no

difficulty determining the correct way to view the slide (the top is the top). The second group puts the dot on the lower left-hand corner in order to indicate how the slide should be placed in a carousel tray for projection. In this case, the dot is placed so it is visible on the slide mount when it is in the carousel slot. Many people not familiar with the image find this confusing. They are not sure if the dot indicates the true top of the image or its correct position when loaded in a carousel tray. Place the colored dot in the upper right-hand corner of the mount: that way you can be sure the top is the top.

If the slides are to be projected, place them, with the dot in the upper right-hand corner, on a light table to sort and position them in the desired order. To place the slide correctly in a carousel tray, position it so the image is how you originally saw it in the camera (dot in upper right-hand corner), turn it upside down (dot now in lower left-hand corner), and drop it in the tray. After all the slides are loaded, project them to make sure they are in the right viewing position. Then make a uniform mark with a felt-tip pen on the upper right-hand

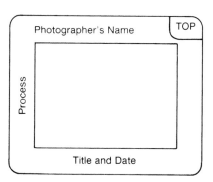

9.9 Slides must be well presented in order to have a chance of receiving a fair reception. Each slide should be clearly labeled with the photographer's name, the date of the image, and the type of process that was used. The top of the photograph should be identified so that it is obvious how to view the image.

edges of the slide mounts sitting in the tray. This line provides a visual indicator for the future that the slides are correctly loaded in the carousel, but it will not be noticeable on the front of the mount.

Masking Slides

Mask out any areas of the slides that should not be seen when projected by using black photographic tape, chartpak tape, or special slide masking tape made of aluminum polyester. Wearing a thin cotton glove, remove the slide from its original mount. Put the slide, emulsion side down, on a clean lightbox. Place the tape on the nonemulsion side (shiny side) of the film. Trim the excess with a pair of sharp scissors. Use only one layer of tape or it may get stuck in the projector. Carefully reinsert the masked slide into a new mount.

Avoid a Bad Reception

Slides or digital files that are not properly made, correctly labeled, numbered, or neatly presented will not receive a favorable welcome at a competition, gallery, school, or job interview. Both methods are at best an imperfect way to view anyone's work, therefore give them your best effort so they present an accurate approximation of the colors, mood, and tone in your work. Always include a cover letter and appropriate support materials, such as a your résumé, an exhibition list, and a concise statement concerning the work. Be selective, decide what is important, highlight important information, and don't bombard the receiver with too much data.

Shipping

Ship slides in transparent polyethylene pages. Put disks in clear plastic cases. Put your name, return address, telephone number, email, and title of the body of work on the slide page. Do not send loose slides or disks. Make sure each image is identified with your name and a number so the person on the receiving end can easily identify which images he or she may be interested in. A separate checklist, referring to the numbered images, should be included providing each image's title, size, process, and presentation size. Use a stiff backing board in the envelope so that the slides cannot be easily bent. Enclose a properly sized return envelope, with the correct amount of postage and a self-addressed shipping label to help guarantee the return of your materials (SASE stands for: self-addressed, stamped, envelope). Write "Do Not Bend!" on the front and back of the shipping envelope. Valuable and irreplaceable materials should be sent by one of the overnight package services; otherwise send them by first-class mail with delivery confirmation.

Copyright of Your Own Work

According to the US Copyright Office in Washington, DC, it is no longer necessary to place the notice of copyright on works published for the first time on or after March 1, 1989, in order to secure ownership of copyright and the failure to place a notice of copyright on work may no longer result in the loss of copyright. However, the Copyright Office still recommends that owners of copyrights continue to place notice of copyright on their works to secure all their rights. The copyright notice for pictorial works should include three elements: (1) the word "copyright" or the symbol for copyright, which is the letter C enclosed by a circle (©); (2) the name of the copyright owner; and (3) the year of the first publication of the image. For example, © Jane Smith 2003. Copyright notice is not required on unpublished work, but it is advisable to affix notices of copyright to avoid inadvertent publication without notice. It is illegal for photographic labs to duplicate images with a copyright notice on them without written permission from the holder of the copyright. For additional information see US Copyright Office, Library of Congress, www.loc.gov/copyright.

Where to Send Work

There is fierce competition for exhibitions, gallery representation, and commercial connections. Prepare yourself to be persistent and for rejection. Numerous publications and websites identify opportunities; they include *Photographer's Market*, which is published every year (www.writersdigest.com); *Afterimage* (www.vsw.org/afterimage); *Art Calendar* (www.artcalendar.com); and *Art*

in America/Annual Guide to Museums, Galleries, Artists, 575 Broadway, New York, NY 10012.

References

American National Standards Institute (www.ansi.org). Request their catalog of photographic standards.

Conservation of Photographs, Kodak Publication No. F-40, 1985.

KEEFE, LAURENCE E., and INCH, DENNIS. *The Life of a Photograph: Archival Processing, Matting, Framing and Storage*, 2nd ed. Stoneham, MA: Focal Press, 1990.

WILHELM, HENRY in BROWER, CAROL. *The Permanence and Care of Color Photographs: Traditional and Digital Color Prints, Color Negatives, Slides, and Motion Pictures*. Grinnell, IA: Preservation Publishing Company 1993.

Chapter Ten
PHOTOGRAPHIC PROBLEM SOLVING AND WRITING

Crewdson thinks: "Twilight is this magic hour between day and night, when ambient and artificial light come together. It's a time of transcendence when extraordinary things happen." Influenced by filmmakers such as Alfred Hitchcock, David Cronenberg, and David Lynch, the making of Crewdson's photographs is an elaborately planned group activity, like a film production, that can involve coordinating 35 assistants and technicians. It reflects his belief that you "do whatever you have to do to make your work." This image, a fusion of documentary and fiction, is reminiscent of *Close Encounters of the Third Kind* (1977) and portrays an alien, exotic, and strange suburban landscape. Crewdson, whose father was a psychoanalyst, comments: "I photograph out of longing and desire. My photographs are also about repression and internal angst."

© Gregory Crewdson. *Untitled*, 1998. 50 x 60 inches. Chromogenic color print. Courtesy Luhring Augustine, New York, NY.

Becoming More Aware/Thinking Independently

Getting ideas to solve visual problems, whether by analog or digital methods, entails becoming more aware and thinking independently. This requires self-discipline and is accomplished by asking questions, acknowledging new facts, reasoning skeptically through your prejudices, and taking on the responsibility of gaining knowledge. It is necessary to believe in your own creativeness. Consider information from all sources. Do not attempt to limit your response to only the rational part of the brain; let your feelings enter into the process. Be prepared to break with habit and take chances. Listen to yourself as well as to others to get satisfaction.

Dealing with Fear

The major block to getting new ideas is fear. Fear takes on endless forms: fear of being wrong, of being foolish, or of changing the way in which something has been done in the past. Fear can be a reluctance to deal with the unknown. It can be brought about by a lack of preparation. Apprehension deters creative development by misdirecting or restraining energy. It is okay to make mistakes; do not insist that everything be absolutely perfect. A mistake can open a window of new possibilities. In *The Act of Creation* (1990), Arthur Koestler wrote: "We find over and over again mishaps which are blessings in disguise." Beginners are not expected to be experts, so take advantage of this situation. Learning involves doing, therefore make that extra negative; make one more print to see what happens. You are the one who will benefit

Journal Keeping

Journal keeping can be a method that helps you sort through life experiences and decide what might be an important issue to problem solve. The exercise of writing down reflections about events

Blacklow tells us: "Journaling, an activity I have engaged in since childhood, is a source for my art, as I attempt to revisit the very moment of creative motivation by using text, drawing, painting, collage, and image transfer. Keeping a journal helps center me. I work on each page only for myself and am not involved in self-conscious thoughts about an audience. Transfer is a fast and simple technique that allows me to remove and relocate a magazine, newspaper, or photocopy image. Ironically, some of the visual strategies and ideas in my journal inspire the art work that I exhibit."

© Laura Blacklow. *Journal Page*, 1979. 11 x 14 inches. Solvent transfer, ink and tape.

experienced each day is an invaluable way to evaluate your performance, set standards, and find new ways to solve difficult problems. Many people resist keeping a journal because they think they are not good enough writers, that they are not good enough writers, that someone will read their innermost thoughts, that their thoughts are petty, or that they have more important things to do. Instead of thinking of a journal as a diary, a book in which you relate the day's events, think of it as a container for self-reflection, self-expression, and self-exploration. Retelling the day's events is not as relevant as the act of finding a way to express your thoughts. Be sure to include any imagery that grabs your attention.

Photography is a Lot Like Baseball

Photography and baseball both require that participants be skilled in the precise placement of objects and the capture of moments in time and space within fractions of a second.[1] There are periods of thoughtful contemplation, followed by bursts of intense activity, and then a return to quietness. Both activities require patience, practice, and study. Both involve performance and control and the comprehension of a spatial language. But most of all, to be a player you must be there and play the game. Warren Spahn, the winningest left-handed pitcher to ever step on the mound, said: "Baseball is a game of failure." The big leagues' best hitters fail about 65 percent of the time; the best pitchers can lose 12 games in a season and hundreds over their careers. Statistics do not always tell the entire story. If a photographer added up the number of frames shot and compared it with the number of satisfying images produced, a typical photographic batting average could be about 1 percent. What is not reflected in an average is all the intangible joys involved within the process of photography that require the integration of abstract ideas and concrete operations. Good photographers overcome their fear and make pictures. Don't be afraid of experience. Being a photographer involves making numerous choices. Choice is what defines who we are and what our work is about. Going to the plate and deciding when to swing the bat, even if it means striking out, is about making such choices. As Ansel Adams said: "Photography is a way of knowing."

Safe at Third, issued by American Tobacco Company, 1911. Chromolithograph with hand-color. Courtesy of Library of Congress Prints and Photographs Division, Washington, DC.

The Problem-Solving Process

Getting ideas means finding ways to solve problems. The process is a continuous intermingling of events (figure 10.1) that includes acceptance, analysis, definition, idea formation, selection, operation, evaluation, and results. Feel free to skip around or go back and forth between steps. There is no definite order; it is dependent on the pattern of your thinking.

Birth of a Problem

Problems arise from every aspect of life. They can spring from our private world of friends, loved ones, children, or parents. They may come from our work world situations of bosses and co-workers. Others are thrust upon us from the outside world due to educational, economic, political, and even accidental circumstances. We cannot try to solve all the problems we encounter. We must be

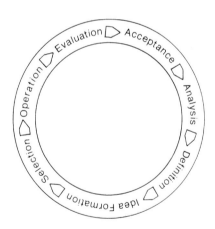

10.1 This is one representation of the problem-solving process as a continuous circle of responsible thinking. There is no definite order for thinking. Feel free to devise a method that is suitable to both the problem and the problem solver. The steps outlined in this chapter can be thought of in linear terms, of taking one step in front of the next until the destination is reached. They may also be taken in a hopscotch manner, by skipping around from one step to another, or by crisscrossing the steps. Don't be afraid to switch models.

Dussinger says of the *String* series: "I examine human relationships and how we communicate with one another. The symbol I use for the visual energy of bonding is a red string. Red also signifies arousal, desire, and emotion, which are parts of our existence. The production challenge involves organizing and directing the models to perform as characters and interact with the string and being prepared for the unexpected. Working quickly and paying attention to details is essential, when using a large-format camera and Speedotron strobes and creating a theatrical appearance that retains the ambience of the bar."

© Camilla Dussinger. *The California Clipper,* from the *String* series, 2000. 24 x 20 inches. Chromogenic color print.

selective about which problems we decide to take on, or be overwhelmed and not be able to accomplish anything.

Acceptance

Acceptance means taking on a problem as a challenge and a responsibility by saying yes to involvement and committing your time and resources to solve the problem. It is like signing a contract that indicates the intention to take charge and see the project through to completion. We can either accept things the way that they are ("I do not know how to do this in color photography") or we can take on the responsibility for change ("I am

going to learn how to do this").

Analysis

Analysis involves studying the problem and determining its essential features and feelings. It includes taking the problem apart, doing research to discover all its ingredients, and working out their relationship to the whole. This is the time to question everything and to generate all the possibilities that are available.

Definition

Definition is getting to the main issues and clarifying the goals to be reached. It entails nonlimiting questioning. Ask yourself what the "real" problem is. Do not get sidetracked by the symptoms of the problem. We must decide where problems may lie and narrow down the information uncovered. This state defines the direction in which the action will be taken in order to solve the problem.

Idea Formation

Idea formation provides ways of reaching the stated goal. Do not fall in love with one idea or assume the answer is known before this process is started. Go out on a limb; defer judgment. Try techniques such as journaling or attribute listing, which tells all you know about the problem, or morphological synthesis, including the internal structure, patterns, and form of the problem and the breakdown of its individual parts. Attribute listing also involves the search for various signs that occur in the problem and the possible arrangements of those signs. Put together all the solutions that have been considered, and keep an open mind to the alternatives.

Selection

Selection is the process of choosing from all the idea options that have been discovered. Now is the time to decide which way is best to reach the stated destination. Keep a backup idea in case a detour is encountered. Do not be afraid to experiment, to take chances, or to try something that has not been done previously.

Operation

Operation is putting the plan into action. The process of doing is as important as the final product. Do not seek perfection, because it is impossible and you will not reach your goal. If the selected idea is not working out, be flexible and attempt something else.

Do not be afraid to make many exposures, as an artist would employ a sketchbook. These recordings act as starting places for your visual ideas. Keep thinking. Do not worry if every picture is not a masterpiece. Do not be concerned about making a mistake; it will be dealt with in the next step of the process. Keep working.

Evaluation

During evaluation the course of action is reviewed. These questions are asked: What was done? What worked? What didn't work? Why did or didn't it work? What could be done to make the picture stronger? Pinpoint the source of any dissatisfaction. If the result does not meet the goals, it is time to do a "reshoot."

Look beyond the obvious. Kofi Annan, the Secretary-General of the United Nations, recounted a lesson in remaining open to what is in front of our eyes. One of his teachers took out a large white sheet with a black dot in the middle, draped it over the blackboard, and asked: "'What do you see?' We all

Culver's publication *A Change of Mind: An Alzheimer's Portrait* (2003) is the result of her documentation of her father and the feeling she had for him and her mother as they struggled through this disease. Culver remembers: "I kept on watching my father as he lay in his special chair and I set up a tripod to make a slow shutter speed photo of him under natural daylight in my parent's living-room, when Joan the aid came along and began to cover him. I continued to photograph this unexpected event and was surprised when I saw the results. The blanket appeared to be an omen of a shroud that was to come, and I knew that it would not be long before he died."

© Joyce Culver. *Dad Being Covered*, 1998. 20 x 24 inches. Chromogenic color print.

answered: 'The black dot.' He responded: 'What about the vast white space?' He was reminding us to look beneath the surface, to bear in mind the larger picture. He was teaching us that there is more than one side to a story, and more than one answer to a question."

Do not hold on to only one idea, as absolutist beliefs can be crippling to creative problem solving. A large part of learning involves how to deal with failure. We learn more from our failures than from our successes. Picasso said, "Even the great artists have failures."

Results

Good results render your ideas and intentions visible. A successful solution is one that fits both the problem and the problem solver. To make this happen, you must be ready to jump in—chance favors the prepared—and become a part of the process called photography.

The successful problem solver keeps a record of what has been done and how it was accomplished. This is empirical knowledge—repeatable results gained from experience.

Problem solving means coming to grips with the true nature of the situation. Simplistic solutions to problems offer the wrong answers for the lazy and the unthinking. Be skeptical of anyone who claims to have all the answers. Some people take a course in photography believing that techniques will make them photographers; this is not the case. To be a photographer, you must learn to think a situation through to a satisfying conclusion based on personal experiences and

Heinecken's inquiry into the limits of photographic form has helped redefine the boundaries of photographic practice. Specifically, his work asked: Does one have to use a camera to make a significant photographic work? Heinecken states: "This relief collage emanates from the saturation of media and the media-driven drama surrounding the social issues of the single mother." He recalls: "The most difficult technical challenge was creating a three-dimensional object out of two-dimensional magazine advertisements."

© Robert Heinecken. *Shiva Manifesting as a Single Mother*, 1989. 96 x 48 inches. Mixed media.

needs that combine the "right" technique for your vision.

The quest for the "absolute" tends to get in the way of good photography. In his book *Perfect Symmetry: The Search for the Beginning of Time*, the physicist Heinz R. Pagels said:

> *Maybe there is some final truth to the universe I do not know. Yet suspending such beliefs opens us to new ways of exploring. Later we can compare our new knowledge and beliefs with the old ones. Often such comparisons involve contradictions; but these, in turn, generate new creative insights about the order of reality. The capacity to tolerate complexity and welcome contradiction, not the need for simplicity and certainty, is the attribute of an explorer.*[ii]

Understanding Photography's Roles

Problem solving and technical abilities communicate nothing to others unless attached to convincing personal beliefs. The big questions deal with the roles photography plays in our lives and society. What must be implicit is that photography's relationship to reality is paradoxical. Conscientious work can provoke without coercing, while providing pleasure that is mediated by the viewer's judgment. Works by artists such as Robert Mapplethorpe and Andres Serrano have been read as advertisements for unnatural acts because some people see the function of photography in a consumer society as promoting products as opposed to provoking controversial ideas. Other artists, such as Robert Heinecken, challenged the notion that it is even necessary to use a camera to make noteworthy photographic work. He falls into a category coined by critic Arthur C. Danto known as a "photographist," which he defined as "an artist who uses photographs for artistic means and whose function is partly philosophical reflection on the nature of the kind of art it exemplifies."

Potent work is often ambiguous and

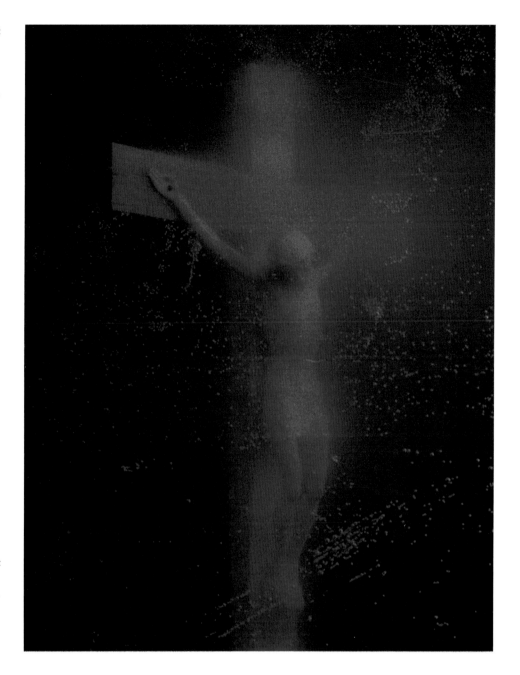

requires interpretation by the viewer. Without being didactic, it can stimulate thinking that leads to an understanding. Such images allow us to be transported to explore other realms while remaining in our habitat, permit us to be transformed, and appeal to our personal freedom and individualism while reminding us of our collective investment in the group. Other times art can resist explanation, which is why it is called art. If an object could be explained in 87 words on an oversize wall label, you wouldn't need the object, just the wall label. Art is

This photograph became a flash point for a conservative crusade to end National Endowment for the Arts (NEA) funding for individual artists and nonmainstream arts and cultural organizations. Why did this piece upset so many people? Is it what you see or what you read? Would anyone have been unnerved had this work been called *Untitled*? Serrano's quandary with his faith has also produced worshipful images, such as *Black Supper* and *Black Mary*, *Black Jesus*. Serrano refers to himself as "a former Catholic and ... someone who even today is not opposed to being called a Christian."

© Andres Serrano. *Piss Christ*, 1987. 60 x 40 inches. Dye-destruction print. Courtesy of Paula Cooper Gallery, New York, NY.

This photograph is from a series dealing with how Jude's childhood home of McCall, Idaho has been transformed into a popular resort destination. But once Jude allowed this image to enter into the public sphere it took on its own identity and meaning. It became a transcendent canine image with great public appeal, which was not Jude's original intent.

© Ron Jude. *Untitled*, from *Near The 45th Parallel*, 1995. 38 x 30 inches. Chromogenic color print. Courtesy of Jackson Fine Art, Atlanta, GA.

not social studies and it cannot be counted on to reveal its meaning at the end of a chapter. At some point it can be perplexing, and it is this bewilderment that remains an unseen part of the art experience. For some this can create the "art jitters," the anxiety of not "getting it." Art appreciation is a complicated process and there can be no epiphanies without trials. You cannot expect to respond to every work of art, but one of the best things about hard-to-get art is that it allows you to create your own narrative, a drama based on allure, apprehension, bewilderment, the sheer pleasure of figuring it out and, and telling others what you discovered.

Images that have integrity allow our imagination to enter a dreamlike state where rational thought is suspended, all while retaining our faculty for judgment and reflection. It is possible to return from this journey to reflect on the choices that habitually define and restrain us. In *The Scandal of Pleasure: Art in an Age of Fundamentalism*, Wendy Steiner says: "Experiencing the variety of meanings available in a work of art helps make us tolerant and mentally lithe. Art is a realm of thought experiments that quicken, sharpen and sweeten our being in the world."

Writing about Images

Being a good visual problem solver involves learning the language of photography. One of the best methods to expand your visual vocabulary is to write about pictures, as this will also increase insight into your own working methods and prejudices and the varied roles photography may play. Begin by going to a major online photographic collection, such as www.eastman.org, or to the library and browsing through the photography and art sections. If you are fortunate to have access to exhibitions, plan on visiting a few different ones. Don't go only to see photography; select a variety of mediums, styles, and time periods. Spend some time leisurely studying the work and begin to write down your

thoughts on your laptop or on 3- x 5-inch blank cards. Now prepare yourself to write a structured review. Begin by selecting work you find positive, appealing, and involving. State your opinions and observations and back them up with specific facts derived from the work. Pretend you are in a court of law; give evidence, not generalizations. Consider the following:

1 Describe the image, including the subject matter and its form. Form entails how the subject is presented. Refer to chapter 12 on the visual language of design. Can you discover the color and/or composition key? How are figure–ground relationships used?

2 Evaluate the technique. Does it work for you? Why? Discuss exposure, use of light, and printing and presentation methods. What would you do differently? Why?

3 Give your subjective reaction. Listen to yourself. What initially attracted you to this work? Did the attraction last? Did the work deliver what you expected? Would you want to continue to look at this work over a period of time? Is the photographer a visual or haptic (see chapter 11, page 212)? Did you find yourself thinking about this piece again? Answer each part with a why or why not response.

4 Interpret the work. Ask yourself: Why was it made in this particular way? What does the work mean? Who made it? What is the point of view of the imagemaker? What was the artist trying to say? Does the imagemaker succeed? Why or why not? Who was it made for? Do the images stand on their own merits or do they require an accompanying statement or explanation? What is your interpretation of the work? Does it tell you a narrative? Does it appeal to your emotions or your intellect? If the work is in a group or series, evaluate how selected images work individually and in terms of the group. Do single images hold their own

ground or do they need to be seen in series? Does the imagemaker use any text? If so, how does it alter your perception of the image's meaning? Which is stronger, the image or the text? Present clear, succinct, and persuasive arguments, citing evidence to back up your thoughts.

5 Incorporate ideas. Examine and define what it is about the work you like/relate to/find moving. Be specific. Then ask yourself how you can integrate these concepts into your own way of working.

6 Do the opposite. Go back to the same body of work and pick an image that you do not care for. Repeat the previous steps to figure out what it is you don't like. Identify specific points and ask yourself what you should do to avoid incorporating these unwanted aspects into your work.

7 Ask someone else. Get the opinion of someone else who is knowledgeable and interested in similar work. Present the work to them. Does the other person agree or disagree with your assessment? Conduct a friendly discussion. Do your opinions hold together? Should they be revised? Can you see the other point of view? What new territory did this other person open for you? How will this affect the way you view the work?

Writing an Artist's Statement

When sending your own work out for review or exhibition, it is necessary to include a statement that concisely explains the conceptual aspects of your work. Basically, an artist's statement explains why you do what you do and what your work is about. A precisely written statement can build a bridge between the artist and the audience, stimulating interest and understanding of your work. Artists' statements vary in form, length, and substance. You may have to consider all or most of the following: your audience, your materials and medium, the subject of your work, the methodologies and theories that have influenced you, and your own background, purpose, or perspective. There are no simple formulas, but the following steps have been put together with the assistance of photographer and educator Kathleen Campbell to provide a starting place for writing a concise, easy-to-read, one-page artist's statement.

1 The purpose of an artist's statement is to clearly and succinctly explain and give credibility to your ideas. Start by discovering what your ideas are and where they come from.

2 Reflect upon your own work and find patterns of interest, then ask yourself the following: What kind of work do you enjoy making and looking at? Do you photograph landscapes or people? Do you prefer to set up subject matter or find it directly from life? Do you gravitate toward cool or warm colors? What ideas, themes, or common denominators can you discover?

3 Select an artist whose work strongly appeals to you and find out what that artist has to say. Review the procedures from the previous section, Writing about Images.

4 Do research. Ideas are built upon other ideas. Your work can share an idea with someone else and still be your own work. Artists get ideas from other artists, history, literature, philosophy, and politics. Where do your ideas come from? What ideas appeal to you?

5 Can viewers interpret your image, not knowing what you intended and not having had your experiences? Keep in mind a photograph is not the same thing as an experience. It is a two-dimensional representation of colors and shapes on a piece of paper. It is a symbol or a metaphor, but not an actual event.

6 Remember that all images have meaning, even if you find requests to explain your work annoying. People will make interpretations whether you want them to or not.

7 Learn the difference between denotation and connotation. Denotation is what images appear to be on the surface, for example a picture of a mountain. Connotation is all the associations you can imagine people might "get" from the picture of the mountain. There are pictures of mountains and pictures of mountains. Are yours cold and intellectual or warm and romantic? Make a list of all the connotations and denotations you can see in your work. Show the work to others and see if they come up with additional ones.

8 Use metaphors. Literal statements lead toward literal interpretations. You are not "illustrating" your idea, step by step, but fashioning a metaphor that involves your use of form and process to convey it (even if you do not discuss this in your statement). For instance, darkness can be a metaphor for a mood. You do not have to beat people over the head with your meaning in your statement if the image creates an interpretable metaphor. Metaphors also can have layers of meaning, so viewers can bring their own insights to the work.

9 A statement should provide a toehold for understanding the ideas behind your images. Don't tell viewers "what they should get" out of your work. Generally images have more than one interpretation so allow others the space to formulate their own interpretation. However, this is not an excuse to avoid articulating your own ideas.

10 Make sure your words agree with what can be seen in your pictures. Do not write about things that are not there. If your words and images do not agree, change either the words or the images until there is coherence between them.

11 Keep it simple and specific. Avoid making negative statements, writing too much, repeating or over-explaining, or using vague generalities, grandiose statements, or incomprehensible language.

12 Only discuss the technical process if it is integrally related to your idea or is unusual and requires explanation. A separate image checklist should state the titles of your work (if any), their creation date, dimensions (height before width), and process.

13 Ask other people who are familiar with your work to critique your statement. Review, rewrite, and recheck the spelling, grammar, and organizational flow of your document. The process of rewriting will also help you gain insight into your work. An artist's statement is a flexible document. You may have more than one, and it should be reviewed and revised each time you use it.

References

BARRETT, TERRY. *Criticizing Photographs: An Introduction To Understanding Images*, 3rd ed. New York: McGraw-Hill, 1999.

STEINER, WENDY. *The Scandal of Pleasure: Art in an Age of Fundamentalism*. Chicago: The University of Chicago Press, 1995.

TURABIAN, KATE L. *A Manual for Writers of Term Papers, Theses, and Dissertations*, 6th ed. Chicago: The University of Chicago Press, 1996.

Endnotes

[1] During the summer of 1839, Daguerre made public his photographic process and the first modern American baseball game, as devised by Abner Doubleday, was played at Cooperstown, NY.

[2] HEINZ R. PAGELS. *Perfect Symmetry: The Search for the Beginning of Time*. New York: Simon and Schuster, 1985, 370.

Chapter Eleven
SEEING THE LIGHT

Norfolk uses Mikhail Bakhtin's term "chromotope" to describe this landscape as "a place that allows movement through space and time simultaneously, and a place that displays the layers of time." The fluorescent balloons provide visual contrast when juxtaposed both with the crumbling remains of a modern concrete teahouse destroyed by years of war, and the warm tones of an early morning desert sunrise.

© Simon Norfolk. *Former Teahouse at the Afghan Exhibition of Economic and Social Achievements*, 2001. 40 x 50 inches. Courtesy of Galerie Martin Kudlek, Koln, Germany.

Looking at a photograph is not like looking out of a window. It requires a system of thought processes to reach a decision. It is not a mysterious, God-given gift but a process involving visual language that can be taught and mastered to stimulate thought and action.

© David Graham. *Mayflower, Philadelphia, PA,* 1984. 24 x 20 inches. Chromogenic color print. Courtesy of Black Star and Laurence Miller Gallery, New York, NY.

How We See

Seeing is an act of perception that helps us to ascertain, experience, learn, and understand our world. It is an individual skill that is conditioned by our cultural standards, education, and physical anatomy.

Our Western industrialized society is dependent on literacy to function. To fully function it is necessary to be able to decipher messages that have been put into a written code or language.

When we begin to deal with pictures, another set of skills is needed to interpret the coded information. We must learn this language to become visually literate.

Visual Literacy

Literacy is based on the quality and quantity of our stored information, yet sometimes we are reluctant to learn to read new images. We tend to accept only the old ways and reject anything that is different or unfamiliar. When we can overcome this fear and begin thinking for ourselves, learning becomes a joyful and invigorating experience. This adds to our storehouse of information that can be called upon when dealing with new situations, thereby increasing our range of responses.

Whatever type of communication is in use, the receiver must be able to understand the code. In the past, pictures showed something of known importance. Traditional picture making used the act of seeing to identify and classify subject matter. This is all many continue to want of a picture maker. Problems arise when something different or unexpected appears and we have no data or mechanism to deal with it. What we do not know or recognize tends to make us nervous and uneasy. This hostility manifests itself in the form of rejection, not only of the work but of any new ideas as well.

Looking at a picture is not the same as looking out of a window. It requires thinking, sorting, analyzing, and decision making. It is a developed system of thought that can be taught and learned.

Social Values

Once formal education begins, Western society greatly reduces the value it places on learning the visual language. For many people art is simply supposed to be pretty, recognizable, and comfortable. People such as these are not aware of the picture maker's function within society as someone who can perceive, interpret, and offer a wider understanding of reality. Yet these people crave the products that these explorations often bring forth. We do not make fun of the scientist in the laboratory even if we do not understand what the scientist is doing because society has sanctioned the scientist's activities. The major difference between art and science is that art offers an intuitive approach to explain reality, while science insists on an exact, objective, rational set of repeatable measurements. Science says there is only one right answer; art says there are many correct answers. The glory of contemporary art and the contribution of the artist citizen to democracy is diversity of thought.

Visual Illiteracy

The value system of our culture reflects the Aristotelian, scientific mode of thought; achievements have to be measured in terms of words and numbers. Our educational system stresses the teaching of the 26 symbols of our alphabet and the numerals 0 through 9. This criterion meets the basic requirements of industrial nations, but needs change. Education should be a process, not a product. Public education continues to ignore visual literacy and the price that has been paid is that many of us do not have the skills necessary to understand the messages that surround us in our media-saturated environment. We lack the necessary data to go through a visual decision-making process. We have become "objects" that can easily be manipulated. We simply react to situations by either accepting them or rejecting them. When we cease to question, analyze, and decide, we have been effectively removed from the process.

The picture maker is an active participant in this decision-making process. Imagemaking offers opportunities for the photographer to interact and comment on what is going on in society. The photographer's work can stimulate others to thought and action. The entire photographic process can make life deeper, richer, more varied, and more meaningful. This process is worth something, even if it cannot always be measured in tangible terms.

Seeing is a personal endeavor, and its results depend on the viewer's ability to decode the messages that are received in a symbolic form. A broad, flexible response helps the viewer to understand that our culture determines the hierarchy of subject matter. Keeping the mind open enables us to uncover all the levels and possibilities of new materials and to view the familiar anew.

The Role of the Photographer

Pursuing the role of the picture maker as the "reconnoiter," journeying out in front of the main body, making observations of unknown or hostile territory, and reporting back the findings to the group, requires a mastery of the basic ingredients of all imagemaking. Understanding essential design elements (see chapter 12, page 231) and how light affects a subject is crucial in learning how to look at and make pictures.

Nix challenges the tradition of photography as evidence by constructing images from her imagination. After learning that deer hunted near uranium extraction plants must be tested with a Geiger counter before they can be dressed out, Nix made this image. Her elaborate set is hand made using such materials as clear resin for casting the deer and expandable foam to carve the mountains.

© Lori Nix. *Uranium Extraction Plant*, 2000. 36 x 60 inches. Chromogenic color print. Courtesy of the Alona Kagan Gallery, New York, NY.

The "visual" photographer's work often reflects concrete themes and tells a narrative story by allowing us to witness events with a minimum of interference. Generally documentary and journalistic work fit into the visual's way of seeing. When working in this made it is considered unethical to alter (electronically or in the darkroom) the content of a photograph in any way that deceives the public.

© Larry Burrows. *DMZ*, 1966. 11 x 14 inches. Dye transfer print. Courtesy of Larry Burrows Collection and Laurence Miller Gallery, New York, NY.

Becoming visually literate is one step we can take in accepting responsibility for affirming our own values. Ultimately it is such small individual steps that can have widespread effects. As people become visually educated, more aware of their surroundings, and able to see the world for themselves, they can participate more fully in making decisions that affect the manner in which the business of society is conducted.

Visual or Haptic— Which Creative Type Are You?

Have you ever wondered how and why photographers make pictures in a specific style or why viewers react more strongly to certain pictures than to others? This section presents some ideas on this subject, spurs on your thinking, and allows

you to draw your own conclusions.

The Work of Victor Lowenfeld

Victor Lowenfeld did the initial work of discovering some of the ways in which we acquaint ourselves with our environment in 1939, while he was working with partially blind people. Lowenfeld found that some of these people used their limited sight to examine objects when they worked with modeling clay. He noticed that others did not use their eyes but rather used their sense of touch. These observations led Lowenfeld to conduct a study of people with normal vision. He found people with normal vision had the same tendencies: some used their sense of sight, while others used their sense of touch.

Lowenfeld determined that the first group took an intellectual, literal, realistic, quantitative approach to things. He called this group "visual." The second group functioned in an intuitive, qualitative, expressionistic-subjective mode. He labeled these people "haptic." Lowenfeld then set out to determine the major characteristics of each of these two creative types.

Visual-Realist Characteristics

Lowenfeld found that "visuals" tend to produce whole representational images. They are concerned with "correct" colors, measurements, and proportion. The visual-realist likes to become acquainted with the environment primarily through the eyes; the other senses play a secondary role.

Visual-Realist Photographers

As a generalization, visual photographers prefer to preserve the illusion of the world. The visual-realist style is an unmanipulated and objective mirror of the "actual" world. It is concrete, unobtrusive, and concerned with what is there. These photographers tend to be observers/spectators. They prefer to use the camera in its time-honored fashion as a recording device that acts as a witness to an event. They go for facts rather than for abstract form. The subject is always supreme. In their work they photograph from eye level and avoid extreme angles. Documentary work is the most obvious style. Visual-realists usually preserve spatial continuity and favor a normal focal-length lens. Their style is open, subtle, recessive, or even informal, and leans toward the unobtrusive and the familiar.

Working Methods of Visual-Realist Photographers

The visual-realists like to print full-frame, uncropped negatives. The code of the visual-realist is that of linear reality. Their pictures reflect concrete themes and often tell a story. The visual-realist uses the "straight" technique and enjoys presenting a wealth of detail.

The picture is usually created at the moment the shutter is released. Darkroom work is kept to a minimum. No unusual techniques are employed, except what is considered to be in keeping with the current tradition. Visual-realists may not do their own processing or printing because they see their primary role as witnessing the world. They use photography to match reality, enabling us to see places and things that we are not able to experience for ourselves. Often they use their work as a call for societal change.

Haptic-Expressionist Characteristics

Haptic comes from the Greek word *haptos*, which means "laying hold of." Haptics are more concerned with their bodily sensations and subjective experiences and therefore are more kinesthetic than visuals. The haptic becomes part of the picture. Emotional and subjective values can express the color and form of objects, rather than how and what they actually look like.

Haptic-Expressionist Photographers

Haptic-expressionist photographers often distort, exaggerate, and stylize the subject for emotional effect. They participate actively in the photographic process and become part of the picture. The haptics, explorers of the inner self, try to liberate

Lowenfeld's "haptic" types tend to incorporate themselves into their work. Emotional and personal values can determine the color and form of the final image, resulting in expressionistic work. Younger photographed this scene on black-and-white negative film and used the cliché-verre process to etch outlines of certain areas in the picture. Next, specific areas of the negative were hand colored with color markers and the result was placed in the enlarger. A pallet of colors was made on a sheet of acetate using color markers, watercolors, and colored acetates. This acetate overlay was contact printed, along with the projected image, onto color paper. Halfway through the developer step, the warm chemistry was dumped and cold chemistry added to shock the paper and give vibrant colors. The object was to create colors that are symbolic of the experience, expression, and imagination of a child.

© Kent R. Younger. *If You Do All Your Homework, You'll Get Good Grades in School*, 1989/90. 11 x 14 inches. Chromogenic color print.

their internal vision rather than reproduce an image of the outer world. They are concerned with the subjective and more personal type of vision. Their approach, which often incorporates private symbols that deal with psychological and spiritual issues, tends to restrict the audience appeal of the work.

Working Methods of Haptic-Expressionist Photographers

The haptics break with tradition and ritual. Their style is self-conscious and conspicuous, and the unfamiliar is of importance. The emphasis is on form. They stress the essential nature rather than the physical nature of the subject. Haptic-expressionists use the camera flamboyantly. It becomes a tool to offer comment on the subject at hand. They manipulate the image if this will heighten the response. They move and rearrange the given reality to suit their needs. Many times, they fragment real space, preferring a closer, more controlled shot.

Haptics frequently practice postvisualization; they consider the darkroom and image manipulation software as creative opportunities to carry out visual research. Experimenting with different cameras, materials, and techniques, their darkroom and/or digital station are places for contemplation, discovery, and observation.

Haptics create their own mini-universe, saturating the image with visual clues and information, attempting to direct and lead the viewer around within the frame.

Photography's Visual Revolution

Photography continues to bring about groundbreaking changes in the arts. It initially freed painters and writers from having to describe objects and happenings and allowed them to move from outer matching to inner matching. It turned art toward the inner processes of creativity in expression, which helped lead to the development of abstract art.

Now digital imaging has given photographers the same options as other artists to alter space-time realities.

The rapid changes in photo-based imagemaking make it difficult to stay current. In this avalanche of transformation it can be comforting to cling to what we know, but this attitude can block the path of creativity. Experimentation in any field is necessary to keep it alive, growing, and expanding. Photographers should be encouraged to experiment for the pursuit of new representational knowledge.

As both a photographer and viewer of photographs, it is important to know that there is no fixed way of perceiving a subject, only different ways in which a subject can be experienced. Photograph your experience of what is mentally and emotionally important, what is actively in your mind, and what you care about during the process of picture making. When looking at other photographs, especially ones that are unfamiliar or that you do not understand, attempt to envision the mental process that the photographer used to arrive at the final image. Regardless of approach, the visual photographers are concerned with the "what" and the haptics with the "how."

The Process of Rediscovery

Photography offers a rapid sequence of rediscovery. A new picture can alter the way we look at a past picture. Feel free to use whatever methods are necessary to

Determine whether you possess the more general qualities of either the visual or the haptic way of imagemaking. Choose a subject and photograph it in that manner. Next, turn that switch inside your brain and attempt to think in the opposite mode. Make a picture of the same subject that reveals these different concerns. Compare the results. What have you learned?

make your picture work, whether they are chemical or digital, previsualization, postvisualization, a preprocess idea, or an in-process discovery. In your work you do not think with your eyes, so give yourself the freedom to question the acceptance of any method of working. Make the chemical and/or digital lab a place and a time for exploration, not a situation in which you display your rote-memory abilities. Do not be too inhibited to walk on the edge. Do not let someone else set your limits. Something unexpected is not something wrong. Enjoy the process of making photographs. Don't turn it into a competition with yourself or others. Randall Jarrell, poet, novelist, and critic, remarked: "A good poet is someone who manages, in a lifetime of standing out in thunderstorms, to be struck by lightning five or six times, a dozen or two dozen times and he is great."

There are major discoveries waiting to be made in photography. Keep your definition of photography broad and wide. If you are able to let your true values and concerns come through, you will be on the course that allows your best capabilities to come forward and be seen. Do not be awed by trendy art fashions, for they are not indicators of awareness, knowledge, or truth. They are simply a way of being "with it." Talking about photography is just that, talking about photography. Words are not pictures. As a picture maker your ultimate goal should be making pictures.

The Color Key and the Composition Key

How is the decision reached about which colors to include in a picture? We each have colors we tend to favor. Notice the colors with which you choose to surround yourself. Observe the colors of your clothes or room, because they are a good indication of your color key.

The Color Key

Your color key is a built-in automatic

pilot. It will take over in situations when you do not have time to think. Everyone has one. It cannot be made; it has to be discovered. The color key reveals the character of a person. It is not a constant; it changes. At one point it is possible to see dark, moody hues; later, bright, happy, and warm colors are prominent. It is all a balancing act that mirrors your inner state of mind. When the picture is composed, the framing establishes the relationship of the colors to one another. These decisions affect how colors are perceived. The colors selected are the ones that the photographer currently identifies with in a fundamental way.

The Composition Key

The composition key is the internal sense of construction and order that is applied when putting the picture parts together. It cannot be forced. Our true

The color key reflects the present fundamental color concerns of the photographer. It is not a constant but varies depending on the concerns, mood, and state of being of the photographer. Kasten's constructivist studio assemblages formally intermix color, line, perspective, texture, and volume to deconstruct hypothetically designed spaces into distinct sectors. By "reorganizing the visual environment," Kasten alters viewer perception by disorienting our customary sense of how things are supposed to look.

© Barbara Kasten. *Metaphase 5*, 1986. 40 x 30 inches. Dye-destruction print. Courtesy of John Weber Gallery, New York, NY.

Visit galleries and museums and look through books, magazines, photo CDs, or online collections to find a body of work by a photographer that you find personally meaningful. Notice the color and composition devices that this photographer uses in the work. Now make a photograph in the manner of this photographer. Do not copy or replicate the photographer's work, but take the essential ingredients and employ them to make your own photograph. Next, compare the photograph that you have made with the work of the photographer. Last, compare both photographs with your other work. What similarities and differences in color and composition do you notice? What can you see that you did not notice before making these comparisons? Now return to the same subject and make an image your way. Compare the results with your previous photographs. Has your thinking been altered in any way? Explain.

sense of design and style is a developmental process. It is a rendition of yourself in terms of picture construction. You are it. It is incorporated into the work and is given back in the final image. Some common compositional keys to begin looking for are the triangle, circle, figure eight, and spiral, along with the H, S, V, and W forms.

Recognizing the Keys

Recognizing these keys is a way to make yourself more aware and a better image-maker. The good photographer can learn to make pictures even in less than ideal conditions. The ability to see that there is more than one side to any situation helps make this happen. For example, you could say it is raining and not go out to

The composition key is an internal sense of design the photographer instinctively uses to structure an image. It reveals the photographer's sense of visual order and style. This sense is not fixed, however, but represents an ongoing visual developmental process. Tress uses his sense of design "to create an image that stimulates viewers' imaginations by transforming ordinary objects into a surreal fantasy world."

© Arthur Tress. *Act II: The Voyage … Where They Came Upon Fantastic Creatures and Strange Botanical Species*, from the *Teapot Opera* series, 1980. 10 x 10 inches. Dye-destruction print.

make a picture, or you could see that it is raining and use this as an opportunity to make the diffused, shadowless picture that has been in the back of your mind. Color and composition keys are meant to offer a guide for understanding how we visually think. They are not hard-and-fast rules for making pictures. They should also show that there is more than one way to see things. When you learn how others view the world, it is then possible to see more for yourself.

Can you identify your personal color and composition keys? Do not expect to find them in every piece. They can be hidden. Doodles can often provide clues to your composition key. If you are having trouble seeing these phenomena, get together with another photographer and see if you can identify each other's keys.

Figure–Ground Relationships

What is Figure–Ground?

Figure-ground is the relationship between the subject and the background. It also refers to the positive–negative space relationship within your picture. "Figure," in this case, is the meaningful content of your composition. "Ground" describes the background of the picture.

Figure 11.1 is a classic example of the figure–ground phenomenon. What do you see first? Can you discern a dif-

ferent figure–ground relationship? What do you think most people see first? Why? What does this tell you about the role of contrast?

Why is Figure–Ground Important?
When the figure and the ground are similar, perception is difficult. The viewer might have difficulty determining what is important to see in the picture. This often occurs when the photographer attempts to show too much. The viewer's eyes wander all over, without coming to a point of attention. The composition lacks a climax, so the viewer loses interest and leaves the image. If you have to explain what you were trying to reveal, there is a strong chance that your figure–ground relationship is weak.

Figure-Ground Strategies

When you observe a scene, determine exactly what interests you. Visualize how your content (figure) and background (ground) are going to appear in your final photograph. Put together a composition that will let the viewer see the visual relationships that attracted you to the scene. Try using different focal-length lenses and angles to alter the areas of focus. Be selective about what is included in the picture. Find ways to

11.1 An example of the figure–ground relationship phenomenon. What do you see first? How can this type of ambiguity affect how the viewer might read and respond to an image? What role do contrast and color play in how you see this image?

both isolate and connect the key visual elements of the composition. Try using a higher shutter speed and larger lens aperture to lessen the depth of field. Experiment with focus and see what happens when spacial visual clues are reduced. Do not attempt to show "everything." Often showing less can tell the audience more about the subject, because they do not have to sort through visual chaos. Try limiting the number of colors in a photograph. A color photograph does not have to contain every color in the universe. Keep it simple and to the point. Wright Morris, commenting about "the problem" with color photography, said:

> *By including almost everything within our spectrum, the color photograph forces upon it the ultimate banality of*

Hagen took one photograph for each of 24 consecutive rides on the Staten Island Ferry in a single day. His images record the duration of a journey and give a collective, stylized interpretation of the cycle of light while reminding us that we often only remember indistinct details. "Each photograph creates an image that contains all time and place experienced during the travel experience using the unique ability of the photographic process to collect light."

© Stefan Hagen. *Crossing the Upper New York Bay—One Day, 8.46 a.m.–9.03 a.m. Manhattan-Staten Island*, 2001. 22 x 28 inches. Chromogenic color print.

The distinct visual difference between the monochromatic trees in the foreground and background, and the brightly colored toys evenly dispersed in the middle ground, is an example of Lavelle's use of figure ground. In this case, the colorful activity in the middle ground represents the "figure" and the surrounding trees are the "ground."

© Frank Lavelle. *Annandale, Virginia*, 2000. 16 x 20 inches. Chromogenic color print.

Williams started this project when her toddler son began his swimming lessons. Williams recalls: "In this small overheated room was a dilapidated pool, made luminous by the natural light which flooded through large south windows. The color of the water seemed to change by the minute." To accomplish a sense of discomfort and distortion, sensations that can accompany learning to swim, Williams used a panorama camera that she "twisted while releasing the shutter." The blurred portions of the image are supposed to reproduce the feeling of actually being in the pool, the natural distortive qualities of water, and the sensation that something is slightly off. "I printed on low-contrast paper to adequately and delicately describe the play of light on the water and the many hues of blue, often so integral to the composition of the photograph."

© Jennette Williams. *Emmet Floating*, from *Off the Deep End* series, 1992. 10 ½ x 24 inches. Chromogenic color print.

'appearances.' That is why we tire of them so quickly. The first effect is dazzling; the total effect is wearying. … Where everything seems to be of interest, the burden of the photographer is greater, not less. The color photograph not merely says, but often shouts, that everything is of interest. And it is not.[1]

Use your abilities to meet the challenge and fulfill the promise that color provides the visual artist.

Natural Light

Light is a paradox, being both permanent and impermanent. Light is ambiguous, for it possesses the qualities of both particles and waves. Light's multidimensionalism shows us that as soon as we think we know the truth about any subject, the light will change and reveal a previously hidden attribute. Light's physical presence demonstrates that everything is in flux and that nothing is as it appears. Light's changeability reveals the complex multilayered matrix of life, signifying the many ways a situation may be viewed and understood.

Good Light

The definition of "good light" rests solely on the intent of a photographer. Have you ever encountered a scene that you knew should make a good photograph, yet the results were disappointing? There is a strong likelyhood that it was photographed at a time of day during which the light did not reveal the fundamental aspects of the subject that were important and attracted you to the scene in the first place. Try photographing the scene again at a different time of day.

What the Camera Does

Your ability to function as a creative photographer depends on your knowledge of how to make your equipment work for you. Any camera is merely a recording device, and it will not reproduce a scene or an experience without your guidance at every stage of the process. The camera can isolate a scene; it can reduce it to two dimensions. It freezes a slice of time and sets it into a frame.

It does not record the sequence of events that led up to the moment that the shutter clicked or your private emotional response to what was happening. These are items you must learn to incorporate into your pictures if you expect to make photographs instead of snapshots. The camera does not discriminate in what it sees and records, but you can and must make such distinctions to create successful images.

The Time of Day/Types of Light

Most photographers are familiar with the old Kodak adage, "Take pictures after ten in the morning and before two in the afternoon." This rule had nothing to do with aesthetics. The purpose of this command was to encourage amateur photographers to take pictures when the light was generally the brightest because early roll film was not very sensitive to light. By breaking this canon you can come up with some astonishing results. The day follows a predictable cycle of light that will influence your images.

Light is the key ingredient shared by every photograph. Before anything else, every photograph is about light. Light determines the look of every photograph you make. If the light does not reveal the perceived nature of the subject, the picture will not communicate your ideas to the viewer. Begin to recognize what light artist James Turrell calls the "thingness" of light, the characteristics and qualities that light possesses throughout the day, and learn to incorporate them into your composition for a complete visual statement.

Before the sun rises above the horizon, our world is basically black and white with colors that tend to be cool, muted, and subdued. This sunrise image was taken from a boat. The photographer used a 200-mm lens with a skylight filter. Dicker comments: "I took a thru-the-lens reading and opened up about one f-stop because experience has taught me the image was lighter than an 18 percent gray card." Recognizing the qualities of light that best reveal the subject, and then correctly interpreting it through exposure, helps to ensure a complete visual statement.

© Jean-Jacques Dicker. *Boy on Kasai River, Zaire,* 1977. 24 x 36 cm. Chromogenic color transparency.

By contrasting the colorful water line with the warm, monochromatic environment of early morning fog, Lavelle gets a compositionally simple and visually dramatic image.

© Frank Lavelle. *Rockland, Maine,* 2001. 8 x 22 inches. Chromogenic color print.

Slankard chose to shoot at midday in order to bring out the contrast and third dimensionality of his subject. His use of the tilt and swing features on a monorail 4 x 5 camera create the distortion and selective focus that give the impression of the landscape as miniaturized, "conveying the idea of a possessable suburban ideal."

© Mark Slankard. *Curb Appeal: cul de sac*, 2002. 20 x 24 inches. Chromogenic color print.

The Cycle of Light and Its Basic Characteristics

Before Sunrise

In the earliest hours of the day, our world is essentially black and white. The light exhibits a cool, almost shadowless quality, and colors are muted. Up to the moment of sunrise, colors remain flat and opalescent. The intensity of the colors grows as the sun rises. Artificial lights can appear as accents and create contrast.

Morning

As soon as the sun is up, the light changes dramatically. Since the sun is low and must penetrate a great amount of the atmosphere, the light that gets through is much warmer in color than it will be later in the day. The shadows can look blue because they lack high brilliant sunlight, because of the great amount of blue from the overhead sky, and because of simultaneous contrast. As the sun rises, the color of light becomes warmer (red-orange). By midmorning the light begins to lose its warm color and starts to appear clear and white.

Midday

The higher the sun climbs in the sky, the greater the contrast between colors. At noon the light is white. Colors stand out strongly, each in its own hue. The shadows are black and deep. Contrast is at its peak. Subjects can appear to look like three-dimensional cutouts. At noon the light may be considered to be harsh, stark, or crisp.

Tischler photographs his subjects in the afternoon, when contrast is at its peak. He shoots through window screens, netting, and scrims, creating grid patterns that become the sharpest focal element of each image. The figures in his photographs are faceless characters that resemble blurred video stills. "The effect of the grids and barriers is such that images are divided, pixelated, and filtered. Subjects and figures are broken apart and reconstructed so that they are both integrated into their environments and isolated within them."

© Matthew Tischler. *Untitled #3*, 2002. 20 x 30 inches. Chromogenic color print.

Afternoon

As the sun drops to the horizon, the light begins to warm up again. It is a gradual process and should be observed carefully. On clear evenings objects can take on an unearthly glow. Look for an increase in red. The shadows lengthen and become more blue. Surfaces are strongly textured. An increasing amount of detail is revealed as the sun lowers.

Twilight/Evening

After sunset there is still a great amount of light in the sky. Notice the tremendous range of light intensity between the eastern and western skies. Often the sunset colors are reflected from the clouds. Just as at dawn, the light is very soft, and contrast and shadow are at a minimum. After sunset and throughout twilight, notice the warm colors in the landscape. This phenomenon, known as "purple light," arises from light from the blue end of the spectrum falling vertically on you from the overhead sky. Observe the glowing pink and violet colors as they gradually disappear and the Earth becomes a pattern of blacks and grays.

At twilight it is possible to observe the Earth's shadow (the dark gray-blue band across the eastern horizon just after sunset). It is only visible until it rises to about six degrees high; after that, its upper boundary quickly fades. The Earth's shadow is immediately visible after sunset because our eastward view is directly along the boundary between the illuminated and nonilluminated portions of the atmosphere. As time passes, we view this boundary with an ever-steepening angle and it shortly disappears. When observing the Earth's shadow, notice the red-to-orange-to-yellow development of color just about at its upper edge, produced as the sun's rays pass overhead and reflect directly back down to Earth. This phenomenon, called

Carr used a long exposure and flashlights with colored gels to create a sense of memory and dreams in this outdoor nighttime scene.

© Christine Carr. *Untitled*, 2002. 19 x 19 inches. Chromogenic color print.

Careful consideration of the lighting allowed the subtle details of the cemetery to show through and create an interesting visual contrast with the imposing presence of the gas pumps. This image was made after sunset, but before total darkness. At twilight, the quality of the light is very soft, and contrast and shadows are at a minimum. These subtle effects can work well with the bright qualities of artificial lights to create contrast and enhance the mood of an image.

© Alec Soth. *Cemetery, Fountain City, WI*, from *Sleeping Along the Mississippi*, 2002. 16 x 20 inches. Chromogenic color print.

This dynamic image was created by making a composite of four negatives, one of the sky and three separate exposures of the same landscape composition under different lighting situations. "I take the most compelling passages of changing light throughout an extended duration of time and weave them into a single composition," says Caponigro. "The result is a dramatic lighting effect never before seen at one time. Yet, a similar sequence of experience has been witnessed countless times."

© John Paul Caponigro. *Oriens*, 1999. Dimensions vary. Dye-destruction print.

the area of sky you want to observe and use the mirror to inspect that region. By holding the mirrored image against a neutral background of your choice, you can compare the colors of different portions of the sky. The backgrounds can also be of other colors or even different shapes and textures, and these combinations can be photographed to alter our traditional way of thinking about the sky.

For more information read M. MINNAERT, *The Nature of Light and Color in the Open Air*, available from Dover Publications (store.doverpublications.com).

The Seasons

The position of the sun varies depending on the time of year. This has a great impact on both the quality and the quantity of the light. Learn to recognize these characteristics and look for ways to go with and against the flow of the season to obtain the best possible photograph.

"counter-twilight," disappears at about the same time as the Earth's shadow.

Night

The world after the sun has set is seen by artificial light and reflected light from the moon. The light is generally harsh, and contrast is extreme. Photographing under these conditions usually requires a tripod, a brace, or a very steady hand. Since an increase in exposure can lead to reciprocity failure and possible color shift, use filters if correction is desired. Combinations of

artificial light and long exposure can create a surreal atmosphere.

Studying the Sky

After looking at a bright portion of the sky, close your eyes for a few moments and allow them to recover from the glare. The color-sensitive area of our vision is easily saturated by intense light and, without short rest periods, our eyes are unable to distinguish subtle color differences. An intriguing way to study specific portions of sky is to use a small mirror held at arm's length. Face away from

Opperman exposed for the light falling on the trees, giving the surrounding clouds and water darker tonal values. The transition between fall and winter is emphasized by the dramatic contrast between the cool blue shadows and the bright yellow and orange highlights.

© Cheryl Opperman. *Seasons Change*, 1996. 20 x 24 inches. Chromogenic color print. Courtesy of Opperman Photographics, Inc., Littleton, CO.

Winter means a diminished number of daylight hours. Bare trees, pale skies, fog, ice, rain, sleet, and snow all produce the type of light that creates muted and subtle colors. Spring brings on an increase in the amount of daylight and the introduction of more colors. Summer light offers the world at its peak of color. Harsh summer light can offer a host of contrast and exposure problems for the photographer to deal with. Fall is a period of transition that provides tremendous opportunities to show the changes that take place in color.

The Weather and Color Materials

There is no such thing as bad weather for making photographs. Fog gives pearly, opalescent, muted tones. Storms can add drama and mystery. Rain mutes some colors and enriches others while creating glossy surfaces with brilliant reflections. Dust softens and diffuses color and line. Bad weather conditions often provide an excellent opportunity to create pictures full of atmosphere and interest. With a few precautions to yourself and your equipment, you need not be just a fair-weather photographer. If the metering looks like it is going to be tough, bring along and use a gray card as a guide. Before going out into any unusual weather conditions be certain to check how many frames you have remaining. If there are only a few left, reload while everything is still dry and familiar.

When photographing under foggy conditions the diffused light can tend to have a cool cast (blue). To bring out warmer tones, shoot in the late afternoon or in the early morning as Mosch did with this image shot at sunrise.

© Steven P. Mosch. *Pointorama: Trees and Fog, Spring Island, SC,* 2002. 3 ½ x 40 inches. Inkjet print.

Fog and Mist

Fog and mist diffuse the light and tend to provide monochromatic compositions. The light can tend toward the cool side (blue). If this is not acceptable, use an 81A warming filter, or photograph in the early morning or late afternoon, when there is the chance to catch some warm-colored light. If the sun is going in and out of the clouds, wait for a moment when a shaft of light breaks through the clouds. This can create drama and break up the two-dimensional flatness that these cloudy scenes often produce.

Because the light is scattered, both colors and contrasts are made softer and more subtle. If you want a sense of depth in the mist, try not to fill your frame completely with it. Attempt to offset it with a dark area. To capture mist, expose for the highlights or use an incident light meter. Bracketing is crucial.

In fog, take a reading from your hand in light similar to that which is on your subject. Then overexpose by 1/2 to one f-stop, depending on how intense the fog happens to be. Bracket your exposures.

Rain

Rain tends to mute and soften color and contrast, while bringing reflections into play. Include a warm accent if contrast or depth is desired. The shutter speed is important in the rain. The faster the speed, the more distinct the raindrops will appear. At speeds below 1/60 of a second, the drops blur. Long exposures will seem to make them disappear. Experiment with different shutter speeds to see what you can achieve. Keep your

In his book *On Fire (2003)*, Schwarm takes advantage of the dramatic lighting effects and adverse environmental conditions such as the controlled fires that occur every spring in the Flint Hills in east-central Kansas. "Fire is an essential part of the prairie ecosystem. Without fire, this prairie would have been forested. Over time, what started as a natural phenomenon became an annual event controlled by man."

© Larry Schwarm. *Earth, Fire, and Water, Z-Bar Ranch, Chase County, Kansas,* 1994. 17 x 17 inches. Chromogenic color print. Courtesy of Morgan Gallery, Kansas City, MO.

camera in a plastic bag with a hole for the lens. Use a UV filter to keep the front of the lens dry. Keep the camera inside your jacket when it is not being used.

When working in constantly wet situations, get a waterproof bag to hold your equipment. Inexpensive plastic bag cases are available at camping stores. These allow you to photograph in wet conditions without worrying about ruining the camera. Carry a bandanna to wipe off any excess moisture.

Dust

Dust can be a bitingly painful experience to photographers and their equipment. Use a UV filter, plastic bag, and lens hood to protect the camera. Use the same shutter speed guide as you would use for snow to help determine how the dust will appear. Dust in the sky can produce astonishing atmospheric effects. If turbulence is to be shown, expose for the highlights. This causes the shadows to go dark and the clouds to stand out from the sky. A polarizing filter may be used to darken the sky and increase color saturation. If detail is needed in the foreground, meter one-third sky and two-thirds ground with the camera meter and bracket one f-stop in either direction.

Heat and Fire

Heat and/or fire is often accompanied by glare, haze, high contrast, and reflection. These factors can reduce clarity and color saturation, but if handled properly they can make colors appear to stand out. In extremely bright situations, a neutral density filter may be needed to cut down the amount of light that is striking the film.

Do not point the camera directly into the sun except for brief periods of time. The lens can act as a magnifying glass and ruin the shutter and light meter. Store the camera and film in a cool place. Heat and humidity can ruin the

color balance of the film before it is even processed. Refrigerate the film whenever possible both before and after exposure. Let the film reach room temperature before shooting to avoid condensation and color shift. Avoid carrying unnecessary equipment if you will be doing a good deal of walking in the heat. Do not forget a hat and sunscreen.

Snow

Snow reflects any predominant color. Blue casts and shadows are the most common in daylight situations. Use a UV filter to help neutralize this effect. If this proves insufficient, try a yellow 81A,

In order to capture the subtle color, tones, and sense of space present during a snowstorm, Allison slightly overexposed the film to ensure sufficient detail in the negative.

© David R. Allison. *New York, NY*, 1999. 16 x 19 ¾ inches. Chromogenic color print. Courtesy of the Kathleen Ewing Gallery, Washington, DC.

81B, 81C, or even an 81 filter. This technique also works well in higher elevations, where the color temperature of the light is higher (bluer).

Brightly lit snow scenes tend to fool the meter because there is so much reflected light. The meter thinks there is more light than there actually is and tells you to close the lens down too far, producing underexposed negatives. Avoid this by taking an incident light reading and then overexpose by 1/2 to one f-stop to get shadow detail. If this is not possible, use the palm of your hand. Fill the metering area with it, being careful not to get your shadow in it. Next open the lens up one f-stop from the indicated reading. To bring out the rich texture of snow, photograph when the sun is low on the horizon. Bracket when in doubt and learn which exposure works the best.

Snow Effects

Slow shutter speeds can make snow appear as streaks. Fast speeds arrest the action of the flakes. Flash can also be employed. For falling snow, fire the flash from the center of the camera. The snow will reflect the light back, producing flare and/or spots. The snowflakes can be eliminated by using a synchronization cord and holding the flash at arm's length off to one side of the camera. This stops the snow and provides a scene comparable to the ones produced inside one of those plastic bubbles that are shaken to make the snow fall. Try setting the camera on a tripod, use a lens opening of f/8 or smaller plus a shutter speed of 1/8 of a second or longer, and fire the flash during the exposure. This stops the action of some of the falling snow while letting the rest of it appear blurred. Bracket the exposures until enough experience is obtained to determine what will deliver the type of results you are after.

Battery Care in Cold Conditions

Check the batteries for all your camera gear before going out into cold conditions and carry spares. At temperatures of 20°F (-6.7°C) or less, there is a danger that all battery-powered equipment will become sluggish. Shutters are affected first, with shutter speeds slowing and producing exposure errors. For instance, if a battery-powered shutter is off by 1/1,000 of a second, and if you are attempting to stop the action of a skier speeding downhill at 1/1,000 of a second, then the exposure would be off by one f-stop. This would not present a serious problem unless you were shooting above 1/125 of a second. In cold conditions, make use of the middle and slow ranges of shutter speeds whenever possible to avoid this difficulty.

Lithium batteries have better cold weather performance, having an operating range of -40°C to +65°C. Carry a warm, spare set when working in cold weather since all batteries tend to drain rapidly in low temperatures. Keep spare batteries warm by putting them next to your body in an interior pocket. If the batteries appear to have expired, do not dispose of them until they are warmed up and tested again.

Cold Weather Lubrication

Mechanical shutters also slow down in the cold because the viscosity of the lubricants thickens as the temperature drops. A camera can be relubricated with special cold weather lubricants if you are doing a great deal of work in extremely cold conditions. These lubricants must be replaced when the camera is used again in normal conditions. Most cameras perform well in cold weather as long as they are not kept out in the elements longer than necessary.

Cold Weather Protection
Simplify camera operations as much as possible. Remove any unneeded accessories that cannot be operated with gloves, or add accessories that permit easier operation. If possible, preload cameras or film magazines before going outside. Avoid using power accessories or an LED screen to conserve power. Do not take a camera that has condensation on it out into the cold until the conden-

sation has evaporated because it may freeze. The camera will cease operating, and the inner components will be ruined. Once outside, avoid touching unpainted metal surfaces with ungloved hands, face, or lips because your skin will stick to the metal. Wear thin gloves so that your skin does not come in contact with the cold metal and you can operate the camera with ease. Metal parts can be taped to prevent this from happening. Do not breathe on the lens outside to clean it because your breath might freeze on it.

When bringing in a camera from the cold, let it warm up before using it so condensation does not damage its working gear. Condensation can be avoided by placing the camera in an airtight plastic bag and squeezing out the air. This prevents the camera from being exposed to the warmer temperature. Condensation forms on the outside of the bag instead of on the lens and camera body. After the equipment has reached room temperature, remove it from the bag.

Static

Because static can occur anytime it is cold and/or dry, it can be the photographer's bane. Rapidly winding or rewinding the film can produce a static charge inside the camera. You will not know this has happened until the film is processed and discover a lightning storm of static across the pictures. Take it easy and go slowly. Do not rewind the film as fast as possible. Do not use the motor drive or auto rewind if possible in these conditions. This helps to prevent those indiscriminate lightning flashes from plaguing you. Keep film warm as long as possible in cold weather since it can become brittle at very low temperatures.

Endnote

[1] Wright Morris. *Time Pieces: Photographs, Writing, and Memory.* New York: Aperture Foundation, 1989, 145.

Chapter Twelve

VISUAL LANGUAGE OF
COLOR DESIGN

Morimura's gender- and culture-bending self-portraits satirically decontextualize Western art icons by inserting an Eastern identity. In the tradition of Kabuki theater in which men play female roles, Morimura masquerades in costumes, wigs, and makeup to challenge stereotypes and unequal power relations by posing as both the black servant and the reclining courtesan in Manet's *Olympia* (1863), thereby interrupting the conventional masculine gaze. In an age of mass-produced images, Morimura's photographs also question the "authenticity" of a work of art.

© Yasumasa Morimura. *Portrait (Futago)*, 1988. 82 ¾ x 118 inches. Chromogenic color prints. Courtesy of Luhring Augustine, New York, NY.

Seeing is Thinking

Seeing is thinking. Thinking involves putting together random pieces of our private experience into an orderly manner. The act of seeing becomes an act of construction, making sense out of the world.

We like what is familiar to us and tend to back away from the unfamiliar. Becoming more visually literate makes us more flexible. Some people think photography is only for recording and categorizing objects. For them the photograph is like a window through which a scene is viewed or a mirror that reflects a material reality. A photograph is nothing more than two-dimensional representation on a surface. It is possible that it shows us something recognizable, but maybe it only shows us lines, shapes, and colors.

> *A work of art encountered as a work of art is an experience, not a statement or an answer to a question. … Art is not about something; it is something. A work of art is a thing in the world, not just a text or commentary on the world. A work of art makes us see or comprehend something singular.*[1]

What is a Good Photograph?

How do you make a good photograph? This is the question everyone wants answered, but it is unanswerable. This book offers a number of ideas that may be of help, but they might get in the way. It is a good question, even if we do not have "the" answer. Keep looking. The search will probably reveal there are

---

Faller clearly defines the scope of her project. "My work is about the aesthetics of everyday life—as opposed to the conventions of the fine arts. Of particular interest are the artifacts of public or private displays and decorations. I want my pictures to function as both image and document. This demands color because it provides so much information about the subject matter."

© Marion Faller. *Halloween Skeletons, Marcellus, NY*, 1989. 16 x 20 inches. Chromogenic color print.

Recipe for Coffee   3/12

L. Prsy '94

Paresky states: "I am a graphic designer with a camera. Letters speak to me. I have photographed thousands of letters that I have contact printed into verbal messages that also document signs and symbols of the American landscape." The text in Paresky's piece is a quote from Charles Maurice de Talleyrand-Perigord (1754–1838) that reads: "Black as the devil, Hot as hell, Pure as an angel, Sweet as love."

© Laura Paresky. *Recipe for Coffee*, 1994. 24 x 24 inches. Dye-destruction print. Courtesy of the Robert Klein Gallery, Boston, MA

many answers to this question. Contemplate what Paul Strand said: "No matter what lens you use, no matter what speed the film, no matter how you develop it, no matter how you print it, you cannot say more than you see."[2]

Discovering What You Have to Say

Good intentions do not make good photographs. The first and most important step in determining what makes a good photograph is to empty our minds of all images that have bombarded us on television and in magazines, newspapers, movies, DVDs, or computers. All these images belong to someone else. Throw them away. Next, toss out the idea that

we know what a good photograph is. We know what is customary: that a good photograph is supposed to be centered and focused; that the subject is clearly identifiable and right side up; that it is 8 x 10 inches and has color (unless it is "old," then it is black and white); that the people are looking into the camera and smiling; that it was taken at eye level; and that it isn't too cluttered or too sparse. It is just right. And we have seen it a million times before. It is known, safe, and totally boring. Throw all these preconceived ideas into the dumpster and start fresh by defining what it is you want to communicate. Most artists make their best work when they have something to prove.

Making a Photograph That Communicates

A photograph is a picture that can communicate your experience to another. A photograph has its own history—past, present, and future—and does not require any outside support; it can stand alone, as a statement. A photograph should be able to communicate something in a way that would be impossible to do in another medium.

Photography is a matter of order and harmony. The photographer battles the physical laws of universal entropy by attempting to control disorder within the photograph. The arrangement of objects within the pictorial space determines the success of the photograph. Order is good composition, which, as Edward Weston said, "is the strongest way of seeing" the subject. The basis of composition is design.

Design includes all the visual elements that make up a composition. Visual design is the organization of materials and forms in a certain way to fulfill a specific purpose. Design begins with the organization of parts into a coherent whole. A good photograph is an extension of the photographer and creates a response in the viewer. A good photograph possesses the ability to sustain a viewer's attention over an extended period of time. If the intentions are communicated successfully, the design of the photograph must be considered effective.

Putting It All Together

Anything touched by light can be photographed. Since it appears so easy when starting out in photography, many of us try to say too much in a picture. We often overcrowd the confines of the visual space with too much information. This can create a visual chaos in which the idea and motivation behind the pictures become lost. Do not assume that anything that happens to you is going to be interesting to someone else. Learn to be selective.

Working Subtractively

When making photographs start by working simply and subtractively. A painter begins with nothing, and through the process of addition the picture comes into being. A photographer, on the other hand, begins with everything. The photographic process is one of subtraction. The critical power of the photographer is in the choosing. When using a camera, the photographer must decide what to leave out of the picture. Ray Metzker said: "The camera is nothing but a vacuum cleaner picking up everything

Digital imaging offers new opportunities for employing the photographer's special license to make pictures happen. Here we see a balancing act of the photographer creating a composition "partly in life and partly by digitally manipulating several transparencies. Various images from multiple sources were scanned and pieced together to get the gestures and expression the way I wanted. This process complements the internal nature of my work, which is more about self-perception in the context of family and cultural history than objective documentation of the present."

© Jessica Todd Harper. *G-Jean with Becky and Kristin*, 2003. 32 x 40 inches. Inkjet print.

within range. There has to be a higher degree of selectivity."

President John F. Kennedy stated: "To govern is to choose." So too in the act of photography, selectivity is everything. Use subtractive composing by going directly for what you want to include in the picture and subtracting all that is not required. This subtractive method of putting the picture together can help you learn the basic visual vocabulary that produces the image. A good photographer is like a magician who knows how to make all the unwanted objects on stage disappear, leaving only the necessary items to create a striking image. For this reason it is necessary for the photographer to have a point of departure.

Point of Departure

If you pick up a camera and go out to do something deliberate and specific, the

possibility of encountering the significant and the useful is greater than if you stand on the corner hoping and waiting for something to occur. Do not be like the photographer described by George Bernard Shaw who, like a codfish, lays a million eggs in the hope that one might hatch. Have a specific direction, but remain flexible and open to the unexpected. A work that continues to say something visually over a long time has what is called staying power. It usually takes years to cultivate this ability. It has almost nothing to do with the technical means of producing a photograph, for the truth is found in how we feel about something. When this feeling is found in the picture, something of significance is expressed. The image possesses meaning. For much of what we see, there are no words. As Albert Camus said: "If we understood the enigmas of life, there would be no need for art."

The Photographer's Special License

When you go out with a camera dangling around your neck, society gives you a special license. Learn to use it. If you went to a football game and started crawling around on the ground like a snake, people would at least find you strange. They may even become alarmed. You could be arrested and hauled off in a straight jacket, labeled as an unfit member of the group.

Now imagine the same scene, only this time you have a camera around your neck. People's responses are different when they see the camera. In this case, they identify you by the camera and dismiss your behavior by saying, "Oh, it's that photographer," or "Look at that photographer trying to 'get' a picture." They may even come over and offer suggestions or give technical advice so that your pictures "come out." Since photography is omnipresent in our society, everyone thinks they are photographers. Use this mindset to your advantage. It is not an excuse for irresponsible behavior or to harass people as the paparazzi do. Learning to strike up a conversation with people is an excellent way to discover what they are doing and why they are doing it. Most people enjoy talking about themselves and can be very accommodating if you learn how to approach them. You can get people to be in your picture, to get out of your picture, to hold equipment, or to just leave you alone. It all depends on the attitude that you project.

Frischkorn used vivid color film and a grid on the ground glass of her 4- x 5-inch view camera, as well as a ruler and a level, to capture the straight stripes on the side of recreational vehicles. Rooted in the tradition of American travel photography, Frischkorn makes a new type of landscape that questions "our relationship to the environment and our drive to conquer wilderness. These audacious panoramic color fields symbolize speed and progress, but also serve as reminders that visiting nature with all the comforts of home is a synthetic experience."

© Shauna Frischkorn. *Travel Master*, from *RV* series, 2001. 14 x 40 inches. Chromogenic color print.

The Language of Vision

The language and tools of vision make use of light, color, shape, texture, line, pattern, similarity, contrast, and movement. Through these formal visual elements, it is possible to make photographs that alter and enlarge our ideas of what is worth looking at and what we have the right to observe and make pictures of. Photography can transform any object and make it part of our experience by changing it into something that can fit into your hand or onto your computer screen to be studied later at your convenience. Important photographers provide the visual tools that express the ideas and stories of their time. The great photographers push out the boundaries of the language and invent new tools for the rest of us to use. In 1947, just before Parkinson's disease cut short his photographic career, Edward Weston had this to say concerning his own experiments in color: "The prejudice many photographers have against color photography comes from not thinking of color as form."

In the *Philebus of Plato*, Socrates comments:

I will try to speak of the beauty of

shapes, and I do not mean, as most people would suppose, the shapes of living figures, or their imitations in painting, but I mean straight lines and curves and the shapes made from them, by the lathe, ruler or square. They are not beautiful for any particular reason or purpose, as other things are, but are eternally, and by their very nature, beautiful, and give a pleasure of their own quite free from the itch of desire: and in this way colors can give similar pleasure.

These eternally beautiful geometric forms of which Plato speaks can be measured or presented in analytical form. They have proved useful to science and engineering, and since these fields have dominated the intellectual landscape for over the past 150 years, they have also had a tremendous influence on imagemaking.

The following categories are offered to provide the basic vocabulary that is needed to communicate in the photographic language.

Line

Line carves out areas of space on either side of it. Any line, except one that is perfectly straight, creates a shape. Closing a line creates a shape. Lines can

Shape is formed by a closed line. Shape is an area having a specific character defined by color value, contrast, outline, or texture with the surrounding area. Epstein relies on shape to create a flowing composition that keeps bringing the viewer back to the beautiful young woman.

© Mitch Epstein. *Carnival Queen*, n/d. 20 x 24 inches. Chromogenic color print.

statements for the purpose of symbolizing ideas. Nature contains mass (three-dimensional form), which is portrayed in photography by the use of line as contour (a line that creates a boundary and separates an area of space from its background).

Shape

Shape is created by a closed line—an area having a specific character defined by an outline, contrast, color value, or texture with the surrounding area. There are four basic shapes:

● **Geometric shapes** include the square, triangle, rectangle, and circle.
● **Natural shapes** imitate things in the natural world: human, animal, and plant.
● **Abstract shapes** are natural shapes that have been altered in a certain way so that they are reduced to their essence. The source of the shape is recognizable, but it has been transformed into something different. This is usually done by simplification, the omission of all nonessential elements.
● **Nonobjective shapes** do not relate to anything in the natural world. Usually, we cannot put specific names on them. They are for the eyes, not the intellect. They represent the subjective, not the rational, part of our being.

Space

Space is an area for you to manipulate in order to create form. There are three kinds of space:

● **Actual space** is the two-dimensional area enclosed by the borders of the camera's viewfinder and the surface on which the image later appears. Three-dimensional spaces are inside and around or within an object.
● **Pictorial space** is the illusionary sense of depth that we see in two-dimensional work such as photography. It can vary from appearing perfectly flat to receding into infinity.
● **Virtual space** exists within the confines of a computer screen or monitor. It may or may not exist in any concrete form.

be majestic, flowing, or undulating. Lines can be used as a symbolic or an abstract concept. They can show you contour, form, pattern, texture, directional movement, and emphasis.

Line, per se, does not exist in nature. It is a human creation, an abstraction invented for the simplification of visual

Texture

Generally, smooth textures tend to create cool sensations and rough textures make for warm sensations. Texture and pattern are intertwined. A pattern on a piece of cloth gives us a visual sense of texture, letting us feel the differences in the surface with our eyes, even though it does not exist to the touch. Texture offers changing sensations either by hand or by eye.

Artists have purposefully introduced three-dimensional texture into media that was once considered to be exclusively two-dimensional. In the twentieth century, the Cubists integrated other materials than paint, such as newspapers and sand, into their paintings. This technique is now known as collage, from the French word *coller*, which means "to glue." Since then other artists have incorporated three-dimensional objects into their work. These works are known as constructions. They are the textural element taken to the limit. The two kinds of texture that we need to be familiar with are tactile texture and light texture.

Tactile is a term that refers to actual changes in a surface that can be felt. They can be rough, smooth, hard, soft, wet, or dry. They possess three-dimensional characteristics.

Variations in light and dark produce visual texture, which is two-dimensional. This illusion is produced by the

Conventional perspective (above) tells us that objects always get small as they recede in distance. Pfahl makes use of pictorial space to set up an illusion that does not agree with our assumptions of reality.

© John Pfahl. *Six Oranges*, 1975. Dimensions vary. Chromogenic color print.

Visual texture (below) plays a major compositional role in Hayashi's panoramic collage that speaks of the death of many industries in the Rust Belt section of America. She states: "I use color machine prints, 3 ½ x 5 inches, to make the composite image. The 35-mm camera is placed on a tripod and pivots around 360 degrees to make the middle row. I angle my camera upward and then pivot around the tripod and then angle the camera downward and pivot around the tripod as I shoot."

© Masumi Hayashi. *Steel Mill, Clay Road*, 1988. 46 x 77 inches. Chromogenic color prints.

Fournier discusses that she "seeks out repetitive visual patterns, for I am drawn to the chaotic or minimal patterns, including textural or minimal music, that contain repetitive loops of sound. This photograph, made while I was standing on a mountaintop near Mt. Saint Helens, may lack the traditional sense of a central focus, but it has a different purpose—to create a meditative state for a viewer."

© Nicole Fournier. *Mountain of Trees*, 2003. 20 x 24 inches. Chromogenic color print.

eye. The relationship of color placement within the composition and the use of depth of field can also determine the sense of visual texture.

Pattern

Pattern is the unifying quality of an object. It is an interplay between shape, color, and space that forms a recognizable, repetitive, and/or identifiable unit. Pattern can unify the composition, establish a balance among diverse elements, or create a sense of rhythm and movement.

The major difference between texture and pattern is degree. Do not get them confused. Pattern can possess visual texture, but not all texture contains a pattern. A single board has texture, but an entire row of boards creates a pattern. Pattern can be found in the repetition of design. In this case no single feature dominates. Its distinctive look is made possible by its repetitive quality. This form of pattern generally serves well as a background.

Surprises are possible when working with pattern. When elements are placed in repetition with other elements over a large area, they create new elements that may not be foreseen. These are often the result of negative space (the space around the design or playing through it). The shapes created by the interplay of the negative space become interesting themselves. Within the pattern these new shapes become apparent and begin to dominate, so that the space or spaces can be the predominating visual factor.

Unity and Variety

A composition devoid of any unifying element usually seems either haphazard

Burtynsky's images of manufactured landscapes are "metaphors to the dilemma of modern existence; they search for a dialogue between attraction and repulsion, seduction and fear." The original negative lacked contrast so it was scanned and corrected, underlining the new ability to use digital technology in the service of conventional photography. Often Burtynsky reinforces the melancholic atmosphere of such images with asymmetric compositions that are weighted to the bottom of his picture frame.

© Edward Burtynsky. *Oil Fields #13. Taft, California*, from the series *Exploring the Residual Landscape*, 2002. 40 x 50 inches. Chromogenic color print. Courtesy of the Mira Godard Gallery, Toronto, Canada and Charles Cowles Gallery, New York, NY.

or chaotic. A totally unified composition without variety is usually monotonous. Unity and variety are visual twins. Unity is the control of variety, but variety provides visual interest within unity.

The ideal composition is usually one that has a balance between these two qualities, diverse elements held together by some unifying device.

The repetition of shape, pattern, or size plus the harmony of color and texture are visual ways of creating unity. The more complex the composition, the greater the need for a unifying device. Variety can be introduced through the use of size, color, and texture, but in photography contrast is a major control—light against dark, large against small, smooth against rough, hard against soft. Dramatic lighting emphasizes these contrasts while soft lighting minimizes these differences.

Balance

Balance is the visual equilibrium of the objects in a composition. Some categories of balance are as follows:

- **Symmetrical, bilateral, or two-sided balance**. If you draw a line through the center of this type of composition, both sides will be an equal mirror image. Symmetrical balance tends to be calm, dignified, and stable.
- **Asymmetrical balance**, such as a composition that has equal visual weight, but the forms are disposed unevenly. Asymmetrical balance is active, dynamic, and exciting.
- **Radial balance**. This type of balance occurs when a number of elements point outward from a central hub, such as the spokes of a bike wheel. Radial balance can be explosive, imply directional movement, and indicate infinity.
- **Balance through color**. The weight of a color can become the focal point in a picture. Warm colors (red, magenta, yellow) tend to advance and/or have more visual weight than cool colors (blue, green, cyan). The majority of landscape is composed of cool colors. Warm colors appear mainly as accents (flowers

Zanisnik says that his "meticulous compositional balance is achieved by paying close attention to cropping, formal design, symmetry, and parallax. I separate my work from contextual photography and its use of both a foreground and a background to communicate a narrative by photographing surfaces that are nearly devoid of linear perspective. This deconstruction of traditional perspective allows color and form to evoke a sense of emphasis and order in an otherwise disengaged urban environment."

© Bryan Zanisnik. *Composition with Line and Shadow*, 2001. 16 x 20 inches. Chromogenic color print.

and birds). A small amount of red can be equal to a large area of blue or green. Much of the landscape in the American West is an exception. There are few trees and the predominant colors are the warm earth tones. During daylight hours with fair weather, the amount of cool color can be controlled by the proportion of sky that is included in the frame. The time of day and weather conditions also affect the amount of cool and warm colors, as the color temperature of the light changes.

- **Texture**. An area of texture can balance a large area of smooth surfaces.

Emphasis

Most photographs must have a focal point or points that provide visual emphasis. There must be some element that attracts the eye and acts as a climax for the composition. Without this, your eye tends to wander and is never satisfied. Focal devices to keep in mind are color, depth of field, isolation, light, position, perspective, and size.

Rhythm

Rhythm is the visual flow accomplished by repetition, which can be evenly spaced points of emphasis. It acts as a unifying device.

Proportion

Proportion deals with the size relationships within a composition. Shapes are proportional to the area they occupy within the composition. An example can be seen when making a portrait. If the circle formed by the head is two inches in diameter on a four-inch background, it will be more disproportional than if it

Rhythm is created by DeWitt through the repetition of shape and color at regular intervals. Original objects (1940s hairnet display heads) were placed on the platen of a Xerox color copier and an electrostatic color image was produced onto heat-transfer paper. A dry-mount press was used to transfer the image to 100 percent cotton cloth. Blocks of images were then assembled using a sewing machine. The finished social commentary takes the form of a traditional quilt with cloth border and backing. DeWitt says: "The repetition of the quilt structure is an ideal stage in which to play out a comment on the multitudes of staged smiles which gleam at us from advertising pages and video screens. The fixed grins and gleaming teeth seem to be more visibly transparent when you see many of them, all gazing sightlessly in concert."

© Rita DeWitt. *Too Many Airbrushed Smiles*, 1984. 81 x 96 inches. Electrostatic color transfers on cloth.

were placed on a 10-inch background.

Correct proportion is generally based on what society considers to be real or normal. Just because something is disproportionate does not make it wrong. On the contrary, it is often attention getting and unique. Because of this, many photographers deliberately change the proportions in a composition to create impact. The position of the camera and the distance of the subject from the lens are the easiest ways to distort proportion. Digital technology makes it easier to make postvisualization modifications such as alterations in proportion and scale.

Scale

Scale indicates size in comparison to a constant standard, the size something "ought to be." By showing objects to be larger or smaller than normal, the viewer is made to see the form in a new way. This encourages the audience to come to terms with it on a new level. Taking the familiar and making it unfamiliar can allow the viewer to see things that were once not visible.

Symbolism

We communicate through the use of symbols all the time. A symbol is anything that stands for something else. Usually a symbol is a simplified image

In the virtual space of the computer, DeLevie blends an authentic record of an event (recorded with a 6 x 7 camera) with the essence of memory (recorded with a Holga) to present a subjective history of a single image. "The historic content of the actual event is digitally rendered and mixed with my own subjective associations so it is no longer a singular representation, but a dynamic collection of viewpoints."

© Brian DeLevie. *Starter Home*, 2002. 20 x 24 inches. Inkjet on canvas.

that, because of certain associations in the viewer's mind, represents a more complex idea or system.

Lines that form letters, words, or musical notes are symbols. A photograph is a symbol. A photograph of a person is not that person but a representation of the person. It stands for the person, which makes it a symbol.

Symbolism is a great power for the photographer. It permits the communication of enormously complicated, often abstract ideas with just a few lines or shapes. Symbols provide us with tools for sorting information and drawing inferences that can aid in more effective communication. Symbols are the shorthand of the artist. Photography is a sign language. Learn to recognize and use the signs to your advantage.

"I am interested in the difference between how much information is needed in an image for a viewer to understand the landscape and how their own memories inform their experience. I use the swings and tilts of a view camera to decrease depth of field. By controlling a very thin plane of focus I draw attention to certain details while allowing colors of the rest of the scene to blur and soften. Changing the scale of the mine gives it a compressed toy-like appearance that produces an uneasy ambiguity based on what is revealed and what is concealed."

© Jeff Van Kleeck. *Ajo Mine*, 2001. 16 x 20 inches. Dye-destruction print.

The following categories of symbol are offered to get you thinking about what they can represent. Symbols are not absolute terms. They all have multiple readings based on factors such as cultural background, economic status, gender, psychological state, and political, religious, and sexual preference. The subsequent symbols and their conceivable meanings are provided only as a starting point. Symbols are highly complex and each image requires its own reading. Reading and decoding images is a fluid process. Based on their set of experiences, different people give different readings, and your own reading can also be subject to change.

General Symbols
The following are some general symbol categories:

● **Cosmic symbols** such as yin and yang (yin: feminine, dark, cold, mystery wetness; yang: masculine, light, heat, dryness), the zodiac (stands for the forces that are believed to govern the universe), and the four humors within the body that control the personality (blood, phlegm, choler, or bile, and melancholy).
● **Magical symbols** such as the Christmas tree, which originated in Rome as a fertility symbol, an emblem of plenty with fruits and nuts decorating it. Cave painting was used to help ensure a successful hunt. Tribal masks were employed for getting the desired results in battle, love, and the search for food. Masks let the wearers both disguise themselves and represent things of importance. This allows people the freedom to act out situations according to the desires of their inner fantasies.
● **Cultural symbols** are mythological

Friedman overcomes his use of such volatile symbols as a Nazi concentration camp prisoner's uniform by sharing his personal history with his subjects and encouraging them to collaborate in the making of the images. His use and understanding of how a 20-mm lens can see a scene enabled him not to look through the viewfinder while photographing. The negative was scanned and adjusted in Photoshop to achieve the desired color contrast and quality.

© James Friedman. *Discussing my life on the run after escaping from Dachau (Germany) concentration camp and eluding my captors, from Self-Portrait with Jewish Nose Wandering in a Gentile World #775,* 2000. 24 x 36 inches. Inkjet print.

or religious concepts that have been changed and incorporated by a culture and become symbolic for a cultural event. St. Nicholas, a tall, serious fellow, is now a fat, jolly, and highly commercialized Santa Claus.

● **Religious symbols** such as the cross, the Star of David, and the Buddha stand for the ideas behind a religion such as faith, generosity, forgiveness, hope, love, virtue, and the quest for enlightenment.

● **Traditional patterns** have been woven into the visual arts for thousands of years. While the pattern remains the same, its context and meaning are altered by the group that makes use of it. The swastika is a good example of how this works. It has been used as an ornament by the Native Americans since prehistoric times. It has appeared as a symbol through the old world of China, Crete, Egypt, and Persia. In the twentieth century, its meaning was totally perverted, from one of well-being to that of death, when the German Nazi Party adopted it as the official emblem of the Third Reich.

● **Status symbols** indicate the exact status or station in life of the owner: wedding rings, military insignia, coats of arms, cars, and clothes.

● **Patriotic and political symbols** in the United States include the Statue of Liberty, the bald eagle, the flag, political parties (elephant and donkey), and Uncle Sam. At a glance they provide a wealth of information and express certain concerns.

● **Commercial symbols** dispense information and/or advertise a service or product to be sold. Examples include three balls symbolizing the pawnbroker, the red-and-white pole signifying the barbershop, international road signs, and logos such as National Broadcasting Company, Shell Oil, and MTV.

● **Psychological symbols** offer a system for investigating the conscious and unconscious processes of the human mind. Sigmund Freud's *The Interpretation of Dreams* and Carl Jung's *Man and His Symbols* are two watershed works that deal with these ideas. Filmmakers such as Ingmar Bergman and Francis Ford

Neon tubes provide the illumination as Iguchi scrutinizes historic Catholic iconography as it may appear in a contemporary context. Iguchi comments that "assimilating current ideas, materials, and techniques to represent traditional imagery sets up an irony that plays with our conventions and expectations."

© Josh Iguchi. *The Last Supper*, 1995. 45 x 102 inches. Chromogenic color print.

Coppola have emphasized the psychological side of human nature in their works.

● **Personal symbols** are created by artists to meet their particular needs. Some photographers whose works reflect these concerns include Man Ray, Lázsló Moholy-Nagy, Barbara Morgan, and Jerry Uelsmann.

Shapes and General Symbolic Associations

Shapes can also have symbolic meaning. Some possible interpretations follow:

● **The circle** is associated with heaven, intellect, thought, the sun, unity, perfection, eternity, wholeness, oneness, and the celestial realm.

● **The triangle** can represent communication between heaven and earth, fire, the number three, the trinity, aspiration, movement, upward, return to origins, sight, and light.

● **The square** may represent firmness, stability, or the number four.

● **The rectangle** often denotes the most rational and most secure. It is used in grounding concrete objects.

● **The spiral** can illustrate the evolution of the universe, orbit, growth, deepening, cosmic motion, the relationship between unity and multiplicity, spirit, water, continuing ascent or descent.

● **The maze** delineates the endless search or a state of bewilderment or confusion.

Color Associations—Some Traditional Effects and Symbolism

Along with shapes, color has symbolic associations that have come down through the ages in Western cultures.

● **Red** portrays sunrise, birth, blood, fire, emotion, wounds, death, passion, anger, excitement, heat, physical stimulation, and strengthening.

● **Orange** shows fire, pride, and ambition.

● **Yellow** indicates the sun, light, intuition, illumination, air, intellect, royalty, and luminosity.

● **Green** depicts the earth, fertility, sensation, vegetation, water, nature, sympathy, adaptability, and growth.

● **Blue** signifies sky, thinking, the day, the sea, height, depth, heaven, innocence, truth, psychic ability, and spirituality.

● **Violet** marks nostalgia, memory, and advanced spirituality.

Baird used "characters" to comment on "the complexity, confusion, and contradiction between pictures and text within an image-conscious culture." Admiring the work of László Moholy-Nagy, Baird worked with "the round image form as a reference to the eye and to photographs, which are round before being cropped in the camera."

© Darryl Baird. *Aqueous Humor # 14*, 2001. 18 x 18 inches in diameter on 20- x 24-inch paper. Inkjet print.

Common Symbols and Some Potential Associations

Consider these symbols and how their meanings can be used in your work.

● **Air** symbolizes activity, masculinity, creativity, breath, light, freedom, liberty, and movement.

● **Fire** represents the ability to transform, love, life, health, control, spiritual energy, regeneration, the sun, God, and passion.

● **Water** denotes feminine qualities, life, and the flow of the cycles of life.

● **The earth** suggests femininity, receptiveness, solidity, and mother.

● **Ascent** indicates height, transcendence, inward journeying, and increasing intensity.

● **Descent** shows unconsciousness, potentialities of being, and animal nature.

● **Duality** suggests opposites, complements, and pairing.

● **Unity** signifies spirit, oneness, wholeness, centering, transcendence, harmony, revelation, supreme power, completeness in itself, light, and the divinity.

● **Centering** depicts thought, unity, timelessness, spacelessness, paradise, the Creator, infinity, and neutralizing opposites.

● **The cross** portrays the tree of life, axis of the world, ladder, struggle, martyrdom, and orientation in space.

● **The dark** illustrates the time before existence, chaos, and the shadow world.

● **Light** stands for the spirit, morality, all, creative force, the direction east, and spiritual thought.

● **Mountains** demonstrate height, mass, loftiness, the center of the world, ambition, and goals.

● **A lake** represents mystery, depth, and unconsciousness.

● **The moon** presents the feminine and fruitfulness.

● **An eye** illustrates understanding, intelligence, the sacred fire, and creativeness.

● **The sun** indicates the hero, knowledge, the divine, fire, the creative and life force, brightness, splendor, awakening, healing, and wholeness.

● **Foodstuffs** represent abundance and give thanks to nature for providing what is needed to sustain life.

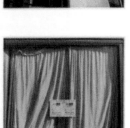   

YELLOW

assignment

DISCOVER YOUR OWN INTERPRETATION

Now that you have read about symbols and some of their possible meanings, choose one or more of your own pictures and make a list of the symbols you discover in them. Write a description that decodes their meaning for others to consider. Remember, the viewer does not have to accept the photographer's meaning, known as intentionalism. Although the opinion of the maker can and should help provide clues for understanding the work, the photographer's interpretation should not be the only factor in determining the meaning or set the standard for other interpretations. Think of what Marcel Duchamp, a co-founder of the Dada group, said: "It is the spectator who makes the picture."

References

CIRLOT, J.E. *A Dictionary of Symbols*, 2nd ed. New York: Philosophical Library, 1971.

DONDIS, DONIS A. *A Primer of Visual Literacy*. Cambridge, MA, and London: MIT Press, 1973.

HORNUNG, C.P. *Hornung's Handbook of Design and Devices*, 2nd ed. New York: Dover, 1946 reprint.

JUNG, C.G. *Man and His Symbols*. Garden City, NY: Doubleday, 1964.

Endnotes

[1] ESTELLE JUSSIM, "The Real Thing," in SUSAN SONTAG *The Eternal Moment: Essays on the Photographic Image*. New York: Aperture, 1989.

[2] PAUL STRAND, "Comments on the Snapshot," in JONATHON GREEN, ed., *The Snapshot*, Aperture 19, no. 1, 1974, 49. Also published as a separate book.

Chapter Thirteen

WORKING COLOR
STRATEGIES

Moving away from the tradition of landscape photography that sets out to idealize and glorify our ideas of nature, Misrach's images of desert fires document the permanent and often negative effects human intervention has on the landscape by focusing on the dueling human forces of destruction and restoration that lead to the fires.

© Richard Misrach. *Desert Fire #1*, 1983. 20 x 24 inches. Chromogenic color print. Courtesy of the Catherine Edelman Gallery, Chicago, IL.

The Angle of View

One of the major tasks of the photographer is to define exactly what the subject is. This capacity to compose is what gives clarity and cohesion to the artist's experience. The angle of view, or vantage point, is one of the most important basic compositional devices that any photographer has to work with in determining how the image will be presented. It is such an elementary ingredient that it is often taken for granted and forgotten. The angle of view lets the photographer control balance, content, light, perspective, and scale within the composition. In color photography it also determines the saturation of the hues and whether or not they form color contrast or harmony. This chapter is designed to encourage you to remove some of the self-imposed limits on visualization and to break away from the accepted, standardized conventions, formulas, and procedures of representation.

Breaking the Eye-Level Habit and Wonderment

Many people just raise the camera to eye level and push the button. A photographer explores the visual possibilities of the scene and attempts to find a way in which to present the subject in accordance with the desired outcome.

Altering the camera position does not cost anything or require any additional equipment, yet it can transform a subject and allow it to be presented in a new and different perspective. It can give the viewer more information, let the subject

Jarboe often utilizes the "eye level of a child" as she approaches the subject of social space for children by photographing lost and abandoned toys. "Spaces, both physical and social, are defined by borders that determine the interaction between different yet interrelated objects and/or people within those parameters. These objects that once belonged in a child's play area now occupy the 'real world' environment of adults. Now at odds with their surroundings in unfamiliar settings, the toys radiate an uncomfortable sensation that offers clues about the colliding of the two spaces."

© Molly Jarboe. *Brush*, 2002. 20 x 20 inches. Chromogenic color print.

In her Statesmen project Miller reconstructs the portraits of those who once ruled our states. "Working close, I was able to isolate the essence of the face. By using an oblique camera angle, I could emphasize the massive head and jaw of my subject. The bronze color results from a mixture of tungsten and daylight sources illuminating the original black-and-white photograph."

© Sybil Miller. *Juneau, Alaska,* from the series *Statesmen—Pictures in the Fifty State Capitols*, 2001. 15 x 22 inches. Chromogenic color print.

be seen in a way that was not possible before, and/or introduce an alternate point of view. It is the difference between seeing and sleepwalking through a scene.

Many times we sleepwalk through life because it is so habitual. We walk down a hall without seeing the hall because we have done it a thousand times before. We are somnambulists, reorienting ourselves. We know what to expect; everything is in check and in place. There is no opportunity for surprise, no chance for the unexpected to enter.

To see you must be awake, aware, and open to wonderment. Peter de Bolla, in his book *Art Matters* (2001), says: "Wonder requires us to acknowledge what we do not know or may never know, to acknowledge the limits of knowledge. It is, then, a different species of knowledge, a way of knowing that does not lead to certainties or truths about the world or the way things are. It is a state of mind that, like being in love, colors all that we know we know." Wonderment can be experienced in ordinary or extraordinary situations and brings with it a sense of amazement, astonishment, awe, and surprise. Being able to visually communicate these powerful feelings is a surefire way of engaging viewers.

When seeing, you are letting things happen and not relying on past expectations and clichés to get you through the situation. Seeing involves being conscious of color and space and learning to organize these elements in a convincing manner. The more you look, the more you can penetrate the subject and in turn are able to see even more clearly and deeply.

Methods of Working

Select a subject that inspires wonderment and proceed to discover how angle and light affect your final visual statement. Here is a suggested method of approach:

1   Begin with a conventional horizontal shot at eye level, metering from the subject. Walk around the subject. Crouch down, lie down, stand on tiptoes, and find a point that raises the angle of view above the subject. Notice how the direction of light either hides or reveals aspects of the subject. Move in closer to the subject and then get farther back than the original position. Now make a shot at a lower angle than the original eye-level view. Try getting the camera right on the ground. Look through the camera; move and twist around, and see what happens to the subject. When it looks good, make another picture.

2   Think about changing the exposure. What happens if you expose for highlights? What about depth of field? Will a small, medium, or large f-stop help to create visual impact? How is the mood altered? All kinds of questions should be running through the photographer's mind at this stage as part of the decision-making process. Answering them requires independent visual thinking. Try not to compete with fellow students. Competition tends to lead to copying of ideas and style. Copying means no longer discovering anything on your own. Watch out for envy as it can also take away from your own direction. The best pictures tend to be those that are made from the heart as well as the mind.

3   Make a vertical shot. Decide whether to emphasize the foreground or background. How will this decision affect the viewers' relationship with the subject?

4   Get behind the subject and make a picture from that point of view. How is this different from the front view? What is gained and what is lost by presenting this point of view?

5   If possible, make a picture from above the subject. How does this change the sense of space within the composition?

6   Change the lens that you have been using. See what changes occur in the points of emphasis and spatial relationships due to depth of field.

7   Move in close. Henri Matisse said: "It's like when you pass a cake shop, if you see the cakes through the window, they may look very nice. But, if you go inside the shop and get them right under your nose, one by one, then you're in business." Look for details that reveal the essence of the entire subject and photograph them. This method of simplification should speak directly and plainly to the viewer.

8   Move back. Make an image that shows the subject in relation to its environment.

9   Now do something out of the ordinary. Using your instincts, make some pictures of the subject without looking into the camera. This can be a very freeing experience and can present composition arrangements that your conscious mind had been unable to think of using.

10   Do not be shy about conveying your sense of wonderment. The camera is society's license to approach the unapproachable in a manner that would not otherwise be deemed acceptable in a normal social situation. Use this license to make the strongest possible statement without being irresponsible or infringing on the rights of others (see the section on the photographer's special license in chapter 12, page 231).

Working the Angles

Here are five basic angles and some of their general characteristics to consider:

●   **The bird's-eye view** is photographed from high above the subject and can be very disorientating. Normally we don't see life from this perspective, thus the subject or event may initially appear unidentifiable, obscure, or abstract. It enables the viewer to hover over the subject from a God-like perspective. The subject appears insignificant, reinforcing the idea of fate or destiny—that something the subject can't control is going to happen. Filmmakers such as Martin Scorsese combine overhead views, ambience, and action into a seamless atmosphere of expectation. Haptic/expressionistic photographers favor shots made from extreme angles. They confine the audience to a particular point of view, which may be very subjective. Wide-angle lenses are often employed with extreme angles to further exaggerate the sense of space.

● **High-angle shots**, though less extreme than bird's-eye views, can provide a general overview of the subject. The importance of the surrounding environment is increased. The setting can overwhelm the subject. As the angle increases, the importance of the subject is diminished. It can indicate vulnerability, a reduction in strength, or the harmlessness of the subject. The angle can deliver a condescending view of the subject by making the subject appear helpless, entrapped, or out of control. It reduces the height of objects and the sense of movement is slowed down. It is not good for conveying a sense of motion or speed. It can be effective for showing a situation that is wearisome or oppressive.

● **Eye-level shots** are more neutral, dispassionate, and less manipulative than high- or low-angle ones. The eye-level shot tends to let viewers make up their own minds about a situation. It presents a more ordinary, normal view of how we see the everyday world. This shot is a favorite style of visual/realistic photographers because it puts the subject on a more equal footing with the observer. A normal focal-length lens is usually used when working in this mode.

● **Low angles** have the opposite effect of high ones. They increase the height of the subject and convey a sense of verticality. They tend to present an added dimension to the sense of motion. The general environment is diminished in importance; the ceiling or the sky becomes more predominant. The importance or visual weight of the subject is increased. A person becomes more heroic and bigger than life. A figure can also become more looming, dominating the

In her exploration of point of view, Lang's models are placed on a tall Plexiglas scaffolding and photographed from below. "The studio construction alters the play of gravity on the subject, making the workings of the body visible. The Plexiglas works as a barrier on both a physical and metaphorical level. It shows exactly how far the body can go, makes visible the limitations of the flesh. We, as viewers, stand on the other side of the Plexiglas. We can look in and see people with their families and friends, see traces of their lives, the choices they have made."

© Cay Lang. *American Body Series #26*, 1990. 20 x 24 inches. Chromogenic color print.

The photographer's vantage point can add information to the composition and increase the viewer's desire to spend time looking at the work by presenting work in a way that is not familiar. This image is part of Evans's Guggenheim Fellowship aerial survey of the nature of the prairie from Canada to Texas. Photographing from both the air and the ground, Evans's intent is to "tell the prairie's stories, past and present, through visible facts and layers of time and memory on the landscape to reveal its use, abandonment, and care."

© Terry Evans. *Silo, North Platte, Nebraska*, 1998. 19 x 19 inches. Chromogenic color print. Courtesy of Catherine Edelman Gallery, Chicago, IL.

visual space, thus making the viewer feel insecure. Photographing a person from below can inspire awe, fear, or respect. In a landscape, it can help to create a sense of greater spatial depth by bringing added importance to the foreground.
● **Oblique angles** occur when the camera is tilted, making for an unstable horizon line. It throws everything out of balance, because the natural horizontal and vertical lines in a scene are forced into unstable diagonal lines. A person photographed at an oblique angle appears to be falling to one side. Oblique angles are disorientating to the viewer. They may suggest anxiety, the imbalance of a situation, impending movement, tension, or transition. They can indicate a precarious situation that is about to change.

Selective Focus

As the keystone of photography has traditionally been based on subject matter, the majority of photographers strive to make pictures that are sharp so that the subject detail can be studied at leisure. The issue of focus was critical in defining serious nineteenth-century artistic prac-

Working with a 4- x 5-inch view camera on the street, Jacobson makes "diffused photographs to explore issues around memory as opposed to making precise rendering of a scene or moment. I produce images that are analogous to how the mind works, often recording images in fragments or traces that suggest we remember little of the information we are exposed to every day. The images relate to poetry as opposed to narrative, hinting at what we hold on to and what we let go of as we travel through life."

© Bill Jacobson. *Untitled* [#3566], 2000. 30 x 36 inches. Chromogenic color print. Courtesy of the Julie Saul Gallery, New York, NY.

tice. During the 1860s, Julia Margaret Cameron's work helped to establish the issue of selective focus as a criterion of peerless practice. The making of "out-of-focus" images was considered an expressive remedy that shifted the artificial, machine focus of a camera toward a more natural vision. Cameron stated that when focusing she would stop when something looked beautiful to her eye "instead of screwing the lens to the more definite focus which all other photographers insist upon." The Pictorialists, who placed importance on how a subject was handled rather than on the subject itself, utilizied soft focus to evoke mystery and de-emphasize photography's connection with reality, which helped their work fit into that era's definition of what consti-tuted art. Recently more photographers have been experimenting with how focus can control photographic meaning.

Contrast with Color

In black-and-white photography, contrast is created by the difference between the darkest and lightest areas of the picture. When working with color materials, the intensity and the relationship of one color to another play a vital role in creating contrast.

Complementary Colors

Complementary colors, opposite each other on the color wheel, make the most contrast. The subtractive combinations of blue against yellow, green against magenta, and red against cyan form the strongest color contrasts. When looking at the reflected colors of a final print some people prefer to use the pigment primary combinations of red against green, blue against orange, and yellow against purple as the basis of their discussion. This allows the photographic print to be examined with the same language as the other visual arts, such as painting.

It is thought that complementary colors create such contrast because of fatigue in the rods and cones of the retina. This is because the human eye cannot accommodate each of these wavelengths at the same time. Think of it as a

zoom lens that is going back and forth between its minimum and maximum focal lengths, while attempting to maintain critical focus. This is what the eye tries to do with complementary colors.

Cool and Warm Colors

Cool and warm colors can be used to create contrast. Warm colors tend to advance and are called active colors. Cool colors tend to recede and are generally more passive. Dark colors against light ones produce contrast, too. Desaturated colors played next to a saturated one make for contrast. Pastel colors can provide contrast if there is enough separation between the colors on the color wheel.

Creating Color Contrast

Color contrast can emphasize the subject if photographed against a complementary background. Areas of contrasting colors can create a visual restlessness that can give a sense of movement within the scene. Active and passive colors can flatten the visual space and bring patterns to the forefront. Warm and cool colors can be used to produce a sense of balance within the picture. Dynamic tension can be built by placing active colors next to each other in the composition.

Color Harmony

Harmonic colors are closely grouped together on the color wheel and present a limited group of colors. Any quarter section of the color wheel is considered to show color harmony. The simplest harmonic compositions contain only two colors that are desaturated in appearance. The absence of any complementary

Dunitz makes use of the play of the cool colors against the warm colors to create color contrast and a vibrant, abstract composition. The image was created by painting titanium and niobium metal sheets with electricity. Applying DC current with a paintbrush dipped in water and baking soda, the metal oxidizes, creating light interference colors. Specific voltages were selected to create each color, and a grinder was applied for texture. The metal sheet, about 10 x 14 inches, was then photographed with a 4- x 5-inch camera.

© Jay S. Dunitz. *Pacific Light #36*, 1986. 40 x 54 inches. Dye-destruction print.

MAKE A PHOTOGRAPH
THAT INCORPORATES ONE OF
THE FOLLOWING COLOR
CONTRAST EFFECTS:

Complementary contrast. Use colors that are opposite each other on the color wheel, such as a yellow building against a blue sky.

Active and passive contrast. Use a warm color against a cool one. The proper proportions of each are critical in making this work.

Primary contrast. The juxtaposition of two primary colors can make for a bright, vibrant, and strong sense of feeling.

Passive contrast. A quiet, easy, restful mood can be achieved by using a neutral background as a staging area. A simple, dark backdrop can be employed to offset a light area and slow down the visual dynamics of the picture.

Complex contrast. Complex contrast uses many contrasting primary colors and requires careful handling or the point of emphasis can become confused or lost in an array of colors. With the proper treatment, the multicolored use of contrast can cause tremendous visual excitement and provide a strong interplay of the objects within a composition, as well as connecting seemingly diverse elements.

colors makes it easier to see the subtle differences in these adjacent hues. Evenness in light and tone can help bring out the harmonic color relationship. Saturated colors that may be technically close to each other on the color wheel can still produce much contrast and interfere with the harmony.

Color harmony is found everywhere in nature. Passive colors tend to be peaceful and harmonize more easily than the warm, active hues.

Frazier used drawing, painting, sculpture, and xerography to make an illusory image that has the qualities of the actual site when viewed through the camera. The final construction is photographed, completing the process of deferring the reality presented in the image. The construction is destroyed after this process is completed. Frazier states: "They [the photographs] picture sites which are part of our culture, and extinct at the same time. They document a Grand Tour never taken. These photoworks create a document of society's propensity toward cultural and political obsolescence. The viewer might be reminded of the temporal nature of all civilizations." In terms of photo history, this image parodies the work of Timothy O'Sullivan and Ansel Adams, as well as traditional tourist snapshots.

© Bill Frazier. *Simulations—Souvenirs from Extinct Civilizations: Canyon de Chelly*, 1987. 20 x 16 inches. Chromogenic color print.

MAKE A HARMONIC COLOR PICTURE FROM ONE
OF THE FOLLOWING AREAS:

Color harmony as found in nature. Pay close attention to the compositional location of the horizon line. Make a landscape that does not follow the traditional compositional rule of thirds. Photograph a scene with little or no sky. Make a skyscape with little or no foreground. Be on the lookout for symmetry in nature. One way to get repetition is to include reflections. This can be especially useful when there is water in the picture. If the harmony produced by cool colors is too uninviting or standoffish, try to add a small area of a muted complementary color. This can draw warmth and interest back into the scene. Look for a detail from the landscape that can provide what you are after in a simplified and condensed manner. Showing less can let the viewer see more.

Urban color harmony. Find a place where people have consciously and deliberately made an effort to blend human-made creations into an overall scheme. Flat lighting can be used to play down the differences in the various color combinations within an urban setting. Smooth, early morning light can be employed for the same effect. Try to avoid the visual hustle and bustle that tends to bring forth visual chaos. Finding scenes of calmness and stillness within a busy cityscape will help to achieve harmony.

Still life is a perfect vehicle for creating a working color harmony. The photographer can assume total responsibility for controlling the arrangement of the objects, the background, the quality of light, and the camera position to ensure a harmonic composition. The sparing and subtle use of filters can enhance the mood of harmony.

Harmonious portraits can be created by simplifying the background, selecting clothes and props to go with the subject, and using neutral colors and similar shapes. Soft directional lighting can minimize complementary colors. Placing tracing paper in front of any light source is a simple and inexpensive way to diffuse the light and gain control. A bare bulb flash can be valuable in a situation of this nature.

Harmony is Subjective

Harmony is a subjective matter, and its effectiveness depends on the colors involved, the situation, and the effect that the photographer wants to produce. The actual visual effect depends on the colors themselves. Blue and violet are adjacent to each other on the color wheel, therefore, by literal definition, in harmony, but the effect that is created tends to be visually subdued. Go to the other side of the wheel and take orange and yellow. These two colors harmonize in an animated fashion.

Harmonic effects can be reinforced through the linkage of colors by repeating and weaving the harmonic colors throughout the composition. This places importance on patterns and shapes within the picture. Soft, unsaturated colors in diffused light have been a traditional way of creating harmonious relationships of colors. Special attention in framing the picture is necessary. Be aware of exactly what is in all corners of the frame. Eliminate any hue that can interfere with the fragile interplay of the closely related colors.

In an urban, human-made environment there is a strong likelihood of encountering discordant, unharmonious colors. This happens when contrasting colors are placed next to each other in such a way as to create a jarring, or even unpleasant, combination to view. Care in the use of light, the angle of view, and the right mixture and proportions of these discordant colors can introduce balance and vitality into a flat or static composition.

Methods to Create Harmony

Basic techniques to orchestrate a mood of unison include using a slight amount of filtration in front of the lens that matches the cast of the color of the light in the scene and desaturating the hues through the use of diffused light, or using a soft filter in front of the lens. Incorporating neutral areas, which provide balance within the picture, can de-emphasize differences in diverse colors. Both contrasting and harmonic colors can be linked together by working with the basic design elements such as repeating patterns and shapes. Look for common qualities in balance, rhythm, texture, and tone to unite the colors.

Dominant Color

Dominant color occurs when the subject of the picture becomes color itself. The painter Paul Cézanne observed: "When color is at its richest, form is at its fullest." Painting movements such as abstract expressionism, color-field painting, and op art have explored different visual experiences that are created through the interplay of color. Works that make use of this method tend to use color itself to express emotions or mood. The color relationships can affect all the ingredients that make up a picture. Colors can be used to create calm or tension. They can create the illusion of depth or make things appear flat.

Simplicity

When putting together a composition keep things simple. Beware of incorporating too many colors into the picture as this can create visual confusion because the different colors will be in competition to dominate. Let one hue clearly predominate. The proportions of the colors in the scene will determine which is the strongest. A small area of a warm color such as red can balance and dominate a much greater area of a cool color such as green.

Dominance may be achieved with a small area of a bright color against a field of flat color. A large area of subdued color can also be dominant. The value of a hue is a relative quality and changes from situation to situation (see section on color description in chapter 1, page 18).

Maintaining a Strong Composition

The dominant color must retain a working arrangement with the main point of interest in the picture. If color is not the subject of it, then it should reinforce and enhance the subject. Don't let the two clash, or the viewer may have a difficult time determining what the purpose of the picture is. Don't send conflicting or confusing messages to the audience. Be straightforward and provide a well-marked visual path for the eye. Strong colors attract attention. Do something with it once you have it. Shape becomes important. Use tight, controlled framing

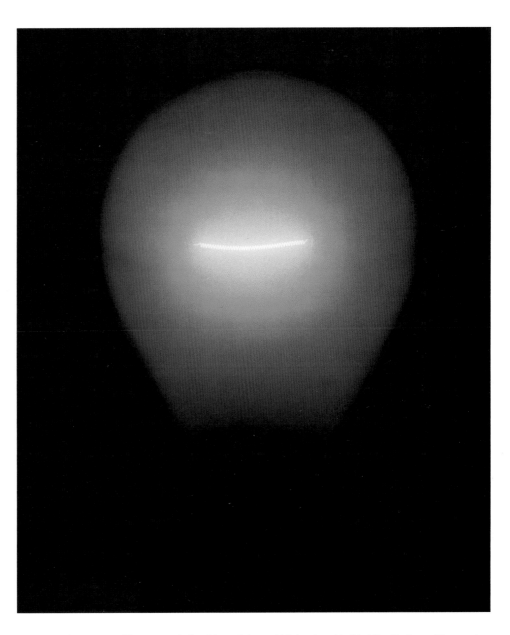

Means used a 60-watt GE tungsten bulb with an Aristo cold light placed behind it with Rosco filters and a variety of exposure times to express the organic nature of the mundane. Means says: "This bulb is full of hot coals—the coals remain when the flames have died down. Its deep blue-black background provides another hot/cold juxtaposition. The filament here is a smile. A bulb smile. A coal smile. A hot smile."

© Amanda Means. *Light Bulb 00050C*, 2001. 24 x 20 inches. Diffusion-transfer print. Courtesy of the Ricco/Maresca Gallery, New York, NY.

to make strong graphic effects. Get close and eliminate the nonessentials. A neutral or even black background can make the color stand out.

Isolated Use of Color

The energy and visual spark of a hue depend more on its placement within a scene than on the size of the area it occupies. Imagine a scene of cool, harmonious colors that are even, smooth, and unified. Now add a dot of red. Pow! It surprises the eye and instantly becomes the point of emphasis. Its solitariness stands out as a point of beauty. Its individuality introduces needed variety into the picture space.

Most colors have the greatest luminance when they appear against a neutral setting. Warm colors visually step forward, adding depth and sparkle to a picture that was flat. On an overcast or dusty day in which everything looks and feels of the same dimension, add a small amount of a warm hue and contrast, depth, drama, emphasis, and variety appear out of this sameness. Warm colors can also be used as dynamic backgrounds that offset and/or balance monochromatic subject matter. Do not underestimate the power a single individual color can have on the entire composition.

Executing a Plan

Often getting this single color in the right place at the right time requires the photographer to be ready in advance. Anticipating the moment greatly increases the chances of this happening. Being prepared also enhances the likelihood of something useful happening. Coordinating the light, background, and proportion of the isolated color requires the photographer to feel confident and comfortable with the equipment and techniques used. Practice and readiness are the prerequisites that let the image-maker take advantage of chance.

Check out the situation carefully. Ask in advance, Which lens is needed to get the correct proportion of that single color into the composition? Be ready to improvise. If the lens that is needed is not available, will getting closer or farther away make it work? Approach each new situation with openness, which allows adapting and accommodating the subject without becoming static or hackneyed.

Getting the right amount of a unified color background is generally one of the first steps necessary to catch this touch of color in the picture. Next comes the actual placement of that hue. Third is being sure of the correct exposure.

For example, a monochromatic sky is the backdrop and the spot of warm color is located on ground level in the shadow area. There are a number of exposure possibilities available, depending on the desired outcome. If detail is to be retained in both areas, take a meter reading from the sky and one from the foreground and average them together. If the sky is f/8 and the ground is f/4, the exposure for that situation would be f/5.6. If detail in the foreground area is critical, expose for the key shadow area by getting in close or tilting the camera meter down so the sky is not included. If the light is similar where you are standing, meter off your hand. The sky receives more exposure than necessary. If this is not corrected for during development, the sky can be burned in when the print is created.

Movement creates visual excitement. Placing the camera on a tripod and using a slow shutter speed to introduce a warm object in motion against a static monochrome setting can produce it.

Monochrome

Some people think that a good color photo must include every hue in the spectrum. Often reducing the number of colors in the composition is more effective than assaulting the viewer with the rainbow.

A narrow definition of a monochromatic photograph would be one that uses only a single hue from any part of the spectrum. In a broader sense it can indicate a photograph that creates the total effect of one color, even though there are other hues present.

When putting together a monochrome picture, the photographer can call into play knowledge, judgments, and understanding of composition that

have been developed in black-and-white photography.

The Personal Nature of Monochrome

Monochromatic photographs can create powerful moods. For instance, when we feel down we say we are blue; we don't say we feel yellow or orange. Utilize such associations in building your image. Monochrome simplifies the composition, so that we tend to react more subjectively and less rationally. The photograph is taken not so much as a document to be read for information, but as an event that elicits a subjective sense of time and place. It can alter the normal flow of time and flatten the sense of visual space.

Exposure is critical to maintaining a fragile color and atmosphere. Monochromes need not lack contrast. Subdued colors and harmonious colors can be employed to give monochromatic impressions.

Color Contamination

When dealing with a monochromatic image, beware of what is referred to as environmental color contamination. This occurs when a colored object within the scene reflects its color onto other items within the picture area. Color contamination can occur when a photographer's bright plaid shirt reflects back onto the subject. Often objects within the composition spill their color onto their neighbor. This is most noticeable when working with white items. It is possible for a white object to make another white object appear to be off-white. Careful observation of the scene, and the arrangement and selection of objects to be photographed, is the best way to deal with this problem.

Aerial Perspective

Aerial perspective occurs when the atmospheric scattering of light mutes colors in distant scenes, so the tones appear progressively paler as the landscape recedes. The blending and softening of colors in this condition can help to create a monotone rendition of a scene. Be aware that aerial perspective also makes distant objects bluer. A UV filter is recommended and you may also wish to use a slight warming or yellow filter to compensate.

Perspective

Perspective allows the artist to give two-dimensional work the illusion of the third dimension and controls the illusion of depth. Light and shadow begin to provide depth, but the actual illusion that one item in the composition is closer to the front than the other is brought about through the use of perspective.

Basic Types of Perspective Control

The following are eight basic types of perspective control commonly used in photography:

● **Aerial perspective** is the effect in which colors and tones become blurred, faded, and indistinct with distance due

As a conceptual artist with a strong leaning toward minimalism, Barth's softly beautiful and mysterious photographs often defy conventions of perception dealing with composition, focus, and perspective. Barth says that to describe her work as out of focus is inaccurate. Instead it is "focused on something outside of the eye." Viewers are encouraged to imagine what the focus is and to insert themselves into the environment she has created.

© Uta Barth. *Ground (95.6)*, 1995. 20 x 17 inches. Chromogenic color print. Courtesy of Tanya Bonakdar Gallery, New York, NY.

to atmospheric diffusion. The colors in the foreground are brighter, sharper, and warmer and have a darker value than those farther away. There is a proportional decrease in luminance and warmth with distance, which can be reduced with a UV and/or warming filter such as the 81A and 81B.

● **Diminishing scale** creates depth by

using the fact that we assume that the farther an object is from the viewer the smaller it seems. By composing with something large in the foreground and something smaller in the middle ground or background, the photographer can add to the feeling of depth. It is also possible to trick the viewer's sense of depth by reversing this order.

when one shape in the picture is placed in front of another, partially obscuring what is behind it. This is a good compositional device to indicate depth.

● **Selective focus** is another method open to photographers to create the illusion of depth. To the eye a critically focused object set off by an unsharp object appears to be on a different plane. Employing the maximum lens opening is a way to separate the foreground from the middle ground and background. Since the depth of field is extremely limited, whatever is focused on appears sharp, while the detail in the remainder of the picture is destroyed. Placing a wide-angle lens so near a subject that it cannot be sharply focused encourages the viewer to actively search the picture for something sharp. Using a longer than normal focal length lens reduces the amount of depth of field at any given f-

● **Position** makes the visual assumption that objects placed in a higher position within the picture are farther back in space than those toward the bottom of the frame. The same rules that apply to diminishing scale apply to position.

● **Linear perspective** happens when parallel lines or planes gradually converge in the distance. As they recede, they seem to meet at a point on the horizon line and disappear. This is called the vanishing point.

● **Two-point linear perspective** can be achieved by photographing the subject from an oblique angle (an angle that is not a right angle; it is neither parallel nor perpendicular to a given line or plane). This is most easily seen in a subject that has vertical parallel lines, such as a building. When viewed from a corner, two walls of the building seem to recede toward two vanishing points rather than one. The closer the corner of the building is to the center of your composition, the more a sense of depth, distance, and space is attained. If the building is placed in one of the corners of the frame it flattens one of the walls while making the other look steep.

● **Overlapping perspective** occurs

Harold-Steinhauser made a "reverse" photogram, which she sepia-toned and softly hand-colored with oil, india ink, acrylic, and oil pastels.

© Judith Harold-Steinhauser. *Tulip Tango*, 1984. 14 x 11 inches. Gelatin silver print with mixed media.

stop. The longer the focal length of the lens, the less depth of field it will have at any given aperture.

● **Limiting depth** can be accomplished visually by incorporating a strong sense of pattern into the composition, which tends to flatten the sense of space in the picture.

Converging Lines

A common problem photographers run into when dealing with perspective is converging vertical lines. For example, when trying to make a picture of the entire front of a tall building, it is possible that the camera may have to be slightly tilted to take it all in or that a wide-angle lens is necessary; both of these options cause the vertical lines to converge. Convergence can be visually pleasing because it emphasizes a sense of height.

If you need to maintain correct perspective and keep the vertical parallel and straight, a perspective-control shift lens is required on a 35-mm camera. On a larger format camera raising the front or tilting the rear allows for perspective correction. It is possible to minimize this effect by moving farther away from the building and using a longer focal length lens. This is often not possible in a cramped urban setting. If negative film is being used, there is one course of action still available. In the printing stage, it is possible to tilt the easel upward to correct the converging vertical. If the enlarger permits, tilt the lens stage as well to maintain image sharpness. Use a steady prop to make sure the easel does not move, focus in the middle of the picture after the easel is in position, and use the smallest lens opening possible to get maximum depth of focus.

Subdued Color

Subdued color photographs tend to possess a uniform tonality and contain unsaturated hues. Soft, flat light mutes colors. Subdued colors can often be

found in aged and weathered surfaces. Color can be subdued by adding black, gray, or white through the use of lighting or exposure or by selecting desaturated tones. Low levels of light reduce saturation. Delicate colors can occur in failing evening light, with shadows adding gray and black. Any form of light scattering, such as flare or reflection, introduces white, thus desaturating the colors. Choice of backgrounds can make certain colors appear less saturated. A limited or low range of tones mutes color and can

"This artificial landscape was photographed with a 4- x 5-inch view camera in the studio on a light table by forming shapes made of Mylar into a 'scene.' I manipulated color, form, and emotional tone to confuse viewers into accepting these synthetic scenes as real, but somehow alien. I used contrasting cool and warm tones, often complementary with selectively placed tungsten lights and colored gels, to create a sense of depth and dynamic tension and thus alter viewer reaction. While the gestalt of the image suggests a common natural subject, further inspection reveals the unfamiliar and evokes the ambiguous nature of reality."

© Janyce Erlich-Moss. *Escape*, 2000. 20 x 16 inches. Chromogenic color print.

be used to induce drama, mystery, sensuality, and the element of the unknown.

Working Techniques

Some techniques to consider when working with subdued color include the following:

● Make use of light that strikes the subject at a low angle.
● Expose for the highlights, which allows the shadows to be dark and deep. Bracket the exposures until you are able to judge the final effect.
● Minimize background detail by using a higher shutter speed and a larger lens opening.
● Intentionally use the subject to block out part of the main source of illumination. This produces a rim lighting effect, which also reduces the overall color contrast and tonal range.
● Employ a dark, simple, uncluttered background.
● Select a major color scheme of dark hues.
● Work with a diffused or weak source of illumination. This often occurs naturally in fog, mist, or storms. This effect also reduces the scene's tonal range.
● Use a diffusion filter. If you do not have one, improvise with a stocking or a piece of cloth.
● Work with a limited color palette.

Colors can express the ideas of contrast. Keasler began documenting orphanages with the "intent of describing a dramatic and emotionally charged subject through subtle, understated photographs. The pictures become tiny descriptive capsules that allow the contrasts and ironies of these worn institutions to speak for themselves."

© Misty Keasler. *Masha and Her Best Friend, Orphanage #16, St Petersburg, Russia*, 2000. 19 x 19 inches. Chromogenic color print. Courtesy of Photographs, Do Not Bend, Dallas, TX.

Colors Attract and Repel

Everyone responds positively to certain colors and negatively to others. This also applies to combinations of colors. Think about what colors are most often

included in your own work. Do these colors appear regularly in other areas of your life, for example in the colors of the clothes you wear or in how you have decorated your living quarters? Which colors do not make many appearances in your work? Are these colors also avoided in other aspects of your life?

Overcoming Color Bias

After making the pictures in the assignment on the next page, look at them and see what associations are created for you from these colors. What effect does

changing the natural color of an object create? Is it possible, by working with a color that you dislike, to see that something beautiful and meaningful can still be created? This teaches us that our preferences and dislikes in color and in life often result from prejudices, which are a manifestation of inexperience, lack of insight, and the failure to think for ourselves. Do you really hate the color orange, or was it your mother's least favorite color? Question yourself about these things. Keep your possibilities open so that you can explore your full potential.

Schorr's pictures of young men use light and shadow to interpret a complex maze of identification and desire. The artifice of Schorr's pictorial space is akin to traditional Western painting within the context of nature. One could assume that a gay man made these images of boyish masculinity, but Schorr is a lesbian. By eliminating desire the ambiguity and awkward vulnerability of these portraits shift focus to androgyny. This counterpoint can lead you into the construction and confusion surrounding gender in dealing with the question of attraction.

© Collier Schorr. *Player*, 1998, 31 x 30 inches. Chromogenic color print. Courtesy of 303 Gallery, New York, NY.

Pairs of Contrast

Use color to make pictures that express pairs of contrast. The object of prime visual importance is not only the actual subject matter in the scene, but also the colors that make up the scene. It is the colors themselves that should be used to express the ideas of contrast.

Counterpoints

Consider these counterpoints: old and new, happy and sad, old and young, large and small, soft and hard, high and low, bright and dull, fast and slow, evil and good, calm and stormy, peaceful and warlike, hate and love, apathy and decisiveness, individual and group, female and male, intimacy and distance, seduction and horror. Counterpoints can also be purely visual in nature, angular and flowing, or sharp and circular. Counterpoints may also be more conceptual, relying on the play of opposites, such as inner and outer reality or the natural and the fabricated.

Chapter Fourteen

THE INTERACTION OF COLOR, MOVEMENT, SPACE, AND TIME

The ability of a photograph to record and act as a surrogate witness to a specific moment in time has been at the heart of photographic practice. While standing in a crowd after the collapse of the twin towers a police officer reminded Meyerowitz that he was standing at a crime scene and no photographs were allowed. "To me," said Meyerowitz, "no photographs meant no history. I decided that my job was to make a photographic record of the aftermath."

© Joel Meyerowitz. *Twin Towers (right panel) 9-25-2001*, from the series Images from *Ground Zero, 2003*. 48 x 60 inches. Chromogenic color print. Courtesy of Ariel Meyerowitz Gallery, New York, NY.

The Search for Time

Most of us, like St. Augustine, think we know what time is until someone asks us to explain it. Even for contemporary scientists the nature of time remains mysterious. In 1905, Albert Einstein's Theory of Relativity revealed that commonly held concepts concerning time were not always true. For instance, Newton's notion that time moved at a constant rate was proved wrong when it was demonstrated that time passes more slowly for rapidly moving objects as compared to slow ones. The conviction that two events separated in space could happen at precisely the same time—simultaneity—was shown to be false. Whether two events appear to happen at the same time depends on the viewer's vantage point, and no one observer has any intrinsic claim to be the authority.

Einstein's work produced even more fantastic conclusions about time. For example, clocks run faster at the top of a building than in the basement. Succinctly, Einstein tells us there is no universal time or no master clock regulating the essence of the cosmos. Time is relative and it depends on motion and gravity. Time and space are not simply "there" as a neutral, unchanging backdrop to nature. They are physical things, malleable and mutable, no less so than matter, and subject to physical law.

The Flow of Time

When most of us think of a photograph, we tend to think only of a tiny slice of time, removed from the flow of life with a frame around it. Everything is still, there is no sense of movement, and that brief instant of time is there for examination. This Western convention of reality, based on Renaissance perspective, has come to dictate that photographs be presented like evidence at a trial—clear and sharp. "The more readable the detail, the better the picture," is a photographic maxim that has been the standard of a picture's worth for many people. This has been based on the assumed modeling of the camera, with its lens and recording material, on that of the human eye, with its lens and retina. Some critical thinkers have challenged this concept by stating:

> The notion that a photograph shows us what we would have seen had we been there ourselves has to be qualified to the point of absurdity. A photograph shows us what we would have seen at a certain moment in time, from a certain vantage point if we kept our head immobile and closed one eye and if we saw things in Agfacolor. ... By the time all the conditions are added up, the original position has been reversed: instead of saying that the camera shows us what our eyes would see, we are now positing the rather unilluminating proposition that,

Whether working with splash-toned, Scotch-taped images or handmade objects that incorporate electro-luminescence, the Starns have constantly rejected the notion that a moment in time can be grasped or that time is precisely linear. *Behind My Eye* opens into a book-like format that embraces the fluidity of time, making us aware of the instability of time and our uncertain grasp of it.

© Mike and Doug Starn. *Behind My Eye*, 1998. 14 x 11 x 4 inches. Mixed media.

if our vision worked like photography, then we would see things the way a camera does.[1]

This chapter calls into question basic photographic axioms dealing with the representation of space and time. This is not meant to discourage photographers from working in this traditional mode, but to encourage growth in unexplored territory. Although the topics are discussed in terms of film, most can be carried out by digital means as well.

Controlling Photographic Time through the Camera

While relativity mathematics shows how the rate of time differs depending on velocity, it does not explain why time seems to pass more slowly, or more rapidly, depending on how boring a given activity is or how eagerly we anticipate a future event. This chapter encourages the photographer to engage with great

riddles that even stumped Einstein, such as the glaring mismatch between physical time and subjective or psychological time.

Another major ramification of relativity is that time is not a series of moments—some of which have not yet occurred—but rather a block in which we exist at a specific position, much like the way we exist at one point in space. The rest of the universe exists even though we are only in one place at one time; perhaps the remainder of time exists even though we have not visited the future. Since Einstein, physicists have generally rejected the notion that events "happen," as opposed to merely existing in the four-dimensional space-time continuum. The discrepancy between the frozen "block time" of physics and the flowing subjective time of the human mind suggests the need to rethink our concepts about time. Most humans find it impossible to relinquish the sensation of flowing time and a moving present moment. It is so basic to our daily experience that we reject the assertion that it is only an illusion or misperception.

By painting black-and-white photographs with oil paint and allowing portions of the original photograph to show through the colored paint, Roberts "marries the two different worlds of photography and painting. For me, the greatest challenge is to 'lose' the photograph with the paint, and then to pull up another image combining the paint and the photo." Her work flows through and connects normally disparate emotional and psychological elements of a journey of self-discovery.

© Holly Roberts. *Two People Watching*, 1991. 15 x 28 inches. Oil paint on gelatin silver print.

During the early days of moving pictures the practice of "reversing" (time), running the film backwards, provided a unique photographic experience that altered a basic concept of how we were taught to perceive our world. As many of Aristotle's theories point out, personal experience and/or intuition is by no means a trustworthy guidepost to scientific understanding. By diverting from standard photographic practice, we can begin to incorporate new ways to thinking about and portraying time using photo-based images.

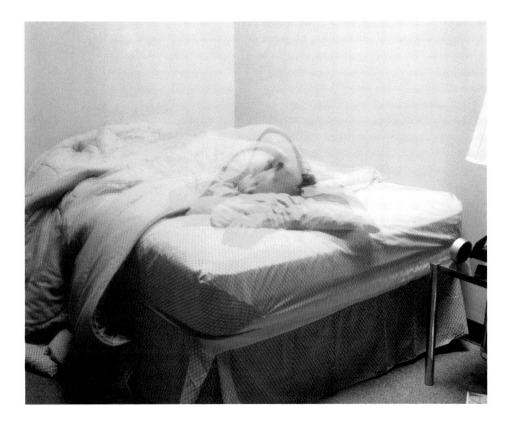

Moss combined long exposures and multiple f-stops to make portraits of his own body over many hours of sleep during the night. His images capture an aspect of everyday life that is not typically observed. "The images allude to several contradictory aspects of being: life and death, movement and stillness, darkness and light."

© Brian Moss. *Where Am I When I'm Asleep? 5-24-01*, 2001. 7 ¼ x 8 inches. Inkjet print.

Breaking Away from 1/125 of a Second

By turning the shutter to a slower speed, that is, increasing the time of exposure, we can increase the amount of time encompassed by the photograph. When the amount of time incorporated into the image is increased, more events become involved in the structure of the composition. This extended play of light on the film can have spectacular results. As light is recorded over a period of time a new fascination with color emerges as the hues swim together and blend into new visual possibilities. A new way of seeing and experiencing is presented to the viewer. Past conditioning has ingrained the concept that the photograph is supposed to be a single frozen moment (the Decisive Moment). Maybe the photograph isn't only a distinct, isolated, moment, but is made up of many moments. The simplest way to begin to break away from the standard 1/125 second mentality is by working with the different methods of dealing with motion.

Stop Action

Stopping the action of an event can be achieved by using a fast shutter speed or flash in conjunction with a high ISO. Consider freezing motion when it offers the viewer the opportunity to see something that happens too quickly for the eye to fully comprehend. It also offers a way to stop an event at a critical point of

Adams has used stop-action photography to give the viewer the opportunity to analyze a camera-created event on two levels: as the story told in the picture and the story of the making of the picture. Adams has this to say: "I am photographed by an assistant as I move around to various positions within the field of a stationary 4- x 5-inch camera (strobes used for this one), wearing different costumes for each exposure. I enlarge the sections in which I appear within each negative, cut them out, and tape them together to form a collage. The pictures are thus continuous scenes (the space does not appear fractured or distorted), in which I play numerous characters visually interacting with each other."

© Bill Adams. *Untitled*, 1989. 44 x 55 inches. Chromogenic color print

the action for further analysis and study, thereby providing the viewer with a new way of visualizing a situation.

Anticipation and timing are crucial to capture the climax of an event. Whenever possible, watch and study the action before shooting. Become familiar with how the event takes place. When shooting a stop-action photo select the appropriate vantage point and lens, then preset both the exposure and focus, taking care to use the smallest aperture to attain maximum depth of field. A wide-angle lens allows more room for error because it has more depth of field at any given aperture than a normal or tele-photo lens.

The telephoto lens can be used to isolate the action. A minimum depth of field separates the subject from the background. Prefocusing or using auto-focus lock becomes critical, because any inaccuracy results in the subject being out of focus.

The shutter speed needed to stop motion depends on the speed of the subject and its direction and distance from the camera (table 14.1). The nearer the subject or the longer the lens, the higher the shutter speed needs to be. A subject moving across the frame requires a higher shutter speed than one approaching head-on or at the peak of its action.

Armstrong makes collages of found photographs, colored papers, and reworked Xeroxes that he rephotographs at various distances, using slow shutter speeds, with the focusing ring of his camera set at infinity to intentionally blur the collage into an integrated, seamless image. "This sleight of hand allows me to conjure a mysterious *tromp l'oeil* world that hovers between the real and the fantastic. The nature of visual perception intrigues me: how the eye continually tries to resolve these images, but is unable to do so, and how that is unsettling. This technique enables me to blend and distill hues, creating rhapsodies of color that are meditative pieces—glimpses into a space of pure color."

© Bill Armstrong. *Untitled, #11*, 1999. 18 x 24 inches. Chromogenic color print.

Table 14.1 **Shutter Speed Needed to Stop Action Parallel to the Camera**
1/125 second: most everyday human activities, moving streams and rivers, tree in a slight wind.
1/250 second: running animals and people, birds in flight, kids playing, balloons and kites, swimmers, waves.
1/500 second: car at 30 miles per hour, bicyclists, motorcyclists, baseball, football, tennis.
1/1,000 second: car at 70 miles per hour, jet airplanes taking off, skiers, speedboats, high-speed trains.

Dim Light and Flash

In dim light, flash rather than shutter speed can be used to stop action. The ability to stop movement is dependent on the duration of the flash. A normal flash unit usually gives the equivalent speed of between 1/250 to 1/500 second. Fractional power settings can supply much faster times, up to 1/10,000 second.

The Blur and Out-of-Focus Images

The blur and out-of-focus images are as inherent to photographic practice as those that are clear and crisp. The blur interjects the suggestion of movement into the picture. This bends the traditional concept of photographic time, producing a miasma image capable of representing a sense of the past, the present, and the future. The blur can eliminate traditional photo-graphic detail, revealing a subject's physical and emotional essence. The blur destroys the notion of a discrete parcel of framed time depicting the past. The blur can provide a sense of suspension in the eternal process of becoming by confronting viewers with change itself. The lack of focus frees the images from the confines of photographic exactitude by offering a different representation of reality.

Begin your experiments by determining what shutter speed is needed to stop the subject's movement in relation to the camera position. A slower shutter speed causes more blur and consequently more contrast between the moving and static areas. This can isolate a static subject from its surroundings. Consider which details are crucial and need to be retained. Decide whether it will be more effective to blur the background or the subject.

Panning furthers the sense of movement in the composition. It concentrates the viewer's attention on the subject while de-emphasizing the background. In this case, flash was used in conjunction with a long handheld exposure. The mixture of artificial and natural light sources allowed the photographer to capture moving subjects in a poorly lit environment. It also provides a sense of place for the subject as well as creating a visually engaging ambiguity of space in the three-dimensional setting.

© Ron Giebert. *Ballroom Dance Competition, Okayama, Japan*, 1987. 7 ¼ x 11 inches. Chromogenic color print.

The Pan Shot

The camera can be intentionally moved to create a blur. One of the most effective ways to convey lateral movement, while freezing the subject and blurring the background, is the pan shot. Range finder cameras are easier to use for this because, unlike a single lens reflex camera (SLR), they contain no moving mirror to black out the viewfinder during exposure. With practice, most cameras can be used with success.

Start out with a subject whose move-ment and speed are consistent. To accomplish the pan shot, use a slow ISO, holding the camera comfortably in the horizontal position. Prefocus on the spot that the subject will cross and set the needed shutter speed. For example, 1/15 of a second can be used to pan a vehicle moving at 30 miles per hour and 1/30 of a second for 60 miles per hour. Correlate the aperture with the speed, using the smallest aperture to get maximum depth of field. Frame the subject as soon as possible. Do not tighten up or hold the camera with a death grip; stay loose.

Make the pan clean and smooth by following the subject with your entire body, not just with the camera. Gently release the shutter as the subject fills the frame and continue to follow through with the motion. Generally, take care not to crowd the subject. Leave it some space to keep moving unless containment is the object. After you learn this technique, try incorporating some variations such as panning faster or slower than the object in motion. Further motion effects can be created by using a slow shutter speed and intentionally moving the camera in nonparallel directions from the subject.

Many random elements enter into these situations that involve long exposures. It becomes a deliberate combination of intent and chance. With practice, it is possible to get an idea of what the final outcome will look like. The unpredictability of these situations adds to their fascination.

Moving the Film

Film movement can achieve the effect of blending colors in motion. Put the camera on a tripod and hand crank the film past the shutter during exposure, using a speed of 1/8 of a second or slower.

Equipment Movement

Equipment-induced movement can provide an exaggerated sense of motion. Consider the following ideas:

● **Use a wide-angle lens** (24 mm or wider). This produces dramatic feelings of motion when employed to photograph movement at close range and at a low angle. The exaggerated sense of perspec-

Jurus's strip photograph blends the subject and colors, achieving the effect of motion in a method that relies on a unique aspect of camera vision. Jurus built his own linear strip camera with a slit shutter to make this image. The film was exposed by cranking it past the slit. In this case the exposure time was about five seconds.

© Richard E. Jurus II. *Zing TA TA*, 1987. 3 ¼ x 10 inches. Chromogenic color print.

tive created by this lens produces distortion and causes background detail to appear smaller than normal, thereby losing visual importance. Conversely, foreground objects seem larger and more prominent.

- **A multi-image prism** that fits in front of the lens is another possibility. Its use requires care because it has been overused. All these ideas can be abused by the unthinking. When a piece of equipment is used in place of an idea, the result is a gimmick. When a photographer has to resort to gimmicks, control of the situation has been lost. Whenever equipment is used to strengthen and support an idea, the imagemaker is working with a technique.

- **The zoom lens** is one of the most popular and useful pieces of equipment available to photographers, but it falls into the same danger category as the prism. When used as a tool, the zoom lens can extend the range of photographic vision. Most commonly used is the zoom during exposure to create the illusion of motion. In this method blurred streaks of color come out of the center of the picture. It is a way to give a stationary subject the feeling of momentum. Put the camera on a tripod, set the lens to its longest focal length, and focus on the critical area of the subject. Start at 1/15 second and then make a series of exposures using even longer times. Be sure to change the aperture to compensate for changes in speed. Zoom back to the shortest focal length as the shutter is tripped. Be prepared to make a number of attempts. Write down the exposure information so that you know which combination produced each picture. Do not depend on your memory. Part of any learning experience is the ability to use the acquired skill in future applications. It helps to practice the zooming technique with no film in the camera until the operation becomes second nature. Once you learn the basic method, it can be combined with other techniques.

- **The pan zoom technique** requires the photographer to pan with the subject while zooming and releasing the shutter. The camera needs to be on a tripod with

A small, on-camera flash was used, and the camera was moved across the subject during a quarter-second exposure. A separate meter reading was used to determine the exposure for the ambient light, and the aperture was set to allow for the fill-flash effect. In this instance, a visual play is set up in which the background appears to have a fluid sense of movement while the subject remains frozen in contradiction to the apparent movement going on behind it.

© Stephen Petergorsky. *Untitled*, 1985. 17 ½ x 12 inches. Chromogenic color print.

a pan head. One hand is used to zoom while the other works the panning handle and shutter. A cable release is helpful, as is an assistant to fire the shutter at your instruction.

- **The tilt zoom technique** needs a tripod with a head that can both pan and tilt. Follow the same basic zoom procedure, but use longer exposure times (start at one second). Try tilting the camera during the zoom while the exposure

is being made, and then try working the pan into this array of moves. The long exposures give the photographer the opportunity to concentrate on this variety of camera moves.

Free-Form Camera Movement

Colored sources of illumination at dusk and after dark give the photographer the chance to weave line and pattern into a

The color shifts that occur in long exposures are produced by the reciprocity failure of the film. Filters and additional exposure are needed for correction, but the unusual color balance can provide a starting visual impact.

© Arthur Ollman. *Untitled*, 1980. n/s. Chromogenic color print.

still composition. With a stationary light source, try using slow shutter speeds (starting at 1/8 second) while moving the camera in your hand. Start by making simple geometric movements with the camera while visualizing the effect of the blending and overlapping of color and line. If the camera being used is an SLR, try to sight above the viewfinder or to not look at all, going by feel and instinct. Using a wide-angle lens should make this easier. If the camera is jerked and waved about too much the resulting color pat-

terns and lines may become confusing.

Moving lights can put color and motion into a static environment. With the camera on a tripod and using small apertures, make exposures at 10, 20, 30, or more seconds. Try not to include bright, nonmoving lights because they will become extremely overexposed and appear as areas with no discernible detail.

Flash and Slow Shutter Speed

The combination of flash with a slow shutter speed permits the incorporation of stillness and movement within the same scene. It is an impressionistic way of increasing ambiguity and mystery. The effects can be varied depending on the amount of flash to ambient light, and by the amount of movement of the camera (if it is handheld), or the subject, or both.

Using a color negative film, begin

work in the early morning or evening, or on a cloudy day when the ambient light level is low. A neutral-density filter is needed when shooting in brighter light. A basic working technique is to cut the ISO rating of the film by one-half and use this new rating to take a normal exposure reading of the scene (ambient light). Set your flash with the same modified ISO rating. Determine the flash exposure based on the distance of the key object(s) in the composition. If the ratio of flash to ambient light is the same, the color palette will be soft. As the ratio of flash to ambient light is increased, the color palette tends to become more saturated. Use an exposure speed of 1/4 second or longer. The flash exposure freezes the subject and the length of exposure time determines the amount of movement that is apparent in the image. Bracketing your exposures and movement is a good idea until you gain a sense of how this interplay works.

Extended Time Exposures

Using the B or T setting, long exposures can be made over a period of time with the camera attached to a tripod. Utilize a cable or electronic release to avoid camera shake. Employ a small lens aperture or a slow ISO to make the exposure longer. For even longer exposures, put neutral density filters in front of the lens. Avoid bright static sources of light. Reciprocity law failure causes a shift in the color balance. Film is suggested for extended exposures because digital cameras are affected by image noise and battery drain.

Clouds, lighting, wind, and passing lights can introduce a sense of motion and create a mood. Other atmospheric effects, such as moonlight and star trails, can be achieved with exposures starting at about 30 minutes and up (see table 14.2). Wide-angle lenses are recommended for increased coverage and the location needs to be away from ambient light sources. Generally include a foreground reference, such as a building or a tree, for scale and sense of place. For maximum star trails, make long exposures on clear, moonless nights. If the moon is too bright, the star trails will not be visible and the image can begin to resemble daylight, although the light from the moving moon may fill in the shadows that would otherwise be cast by the sun in a daylight photograph. An FL-D can cut the garish green color cast from the fluorescent light in office buildings that may be included in nighttime cityscapes.

Table 14.2 **Star Trails Exposures at f /2.8, ISO 50**	
No moon	1 ½ hours minmum
Quarter moon	1 hour
Half moon	30 to 60 minutes
Full moon	10 to 20 minutes

Rephotography

Rephotography is when a photographer returns to a subject that had been previously photographed and attempts to make the exact picture again to show how time has altered the original scene. Precise records are maintained so the returning photographer can more easily duplicate the original scene. The original photograph and the new one are usually displayed next to each other to make comparison easy.

In another form of rephotography, the photographer returns to the same subject over a period of time. Examples of this would range from making a picture of yourself every day for a week, to Alfred Stieglitz's photographs of Georgia O'Keeffe that span decades. The relationship of the photographer and the subject is pursued over a period of time. The results should represent the wide range of visual possibilities that can be produced from this combination due to changes in feeling, light, and mood.

Multiple Exposure

Making more than one exposure on a single frame offers another avenue of exploration. Try it out in a controlled situation with a black background. Light the setup, mount the camera on a tripod, and prefocus and calculate the exposure based on the number of exposures planned. A good starting point is to divide the exposure by the number of planned exposures. For example, if the normal exposure is f /11 at 1/4 second, two exposures would be f /11 at 1/8 second each. A camera with automatic exposure control can do the same thing by multiplying the speed of the film by the number of exposures and then resetting the meter to that new speed.

Try varying the amount of exposure time. This can give both blurred and sharp images as well as images of different intensity within one picture. Repeated firing of a flash provides multiple exposures when the camera shutter is left open on the T or B setting. Move the subject or the camera to avoid getting an image buildup at one place on the film.

Sandwiching Transparencies

A simple way to work with more than one image is to sandwich transparency film into a single slide mount. Transparent color tints can be added to modify the atmosphere. Tints can be made from any transparent medium or by photographing discrete portions of a subject, such as the sky or a wall. Bracketing provides a range of color choices from supersaturated to high-key. An internegative can be made of the final result and used to make regular chromogenic color prints. This can also be done by scanning two or more frames of film or building layers using imaging software.

Expose the Same Roll Twice

Another multiple exposure idea is to run the film through the camera twice. Cut the ISO rating of the film being used by one-half. Try photographing the same subject from a different point of view, at a different time of day, closer up, or farther away, or photograph an entirely different subject. If you want the frames to line up, mark or cut a small, V-shaped notch on the edge of the film. Make a pencil mark inside the camera body, below the film plane, which will serve as a guide to realign the film. Make a contact sheet of the roll and examine it carefully. What new ways of seeing and composing has chance provided? How can this new knowledge be applied to other, maybe more controlled shooting situations to expand your visual limits?

Painting with Light

Using light as a paintbrush requires setting the camera on a tripod with a medium to small lens aperture. Start with a subject against a simple backdrop in a darkroom. Prefocus the camera, then use a small pocket flashlight with a blind to control the amount and direction of the light. Leave the lens open (use the T setting or the B setting with a locking cable release). By wearing dark clothes, the photographer can quickly walk around within the picture and

Daily Portrait began in 1978 with photographs that formed a dialog between Jeffrey Fuller, Madigan, and a beech tree on the shore of Lake Michigan, and has been in continuous progress. With the birth of their children, *Daily Portrait* has shifted to include their developing relationships. Madigan says: "Every day, a snapshot portrait is made of each child, and I often photograph them together. Every season marks a shift in *Daily Portrait*. From March 21 to June 21 during the years 1982 to 1988, I photographed my children in front of this magnificent azalea bush. *Daily Portrait* makes a cyclic journey tangible through the photographs as evidence. It is an attempt to touch the absolute through constant change." "What is eternal is circular and what is circular is eternal," said Aristotle.

© Martha Madigan. *Daily Portrait, Daniel and Claire and the Azaleas*, March 21–June 21, 1988. 80 inches in diameter. Chromogenic color prints.

draw with the light without being recorded by the film. Imagine how the light is being recorded. Since the final effect is difficult to anticipate, be prepared to make a series of exposures. Vary the hand gestures used with the light source to see what effect will be created. Colored gels can be applied to any light source in order to alter its color output. The gels can be varied to introduce a variety of hues into the scene. As experience is gained, more powerful light sources, such as strobes and floods, can be used to cover larger areas, including outdoor scenes.

Slide Projection

A slide projector with a zoom lens can also be used to paint a scene with light (by placing a colored gel or gels over the lens) or to project an image onto a scene to create a visual layering effect. Try using old slides, making new slides of the same subject, using black-and-white slides, appropriating images or text from other sources, projecting more than one image, projecting different images into different parts of the composition, or using the zoom lens to vary the size of

Bernstein created this image by making four separate exposures. Bernstein explains: "Using a copystand, all the pieces are placed on black and photographed on one piece of film. I draw a simple acetate mask and place it in the viewfinder of my Hasselblad for placement. Extension tubes and Proxar filters allow me to work close-up. I used a photograph of Alois Brunner (Nazi war criminal) to create an image of a serial killer stalking female victims. Secrecy is maintained as sins are committed."

© Audrey Bernstein. *The Sin*, 1993. 30 x 30 inches. Dye-destruction print.

The first exposure for this photograph was made of a mural by O'Gorman in Mexico City. The second exposure was made in a market in San Cristobal to fashion a cinematic narrative of time and culture. This multiple exposure process involved exposing portions of a roll on fragments of murals, making notes, rewinding the film, and later re-exposing it in a random frame overlay. The uncut roll is edited to slightly less than two frames to make the final image. Full-color saturation is achieved by exposing Kodachrome 64 at ISO 125 and re-exposing it at ISO 185. The layering of colors, masses, and spaces forms its own contrast mask, thus cutting the inherent contrast in both the Kodachrome film and the Ilfochrome Classic printing process.

© Lorne Greenberg. *Victims of the Colonial Regime*, 1988. 5 ½ x 14 inches. Dye-destruction print.

By incorporating long exposures and painting with light through the use of multiple handheld flashes, Shank transforms a natural landscape into a surrealistic scene. The long exposures bring out the changing colors of the sky, and the chairs are individually lit with the handheld flashes, altering the everyday object to a level of personification.

© Christine Shank. *Untitled*, from the *visual dramas* series, 2002. 20 x 24 inches. Chromogenic color print.

the projection. For a naturalistic color balance, make certain the type of film or color balance setting used matches the color of the light source. Filters in front of the camera lens may be necessary to make color corrections.

Postvisualization

The darkroom offers the photographer a postexposure opportunity to expand and induce movement and time into a still scene. Application of these postvisualization methods can break the photographic idea that time is a mirror rendering the appearance of nature into the hands of humans. These methods let the photographer increase the possible modes of exploration with the work. These techniques include the interaction between positive and negative space, and interaction between different aspects of the same event, the interaction between static structure and movement, and interaction between the viewer and the object being viewed. Be ready to experiment and rely on intuition. Many of these methods can also be accomplished using digital imaging software.

Moving the Easel

When moving the easel, prepare to print in the normal fashion. Calculate the proper exposure, giving the print 75 percent of that figure. Make a second expo-

Walking the streets of Berlin, Attie kept asking himself, "Where are all the missing people? What has become of the Jewish culture and community which had once been at home here? ... I wanted to give this invisible past a voice." Attie projected prewar photographs of Jewish street life in Berlin onto the same location today in order to introduce fragments of the past into the present. Using photography as an archaeological tool Attie explores the presence of absence. "By attempting to renegotiate the relationship between past and present events, the aim of the project was to interrupt the collective process of denial and forgetting."

© Shimon Attie. *Almstadstrasse/Corner Schendelgasse, Berlin: Slide projection of former Jewish religious book salesman (1930)*, 1992. (On-location installation). 20 x 24 inches. Chromogenic color print. Courtesy of Nicole Klagsburn Gallery, New York, NY.

sure of the remaining 25 percent and move the easel during this time. This ratio may be altered to achieve different results. The easel may be tilted during the exposure or the paper can be curled and waved outside of the easel for additional effects. The easel can be placed on a device such as a "lazy Susan" and spun to create circular motion.

Moving the Fine Focus

Moving the fine focus control on the enlarger is a method of expanding the picture. Give the print two-thirds of its required normal exposure time. For the remaining one-third exposure time, move the fine focus adjustment on the enlarger. To give yourself more time to manipulate the fine focus control stop the lens down and increase the exposure time. The outcome will be determined by how fast the fine focus control is moved, how long it is left at any one point, and the proportion of normal exposure to moving exposure.

Painting the Print with Light

Painting the print with light can be accomplished with a small penlight fitted with a handmade opaque blinder. The blinder acts as an aperture to control the amount of light. If this is done during the development stage of the print it produces a partial Sabattier effect (see chapter 16, page 321). Different transparent filters can be placed in front of the flashlight to alter the color effects. This technique can often be effective when combined with other methods, including the masking of specific portions of the image.

Multiple Exposure Using One Negative

Exposing one negative a number of separate times onto a single piece of printing paper can vastly alter the perception of time within the picture. Many variations are conceivable.

● Reduce the size of the picture and

The negative was etched using a knife, the fine focus control on the enlarger was moved during exposure, and the resulting print was painted with light during the exposure phase of processing. A red filter and masking were used to control the areas that were struck by light. Synthetic color was added later with an airbrush.

© Robert Hirsch. *David*, 1984. 16 x 20 inches. Gelatin-silver print with enamel paint. Courtesy of CEPA Gallery, Buffalo, NY.

print it a number of times on a single piece of paper. Let parts of each picture overlap to form new images.
● Vary the size of the picture as it is printed on the paper.
● Change the exposure times in order to create a variety of densities.
● Print the full frame on part of the paper and then print different parts from the negative onto the paper.

Combination Printing

Printing more than one negative on a single piece of paper jettisons the traditional picture vision and embraces a far more complex image of reality. This is commonly done by switching negatives in the enlarger or by moving the paper to another enlarger and easel that has a different negative set up for projection. Opaque printing masks are used to block out different parts of the paper in order to control the areas of exposure.

Combination printing can also involve combining a negative with a photogram or varying the exposure time of different parts of the print. Determine the proper exposure and give a percentage of it to the paper, then mask certain areas and give the remainder of the exposure.

Digital software also permits the compositing of scenes to form a new one.

Multiple Filter Packs

Making use of more than one filter pack can transform the picture's sense of time. Start with a negative that contains a basically monochromatic color scheme and simple linear composition. Print one area of the picture with the normal filter pack while holding back the exposure on another part of the print. Now change the filter pack.

Consider working with complementary colors. Print in the area that was

dodged out during the first exposure while holding back that part of the print that was already exposed.

The Cinematic Sequence

The cinematic mode of picture making, in which each new frame implies a new episode or another step, modifies the way photographic time is perceived. It is concerned with the interaction among the objects of the composition. The space between objects can become part of the same structure as the objects. Forms actually reverse themselves. The topics covered in this section can be done using either film or digital methods.

The vitality of movement can be conveyed through the use of traditional still pictures linked together to form a cinematic sequence of events. This group of pictures is designed to function not individually but as a group. The sequence must be able to provide information that a single image would be incapable of doing. A sequence can tell a story, present new information over an extended period of time, or supply a different point of view.

The Matrix-Grid

The grid can be used as a device to lead the viewer through the details and visual relationships of a scene. Photograph a person or object so that the pictures have to be combined to make a complete statement. The pictures do not have to be made from one frozen vantage point but rather from a general point of view. It is possible to incorporate a number of variations of the subject into one single statement. Try it with Polaroid film for instant feedback. Imaging software has greatly simplified the process of making picture grids.

This type of picture invites the audience to spend time looking at it because the sense of time is fluid; it cannot be taken in all at once. The viewer must take many separate glimpses and build them up into a continuous experience, much as we see the actual world around us.

Many Make One

"Many make one" describes the visual process of photographing a scene in numerous individual parts and then fitting these single pieces of time together to create one image. The single pictures

of the original scene are not made from a specific vantage point but a general one. This encompasses different points of view over an extended period of time.

The focus may also be shifted to emphasize important elements of each single frame. Take all the prints and spread them out on a big piece of mat board. Begin to build an entire image out of the many components. It is okay to overlap pictures, discard others, and have open spaces and unusual angles.

Try not to crop the single pictures because a standard size seems to act as a unifying device. When the arrangement is satisfactory, attach the prints to the board. They do not have to be flush.

This method of picture making can expand the sense of space and time that is often lost in an ordinary photograph. It breaks down the edges of a regular photograph. It expands the frame beyond the conventional four perpendicular edges and can bring the viewer

Using tapestries that illustrate memorial events as a model, Berger weaves multiple images into a coherent visual field that reflects a unity of how we see and process the multiple perceptions that make up daily life. A loom, like a computer, was one of the first machines to give precise, grid-like, algorithmic repeatability and organization to the structure of time within visual works.

© Paul Berger. *Warp & Weft: Figure, Tree*, 2002. 35 x 47 inches. Inkjet print.

An incredible painterly sense of time, space, and place is woven by Hockney's masterful application of the "many make one" method. Exposing 650 rolls over a nine-day period, Hockney used about a thousand single images to create a new photo-based interpretation of the originally seen landscape.

© David Hockney. *Pearblossom Hwy. 11–18th April 1986* (2nd version). 78 x 111 inches. Chromogenic color prints.

right into the picture.

Contact Sheet Sequence

The contact sheet sequence is a modified technique of using many single contact-size images to make a statement. Pick a scene and imagine an invisible grid pattern in front of it. Photograph that scene using this invisible pattern as a guide. Process the film, then arrange the nega-tives into the desired order based on your grid pattern, and contact print them to form a complete image.

Joiners

Joiners are created when a number of separate images of a scene are combined to make a whole. The subject can be divided into separate visual components and photographed individually. Each part provides information about the sub-ject that could not have been included if the subject was shot in a single frame. These additional exposures should alter how the subject is perceived. This includes its relative position in time and space, changes in vantage point and angle, and variations in subject-to-cam-era distance. Single prints are made, laid out on a mat board, arranged, fitted, or trimmed, and then attached into place.

Slices of Time

Slices of time occur when a single scene is photographed a number of separate times to show the visual changes that can occur over a period of time. Intentional alter-ations in light and placement of objects can be made each time the scene is pho-tographed. Prints can be butted together, overlapped, or cut into slices and pieced together.

With practice the pieces may be cut into a variety of different sizes and shapes. Keep each cut picture separate. Select one of the pictures to be the base print. Arrange it on a mat board and begin to combine the slices from the other prints into the single base print. When com-plete, attach the slices to the board.

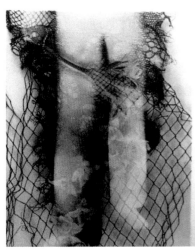

Working from her Mexican American culture, Vargas makes double exposures to represent the duality of time: life and death presented at once. "Death is simply a part of the cycle of living. I depict the starkness of death within the complement of beauty. People look at the soft colors and find there's a little death waiting inside; or they look at the harshness of death and find life waiting for them in the seduction of the colors."

© Kathy Vargas. *Missing #1* (left panels), 1992. 48 x 20 inches. Gelatin-silver print with mixed media.

Composite Pictures

Composite photographs occur when visual elements from various sources and mediums are intertwined and then cut out or pasted on a common support material and rephotographed to obtain the final image. If the picture is not rephotographed, it is considered to be a montage. Pictures of astonishing paradox can be produced using this method, especially when manual and digital techniques are used in tandem.

Photographic Collage

A photographic collage is made when cut

Working both manually and digitally, Hutchinson integrates broken fragments taken out of time to craft tangible realities that describe complex psychological spaces dealing with self-identification. "All my mark making is done before the computer and all of the blending and scaling of the different layers is done with Photoshop."

© Ambler Hutchinson. *Untitled* [slide #20, image description: girl with scissors], 1999. 17 x 9 inches. Inkjet print.

Deschamps built an assemblage in which "the colors of the images and the colors of the wood harmonize. I want to achieve an interplay between illusion and reality, between the photographic image and the materials used to construct the piece. The whole should appear organic and complete in its own little world that evokes a feeling of distant and mythical South Seas."

© Francois Deschamps. *The Oldest Woman of Yadrana*, 2000. 9 x 26 inches. Chromogenic color print with mixed media.

or torn pieces from one or more photographs are pasted together, often with three-dimensional objects, to produce the final picture. The picture is not rephotographed. In this technique no attempt is made to hide the fact that it is an assemblage.

Three-Dimensional Photographs

Three-dimensional photographs can be made by emphasizing one attribute of a subject—color, pattern, shape, or texture—and having it physically come off the flat picture surface. This exaggeration in time and space calls attention to that aspect of the subject while de-emphasizing its other qualities.

Photo-Based Installations

Photo-based installations comprise an entire arrangement of objects, not just a group of discrete images/objects to be viewed as individual works, presented as a single work. Installations provide viewers with the experience of being in and/or surrounded by the work, often for the purpose of creating a more intense sensory realization, and may

include still and moving images, computer screens, music, and sound. Precedents for installations can be found in the Pop Art era of the late 1950s and 1960s, such as Allan Kaprow's "sets" for Happenings or Red Groom's theatrical environments such as *Ruckus Manhattan*. Most installations are unsaleable and generally are exhibited and dismantled, leaving only photographic documentation of their existence.

Public Art

Art history is filled with more examples of public than private art, ranging from the frescos and sculpture of religious

Modrak built busts that seem life-like and statuesque, but have all the details and scars of daily life. "Piecing together figures allowed me to work sculpturally, to construct fragile and fantastic being, to include photographic minute details, and simultaneously question the static representation offered by conventional reality through a viewfinder."

© Rebekah Modrak. *Portrait (Babachou)*, 2000. 33 x 32 x 19 inches. Chromogenic color prints and mixed media.

centers, to the commemorative statuary of public squares. The dissolving of Modernist notions of purity of form and the rise of government initiatives, such as the percent-for-art programs that set aside a certain percentage (usually 1 percent) of a construction budget, led to an increase in artists' projects in public spaces. Changing attitudes by artists who give up the absolute control of the studio and who collaborate, as well as new technologies, have made it easier to

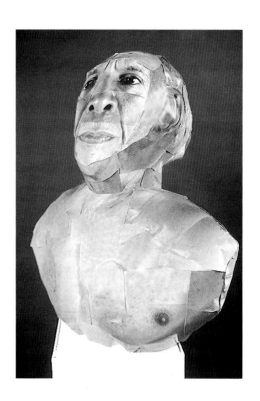

bring artworks outside the traditional context of museums and galleries and into daily life. Work is shown in centers of public transportation, city streets, and workplaces, and is seen by people outside the art and academic worlds. Part of the fun and power of public art is its ability to enter into the space of everyday life by catching you by surprise—an audience not intending to be an audience, which often accidentally challenges the status quo.

Penetrating the Photographic Mirror

Being able to understand this type of nontraditional photographic time means continuing to penetrate the mirror of reality. Whenever traveling into the unknown we can hope to be rewarded with understanding. Ironically, the information that is brought with you may prove to be invalid in new circumstances. As T.S. Eliot said: "Time the destroyer is time the preserver." Be prepared to expand your previous concepts of how reality is composed.

Byrd's work is autobiographical, but "rather than documenting my daily experience, I have chosen to use photography to create visual metaphors for what happens to me. Since my work stems from the relationship between reality and fantasy I use applied colors (toners, pastels, and paint) on black-and-white photographs." The repetition of hanging 300 gold-leafed razor blades with red thread relates to the performance aspect of Byrd's work. "The blades would move with each gentle breeze as people walked by. They looked surprisingly like butterflies fluttering above the body. I only cut myself three times."

© Jeffery Byrd. *Untitled*, 1993. 75 x 36 x 24 inches. Gelatin-silver print with mixed media.

Requiem for September 11th was commissioned by CEPA Gallery for the Market Arcade Building in downtown Buffalo, New York, to commemorate the first anniversary of the terrorist attacks of September 11, 2001. This large-scale public art memorial project consists of 45 white translucent fabric banners, each 16 feet long and four feet wide, suspended in two columns 12 feet above the arcade floor. The site-specific installation—designed to mimic the twin towers of the World Trade Center—represents each of the victims of September 11 with hand silk-screened images and text culled mostly from the *New York Times Portraits of Grief* series. Embodying the power of public art, this memorial simultaneously offers a moving tribute to all who died on 9/11, as well as a site for the living to reflect and grieve.

© Tatana Kellner. *Requiem for September 11th*, 2002. 16 x 10 x 44 feet. Silkscreen on fabric. Courtesy of CEPA Gallery, Buffalo, NY.

Eliasson creates relationships by photographing specific geographic phenomena in his native Icelandic environment. The grid of images becomes more than the sum of its parts as the rhythmic orchestration abstracts nature into a bodily illusion, encouraging viewers to look harder, see more, feel wonder, and expand their concepts of what makes up reality.

© Olafur Eliasson. *The Fault Series*, 2001. 103 ½ x 146 inches. Chromogenic color print. Courtesy of Tanya Bonakdar Gallery, New York, NY.

Often the most important aspects of a scene are hidden because of their familiarity and simplicity and our own lack of knowledge. When an urban dweller drives by a field with cattle in it, the urban person sees a field with cattle in it. When a farmer drives by the same field the farmer sees something entirely different. The farmer can identify the breeds of cow and knows what condition the cows are in, what is planted in the field, and how the crop is growing. Both are viewing the same scene, but the farmer's broader knowledge and understanding of what is there allows the farmer to read more of the visual clues that are in the scene. This provides the farmer with a richer and more accurate account of the scene.

By extending our picture-making endeavors we create new ways to look at the world and enlarge our understanding of its complex system of interaction.

assignment

Select one of the methods discussed in this chapter and render it using only chemical and handmade methods. Then pick another topic and complete it using only digital techniques. Now select a third topic and execute it by combining both approaches and compare the results. What differences do you see in the final images and how might this affect viewer response? What are the advantages and disadvantages of each way of working?

References

Detailed information about many of the processes discussed in this chapter is available in HIRSCH, ROBERT. *Photographic Possibilities, The Expressive Use of Ideas, Materials & Processes*, 2nd ed. Boston, MA: Focal Press, 2001.
For information concerning time and space see: HAWKING, STEPHEN W. *A Brief History of Time: From the Big Bang to Black Holes*. New York: Bantam, 1988.

MORRIS, RICHARD. *Time's Arrow: Scientific Attitudes Toward Time*. New York: Simon and Schuster, 1985.

RUSSELL, BERTRAND. *The ABC of Relativity*, 4th ed. New York: New American Library, 1985.

SHELDON, JAMES L., and REYNOLDS, JOCK. *Motion and Document Sequence and Time: Eadweard Muybridge and Contemporary American Photography*. Andover, MA: Addison Gallery of American Art, Phillips Academy, 1991.

Endnotes

[1] JOEL SNYDER and NEIL WALSH ALLEN, "Photography, Vision, and Representation," *Critical Inquiry* 2, no. 1, Autumn 1975, 163–64.

Chapter Fifteen

COLOR PROJECTS

Golden created a composite mask in which her own face peeks through a partially torn and crinkled fashion magazine photograph to explore the effects of advertising on popular beliefs and fantasies about women. Golden thus points to the way women are defined by youth culture and the fear of ageing. Her layered technique generates a sense of temporality in relation to personal history, implying that the construction of the present self is the result of past actions.

© Judith Golden. *Rhinestones*, 1976. 14 x 11 inches. Gelatin silver print with oil paint and glitter.

Self-Portraits

Since the time of German artist Albrecht Dürer (1471–1528), artists have expressed many inner concerns through self-portraits. They have shown awareness of their own appearance and traits, producing evidence that will probably outlive them of the complexity of their lives. Their portraits continue to gaze back at the viewer in another time and place. Self-portraits can show you as you are or may reveal an ambition of yours to be something other than your ordinary self. These pictures often reveal the secret self. In recent times, some artists have been using the self-portrait as a means of assuming historical guises to confront and challenge archetypes and stereotypes that have been formulated about the roles men and women play within society.

Making a Self-Portrait

With these ideas in mind, make a self-portrait. The photograph should express self-awareness and reveal something that is important for others to know about you. A good way to reacquaint yourself with yourself is to sit down in front of a mirror alone, without any outside distractions. After studying your image in the mirror, get a pencil and paper and make a series of contour drawings. To make a contour drawing look into the mirror and draw what you see and feel without looking at the paper until you have finished. Based on what you learned from making the contour drawing, make a photographic portrait of yourself.

Portrait of an Other

Portrait of Another Person

Next, make a photographic portrait of someone you know following these same

Sherman's use of self-portraits reveals her secret ambitions, dreams, fantasies, and hopes within the framework of a media-image-saturated society. This work also shows the fun of dressing up and playacting before the camera.

© Cindy Sherman. *Untitled #131*, 1983. 34 1/3 x 16 1/2 inches. Chromogenic color print. Courtesy of Metro Pictures, New York, NY.

guidelines. This photograph should present information to the viewer that shows something important about this person's character. Try photographing yourself and another person in the same surroundings. Compare the resulting differences and similarities.

Environmental Portrait

Make a portrait that shows the viewer how the individual interacts with his or her environment. Consider showing only one part of the sitter's surroundings so as not to diminish the importance of the person.

Portrait of an Object

Compose a photographic portrait of an object that tells your audience something about your feelings and relationship toward it.

Here are technical considerations that will guide you through this process:

- **Camera** Any.
- **Lens** What will best fit the situation.
- **Light** Make all your pictures using daylight as your only source of illumination. Do not use any artificial light, including flash.
- **Image size** Print the full frame of your negative; don't force it to fit the standard 5- x 7-inch or 8- x 10-inch size. Make the size of your print fit the concerns of the subject. Don't try to fit them into an arbitrary size.

Kline relates: "By including a few specific objects in a very specific light I hope to stimulate a resonant synergy between the viewer and the environments beheld. In order to successfully communicate the emotional essence of these solitary places, it becomes crucially important to control the Kelvin temperature relationship of the scene's varying light sources. The color of light, the feel of a room, the sense of time, and the season outdoors all combine to provoke the many buried memories we all carry. Much of my approach has been affected by the contemporary American short-story writers such as Raymond Carver, Grace Paley, and Gordon Lish."

© Jon Kline. *Attic Train*, 1989. 30 x 40 inches.
Chromogenic color print.

Barney's photographs are elaborately staged tableaus, echoing the daily lives of her close circle of family and friends who are in fact her subjects. She shoots with a 4 x 5 camera and makes richly colored, large-scale prints of the kinds of mundane scenes we are used to seeing in photo albums and scrapbooks. Her photographs comment on the daily rituals and customs of upper-class, Anglo-American life.

© Tina Barney. *Sunday New York Times*, 1982. 48 x 60 inches. Chromogenic color print. Courtesy of Janet Borden Inc., New York, NY.

Lê's work is about "trying to establish my identity in relation to the culture I have entered. As a Vietnamese living in a Western society, educated in Western institutions and surrounded by Western popular culture, I am a product of both East and West. Through my work, I explore the exchange and interweaving of cultures and identities from a bicultural perspective."

© Dinh Q. Lê. *Self Portrait After Bosch, The Haywain*, 1991. 40 x 57 inches. Chromogenic color prints and tape.

● **Point of view** Break with tradition and make some photographs that are not at eye level.

Ideas Make Photographs

Think before starting to make this series of images. Develop an idea and let it lead you through the process. Edmund Carpenter said: "Technique cannot conceal that meaningless quality everywhere characteristic of art without belief." Techniques well learned can help us to speak, but some of the greatest thoughts have been expressed by the simplest means. Ideas, not equipment, create powerful photographs.

View from Within/Portrait as Social Identity

There has been much interest in using photography to represent groups of people who in the past had their visual identity created from outside rather than from within their own social group. Historically, photography has played a major role in shaping how different groups of people are perceived. Beginning with nineteenth-century ethnological studies such as John Thompson's *The Antiquities of Cambodia* (1867) and *Illustrations of China and Its People* (1873–74), outside observers have brought back exotic images that reconfirmed the pre-existing attitudes, prejudices, and stereotypes of those in power. Thompson made pictures for people who considered "the other" to be primitive and inferior. His work reflected the values of the British colonial system, which believed it had the right and the duty to govern other lands and enlighten the natives of its colonies to Christianity and the monarchy. Such practices helped to objectify and exploit the native populations, which had no control over how they were pictured or the contexts in which their pictures were deployed within the society at large.

Your assignment is to examine how the practice of photography can become part of the process of dismantling preconstructed notions and shape a new portrait that more closely reveals how a group currently would like to represent itself. Make images of members of your specific cultural subgroup(s) or of those with whom you have shared similar circumstances. The purpose is to provide a contextualized reading from the point of view of that private experience within your particular subculture. Discover ways to express an understanding of the social rituals of your group that allow you to deliver intimate, firsthand accounts of the group's values—a view from within rather than a gaze from without. There should be a sense of comfort, ease, and openness between you and your subject. The pictures should be a result of your bond to the group, and should display an innate sense of trust with the subjects. Through such work it is possible for groups to begin to reclaim control over their own image by modifying misrepresentations that have previously been placed in circulation.

Representing Rituals

Try concentrating on specific rituals that provide your group with a common, cohesive experience. Ritual is an act of bonding. It provides a way for us to forge a loyalty that transcends our individuality. It is a uniting force that allows us to blend into a community that shares common ambitions, despairs, dreams, passions, and values. It reveals how the act of photography can supply the power of ownership over how our visual image is defined.

Make photographs that question historical depictions and in turn realize and discover your group's own stories. Reject being embarrassed by cultural features that do not fit into mainline esteem. Examine a heritage that may have been intentionally concealed out of shame and ridicule. Ask the question: What does it mean to be a member of this specific circle?

The results are often private stories, based on personal involvement within a specific community, which have the capacity to expand outward, encompassing the universal in a narrative tradition that embraces the collective of human nature. Such work can function as an act of reclamation and provide a new telling by recognizing that the earlier legends were incomplete. It also implies that the community is an ongoing process, which requires the participation of each new generation to keep the story alive and relevant. The picturing and preserving of rituals extends the time that the participants can spend celebrating and contemplating their own values. Your images can proclaim that what is of worth is of our own creation, thus recognizing differences through the process of deconstructing myths. This picturing of core experiences can provide an infrastructure of social events that becomes part of the group's consciousness. The alteration in self-perception can help provide the strength and confidence necessary to reformulate a community's social identity.

Who is Qualified to Speak?

Working in the arena of social identity raises some difficult questions. First, who has the right to speak/represent a particular group? Must you be African American to make work about slavery, or gay to comment about sexual preference? Second, does having a strong identification with a specific group give you the ability to make images about that group? Third, is it possible to have a memory of something you never experienced? Can Jews born after World War II produce compelling commentary about the Holocaust? Finally, who determines the validity of such experiences and bestows the credentials to make legitimate images?

What is Reality: What is a Hot Dog?

It is estimated that Americans consume an average of 80 hot dogs per person per year. It is clearly a national pastime. Pretend that aliens from another planet have contacted the United States government. They communicate only through

McGovern's series of images depicting young people who live their fantasies of greatness through professional wrestling illustrates how photography can create identities and blur fiction into fact. "But look beneath the surface of their bravado and there are signs of the vulnerable and slight young person, trying desperately to find his or her way in a world where image rules."

© Thomas McGovern. *Under Pressure and Iceman John Black*, from *Hard Boys and Bad Girls*, 2002. 15 x 22 inches. Chromogenic color print.

Above, Neal has visually conveyed the attributes of eating a hot dog in a warm, humorous manner.

© Ellen Neal. *Untitled*, 1985. 8 x 10 inches. Chromogenic color print.

Below, the hot dog is disguised by altering its traditional context. Bosworth comments on his approach: "A photographer's stockpile of props often becomes a large portion of their visual vocabulary. The more formally pleasing, easily manipulated, or recognizably symbolic objects become the most common part of that vocabulary. As I have never stopped playing with toys, they are still a part of my environment. When I interact with toys, I tell myself things that I did not know. Although they are a vocabulary which I use for myself, I would like to widen this conversation to include others."

© Michael Bosworth. *Untitled*, 1991. 24 x 36 cm. Chromogenic color transparency.

pictures. They have no spoken or written language. They want to know only one thing: What is a hot dog? The President does not know if the aliens' intentions are peaceful or warlike, and calls on you to solve the dilemma. See your assignment, right.

Photographic Reality

The photograph has become a major part of our decision-making process. Its inherent ability to transcribe external reality enables it to present what appears to be an accurate and unbiased validation of a scene. While photography is expert at expressing events, it also subtly interprets events by constantly interacting and integrating with the current values of the society at large. In reality, the so-called impartial lens allows every conceivable distortion of reality to take place. Even in the Photoshop age people

Grant conveys: "My work consists of previsualized imagery created from my journal that contains writings and sketches synthesized from confronting personal issues, relationships, dreams, and inner preoccupations." Some of the issues raised in this piece include tensions between longing and being repulsed, wanting acceptance but not seeking it, father and daughter difficulties, older man and young women, the strain between male/female relationships. The work in this series was created by dissecting 4- x 5-inch color negatives and enlarging them into nine segments. The segments are each 20 x 24 inches, some of the panels are printed backwards, some are placed out of order, and some are enlarged more than others. The images are then reassembled to make up a whole image.

© Susan Kae Grant. *Accept*, 1989. 5 x 6 feet. Chromogenic color prints mounted on aluminum.

continue to believe in the authority of the photograph. Traditionally we knew that painters inserted or left out objects that were in the original scene to depict a scene from their imagination, and photographers were not supposed to do

MAKE A PHOTOGRAPH THAT USES THE POWER OF COLOR TO DEAL WITH EACH OF THE FOLLOWING THEMES:

● *Produce a picture of something that bothers you or that you find disturbing. Use your fears or neuroses for a chance at development and growth. Consider these possibilities: Can your pictures be used to confront something that makes you unhappy? Is it possible for the act of photography to lead to a new understanding of this situation? Can a picture increase your knowledge of the world? Can the act of picture making produce a change in your attitudes about something or make you more sympathetic to a particular cause? Do not be like the dog that runs in circles chasing its own tail. Use the picture-making experience to break out of your habits and routines and see.*

● *Construct a photo of an inner fantasy. Let your creative energy spring from yourself. Your own ideas and experiences communicated directly to another are always more important, instructive, and powerful than the secondhand imitation of someone else's style. Let them out in your imagemaking. Keeping them inside can make you aggressive, crabby, irritable, or depressed. People can become intolerable when they cannot be creative. Bring forth yourself.*

● *Construct a photograph or a series of photographs that recall an important aspect of a memorable dream. It is okay to set things up to be photographed. You are the director. Do not take what is given if it is not what you want. Take charge. Do it your way and do it right.*

● *Use photography to politicize a social issue that you feel strongly about. Such topics can deal with war, women's issues, people from different ethnic groups, or AIDS. Address issues with which you have direct personal experience. Ask yourself if these images are being made solely to express your own feeling or if you want other people to seriously consider adopting your position. Approaches can be varied to meet the needs of specific viewing groups. Think about the type of response and reaction you want the viewer to have. This may be new material or something the audience does not completely or deeply understand. If you want your audience to be sympathetic, figure out a way not to alienate it. If this is of no consequence, then fire away.*

● *Make use of photographic means to portray a psychological drama. What is it you want to suggest? Do you need a literate, explicit narrative or can your concepts be implied? Are you raising questions or seeking answers? What do you want your audience to realize?*

Some things that concern photographers do not visually coexist in the natural world. Skoglund constructs fantasy installations for the purpose of being photographed. She uses color contrast as a method of portraying adult anxieties in a childlike context. In discussing her working method Skoglund says: "I find photography to be convenient as a unifying device for a variety of disparate mediums. It is, in a sense, a container to put many meanings in, with its own shape and rules and behavior."

© Sandy Skoglund. *Revenge of the Goldfish*, 1981. 30 x 40 inches. n/p. Courtesy of Castelli Graphics, New York, NY.

that. Digital imaging has blurred this profound psychological difference between photography and painting, yet we continue to bestow on the photograph the power of authenticity. We want to believe photography can recre-

ate the original scene with absolute fidelity because this makes us feel better. It rescues and saves the past, often lending it dignity and romance, and makes us feel a little less mortal.

Although seemingly silly on the surface, the hot dog assignment demonstrates not only how the camera can capture infinitesimal detail and accepted proportion, but also how these same features can be employed to "lie" or distort what is before the camera, with or without digital assistance. What questions does this raise in your mind about the role of the photographer, the use of the picture, and the subjective nature of the medium? What impact has digital imaging had on the believability of the photo-based image?

Internal Color Events/What is Important in Everyday Life?

Photography is the medium that is used to tell people about their world, and is the prime communicator of human emotion. Photography is with us in our daily lives through television, magazines, newspapers, movies, DVDs, and computers. It reaches out in all directions, even encompassing those who do not want to be touched. Many people still seem to only think of photography for its documentary abilities. For this project use the camera to probe the inner realities of your mind rather than the outer reality of the street.

Fabrication

This section raises an important issue confronting the contemporary photographer. In the past, most photographers went out and "found" things to photograph in the natural world. Today a sizeable segment of the photographic community has rejected the notion that the only photograph is a found one. In order to achieve and show their concerns, many people create and stage productions whose sole purpose is to be photographed. People, animals, and objects are collected and arranged, sets may be painted, lighting can be altered and/or controlled, the photographs are made, and the stage is dismantled, leaving no evidence, except the photograph, that the event ever occurred. The final result may not be a traditional, two-dimensional representation but a three-dimensional installation.

assignment

Fabricate your own environment. Arrange the existing objects, rooms, space, and light to create an environment for the sole purpose of photographing the manipulated event. Digital software may be used to enhance your effect, but not as its source of creation.

For more information see
HOY, ANNE H. *Fabrications: Staged, Altered, and Appropriated Photographs.* New York: Abbeville Press, 1987.

As part of a series that addresses some of the social, political, and cultural issues of contemporary life, Kaida declares: "This staged tableau is ideologically feminist. It's postmodern in that it attempts to deconstruct the female as object, the nude as female centerfold (here replaced by a male nude) in high art and popular pornographic sources." Some feminist theorists have argued that traditional visual and verbal representations of women do not represent a biologically given "feminine nature." Instead, women have to adapt and take on the roles that these societal representations portray. Hence, deconstruction (tearing down) of these models becomes important.

© Tamarra Kaida. *Centerfold*, 1988. 24 x 30 inches. Chromogenic color print.

Goodine expresses: "I sometimes dream the structure of work and then choose a cast of characters to play out the particular scene. It resembles living out a myth: we all carry out personal myths with only brief glimpses of recognition and in that split second of perception a spark flies up and with it a complete history of emotion. Yes, it is a stage. Yes, it is a symbol. Yes, it is real."

© Linda Adele Goodine. *Infant Joy*, 1987. 4 x 5 feet. Dye-destruction print.

Words and Photographs

In Western culture we are surrounded by words. More and more through the media we find the combination of pictures, screens within screens of images, and text all simultaneously compete and play off of each other at the same time. The existence of separate sets of symbols forces the brain to deal with contending sets of messages. This juxtaposition can be effectively used to convey additional straightforward information, humor, irony, and surreal spatial arrangements, or to create conditions of fantasy and meaning that would be impossible with only one set of symbols. The combinations give the artist more power to delve into psychological relationships, while also showing the major characteristic of photography, its adaptability in a multitude of situations. Notice how dependent the meaning of an image is on its accompanying text. Wright Morris, who has spent more than 50 years investigating the wily synergy between words and photographs, said: "The mind is its own place, the visible world is another, and visual and verbal images sustain the dialogue between them."

The combining of images and text can be an attempt to get past the barrier between image and spoken language. We

Letinsky is concerned with the way single moments can suggest psychological dramas. "I am striving to depict emotionally more uncomfortable, sometimes explicit situations between heterosexual couples. My photographs show couples in the midst of realizing their seductions, for better or for worse. ... My intention is to picture what sexual intimacy can look like between adults. ... I address questions concerning identity and representation, foregrounding women as protagonists; I have drawn upon feminist theory to examine gender roles, power relationships, and the gaze that activates it and who receives it."

© Laura Letinsky. *Untitled*, 1992. 35 ½ x 28 ¾ inches. Chromogenic color print.

Nagatani and Tracey fabricate environments in order to photograph them. This allows them to densely pack recognizable symbols from our society into a controlled situation that permits elaborate commentary from the artists.

© Patrick Nagatani and Andrée Tracey. *34th & Chambers*, 1985. 24 x 60 inches. Diffusion-transfer prints (triptych).

tend to think in pictures but in order to communicate we generally have to transform these images into thoughts and the thoughts into language. During this process the flexibility, plasticity, and texture of the image is often a casualty. This process is further complicated as viewers translate this collection back in their minds. Translation errors and personal bias make it unlikely that the received message will exactly match what was sent. Marcel Proust believed that we pack the physical outline of what we see with our own previously formed ideas, so what we essentially recognize (or don't) is ourselves, and this is also why we fall in love with our own creations.

What do you notice happening when you combine pictures and text? Does one overwhelm the other? Do you want to strike a balance between the two? Is there a blending or a duality of the two

Kruger says: "I work with pictures and words because they have the ability to determine who we are, what we want to be, and what we become." Her work asks: Who speaks? Who is silent? Who is seen? Kruger also recognizes the changing usage and reality of the photographic message and designs work to function in numerous environments, including book form, gallery wall, installation, and billboards.

© Barbara Kruger. *Installation*, 1991. Courtesy of Mary Boone Gallery, New York, NY.

symbols? Should you give more weight to one than the other? How does the addition of text affect the direction in which you read the work? Which do you read first? In a literate culture which has more importance? How can you effectively play one off against the other? If you want to ensure the supremacy of the photograph, use your words as a support and not as a crutch to hold up a weak photograph. Let them supply information that enhances your imagery. If this is not a concern, create arrangements that challenge the traditional relationships between pictures and words. How does the meaning of an image change when text is added or the original text altered? What differences in effect do you see between manual and digital ways of working? Finally, as a photographer, how important is it to be led by images—the internal visual impulse— as opposed to words?

The Camera

The camera is the key component that makes up photographic vision. Until recently the job of the camera has been primarily to make an "acceptable" and recognizable depiction, based on established visual conventions, of what is seen. The early camera, called the camera obscura, was designed to imitate the visual ideas of perspective and scale that were formulated during the Renaissance. Even today, the combination of camera and lens, whether film or digital, determines many of the basic characteristics of the final photographic image, including field of view, depth of field, sharpness, tonal range, and graininess. A knowledgeable viewer can often identify the fingerprint of the camera used to make an individual image. Because the camera plays such a vital role in the formation of

The panoramic format allowed Goldberg to expand the ordinary photographic viewpoint and capture not only the main subject, but also the context of the farm, pasture, and rainbow in the distance.

© Gary Goldberg. *Cow and Rainbow, Wichita Falls, Texas,* 2003. 8 x 22 inches. Inkjet print.

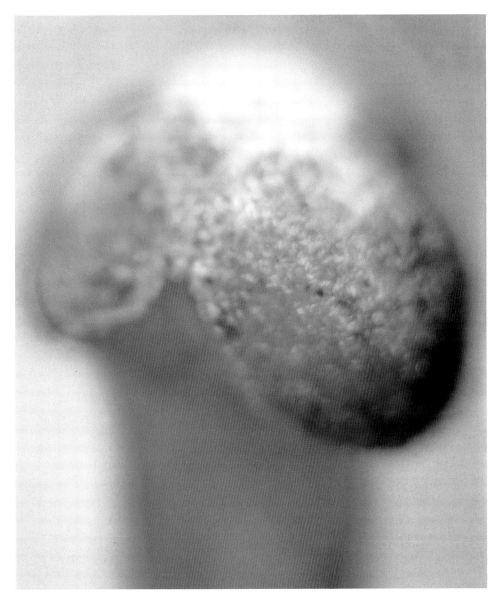

the final picture, photographers must be sure that the type of camera they use supports their personal aesthetic goals. No single camera can produce acceptable results in every situation. This is because the standard of what is acceptable is dependent on a variety of factors, including the subject being photographed, the audience, the purpose for which the picture is being made, and the desires of the photographer. Photographers should learn about the differences in cameras, their strengths, and their drawbacks so that they can make intelligent choices to achieve the desired outcome, and when possible experiment with different types of camera.

By attaching a child's microscope lens to a 4 x 5 camera and extending the bellows all the way, Formica was able to capture microscopic images on film. Enlarging the images on 20 x 24 paper made "the small details of nature transform themselves into something monumental and symbolic."

© Jennifer Formica. *Stigma,* 24 x 20 inches. Chromogenic color print.

A photograph can only look like how the camera saw what was photographed. Or, how the camera saw the piece of time and space is responsible for how the photograph looks. Therefore, a photograph can look any way. Or, there's no way a photograph has to look (beyond being an illusion of a literal description).[1]

Although a camera may shape the construction of an image, it is the private individual response to a situation that gives an image its power.

Special Camera Formats

Besides the familiar SLR, range finder, and twin-lens cameras, there are a number of cameras you can work with, including the following:

● **Medium formats,** such as the 6 x 4.5 centimeter, 6 x 6 centimeter, 6 x 7 centimeter, and 6 x 9 centimeter, which provide a larger image while still retaining the convenience and versatility of a handheld camera.
● **View cameras,** such as the 4 x 5 inch, 5 x 7 inch, and 8 x 10 inch, which offer the largest film area and the greatest amount of perspective control, but do require the use of a tripod.

Savedge captured the original scene using a disposable waterproof camera and scanned 12 of the resulting negatives. Next she used Photoshop to eliminated distracting items such as sports logos. Then she brought the images together in a long composition and elongated them to "create a feeling of timelessness of place and person."

© Anne C. Savedge. *Niagara Frieze*, 1999. 18 x 80 inches. Dye-destruction print.

● **Toy cameras,** such as the Holga, which challenge the accepted standards of image quality and encourage playfulness and simplicity.
● **Disposable cameras,** which provide inexpensive ways to experiment with different imagemaking. They include waterproof, underwater, and panorama cameras.
● **Homemade cameras,** such as the pinhole camera (covered in chapter 16, see page 320), which you can construct to suit your own way of seeing.
● **Panoramic cameras,** which are used to expand the ordinary photographic viewpoint.
● **Sequence cameras,** which make a series of exposures over a specific amount of time, either on one piece of film or on consecutive frames.
● **Stereo cameras,** which allow the imagemaker to work with the illusion of depth.
● **Underwater cameras,** which allow the camera to be used in wet conditions or submerged in water.
● **Microscopes** with cameras attached, which produce photomicrographs.
● **Telescopes** equipped with a clock drive and a camera body attachment mount, which can be used to make images of the sky at night.

Whenever the opportunity presents itself, try to work with a camera format different from the one you normally use. Compare the results. Notice how the camera itself affects what you look at, how you see and interpret the results.

For more information on cameras see ADAMS, ANSEL. *The Camera.* Boston, MA: Little Brown, 1983 and HIRSCH, ROBERT. *Photographic Possibilities: The Expressive Use of Ideas, Materials & Processes,* 2nd ed. Boston, MA: Focal Press, 2001.

Landscape Defined

The term landscape originates from the Dutch word *landschap,* meaning "landship." It represented a segment of nature that could be taken in at a glance, from a single point of view, and encompassed the land as well as animals, buildings, and people. In *Discovering the Vernacular Landscape,* John Brinckerhoff Jackson defines the landscape as an artificial collection of manmade spaces on the Earth's surface that have been devised to meet the human need for organizing time and space. Since the nineteenth century there has been an aesthetic movement to separate nature from humanity. The images from publications such as the Sierra Club, glorifying pristine, unpeopled, transcendental nature, have come to be the publicly accepted definition of the landscape. John Szarkowski, former Curator of Photography at the Museum of Modern Art in New York, said that people are thankful to Ansel Adams because his pictures stirred our collective memory of what it was like to be alone in an untouched world. This may be, but it leaves out the way the majority of people see the landscape.

Traditional Viewing Concepts

Many people still see the landscape through the English-gentleman concepts

Goin's *Nuclear Landscapes* represent the artifacts and sites that encompass the myth and political ritual surrounding the nuclear age. The title of this piece is branded on the image to reflect a nuclear impact. "This allows the photographs to maintain their context while in a viewing circumstance whereby the full sequence and narrative [from the book] is absent. Given that these landscapes are also branded, it made aesthetic sense to present this disharmonic element. No one need judge these scenes as celebratory!"

© Peter Goin. *Orchard Site*, from *Nuclear Landscapes*, 1991. 11 x 14 inches. Chromogenic color print. Accompanying caption in *Nuclear Landscapes* reads: "Abandoned and scarred peach or apricot orchard from the Hanford farming area."

of the sublime, the beautiful, and the picturesque as presented by Edmund Burke and John Ruskin. Briefly, some major aspects of the sublime include astonishment, confusion, darkness, infinity, monsters, obscurity, silence, solitude, terror, and vastness, with its major colors being blacks, browns, and deep purples. The quality of light can be intense and directional, with great play between the shadows and highlights. The beautiful is less strong, being rounded, smooth, and well proportioned without surprise or terror. It is admirable but not as capable of arousing such great passion. The colors of beauty tend towards the warm hues and favor a softer, more diffused light. The picturesque is a series of motifs that were used by artists wishing to elicit known responses from the audience. The picturesque provided a structure for seeing what in nature would make a good picture. Far less threatening than the sublime, it provided a more complex view of nature based on the then-popular ruin of the world theory. Typical picturesque subject matter features shattered trees, rotten stumps, overgrown foliage, rushing brooks, and tumbled-down structures. Detail and texture are of paramount concern when used within the confines of academically approved compositions (the rules of painting).

For over a hundred years, Gustave Courbet's so-called realistic landscapes, emphasizing subjects of immediate, pre-ordained appeal, served the public as the exemplifier of many of these notions, including the one that nature had to be improved upon in the interest of the ideal. Although Courbet stated that "painting is an art of sight and should therefore concern itself with things seen. (Show me an angel and I will paint one)," it was nevertheless vulgar to portray what one saw. In *Landscape Into Art*, Kenneth Noland cuts through the numerous falsehoods surrounding Courbet's concentration on the tangible reality of things with his observation that Courbet "cheerfully substituted a false sensation for a real one, and the remarkable thing is that his false sensations are exactly those which have satisfied the popular eye ever since." Such academic guidelines of "good taste" continue to influence us today with models and expectations of how photography should be judged.

Photography and the American West

Beginning with Solomon N. Carvalho's daguerreotypes (now lost), made on the 1853 Frémont expedition, photography has been the instrument that awakened America to the sublime and mysterious landscape of the "West." Throughout the twentieth century photography has been the keeper of the flame, shaping the ideas and perceptions of the Great American West. The major religions of the Western world were all born in the desert. In *Satanic Verses* (1989), Salman Rushdie says: "God is in the desert." So too in America, God must be in the West. The American West has become a visual concept for a spacious, waterless wonderland of repeating geometric shapes, dominated by a horizon line where the earth meets the sky. It is a place of personal freedom that is also cruel, harsh, bright, clean, sharp, and completely unforgiving; one wrong move and you could be in serious danger. This wild and tough image, which dominates the American psyche and character, has been generated by photography and has become one of America's major cultural exports.

The Landscape Today

Contemporary landscape has broader parameters than it did in the past. The

Misrach's 8 x 10 view camera series, *The Desert Cantos*, subtly reveals the atmospheric conditions, light, and color of a place without idealization. By making photographs that look beyond the obvious and do not perpetuate a myth of unsullied nature, Misrach confronts us with "what we have done to the wilderness."

© Richard Misrach. *Outdoor Dining, Bonneville Salt Flats*, 1992. 40 x 50 inches. Chromogenic color print. Courtesy of the Catherine Edelman Gallery, Chicago, IL.

successful landscape can convey a sense of time, place, and human experience. Some photographers pay homage to the beauty and grandeur of nature by making views that give the audience a sense of actually looking at the scene without any political message. Today many photographers specialize in recording how the landscape is shaped by human presence (the social landscape), combining ethics and aesthetics. More and more the landscape becomes a site to express the personality, ideas, and social/economic/political concerns of the photographer. Here the quest becomes making the unsavory truth, the thing we would like to ignore, into something that challenges the viewer and provokes thought within the landscape tradition. In his book *Why People Photograph* (1994), Robert Adams comments:

If the state of our geography appears to be newly chaotic because of heedlessness, the problem that this presents to the spirit is, it seems to me, an old one that art has long addressed. As defined by hundreds of years of practice—I think history is vitally important—art is a discovery of harmony, a vision of disparities reconciled, of shape beneath confusion. Art does not deny that evil is real, but it places evil in a context that implies an affirmation; the structure of the picture, which is a metaphor for the structure of Creation, suggests that evil is not final.[2]

BASIC WORKING CONSIDERATIONS

Decide what your landscape subject is, then spend time looking at the subject and determine the essential qualities you want to convey. Now consider these points:

- *What type of light and recording media will best realize your ideas? Would low, directional light, revealing pattern and/or texture, be effective, or would a clear, hard, contrasty midday light show the qualities you find essential?*
- *Identify the key colors and decide the most effective method to convey them.*
- *Would a wide-angle lens, emphasizing a great deal of depth with an exaggerated foreground, be effective, or would a telephoto lens, concentrating on detail, compressing and foreshortening the space, do the job? Would a detail shot or a panorama better express your idea?*
- *Should the point of view be horizontal, vertical, or oblique?*
- *Using your camera position, how should you compositionally control the spatial relationship of the foreground, midground, and sky? Should the sky or the ground dominate? Do you want a dramatic or naturalistic point of view?*
- *How can perspective be applied to draw the viewer into the scene?*
- *How does setting up spatial relationships affect the psychology of the picture?*
- *Which key elements will be used to determine how to control the exposure? Will a filter, such as a polarizer, add strength to the image?*
- *How will you convey a sense of scale? Do you want to use a human figure as a contrast to the size of natural forms? Or would it be better to play natural shapes off against each other? Remember the human figure is visually very powerful, and it immediately attracts the viewer's eye.*
- *What type of focusing techniques will be employed? Will you go for maximum depth of field or make use of selective focusing to direct the interest of the viewer? Is it necessary to clearly separate the subject from busy or confusing surroundings?*
- *How should the print be made? What would happen if you increased or decreased the exposure time? What about burning, or dodging, including edge burning?*
- *Is one image enough or would a group or collage/montage/slide show/website be more effective?*
- *How will the presentation affect the viewer's response?*

Follow up. Make and carry out all your initial decisions. Then return to the same subject and begin to reconsider your first thoughts. For instance, how would changing the angle of view or extending the exposure time affect the outcome? Make a new group of pictures based on your second group of thoughts. Compare the two. Are your first ideas always the best? What did you learn from the second effort? What would you do differently if you photographed the scene a third time? Keep asking questions and trying new ideas until the results are satisfying. When we think of making landscape photographs, we think about traveling somewhere, of taking a voyage. The curiosity of exploration has been responsible for many of the concepts we hold about the landscape. But what do such images reveal about the inner journey of the photographer? Do we go out of ourselves in an attempt to discover what is within us?

For additional information see JUSSIM, ESTELLE, with ELIZABETH LINDQUIST-COCK. *Landscape as Photograph*. New Haven, CT: Yale University Press, 1985; CLARK, KENNETH. *Landscape Into Art*, new edition. New York: Harper & Row, 1976; JACKSON, JOHN BRINCKERHOFF. *Discovering the Vernacular Landscape*, New Haven, CT: Yale University Press, 1984; SCHAMA, SIMON. *Landscape and Memory*, New York: Alfred A. Knopf, 1995; POOL, PETER, ed. *The Altered Landscape*, Reno, NV: University of Nevada Press, 1999.

These are all legitimate means in which to consider the landscape. Regardless of which approach you take, there are a number of common basic considerations to think about (see assignment).

The Power of Nature: Visceral vs. Theoretical

Most photo-based imagemakers do not spend much of their time discussing Hegel, Descartes, or Derrida. What they do discuss is what work gets shown in the major venues and what work is ignored. During the past few decades photography's critical dialogue has been dominated by European academic theoreticians whose postmodern philosophies appear to maintain that there is greater value in the role of the interpreter than in that of the maker. Intolerant of non-political interpretations and any non-material focus, the deconstructionists disallow any firsthand experience of aesthetic pleasure. Their theories are a continuation of the mechanical philosophy of the sixteenth and seventeenth centuries, in which people are viewed as isolated (alienated) observers and not as active participants in the cosmos. Their coolly academic approach brings a foreign sensibility and class-consciousness that deconstructs American mythology but replaces it with nothing, leaving a void without a sense of community or hope. Theirs is the art of elite specialists, divorced from the public, who delve into the relationship between art and art, art and the idea of art, but not art as a revelation of nature. For them art is not an investigation of nature, but an investigation into the nature of investigation.

The shift to the puritanical right in American culture and politics makes it vital for artists not to throw up their hands and say they have no answers, for to do so is to cede the issues of humanity and spirituality to only the political conservatives. Under such circumstances, it is imperative for American artists to offer countermeasures that deploy fundamental American strengths and engage the belief in the power of nature as an effective weapon against blaming, stereotyping, and pretentious standards.

Still Life

A photographer can undertake exciting explorations without traveling to exotic, far-off places. The studio can provide a setting for contemplating visual problems. The tradition of still life was established in the beginning of photography by Daguerre and Talbot and can be traced back to fifteenth-century painting. Today still life is pursued in both the artistic and commercial photographic communities and has laid the infrastructure for advertising and product illustration photography. The challenge is to build an image, from the camera's point of view, that delivers a distinct outcome.

Still-Life Considerations

Visit the library and search the Internet to look at work done for commercial and artistic purposes by photographers and artists using other media, especially painting. Analyze what you are attracted to and repelled by in these images. Consider taking a simply done advertisement and duplicating it to learn some of the basic technical problems in doing still life. Now formulate your own still-life vision. Picking a theme can provide structure for the entire operation.

Still life affords the opportunity to control all the elements within the composition. You can work entirely alone, setting your own pace, without the distractions and problems characterized by working with live models. Working with still life can provide a sense of privacy and meditation that permits a great deal of concentration. Consider using a view camera because the adjustments it offers (swings, tilts, and rising front) can increase the control over the final image (especially depth of field). Polaroid materials and/or digital media can be used

In *The Drive-In Theater* series, Nakagawa uses the idea of a frame within a frame. "I digitally paste images I have photographed, representing some aspect of American culture, onto abandoned and decaying drive-in screens. The nostalgic mythology of the drive-in theater is juxtaposed with explicitly public and political messages. Similarly, the commercial nature of the billboard is subverted. The series proposes a critical inspection of Western society from my viewpoint, which is Eastern in origin and Western by immersion."

© Osamu James Nakagawa. *K.K.K.*, from *The Drive-In Theater* series, 1992. 26 ½ x 40 inches. Chromogenic color print.

with the view camera to make test shots. Collect and organize your objects and props. Select a location. It can be the corner of a room or a larger studio space. It can be beneficial if you have a spot where the setup can be left undisturbed. This allows you the time to study, linger, and interact with your construct before shooting. It also lets you go back and make adjustments after the first round of photographing has been completed. Pick the background setting. It may be a seamless paper or a personal construct. Play with the objects. Stay loose and try different compositional arrangements. Look for combinations of colors, shapes, and textures that promote the theme. Once the composition is set, decide what are the prime factors to be revealed. Is precise detail important? Which recording media's characteristics best suit the needs of this still life?

What type of lighting is required to accomplish your goal? Should you use natural, artificial, or a combination of both types of light? Will more than one

Under the guise of the traditional still-life genre, Whaley manufactures a composition that alludes to the richness and bounty of the natural world. But that's where the affinity with the historical still life ends. The conflict between science/technology and the natural world is addressed through the use of nonsensical devices; pointing out there is something wrong with a system that in its quest for knowledge often destroys that which it is examining.

© Jo Whaley. *Analytical Behavior*, 1994. 16 x 20 inches. Chromogenic color print.

dled determines whether the composition seems to glow with a lifelike aura or remains flat and lifeless.

How will the final piece be presented? Will postvisualization techniques, including digital enhancement, help to strengthen the message?

The Macro Lens

Beginners often attempt to make still-life photographs using a 35-mm camera with a macro lens. This can prove unsatisfactory because of its flat-field optics, designed to give a nearly flat image surface to accurately match the film surface at the focal plane, and lack of depth of field. The macro lens is excellent for doing flat-field work, such as copying and making slides of original prints, but even stopped down to f /32 will probably lack the depth of field often critical for a successful still life. The shorter focal length macro lenses (in the 50- to 60-mm range) provide more depth of field at any given aperture than their longer focal length (100 plus-mm range) counterparts. The same depth of field problem will also be encountered when using an add-on close-up lens, reversing ring, or extension bellows. If this is not acceptable, you should consider using a view camera.

The macro lens can also serve as a postmodern tool. Try re-photographing small sections of images using intrinsic photographic methods such as angle, cropping, focus, and directional light to alter the original's context and meaning. These new images can also be digitally manipulated.

light be needed? Start with only one main light. What direction should it come from—front, side, top, or bottom? Are reflectors or diffusers required? Use a second light only to bring out the background or reduce shadows. Watch out for double shadows when working with two lights, because overlapping tends to make visual confusion. What about filters or colored gels? What type of psychological atmosphere do you want to

create? Where and how should your exposure reading be determined?

The direction and quality of light is determined by numerous considerations such as the mood, the message, and personal aesthetic tastes. The challenge in lighting is to reveal the natural properties of what is being photographed. Opaque, translucent, and transparent objects each require special considerations. How the combination of these properties is han-

The Human Form

The human body has proved to be a challenging and controversial subject since the beginnings of photography. Some of the interest in the human body has been solely prurient, as in the making of pornography. But the nude has long been a venerable subject for artists. The vitality of the genre can be seen in the diverse ways that the human form has been portrayed: beautiful, delicate, soft, whole, inviting, sculptural, hard, unavailable, horrific, broken, fractured, faceless—the list goes on.

In the early nineteenth century, the traditional male nude became a taboo subject and photographers, like other artists, began to concentrate on the female form. It was also considered to be objectionable to show pubic hair. This convention is still enforced in many areas. Only recently has the male form been reintroduced into the public arena, often with a great deal of public outcry, as witnessed in the work of gay photographers such as Robert Mapplethorpe.

Decide what is important to reveal and how you can go about it. Do you want to show the entire figure or part of it? Is it going to be realistic or abstract? Should the color scheme be cool or warm, high key or low key? Is the sense of texture important? Will soft, indirect light, good for revealing subtleties of form through tonal graduations, be effective? Or would stronger, directional light, creating more contrast, darker shadows, and a bolder more graphic mood, meet your intentions? What mood do you want: innocent, dramatic, sensual, romantic, erotic, secretive, provocative, vulnerable, loving? How can choice of camera lens and position be employed to create this psychological effect? Should focus be sharp or diffused? What type of background will work? Will you need props? Pick a human form that personifies your idea. Establish a good working rapport with the model(s). Explain to the model what you are looking for. Offer direction without being a bully. Be willing to take suggestions. Leave any hidden agendas or expectations somewhere else, and concentrate on making photographs.

For more information on the human form see EWING, WILLIAM, ed. *The Body: Photographs of the Human Form.* San Francisco: Chronicle Books, 1994; GILL, MICHAEL. *Image of the Body: Aspects of the Nude.* New York: Doubleday 1989; PULTZ, JOHN. *The Body and the Lens: Photography 1839 to the Present.* New York: Harry N. Abrams, 1995.

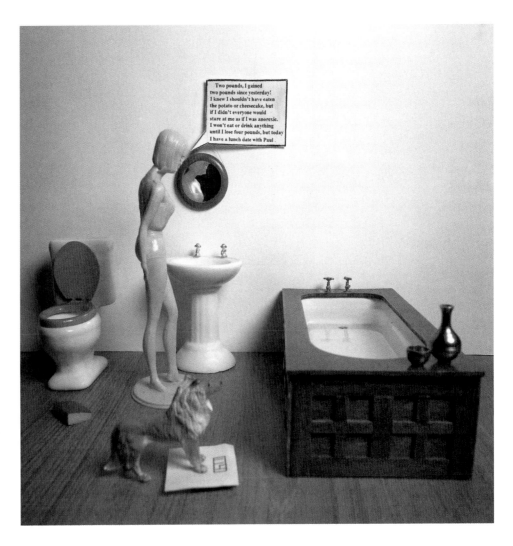

Using a macro lens extender, De Marris takes close-up photographs of plastic figures in handmade sets. Her images create scenarios of stereotypical behaviors of the "Pink People" she uses as stand-ins for those in a community who have financial and influential means to make noteworthy social and political changes. "The scenarios are intended to describe various 'Pink People' relationships and how they unconsciously relate or cope in varied social situations."

© Pamela de Marris. *Pink People Series: Tossed Salad,* 2001. 43 x 43 inches. Duraflex print. Text reads: "Two pounds, I gained two pounds since yesterday! I knew I shouldn't have eaten the potato or cheesecake, but if I didn't everyone would stare at me as if I was anorexic. I won't eat or drink anything until I lose four pounds, but today I have a lunch date with Paul."

Pictures from a Screen

Making pictures from a television screen or monitor offers the photographer the opportunity to become an active participant in the television medium instead of being a passive spectator. The camera can be used to stop the action on the screen or extend the sense of time by allowing the images to blend and interact with each other. The literalness of photographing directly from the screen is both its strength and its weakness.

To make pictures from a television or monitor screen try following these steps:

1 Make certain the screen is clean.
2 Place the camera on a tripod. A macro or telephoto lens can be used to fill the entire frame or to work with a small area of the screen and minimize the distortion produced by a curved screen.

Hafkenscheid's work was inspired by glimpses into other people's homes. "At night when the curtains are open, living rooms often resemble a small theatre. This theatre aspect is emphasized by the quality of light [a combination of ambient and flash]. ... These images are intended to be voyeuristic and seductive and to provide windows into private moments in the subject's home environment."

© Toni Hafkenscheid. *Greg and Gordon*, 1992. 30 x 30 inches. Chromogenic color print.

Once the correct shutter speed is determined, make all exposure adjustments by using the lens aperture.

With daylight-balanced color film, the resulting image will probably have a blue-green cast. This may be partially corrected by using a CC30R, CC40R, or 85B filter, with appropriate exposure compensation, at the time of initial exposure.

Different films deliver a variety in color renditions due to the film's spectral sensitivity and dye-image formation system. If color film is used to photograph a black-and-white monitor, the resulting image may have a blue cast.

If no screen lines are wanted, the image will have to be captured by using a film recorder that makes its image based on electronic signals rather than from a screen.

A videocassette recorder (VCR) or DVD player gives the photographer the chance to be selective about the images on the screen and also provides the ability to repeat the image on the screen until it can be photographed in the manner that is desired. The VCR and DVD can be effective visual arts teaching tools, as demonstrated by Quentin Tarantino, director and screenwriter of *Reservoir Dogs* (1992) and *Pulp Fiction* (1994). Tarantino used them as a poor person's film school to instruct himself about filmmaking while working in a video rental store.

Alternative Modes

Nonstraightforward representations from the screen are possible using the following methods:

● Vary the shutter speed from the standard 1/30 of a second.
● Adjust the color balance of the screen from its normal position.
● Vary the horizontal and vertical hold positions from their standard adjustment.
● Use a magnet to distort the television picture. Be aware that this could put the television out of adjustment, requiring a repair person to correct it. Try this on an old set that you no longer care to use.
● Make a series of multiple exposures

3 Turn off the room lights and cover windows to avoid getting reflections on the screen. A black card put in front of the camera, with a hole cut in it for the lens, helps to eliminate camera and other reflections. If available, use a "hood" device (designed to capture images directly from a computer screen) with a camera attachment to cover the screen area and block out ambient light.

4 Adjust the picture contrast to slightly darker (flatter) than normal for an accurate, straightforward rendition.

5 Adjust the color to meet your personal considerations.

6 Most monitors generate a new frame every 1/30 of a second. If the shutter speed is higher than 1/30 of a second, the leading edge of the scanning beam will appear on the picture as a dark, slightly curved line. If you do not want this line, a shutter speed of 1/30 of a second or slower should be used. Experiments should be carried out with shutter speeds of 1/15 and 1/8 of a second since the shutter speeds of some cameras may be faster than indicated. If the image being photographed is static or can be "frozen" on the screen, try using the slower speeds to ensure the frame line is not visible. Cameras with a leaf-type shutter may synchronize better with the monitor's raster lines.

from the screen onto one frame.

● Put a transparent overlay of an image or color in front of the screen. Make your own using litho film.

● Another possibility for incorporating images into a picture is to project a slide or slides onto a scene, rather than onto a screen, and then to rephotograph the entire situation. A zoom lens on the slide projector can be useful in controlling the image size.

● Movie theater screens, including drive-ins, can also provide the photographer with a rich source of imagery to call upon.

● Create images using a digital imaging program.

● Incorporate the screen image with its surroundings or other events.

● Fabricate a situation to be photographed that includes a screen image.

Postcards

The postcard format, about 3 ¼ x 5 ½ inches, first appeared in Europe in 1869. At the turn of the twentieth century, free rural delivery; reduced rates for cards; small, folding, handheld cameras; and the new postcard-size printing papers con-

A macro lens was held at an extreme angle to the surface of the television to inject the image distortion. The unnatural color is achieved by adjusting the color, contrast, and tint controls of the television set. The print is mounted on a Voice Print frame, a device capable of recording and playing back a 10-second sound bite. The sound is recorded from a prerecorded video segment. The satirical photograph becomes an interactive piece; viewers can repeatedly hear the sound segment by pushing a small "play" button on the frame.

© Diane Bush and Steven Baskin. *Jesus Removes All Human Ingenuity*, from the *Televangelist* series 1995. 5 x 7 inches (image), 11 x 14 inches (framed). Chromogenic color print with Voice Print frame. The sound bite says: "Jesus removes all human ingenuity, all human 'intuity.' He removes all innovations from man."

tributed to making the postcard immensely popular. Before the rise in technology led to telephones and mass-circulation picture magazines, postcards were a fun and inexpensive way for people to keep in touch.

The postcard's form and style are in the folk art genre and throw to the winds all the sacred rules of picture making. Many cards possess an amazing sense of irreverent good humor in how the subject is depicted. Originally the postcard was of a highly personal nature. People went to a local photographer's studio and had their own cards made that dealt with subjects of current importance in their lives. Portraits were popular and

327 Footfall   J. Mead '92

Working in the postcard format, Mead used numerous depictions of Niagara Falls including postcards, a matchbook cover, a chromolithograph, and a color Instamatic print he made of the falls as a teenager. "The inclusion of shredded US currency and bar coding refers to the commercialization of the Niagara Falls area. The title is derived from the fact that the average height of the American and Canadian Falls is 327 feet. The choice of scale is very deliberate. It invites close inspection and encourages a greater level of intimacy with the work."

© Gerald C. Mead, Jr. 327 *Footfall*, 1992. 3 ½ x 5 ½ inches. Mixed media.

included all members of the family from the new baby to the dog. These were then sent to friends and relatives. The latest incarnation of this phenomenon can be seen on millions of personal websites. At present most postcards are commercially printed and mass circulated. They serve primarily as documentation, offering evidence that you were in a certain place, at a certain time, and this is what you saw. Being able to write a message on the back of a postcard makes it more personal. It is a form of simple communication that is quick, cheap, educational, and often entertaining. Commercially printed postcards are used by the travel industry to provide pictorial stereotypes. They have become part of the tourist experience. People tend to value the kind of scenery that has been aesthetically validated in travel brochures, advertisements, and other mass media visuals. When tourists encounter the original scene they often want to confirm its "picturesque" value

by making a snapshot of it or buying a postcard depicting it. Today postcards are also commonly used by photographers (and other artists) to announce the openings of exhibitions of their work.

Stereo Cards

Sir Charles Wheatstone discovered the stereoscopic effect in binocular vision (using both eyes at once). In the 1830s he invented both the reflecting (mirror) and refracting (lens) stereoscopes for use with hand-drawn designs. Photography provided answers to many of the difficulties of these hand-drawn designs. Stereo pictures were tremendously popular from about 1854 to 1880 and again from about 1890 to 1919, with millions of cards and viewers sold.

How the Stereo Effect Is Achieved

Stereo cards create a three-dimensional

effect by taking separate photographs of a subject from two lateral viewpoints 2½ inches apart, which is the average distance between the human eyes. This is accomplished with a twin-lens camera with an interlocked double shutter that makes two images of the subject at the same time, side by side on the film. Stereo cameras can also produce a three-dimensional effect by interlacing the images with one another through the use of a lenticular screen.

It is also possible to produce stereo pictures of subjects that contain no movement with a regular camera. This is done by making the first exposure of the subject and then shifting the camera exactly 2 ½ inches and making the second exposure. It may be moved to either the right or the left, but be certain to move it in the same direction every time. If this is not done, it gets confusing which is the right-eye view and the left-eye view. If they are mixed up the stereo effect will not work. There are also stereo devices that can be attached to the front of the camera lens and permit simultaneous exposures with a conventional camera.

Stereo images on a computer can be viewed with 3-D glasses that have one red and one blue lens. These can be made at home with medium-density red and blue cellophane (red lens over the left eye and blue over the right). The results can be outputted (see Digital 3D below).

The Effect of Distance

The normal stereo effect starts at about five feet from the camera and is exaggerated at closer distances. Stereo infinity is the distance that the stereo effect ceases. This can range from 200 to 1500 feet and is dependent on the number and variety of visual depth clues that are included in the view. The hyperstereo effect, in which the depth and size of the objects are exaggerated, occurs when there is too great a separation between the picture-taking viewpoints. It is generally noticeable in the foreground of the picture. Improper separation of the images on the viewing card can also produce this effect. Pictures up to 2 ½ inches wide can be mounted in

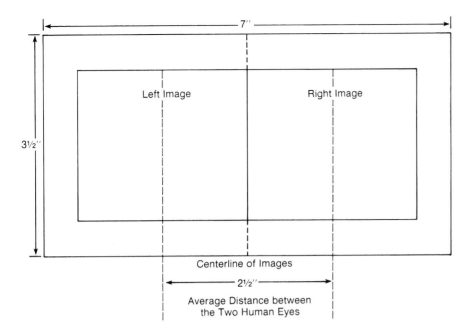

Digital 3D

The following is a basic digital method used by artist Michael Bosworth to make single, three-dimensional images that are viewed with special colored glasses.

Three-dimensional images can be digitally printed with red/blue or red/cyan ink. Seen through a red filter, red ink and white paper appear much the same. A red filter will block all blue color, causing an image printed with cyan ink to appear black. Red and cyan overlapping images will be seen independently when viewed with cyan and red filters, creating the illusion of depth.

In his images of Niagara Falls (see figure 15.2), Bosworth used a single camera to make two exposures from different perspectives. A camera was placed on a tripod with a device allowing the camera to be moved from side to side to create images from two perspectives. Stereo illusion works if the subjects of two images occupy nearly the same space in both images. If the subject changes position between exposures, the illusion will not work. Usually, a stereo camera uses two lenses to make two simultaneous exposures of the same scene. Although the water pouring over the falls was continually moving, a shutter speed lasting several seconds caused the water to take on a constant form. The smooth blur of the water occupied the same position in each exposure taken minutes apart.

After developing the black-and-white film, Bosworth selected and digitally scanned two negatives, producing a pair of grayscale images. Using Adobe Photoshop, a new CMYK file of the same resolution and proportions as the grayscale images was created. One of the grayscale images was copied and pasted

a simple viewer with the proper distance between their centers. Larger images, having more than 2 ½ inches between their centers, need to be viewed in a stereoscopic viewer with a lens or prism to compensate for this distance, which is greater than that between human eyes.

Stereo Card Size

Following the model card in figure 15.1, make a standard 3 ½- x 7-inch stereo card that is designed to be viewed in the basic refracting stereoscope. This style was devised by Sir David Brewster in 1849 and was improved into its current form by Oliver Wendell Holmes in 1861. It consists of a T-bar with a handle beneath the stereoscope body. A hood at one end of the bar contains two short-focus spectacle or prism lenses; a crossbar at the other end holds wire clips in which the card with the stereo photographs is inserted. The crosspiece can be moved back and forth along the bar for focusing. An opaque divider extends partway along the T-bar between the lenses, preventing each eye from seeing the opposite image. The stereo effect can be seen without a viewer. A simple opaque divider can be placed between the two images, maintaining the focus of

the left eye on the left image and the right on the right image. Inexpensive twin plastic lenses, held up to your eyes, are also marketed.

15.2 Harkening back to Gustave Le Gray's stop-action wave photographs, Bosworth observes: "The mighty Niagara River is both sublime and consistent, allowing it to be photographed in stereo with a single camera. Viewed without optical devices, the composition and form take on an abstracted quality. Glasses with red and blue colored lenses resolve the overlapping images to give an illusion of space, although one that is amorphous and lacking in a sense of human scale. This absence of distinction reflects the common struggle of art to describe the world in human terms while scientific definitions are often beyond human scale."

© Michael Bosworth. *Niagara XX*, 2001. 20 x 30 inches. Inkjet print.

text, drawings, marks, and appropriated materials into a variety of formats. Since the late 1960s, photographers have been rediscovering the idea of the book as a way of working. They have dealt with themes of a narrative and diaristic nature as well as those of sequential time, dreams, friendship, and social and political issues. Many photographers who were denied access to the traditional outlets, such as museums and galleries, began to cut and paste and make use of quick-copy centers, rubber stamps, and old, unwanted printing equipment. The

into the cyan channel of the new file, while the other grayscale image was pasted into the magenta and yellow channels. With all channels displayed, the resulting image appears as a pair of red/cyan overlapping photographs. Printed in ink and viewed with cyan/red glasses, the image provides the illusion of depth.

Artists' Books and Albums

The idea of illustrating books with photographs appeared shortly after the invention of photography. Anna Atkins's *Photographs of British Algae: Cyanotype Impressions* (1843–53) and William Henry Fox Talbot's *The Pencil of Nature* (1844–46) are examples of paper prints being hand pasted into books. The images had to be added by hand since

there was no perfected method for direct reproduction of photographs until the halftone process of the 1880s.

The carte-de-visite, French for visiting card, was a 2 ¼- x 3 ½-inch photograph, usually a full-length portrait, mounted on a 2 ½- x 4-inch card. It was introduced in the early 1850s and became a fad during the 1860s in America and Europe. Millions of "cartes" were made of individuals, celebrities, and tourist attractions. People did not use them when they called but exchanged and collected the cards, keeping them in albums with special cutout pages for easy viewing. The birth of the photo album can be traced back to this custom.

The mixed-media work of Lady Filmer, who cut and pasted cards into designs that were interlaced with watercolor and text, is an early prototype of an artist-made book (circa 1864).

The artist-made book can bring together a play between photographs,

handmade book has provided an inexpensive alternative, artist-controlled method of getting the work out to a larger audience. There are workshops, classes, conferences, printers, distributors, and bookshops that specialize in artists' books.

Digital imaging methods are providing access to previously inaccessible imaging and printing techniques and can include elements of performance through video and sound. Interactive programs, embedded in a CD/DVD or other storage device, may require the viewer to make choices that determine the content or outcome of a work and are modified with each viewing.

In addition, special hinged paper, such as that made by Stonehinge Systems (www.stoneeditions.com) is designed for digital printing and has a companion digital album cover set, translucent interleaves, and binding hardware that simplifies production.

Sligh works with various photographically based prints, artists' books, video, audio, sculpture, and writing to explore the intersection of memory and history, reality and myth. "I am interested in the visual tensions which result from the integration of machine-generated and handmade image and text." Her starting points can be anything, a found photograph, a memory, a word, an interaction, a place, almost anything that resonates with her. From there she does research in libraries and archives. "This leads me to shoot more photographs and conduct interviews." Sligh uses copiers, computers, drawing, and writing to combine repetitious elements of marks, words, and photographs into one frame. Successive and simultaneous time elements are brought into the present in one frame, one place, or one event.

© Clarissa Sligh. *What's Happening with Momma?* (interior view), 1987. 11 x 36 inches. Van Dyke brown prints.

Create and Evaluate Your Own Assignment

This is the opportunity to make that picture you have been dreaming about and then measure the plan against what was accomplished.

Guide to Evaluation—Before Photographing

Before you make any pictures, consider the following:

1 Write a clear, concise statement of the specific goals you intend to accomplish.
2 Describe and list your purposes, both objective and subjective, and how you plan to reach them.
3 What problems do you anticipate? How do you propose to deal with them?

For more information on artists' books see LYONS, JOAN, ed. *Artists' Books: A Critical Anthology and Sourcebook.* Rochester, NY: Visual Studies Workshop Press, 1985; SMITH, KEITH. *Structure of the Visual Book,* 3rd Edition, *Text in the Book Format,* and *Bookbinding for Book Artists.* These titles plus others are available directly from the author, www.keithsmithbooks.com. Also see DRUKER, JOHANNA. *The Century of Artist's Books,* 1995 (available from D.A.P.); HOLLELEY, DOUGLAS, *Digital Book Design and Publishing,* Rochester, NY: Clarellen and Cary Graphic Arts Press, 2001.

Guide to Evaluation—After Photographing

After making your pictures, answer these questions:

● **Achievement** How many of the stated objectives were attained? How well was it done? Are you satisfied? What benefits have been gained? Has new knowledge been acquired? Have new skills been developed? Have any attitudes been either changed or reinforced? Has the way in which you see things been altered?

● **The unexpected** What were the unforeseen benefits and problems that were encountered? Did anything happen to alter or change the original plan? How do you think you did with any unplanned events? Was there anything

that you should have done to make a better picture that you did not do? How will this help you to be a better imagemaker in the future?

● **Goals compared to achievement** Compare the final results with the original list of goals. What did you do right? What did you do wrong? What are the reasons? What would you do differently next time? Were the problems encountered of an aesthetic or technical nature? Which were more difficult to deal with? What has been learned? How has it affected your working methods? Make yourself the teacher and measure how well you met the objectives of your assignment. What grade would you give a student who had completed this project if you were the teacher? Why? Be specific.

Mari is a Brazilian photojournalist doing an ethnographic documentation of the Yanomami Indians, who are regarded as the last Stone Age tribe living in the Amazon and currently facing anthropological genocide. He says: "Due to the current rapid destruction of their culture, I believe that it is of immense cultural importance that a comprehensive photographic record be made of the Yanomami lifestyle in order to preserve for future generations the knowledge of their culture."

© Antonio Mari. *Ray Ban Acculturation*, 1995.
7 ⅝ x 11 ½ inches. Inkjet print.

Endnotes

[1] GARRY WINOGRAND, "Understanding Still Photography," in *Garry Winogrand* (portfolio). New York: Double Elephant Press, 1974.

[2] ROBERT ADAMS, *Why People Photograph*. New York, NY: Aperture, 1994, 181.

Chapter Sixteen

SPECIAL COLOR MATERIALS, PRACTICES, AND PROCESSES

Fuss says: "The lens is a manipulation of an image. To me the photogram is a non-manipulation of the object and the interaction of the object with light and the direct recording of that. To me that's pure photographic imagery. It's a different language of light. The one with the camera has seemingly a lot more detailed information, but I find that there is information of a different kind that is no less rich."

© Adam Fuss. *Untitled*, 2001. 61 ¾ x 50 ¼ inches. Dye-destruction print. Courtesy of Cheim and Read, New York, NY.

Polaroid: Instant Manipulation

Altering a Polaroid print as the image is developing lets you interact with the picture during the part of the process that is supposed to be automatic with no human intervention. The dyes beneath the plastic coating of Polaroid Time-Zero film are the most malleable both during and after development. Spectra prints can be manipulated to a lesser extent. Any type of stylus can be used to push and pull the dyes under the plastic covering (figure 16.1). Pencils, dowels, clay-working tools, dental tools, burnishing tools, spoons, butter knives, coins—anything that can apply pressure directly to the print surface is worth trying. The secret of a good manipulation is knowing when to stop. Do not get carried away. Avoid creating more chaos; we already have enough of it in this world. Make some extra pictures to play and loosen up with before you get down to business.

Time-Zero Manipulation Approaches

If you have never attempted this process, try photographing a still life or a scene that is repeatable. There are several ways to manipulate this film. The easiest is to allow the image to develop for only about 15 seconds. As soon as the outlines of the image become visible, you make your choices as to which areas to work on and how to alter them. This method is the quickest and relies on your first inclinations. For a general blurring and softening of the entire image, begin lightly manipulating the surface with a blunt tool before the image becomes visible. As the image develops use a more pointed tool for outlining areas and objects. Different amounts of pressure can produce black or white lines. New colors can be blended by applying a slightly heavier, pointed pressure to mix the layers underneath. Blues and reds can be produced during this time. During the next five minutes, use a blunt- or fine-tip tool to blend, distort,

and stretch the image. Try varying the pressure and using both circular and short stroke motions.

If you prefer a more contemplative method, make a number of exposures and allow one to remain unmanipulated as a guide. Permit the print to fully develop. Then take a stylus and gently trace over the image to see which areas are the most receptive to manipulation. Gently start rubbing, in a circular motion, on the background and light-colored areas before tackling the more detailed aspects of the picture. Wherever pressure is applied, it loosens the dyes and brings to the surface a bit of white reflective pigment that is under the picture. Rubbing on dark colors tends to turn these colors a gray-white. Consider leaving a dark area unmanipulated to create contrast and juxtaposition with the altered part of the image.

Compositions that are predominantly one color don't offer as much opportunity for alteration. Look for a picture that can provide a variety of shapes and tones for experimentation. As for color relationships, the film responds strongly to blue, green, and red. Take your time. Be gentle. Do not rush. It is okay to be subtle. The entire print does not have to be manipulated. The final picture will be textured with bumps and waves. Do not forget it is fine to ignore all this and just jump in and see what can be discovered.

Another method of manipulation involves puncturing a small hole behind the image during the initial development stage and, while watching the image develop, moving the dyes around using a needle or paper clip inserted through the hole.

Another possibility is to use an X-Acto or other utility knife to cut open and peel a fully processed image apart. Next, run cool water over the image to remove the white, chalky coating. The longer you wash, the more of the image will be removed. Now apply water-based dyes, such as Dr. Martins (docmartins.com), with a brush or cotton swab. Color markers can also be used. These images are best viewed as transparencies. Build small lightboxes for

display so they can be lit from behind. Boxes can be constructed so the images can be interchanged, combined, or shown in small groups. Wear gloves when disassembling this film as it contains a caustic developer gel. If you get any developer on your skin, immediately wash it off with running water. Children should perform this process only if they are under direct adult supervision.

Also note that the backside of Polacolor film can be manipulated by applying pressure to selective areas during development by using the same tools as in Time-Zero manipulation.

Subsequent Manipulations

It is possible to wait a couple of hours after you have shot to begin alterations. It will be necessary to soften the dyes again. This is done with the application of heat. A home hand iron works great. Hair and print dryers, hot plates, and dry-mount presses work too. But be careful; too much heat causes the plastic surface to bubble, buckle, or crack. If you do not want these effects, cover the picture with some clean, smooth sheets of paper. Then apply low heat for a few seconds at a time until the dyes soften.

Manipulation lets the photographer re-enter into part of the photographic process from which they had been excluded. It gives the photographer more freedom of choice in determining the final outcome of the picture and increases the options. Avenues for subjective feeling are now able to enter into an automatic technical process. The artist can build more time into the picture. Instead of 1/125 second of time, the photographer can continue to be involved with the image for longer blocks of time. This can give the photograph more life and involve the viewer for longer periods of time.

As these are small, one-of-a-kind images, they can be copied onto conventional film to make more prints or enlargements.

Most Polaroid materials duplicate well onto 4- x 5-inch transparency film, and these "interpositives" can make great small-sized prints.

Polaroid Transfer Methods

The transfer process allows a previously made image to be relocated onto another receiving surface. Magazine transfers, the kind often done in grade school, are the most familiar. Postmodernistic trends have brought about a renewed interest in transferring images. The Polaroid transfer method is capable of producing soft, fully rendered images or fractured, partially rendered images. Other postvisualization methods, such as handcoloring, can be incorporated into the process of transforming the image to provide a more subjective response to the subject. Although any size Polaroid film can be used, Polacolor films provide a simple avenue to begin experimentation. The Polacolor ER films, such as Type 669, 59, 559, or 809, as well as Polacolor 64 Tungsten, deliver the most constant transfer results. Type 59 is excellent for beginners, while Polaroid Pro 100 is not recommended for transfer applications. Inkjet printers can also be used to make transferable images.

The Polaroid transfer process can be carried out under ambient light. A few simple safety precautions are in order since Polaroid did not design their films for this purpose. Wear gloves during this process; the film contains a caustic developer gel. If you get any developer on your skin, immediately wash it off. For this reason this process is not recommended for children. To transfer an image from Polacolor film to another surface follow these suggestions:

1　Select a receiving support, such as watercolor paper, but different support materials, such as vellum, rice paper, wood veneer, or even other photographs. Cold-press papers, which have large pores, deliver more texture and less detail. Heat-press papers, which have smaller pores, provide a smoother image with more detail. Paper may also be treated with a gelatin for enhanced detail. For the sharpest possible image with the most color saturation, tape down the receiving support material before starting the transfer process. Natural fabrics, such as broadcloth, linen, silk, and even wood, can be used. They may require more wetting and pressure. Additional pressure can be applied by putting a heavy weight, such as a brick, on top of the transfer after you have completed the rolling process. If you do not want the characteristic "ooze" of excess developing chemicals around the outside of the image to show, use tape or rubber cement to mask out the nonimage area.

2　Immerse the paper in a tray of distilled water (100°F, 38°C) for about 60 seconds for 80-lb. paper, two minutes for 140-lb paper, and five minutes for 300-lb paper. Differences in the pH level of the water will affect the outcome. Remove the paper and drain. Place the paper on a flat, dry surface, and use a squeegee to remove the excess water. Other methods include using a brush, cotton ball, or portable steamer to dampen the paper. If the paper is too wet, the dyes can liquify and run. Try dry paper to see the different effect it makes.

3　Make sure the rollers and exit slot of the film holder are clean. Wipe them down with a damp, lint-free cloth before processing. Expose the Polacolor film and pull it through the film holder. Cut off the clipped end of the film pack, known as the trap end, with a pair of scissors. Wear gloves and avoid getting any of the processing chemicals on your skin.

4　Try variations in the processing time. Many workers prematurely peel the film apart to stop the migration of the dyes. For example, if the film is peeled apart after about 10 to 15 seconds (at 70°F, 21°C), the negative retains almost all the cyan dye, about half of the magenta, and almost no yellow. This is why the Polacolor transfers look cyan. This can be corrected by using 10CC to 20CC red filtration at the time of exposure. If you peel sooner than 10 seconds the negative may be fogged by light. Do not touch the negative at this time as the heat from your fingertips can produce fog marks (white ovals).

5　Normally you would save the positive and throw out the negative, but in this case save the negative for transferring. Immediately place the negative, face down, onto the receiving material, and apply an even, medium pressure with a hard roller (soft rubber brayer) or squeegee (waiting causes the dyes to dry out). Do this four to six times in one direction, rolling smoothly, and stop just before the end of the Polaroid image. After placing the negative on the receiving material, cover it with a piece of clean, smooth paper, which acts as a buffer and delivers a more even and complete transfer. Shadow areas may require more pressure than highlight areas to transfer. Controlled levels of pressure can be applied to specific areas with a smooth, round tool, such as a spoon. Too much pressure can distort the darker areas while too little pressure can create tiny white dots.

6　Wait about two minutes. Keeping the negative warm, with low heat from a hair dryer, prevents the image from lifting off when you peel the negative back. Then carefully and slowly peel the negative back diagonally from one corner to reveal the transfer image. Don't let the negative fall back onto the receiving material. The blade of a utility knife can be gently slipped under a corner of the negative to lift the corner from the receiving material in order to reduce smudging and keep the edge of the image clean. Allow to air dry.

7　Consider doing posttransfer work. While the image is still wet, a foam brush can be used to clean up the edges and remove excess dyes. A knife can be used to scrape away designated areas. Watercolors can be

applied while the surface is wet or after it is dry. Permit the transfer to dry on a flat surface. Once dry, fine sandpaper can be used to eclipse areas of the image while graphite can be applied to highlight others. Colored pencils and pastels work well on dry images. A neutral acrylic mat varnish may be used to protect and seal the finished work. Brighter colors can be obtained by immersing the finished transfer in a working solution of stop bath or distilled white vinegar diluted one part vinegar to four parts water. Agitate for 30 to 60 seconds. Rinse for two to five minutes. If bubbling occurs, reduce the time in the acid or increase the dilution ratio.

Polaroid Emulsion Transfer

Emulsion transfer is a process for removing and transferring the top image layer of Polaroid ER films (Types 108, 669, 59, 559, 809) or Polacolor 64 Tungsten onto another support surface. European imagemakers began experimenting with the process during the 1980s, but it did not gain access into American photographic practice until the 1990s.

Basically, an exposed sheet of Polaroid ER film is submerged in hot water until the emulsion can be separated from its paper support and then transferred onto another surface, including ceramics, fabric, glass, metal, and wood. Three-dimensional surfaces can also be used. The process removes the image from its normal context and destroys the traditional frame, while adding a sense of movement and elements of the third dimension into the image. The following steps are provided as a gateway to this nontraditional process.

For additional information see: THORMOD CARR, KATHLEEN. *Polaroid Manipulations*. NY: Amphoto Books, 2002.

Inkjet Transfers

Inkjet printers can be utilized for making transferable images by using a waxy paper such as computer label sheets, or a release paper that is used as a protective overlay in dry-mount operations. Follow this procedure:

1 Put the transfer paper, shiny side up, in the printer. Be sure to remove any labels that might be on the paper.

2 Adjust the image settings to print about 20 percent darker and 5 percent higher in contrast than normal.

3 Select the highest quality printing mode and print the image. The image will look very dull.

4 Briefly soak a piece of blank receiving hot-press printmaking or watercolor paper in a tray of water, remove it, and blot excess moisture with a paper towel or cloth. If the paper is too wet, a dot pattern will result. Cold-pressed papers will deliver a softer effect.

5 Place the inkjet print face down onto the damp receiving paper. Hold firmly in place, then gently rub the back of the transfer paper and carefully lift it off.

6 A soft or foam brush may be used to blend and manipulate the inks.

7 Watercolor paints or pencils can be applied on either a wet or dry print. Pastel chalks may be used on a dry print.

8 Dry the print with a hair dryer or face up on a plastic air-drying screen.

For details see ENFIELD, JILL. *Photo-Imaging*, NY: Amphoto Books, 2002.

The Emulsion Transfer Process

Emulsion transfers can be made onto any clean, smooth surface, including glass or sheet metal. Fabric support should be stretched and mounted, since folds in the material can produce cracking when the emulsion dries. The emulsion can be transferred in sections by

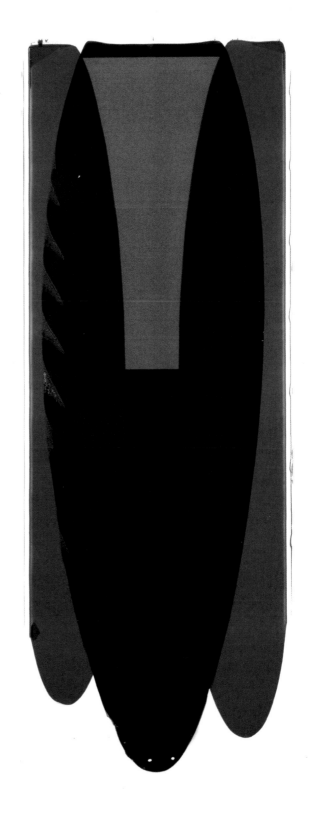

Carey approaches photography as picture making rather than picture taking. "My term 'pull' describes the act of pulling the film through a 20- x 24-inch Polaroid camera, while the 'rollbacks' are prints that are refed through the camera for another exposure. People often ask 'How was this picture made?' and 'What is this a picture of?' These question confront photography as process and challenge the expectation that photographs depict reality."

© Ellen Carey. *Blue Pull with Red Rollback*, 2002. 70 x 22 inches. Diffusion transfer print. Courtesy of Jane Baum Gallery, New York, NY.

tearing it with your nails or cutting it while soaking. The print can also be cut into pieces before its first submersion. All steps may be carried out under normal room light. (See figure 16.1 for visual outline of this process.)

1 Expose and process Polaroid Type 669, 59, 559, or 809 film and let it dry for eight to 24 hours or force-dry with a hand hair dryer. Besides using a camera, exposures can be made onto positive transparency film and projected onto Polaroid ER. This can be done with the Polaprinter, the Vivitar slide printer, the Daylab II, a colorhead enlarger, or a copystand.

2 Cover the backside of the print with plastic contact paper or with a coat of spray paint and allow to dry. This prevents the back coat of the print from dissolving during the submerging process. Trim the white borders of the print if you do not want them to transfer.

3 Fill one tray, larger than the print, with 160°F (71°C) water. Fill a second tray with cold water. Place a sheet of acetate or Mylar on the bottom of the cold-water tray.

If transferring onto watercolor paper, use a foam brush to moisten (but do not soak) the paper with room-temperature water. Put the paper on a clean, smooth piece of glass and squeegee it onto the surface, taking care to remove bubbles and/or wrinkles.

4 Submerge the print face up in the tray of hot water for four minutes with agitation. The water should be allowed to cool. Using tongs, remove the print from the hot water and place it in the tray of cold water. This quick dunk, just prior to placing the emulsion down, provides a lubricating layer helpful for manipulation.

5 Lightly massage the emulsion with a pushing motion from the edges of the print toward the center (see figure 16.1a). Slowly and carefully lift the emulsion and peel it

(a)

(b)

(c)

(d)

(e)

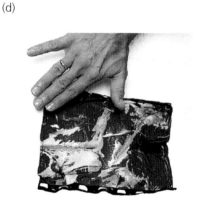

(f)

(g)

16.1 These images visually outline the procedures involved in making a Polaroid emulsion transfer.

Polaroid Emulsion Transfer Process. Courtesy of Polaroid Corporation, Cambridge, MA.

away from its paper support base (see figure 16.1b). Keep the emulsion that is being released from its support under the water. Now reverse the image (so it will not appear backwards when transferred) by bringing the emulsion back over itself (like turning down a bedsheet). Leave the emulsion floating in the water and dispose of the paper support. Hard water can make the emulsion difficult to remove. If this is a problem try using bottled spring water.

6   Take hold of two corners of the floating emulsion with your fingers and clamp it on the bottom of the tray (see figure 16.1c). Holding the emulsion, lift the acetate in and out of the water several times to stretch the image and remove the wrinkles (see figure 16.1d). Repeat this on all four sides, always holding the top two corners. Once stretched, you can dunk the image to purposely let the water curl and fold it. When you are satisfied with the image, remove it from the water and place it on your transfer surface, making sure the acetate or carrying material is on top.

7   Rub the image with your fingers and carefully remove the acetate (see figure 16.1e).

8   Smooth and straighten the image until it looks the way you want it (see figure 16.1f). At this point the emulsion can also be resubmerged in and out of cold water to perform additional manipulations. When completed, roll the image with a soft rubber brayer from the middle outward (see figure 16.1g). Begin using only the weight of the roller and gradually increase the pressure after all the air bubbles and excess water have been removed. Generally the operation is considered complete when all the folds appear to be pressed down. However, other rubbing tools and techniques may be used to achieve different effects.

9   Hang to dry. The transfer may be flattened in a warm dry-mount press.

Pompe used a Daylab to convert her digital montage (top) into a Polaroid from which she did an emulsion lift (bottom) onto different types of cotton rag papers. Pompe says: "the small size of the new image and its unpredictable edge creates a feeling of intimacy and helps transport the viewer into a fragile, magical landscape."

© Kathleen Pompe. [A] *Doors of Perception*, 2000. 10 x 13 inches. Inkjet print. [B] *Doors of Perception*, 2002. 3 x 4 inches. Diffusion transfer lift.

Making Black-and-White Prints from Color Negatives

The time will come when you need to make a black-and-white print from one of your color negatives. Maybe one of your pictures is going to be reproduced in the local newspaper, or a client may want a black-and-white print from a job that you did in color. You may make a photograph in which the composition appears strong but the colors do not work well together. It could be that the picture will work better in black and white, rather than in color. In certain situations, shades of gray communicate better than colors.

Basic Problems

There are some basic problems that need to be overcome to make a good black-and-white print from a color negative. If you print a color negative on regular black-and-white (blue-sensitive) paper, there will be a loss of contrast. The colors from the negative will not be reproduced in the correct shades of gray. Most commonly, reds print too dark, which is noticeable in the skin tones of the print, and the blues appear too light, revealed in the tonality of the sky. Such a print will not look natural. Also, regular black-and-white paper produces a much grainier image because it only responds to the cyan dye layer of the color negative. This creates gaps in the grain pattern because the paper cannot record the dye image from the magenta and yellow layers of the negative. As a result the grain has a very coarse appearance. It should be noted that imagemakers have made use of these characteristics to produce unusual effects.

Black-and-White Prints from Color Paper/Ektamax RA Paper

There are a number of ways to overcome these problems. You could make a color-corrected black-and-white negative on panchromatic film, but this is a difficult and time-consuming process. The sim-plest solution is to use a color paper such as Kodak's Ektamax RA Professional, which allows the direct production of neutral-tone black-and-white prints from color negatives in the normal RA-4 color process. Oriental Hyper Seagull Black & White (gloss and matt surface) is a similar product. Also available is Oriental Hyper Seagull Sepia, which allows you to make a sepia tone print from a color negative.

Ektamax RA is a resin-coated paper that is similar to panchromatic paper, such as Kodak Panalure Select RC Paper, grade M for medium-contrast commercial applications. The starting filter pack remains the same as used for printing color negatives (or use 45M and 45Y as a starting place). Limited contrast control can be obtained by altering the filter pack. To lower contrast, subtract 20M and 20Y. To increase contrast, add magenta and yellow. Adding more than 20 units of magenta or yellow can affect the red color lightness reproduction. The presence of any color cast in the image may indicate that your process has a developer or bleach-fix problem. Ektamax is good for quick and general work, but panchromatic paper continues to offer more versatility and contrast control over the final image.

Black-and-white negatives can be printed onto this paper at normal filtration by sandwiching a clear piece of processed C-41 film to provide the missing orange mask. Without this mask you run the risk of having the neutral tones show a distinct color cast (this can be used as a method to introduce monochromatic color into a black-and-white print). Without the mask, use a filter pack of 80M and 110Y as a starting place.

A color print can also be scanned and converted to grayscale and then out-putted as a black-and-white print.

Panchromatic Paper/Panalure

Panchromatic enlarging paper, such as Kodak's Panalure, is sensitive to green and red as well as to blue light.

Panalure Select RC is a warm black-tone, medium-weight, developer-in-emulsion, resin-coated paper, available in a glossy (F) surface and a fine-luster (N) in an M (medium) grade for negatives of average contrast. It incorporates a developing agent and is designed for machine development in an activator-stabilization processor, but it may be tray processed.

Since Panalure paper is panchromatic (sensitive to all the colors of the visible spectrum), it should not be handled under a standard black-and-white safelight. The regular #13 color safelight is recommended. Keep safelight exposure to a minimum. If you do not have a #13 safelight, simply do not use a safelight.

Processing

Panalure can be developed in a normal black-and-white developer such as one part Dektol to two parts water (1:2) or

---

a s s i g n m e n t

FOR THIS PROJECT, MAKE THE FOLLOWING PRINTS FROM A SINGLE NEGATIVE:

1. Perfect color print (figure 16.2).
2. Panchromatic print; use filters if necessary (figure 16.3).
3. Print on regular black-and-white paper (figure 16.4).
4. Color paper processed in black-and-white chemistry (figure 16.5).
5. Ektamax print (not shown as the subtle differences are lost in the reproduction process involved in making this book).
When you have completed all the prints, compare all the black-and-white prints to the original color print and see which one works best. Pay close attention to the red and blue colors to see which offers the best translation. Learn all you can about the different ways that the photographic processes can be put to work for your picture ideas. There is no telling when you might need one or where it might lead you.

16.2 A normal well-crafted color print. Compare it with figures 16.3 to 16.5 to see how it translates into a black-and-white image.

© Paul Marlin. *The Bagheads*, 1987. 8 x 10 inches. Chromogenic color print.

16.3 This figure offers an excellent translation of the color print. This print was made on Panalure paper, a panchromatic paper sensitive to green and red light in addition to blue light. This provides an accurate tonal rendition of all colors into shades of gray.

© Paul Marlin. *The Bagheads #2*, 1987. 8 x 10 inches. Gelatin-silver print.

16.4 This print was made on a normal fiber black-and-white paper that is sensitive to blue light. There is a reduction in the tonal range and the colors are not reproduced in the correct shades of gray. Notice how the outline around the sign letters comes up looking white.

© Paul Marlin. *The Bagheads #3*, 1987. 8 x 10 inches. Gelatin-silver print.

16.5 This photograph was made on color paper that was processed in a normal black-and-white process. There is a noticeable loss of image quality and contrast when compared with the Panalure print. It will do in an emergency and produce an acceptable halftone for reproduction purposes.

© Paul Marlin. *The Bagheads #4*, 1987. 8 x 10 inches. Chromogenic color print.

one part Selectol to one part water (1:1). Normal development temperature is 68°F (20°C). Standard development time for Dektol is 1 ½ minutes. Selectol's development time is two minutes. Both have a useful range of one to three minutes in the developer. All the tones produced will be warm blacks. All processing procedures are the same as for any regular black-and-white paper. Contrast can be slightly modified by choice of developer and how it is mixed. To increase the print contrast, use Dektol mixed equally with water (1:1), or even use Dektol straight and print using a condenser-type enlarger. To decrease print contrast, use one part Dektol to three (1:3) or four parts water (1:4). If this does not do it, switch to one part Selectol or Selectol Soft to one or two parts water (1:2) and print using a diffusion or cold-light-type enlarger.

Begleiter brings the illusion of movement to his photographs of still plant life. By using color infrared film the deep greens of healthy foliage will record as magenta, creating an intense color contrast against the blue sky. "By adding a polarizing filter, I brought out the clouds and darkened the sky, bringing out the visual movement I seek in my work."

© Steven H. Begleiter. *Palms I*, 1998. 24 x 30 inches. Chromogenic color print.

Color Infrared Film

Kodak Ektachrome Infrared (EIR) is a false-color reversal film that records electromagnetic radiation waves. Originally EIR was designed for camouflage detection by aerial photography, but the unusual color effects of this material can be used for artistic, fashion, illustration, or pictorial photography.

EIR film is made up of three layers of emulsion that are sensitive to red, green, and infrared instead of the standard sensitivity to blue, green, and red. In addition, each layer also contains a blue dye, necessitating the use of a yellow filter. When this film is processed the green layer responds to form blue, the red produces green, and the infrared makes red.

Infrared waves cut through haze and mist, making it effective to photograph scenes that encompass great distances, especially aerial photography. EIR film can record infrared waves in darkness if there is an infrared light source, but note that fluorescent lights do not emit infrared radiation.

EIR film should be loaded and unloaded in total darkness because it lacks an anti-halation layer. It should be refrigerated before and after exposure, but let it reach room temperature before exposing or processing it. After rewinding the completed roll, return it to its container and process as soon as possible.

Filtration and Color Balance

A Wratten filter No. 12 (deep yellow) is recommended in daylight or the results will look cyan. Other yellow filters can be used to achieve different effects, but a deep yellow works best. The addition of a polarizing filter to the yellow filter can give foliage a deeper red or darken the sky dramatically. When working with tungsten light sources of 3200 K or 3400 K, a 50 CC cyan and the yellow filter is the suggested starting place for pictorial results. To increase magenta or decrease green add a cyan filter; to increase red or decrease cyan add a blue filter; to increase yellow or decrease blue add a magenta filter. When high levels of

Panalure paper can be toned with warm toners such as Kodak's Sepia and Brown toner.

Use of Filters

Normally exposures are made using only white light. On a color enlarger start out with all the filters set on zero. You can use dichroic or CC filters during exposure of the Panalure paper to change the gray tonal values in the final print. The filters work in the same manner as they would if they were used on a camera with black-and-white film. If you want to make a gray tone lighter, use a filter of the same color as the photographed object. For example, if you made a picture of a yellow flower and wanted the gray tonal value of the yellow to be lighter in the final print, you would add yellow filtration. If you would like to make a gray tonal value darker, use the filter of the complementary color of the subject photographed. To make the yellow flower darker, add blue filtration.

Black-and-White Prints from Regular Color Paper

What if there is no panchromatic paper available to make a black-and-white print? The standard color negative papers are panchromatic. It is possible, by altering the development process, to make a black-and-white print on color paper. There will be a loss of image contrast and quality when compared with Panalure paper.

Expose the color paper normally, as if making a regular color print. Instead of processing it in the color process, do so in a standard black-and-white process. Use fresh, undiluted Dektol because the prints made in this manner tend to be flat. No color developer is used. Dektol processes the metallic silver and the fixer removes the unexposed and undeveloped silver halides. Do not use a color bleach-fix because it removes all the silver. This procedure exhausts the chemicals rapidly, and they should be replaced often.

infrared are present, as with chlorophyll-rich plant life, what appears to be green to the eye records as red.

Exposure, Focusing, and Processing

Because this film is sensitive to infrared, a regular ISO rating cannot be applied. Most meters will not measure infrared. A daylight starting point is 200 ISO with a Wratten filter 12. Use 100 ISO under tungsten light with a 50 CC cyan filter. Due to the uncertainty of actual infrared conditions, bracketing is a good practice in 1/2 f-stop increments. At shutter speeds of 1/10 second or longer reciprocity failure can occur. To correct for this, increase the exposure about one full f-stop and add a CC20 blue filter.

Since EIR film focuses on the reflective blue color there is no need to make focus adjustments as with black-and-white infrared film.

EIR film can be processed in E-6 with no safelights or inspection.

Chance

EIR film has many variables, which means that chance enters into your calculations. Experimentation is in order. To obtain repeatable results it is advisable to keep a written record of your exposure and filtration of your exposures. Make pictures that include foliage, sky, human skin, and water, and observe the effects this film produces on these subjects.

For additional information see BEGLEITER, STEVEN. *The Art of Color Infrared Photography*, Buffalo, NY: Amherst Media, 2001.

Criterion Photoworks, 119 East 4th Street, Minden, NE 68959 sells an infrared film that it processes as a negative.

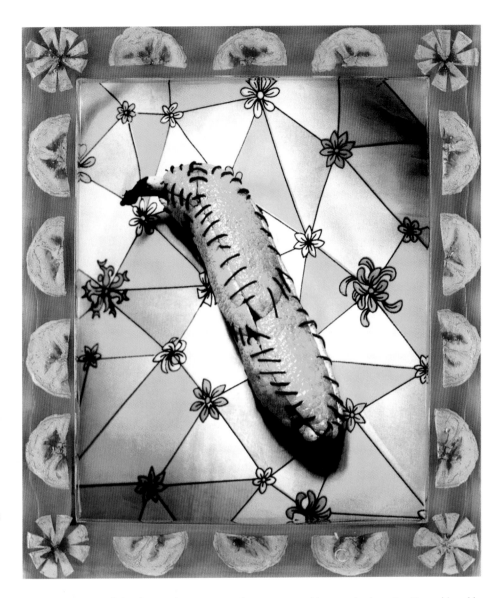

Karady makes use of the changes in contrast, grain structure, and increased color saturation achieved by processing slide film in C-41 chemistry to play with photographic representation's relationship to reality and truth. In her *Surgically Altered Fruit* series, Karady fabricated fruits and photographed them to emphasize the artifice inherent in photographic practice: "In context with our current technological society this work evokes genetic engineering, plastic surgery, and computer-manipulated photographs, all of which have shaken our notions of truth. Metaphorically they evoke the body and the experience of clothing or reinventing one's self through the recreation of one's exterior appearance. Just as the skins mimic the idea of the shapes of the fruit inside, we desire to take attributes of the other through similar mimicry and masquerade."

© Jennifer Karady. *Banana Honeydew*, 1995. 6 x 7 inches. Chromogenic color print with polyester resin and fruit frame.

Cross-Processing/ Slides as Negatives— E-6 at 1200

Astonishing visual events can be produced by taking color slide film and processing it to produce negatives. It is possible to push the film up to a speed of 10,000, dramatically increasing the color saturation, raise the level of contrast, and create a pointillistic grain structure à la the French neo-impressionistic painter George Seurat.

For the most spectular effects, get a 36-exposure roll of Kodak Ektachrome 200 Professional film. Set the film speed at 1200. In most situations ISO 1200 produces satisfactory results, but bracketing your exposures 1/2 f-stop and one full f-stop in both directions is suggested until experience is gained. If you push the film higher, be extremely careful in your exposures to retain acceptable shadow detail. You will be able to shoot in very low levels of light or use very

Litho films can be employed in many operations involving color imagery. Seeley summarizes his method: "Bits of ribbon, florist wires, cut paper, and other objects or drawings are arranged on a lightbox and photographed using a 4- x 5-inch enlarger as if it were a copy camera. The unexposed 4- x 5-inch litho film goes into the carrier, and the lightbox is switched on to initiate a series of silhouette exposures. The litho negatives are then tray processed. These negatives are enlarged onto 16-x 20-inch litho film. Three to five copies of this master positive are modified by the addition or elimination of specific areas so that they may serve as separations for the addition of color in the final printing process. Each color separation is then conventionally screen-printed on paper. The final prints are the result of three to five layers of color ink, normally printed on black paper."

© J. Seeley. *Flatware, Red State*, 1985. 16 x 20 inches. Photo screen print on paper.

high shutter speeds to stop action.

Contrast will be greatly increased, as in all push processes. A scene of low contrast will come out to be one of at least average contrast. A scene of high contrast will come out looking like it was shot on litho film.

There will be a noticeable increase in color saturation. Colors can begin to vibrate, look very intense, take on a "Day-Glo" appearance, and become deeper and more brilliant. The grain will appear quite oversized. You can literally pick out the different points of color.

Overall, the composition will tend to become more abstract, bold, impressionistic, and striking. The process is great for creating a mood. It is not suited for a situation that requires clarity and sharp detail. It should offer the opportunity to see things in a different manner. Predawn, after sunset, and night now become times that are accessible for you to photograph. This is not the time to go and shoot by the beach at noon. With these posterlike colors, the images tend to cry out to be printed bigger than normal. Consider getting some larger paper to print on if you find these images successful.

Double Development Procedures

After exposing the roll, the film will be developed twice, once in a special black-and-white process and then a second time in the normal C-41 color process (table 16.1). After completing the black-and-white process you can either dry the film and carry out the C-41 process at a later time, or continue on and complete both processes in succession. Be certain not to use any type of wetting solution like Photo-Flo if the film is dried before doing the C-41 process. At this point, watermarks do not matter because the film will be developed again and the wetting agent can cause difficulties in the color development.

Color Development

After completing the special black-and-white process develop the film again in the regular C-41 process, following normal C-41 procedures. The C-41 color-developing process adds the color couplers, and the density and color saturation will appear more normal. The entire C-41 process may be carried out under normal room lights. Be certain to maintain accurate temperatures.

Evaluation

After the film has dried inspect it. It appears pink because the slide film does not contain the orange mask as do regular color negatives. Make a contact sheet to see exactly what you have to work with. The highlights should be fairly dense and bold and the shadow detail will look thin. The colors should be intense with the grain quite visible. Negatives with good detail in the shadow area and with highlights that are not blocked indicate proper exposure. You should have exposures at 600, 800, 1200, 1800, and 2400. Check to see which film speed worked best.

Printing

Because there is no orange mask you will probably have to add about 20 to 30 units of yellow to your regular starting

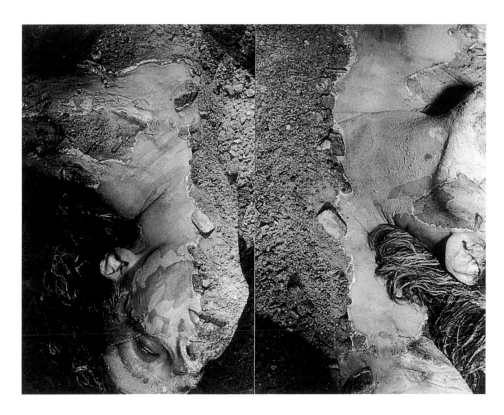

Notari finds another way to sandwich black-and-white and color negative films. She declares: "I combine a black-and-white negative of my figure (covered in a layer of clay slip) with a color negative of a textured ground to create a color image which transforms into an abstract or imagined experience and space. By sandwiching the negatives, each image transmutes into a symbolic vision beyond what an individual image can offer."

© Carrie Notari. *The Eternal Return: The Myth of Persephone*, 1989. 9 x 14 inches. Chromogenic color print.

Table 16.1	Development Procedures for Processing Transparency Film as Negative Film		
First Development Process Black-and-White Development Chart After black-and-white development is completed, the same roll of film must be developed for a second time following regular C-41 procedures.			
Solution	*Time/Temperature*	*Agitation*	
1. Acufine (1,200)	12 min	75?F	30 sec*
Acufine (10,000)	25 min	75? F	30 sec
2. Water stop	30 sec	75°F	Continuous
3. Color film fixer or black-and-white fix without hardener	5 min	75°F	1 min
Remaining steps can be carried out under normal room lights.			
4. Wash	15 min	75°F	
5. Bleach (C-41)	15 min	75°F	1 min
6. Wash	30 min	75°F‡	
7. Dry	Room temperature§		
Second Development Process			
C-41 Color Development Follow steps in Kodak E-6 Process, as listed in table Table 5.1 [NEW]			

* Agitate continuously for first 30 seconds and then for 5 seconds every 30 seconds.
† Agitate continuously for first 15 seconds and then for 5 seconds every 10 seconds.
‡ Water must be constantly flowing. If the wash is not complete it is possible to contaminate the color chemistry.
§ At the end of this process your negatives will appear extremely thin, with a light creamy pink color cast. This is normal.

filter pack (or sandwich a clear piece of processed C-41 film over your film). A low-contrast scene should print like a normal negative. A contrasty scene may require exposure times of over a minute. Although the colors will be much more saturated and the grain very noticeable, the overall color balance of the scene should remain the same as you saw it. This process does not create false colors as with infrared, but it enhances what is already there.

Use this process to step into some new areas that you had felt were off-limits with your conventional use of materials. Normally you would use color materials to depict a scene. Now is your chance to open up and express your feelings and mood about a subject.

Alternative Cross-Processing Method

E-6 film such as Fujichrome MS 100/1000 Professional multispeed can be cross-processed in C-41 chemistry to achieve an artificial, hyperenhanced color scheme with intense contrast, although the effect is not as intense as with double development. Expose the film and have it processed at ISO 400 or 800 in the C-41 process. Bracketing is recommended.

Litho Film: Color from Black and White

Litho films offer photographers a wide array of possibilities in altering and enhancing their vision. Here are some of the basic methods that can be applied in the making of color photographs.

Bas-Relief

Bas-relief is a technique that creates the illusion of the third dimension in a two-dimensional photograph by emphasizing the shadow areas of the picture. The effect is achieved by placing a normal continuous-tone negative in contact with, but slightly out of register with, a high-contrast positive of the same negative. Variation in the registration method alters the intensity of the effect. The negative and positive are then placed in the enlarger together and printed with a single exposure onto a piece of color paper.

The tonal range can be sharply reduced to produce extremes in the highlight and shadow areas. The final print will be a simplified version of the original scene; there will be no subtle details. The image will be graphic. Line and shape become the key compositional elements. Colors appear bold, bright, and striking. Be visually dynamic in the selection of the composition.

Tharp has found yet another method to incorporate black-and-white film into her color imagemaking. She tells us: "I borrowed my parents' wedding album and rephotographed it with black-and-white negative film and color slides. I then took the slides and projected them onto myself creating a tatoo-like image on my skin (and made photographs of this setup on black-and-white negative film). This was processed and printed onto color paper. I get great tonal ranges and have the capability to make a print slightly sepia or bluish in coloration."

© Deborah Tharp. *Self-Portrait with Mother*, 1988. 24 x 20 inches. Chromogenic color print.

Litho Production Materials

The production of both positive and negative lithos from the original through the use of both contact printing and projection printing is done to make the final pictures. It is possible to work from either a negative or a slide. You will need the following materials: an original continuous-tone color negative, two clean pieces of 11- x 14-inch glass, color paper, litho film and developer, and a red ortho safelight filter (1A).

All darkroom procedures with litho film must be carried out under a red 1A filter. With the exception of the developing and washing of the film, the darkroom procedures are the same as for regular black-and-white printing. Mix all chemicals beforehand and allow them to reach an operating temperature of between 68° and 72°F (20° and 22°C). Process in trays that are a little larger than the size of the film used.

Start readying the chemicals by preparing a working solution of litho developer, following the manufacturer's mixing directions. Make sure that there is enough solution to cover the film completely. Next, make up a tray of stop bath, then prepare a tray of paper-strength fixer. Have a deep tray for washing. Finally, mix a tray of wetting agent, such as Kodak's Photo-Flo, with distilled water.

Making the Contact Positive

When the chemicals are prepared and at operating temperature set the enlarger to 8- x 10-inch print height, and then over a clean opaque surface, place the clean negative on top of an unexposed piece of litho film, emulsion to emulsion. The lighter colored side of the litho film is the emulsion side. The dull side of the negative is its emulsion side. Put a clean piece of glass over this entire sandwich. Dust creates pinholes that have to be retouched.

Set the enlarger lens to f /11 and make a test strip. The exposure time should be similar to the time used for making an 8- x 10-inch proof sheet. White light, without any filters, is used to expose the litho film.

Develop the litho film by sliding it into the developer emulsion-side up. Agitate the tray by lifting one corner and setting it back down. Lift another corner and repeat. Complete development takes 2 minutes and 45 seconds. The dark areas should be totally opaque. Develop by visual inspection under the safelight and pull the film when the density appears correct. Do not develop for too short a time because streaks and pinholes may appear in the opaque areas. If the image comes up too rapidly reduce the exposure time and try again. If the den-

a s s i g n m e n t

THE SERIES OF LITHOS OUTLINED BELOW CAN NOW BE USED TO CHANGE THE ORIGINAL IMAGE IN VARIOUS WAYS. MAKE THE FOLLOWING COLOR PRINTS USING A COMBINATION OF THE NEGATIVES AND POSITIVES YOU HAVE MADE:

1. *A straight print from the original continuous-tone color negative. This acts as the standard of comparison for the rest of the prints that will be made using the lithos.*
2. *A bas-relief print. On a light table place the litho contact positive with the original negative. Carefully arrange the two just slightly out of register, so they do not exactly coincide. When a pleasing registration is obtained, tape the two pieces of film together. Put this sandwich into the negative carrier and place it in the enlarger. Make a color print following normal working steps.*
3. *A high-contrast bas-relief print. Arrange the 8- x 10-inch litho negative and positive slightly out of register and tape them together. On a clean opaque surface, lay the film sandwich on top of an unexposed sheet of color paper. Make a test print to determine the correct exposure, then make the final print.*
4. *A high-contrast black-and-white negative or positive. Make a contact print using the 8- x 10-inch litho negative. Adjust the filter pack to make three prints that have entirely different color balances. Record the filter pack information so that you will know how to alter colors with black-and-white film. Some typical filter packs and the colors that they will produce include:*

$$150Y = purple$$
$$150M = yellow\text{-}green$$
$$150C = sepia$$
$$150C + 60Y = red$$
$$150C + 60Y = yellow\text{-}brown$$

5. *A high-contrast black-and-white positive. Follow the same procedure as for print number 4.*
6. *Carbo print hues (optional process). To produce colors that have a flat tonal range, such as a copy of an old* Fortune *magazine, make two black-and-white positives from the negative. Sandwich all three together and make a print.*
7. *An offshoot of this process is to make a color print from a regular continuous-tone black-and-white negative. The color filter pack information gained from the litho film should apply.*
8. *What other ways can litho film be incorporated into color photography?*

sity is too light after 2 minutes and 30 seconds, increase the exposure time.

When the development is complete lift the film out by one corner and slip it into the tray containing a working solution of stop bath. Agitate the film gently for about 10 to 15 seconds in the stop bath. Lift the film out, drain it, and put it into the tray of fixer.

In the fixer, agitate the film constantly and gently. In about 60 seconds

the image will start to clear. Note how long it takes for this to occur. The total fixing time will be about twice the clearing time.

Rinse the film off, then inspect it in white light for proper exposure and processing. Do not attempt to judge it under the red safelight, because it will appear darker in the developer than in white light. If everything looks good continue to the next step. If not, decide what the trouble is and redo the process.

Wash the film for at least five minutes. To preserve the film for a longer time, use a hypo eliminator and then wash the film again for at least 10 minutes. Handle wet film with care to avoid scratching it.

After washing prepare a wetting agent mixed with distilled water and apply for at least 30 seconds.

Hang the film by one corner in a dust-free place to dry. Excess water can be removed with a Photo-Wipe on the nonemulsion side. This helps to get rid of processing debris, streaks, and watermarks and speeds up the drying time.

After the film is dry, make a contact positive based on test information. Burning and dodging can be employed.

Retouching
Opaque can be applied with a spotting brush to retouch litho film. Any place where opaque is applied the light will be blocked. The opaque eliminates dust spots, pinholes, scratches, and any unwanted details by simply painting over them. Work on the base side of the film. Opaque is water soluble and can be removed with a damp Photo-Wipe if a mistake is made.

Litho film is versatile and can also be collaged, drawn on, scraped, and scratched to make an image.

Making a Litho Projection Positive

While the litho contact positive is drying, make an 8- x 10-inch positive from the same original negative using the following procedure: Place a clean negative in the carrier and put it in the enlarger, which should already be set to the 8- x 10-inch format. Then focus and set the enlarger lens to f /11 and make a test strip. The exposure time should be close to the time used to make the positive litho contact. Repeat the processing procedures and evaluate.

Now proceed to make an 8- x 10-inch projection positive based on the test information.

Making Litho Contact Negatives

To make a litho contact negative, take the dried litho positive contact and place it, emulsion to emulsion, with an unexposed piece of litho film on a clean opaque surface and cover with glass. Repeat the processing steps.

Take the dried 8- x 10-inch litho positive and repeat the previous steps.

At this point you will have an original color negative, a contact litho positive, a contact litho negative, an 8- x 10-inch litho projection positive, and an 8- x 10-inch litho negative.

Litho Paper and Color

Special litho papers, such as Lith deliver a noticeably gritty grain structure and warm tones that can be controlled by varying the concentration of the litho developer. The gritty grain effect is enhanced by overexposing the paper, starting at about two f-stops and using a diluted developer for an extended time (roughly doubling the dilution rate doubles the development time). Print development must be done by inspection, learning to judge the exact moment to pull the print from the developer and get it into the stop bath with only red safelight illumination. For example, the exposure might be f /4 at 60 seconds,

The figure was intentionally grossly overexposed with an electronic flash. The gritty grain, extreme contrast, and brown tones were produced by varying the exposure and development times of the litho paper in Super Kodalith developer.

© Robert Hirsch. *Demon-Dream*, 1973. 16 x 20 inches. Gelatin silver print. Courtesy of CEPA Gallery, Buffalo, NY.

16.6 An offshoot of the photogram, the chemogram juxtaposes a camera-made image and painting with chemicals. A print was made from two negatives. As it developed, it was worked with a brush very close to the safelight to produce the Sabattier effect. Next it was painted with stop bath in some areas. The lights were turned on and thiourea and sodium hydroxide were introduced. After the print was fixed, hypo cleared, and washed, it was soaked in a gold protective solution (GP-1) for eight hours, and then rewashed and dried.

© Nolan Preece. *Au Descends on Ag*, 1989. 16 x 20 inches. Gelatin-silver print with applied chemicals.

developed for 50 seconds. Images are unique and can have endless combination of warm tones and colors, including shades of peach, pink, purple, and red.

Other papers can also be used. In such cases, dilute the litho developer 1:4 or 1:6 and expect exposure times of three to 10 minutes. Fixing and washing procedures remain the same. Experimentation with exposure times and developer dilution is in order with this process, following the general guideline for exposing for the highlights and developing for the shadows.

The Sabattier Effect

The Sabattier effect, often referred to by the misnomer of solarization, is the partial reversal of an image caused by exposing it to light during development. The result contains both negative and positive colors and tonalities.

This effect was first observed in the making of daguerreotypes in the 1840s. Armand Sabattier, a French scientist, discovered what caused this phenomenon in 1862. The process is one that is still not completely understood by scientists today.

The results of this effect are never the same. Many photographers have been attracted to the process because of the expressive uniqueness of each image, the influence that chance plays in the creation of the picture, and the mysteries that continue to surround, defy, and frustrate rational scientific explanation.

The Sabattier effect can be carried out on either negatives or prints. This section deals only with prints since the process does not put the original negative at risk and offers many picture possibilities for someone attempting the method for the first time. Negatives that have been

sabattiered do tend to produce more dramatic results than those made directly on a print from an unaltered negative. In order to preserve the original negative, those wishing to sabattier the negative often make copy negatives from the original. The copy negatives are sabattiered at various times and distances in order to produce a wide variety of effects.

The Sabattier effect occurs when a burst of light strikes the paper or film during the development cycle. This fogs the paper or film and reverses the colors and tones. By controlling the duration and intensity of the burst of light, it is possible to control the extent of the effect. Too much exposure produces black by converting all the silver halides to silver. Too little exposure does not change enough of the silver halides to produce the desired results.

A definite demarcation, known as a mackie line, is produced at the boundary between the reversed and unreversed areas. If it were not for these lines, the print would appear to be a positive version of a very dense and fogged negative.

What to Look For

Scenes that contain higher than normal contrast and possess a wide range of tonal differentiation are good candidates with which to begin experimentation. Images that have a strong sense of pattern or have distinct shapes will show noticeable changes. This will also make up for the loss of detail and subtlety of tone that accompanies this process. Since light-colored subjects contain more unconverted silver halides than darker ones, they generally respond more strongly to re-exposure. When this technique is successfully carried out, the image can appear more graphic, with light glowing areas competing against dark mysterious spaces that contain a surreal sense of place, space, and time.

Sabattier Procedure

The Sabattier effect can be produced without any special chemicals or equipment. The print should be developed in a tray because it offers the greatest control, but a drum can also be used. Make the print on the highest contrast paper obtainable. Mix the chemicals to regular strengths, but add a tray of water between the developer and the bleach-fix. Expose the print normally. Develop it for about one-half to three-fourths of the normal time. The print should contain essential shadow detail without full development of the highlights or mid-tone areas. At this point, remove the print from the developer and place it in a tray of water for up to 30 seconds with agitation. This dilutes the developer tremendously, but it does not completely stop the action of the developer. Next, take the print out of the water bath, drain it, and place it on a clean sheet of Plexiglas, glass, or an unribbed darkroom tray. Squeegee the excess water from the print and put it and the backing under a light source for re-exposure.

Tuckey discusses his use of the Sabattier effect: "I took this shot of native Indian men who were inducted into the Guatemalan military, where an effort is made to separate the people from their cultural roots. By solarizing this print, I hoped to evoke some of the emotion I felt while observing this scene. While processing, I flashed the print with a small pocket penlight for an instant (half a second) at one minute into its development. I was using a Jobo tube and simply removed the lid (in the dark) and shone the penlight in, producing an uneven Sabattier effect. Fortunately, the most dramatic color shifts took place in the highlights—the white uniforms of the conscripts."

©John Tuckey. *Two Faces of Guatemala*, 1991. 8 x 13 inches. Chromogenic color print.

Sources of Re-exposure

A variety of light sources can be used for re-exposure. Plug the light into a timer for accurate re-exposure control. A small light, such as an architect's lamp with a 15-watt bulb, placed about four feet above the print, works well. The enlarger can also be used as an accurate, control-lable, and repeatable source of re-exposure. It also presents the opportunity to easily work with either white light or, by dialing in filters, colored light. Coloring the light source increases the range of effects that it is possible to achieve. Place a towel on the baseboard of the enlarger to catch any dripping water. Remove the negative from the carrier before re-exposure. Refocus the enlarger if the negative is returned to make another print. An electronic flash with a diffuser may also be used as a light source.

Degree of Effect

The degree to which the Sabattier effect takes place is determined by when the re-exposure takes place and its duration. The earlier the picture is re-exposed and/or the longer or brighter the light, the more intense the reversal becomes in the final print. Re-exposure time is a matter of seconds or a couple of bursts from the flash. A digital timer allows exposures to be made in fractions of a second, providing even greater control.

Procedure after Re-exposure

After re-exposure, the image can sit for up to 30 seconds. This can serve to improve the overall contrast and enhance the edge effects that are created along the borders of the different densities.

Now place the picture back in the developer and continue to process normally. The results cannot be judged until the entire process has been completed.

Trial and error is the rule. Nothing is predictable. Not all pictures are suited for this technique. Do not force the method onto a picture. Wait for a situation in which this technique can be used to enhance the statement. Some control can be gained by using a constant light-to-image distance from a timed light source, but careful record keeping of exact working procedures, experience, and experimentation provide the main guideposts.

Photograms

A photogram is a cameraless image created by placing a two- or three-dimensional object on top of light-sensitive material, and then exposing the entire setup to light. After development the image reveals no exposure effects where an opaque object was in touch with the emulsion. Instead, it produces an outline of the object.

A wide variety of tones and colors is produced where translucent objects were placed on the emulsion and where partial shadowing occurred under opaque objects that were not totally in contact with the emulsion. Areas that were left uncovered receive the maximum exposure and do not record any detail.

The early explorers for a workable photographic process, Johann Schuluze in 1725 and Thomas Wedgwood and Humphry Davy in 1799, all began their experiments with cameraless images. The technique remained dominant until 1918, when Christian Schad, a Dadaist painter, used this method to make abstract images known as schadographs. Man Ray followed with his rayographs, and then László Moholy-Nagy with what we now call photograms.

Color Photograms

Color offers expanded possibilities for the creation of photograms. Photograms can be made on any light-sensitive material. Color paper offers a starting place for beginning experimentation. Paper is easy to work with and it can be handled under a safelight, which enables you to see where to place the objects. It can be processed quickly so the results are immediately known.

To get the feel and look of a frantic shopping spree Burchfield rehearsed and directed live models and various objects on eight pieces of dye-destruction paper. The photogram was created as Burchfield walked into and around the picture space exposing the paper with a penlite flashlight and colored gels for about 20 minutes.

© Jerry Burchfield. *Art and Commerce*, 1986. 8 x 16 feet. Dye-destruction print.

The photogram is used here by Barrow as a vehicle of inquiry into the nature of photography itself. The spray-painted colors on the image call attention to the fact that photography is not a depiction of reality but an extension of our own private experiences and perceptions.

© Thomas Barrow. *Location of Zeroes 2*, 1981. 16 x 20 inches. Gelatin-silver print with enamel spray paint. Courtesy of Andrew Smith Gallery, Santa Fe, NM.

The choice of objects to use in photograms is endless. Give it some serious thought and don't just use what happens to be in your pocket. There are natural objects such as plants, leaves, flowers, feathers, grass, sand, and rocks. Consider using artificial objects such as colored glass, or make your own materials. These can include cut paper in a variety of colors and shapes. They may be either translucent or opaque. Here are some additional ideas:

● Liquid-colored inks, such as Dr. Martin's, can be put on a piece of thin glass and exposed through onto the paper. The thickness of the glass affects the outcome. Both inks and objects can be combined.

● Different-colored light sources can be used to make various color effects.

● The color enlarger can be used as the source of exposure. Try changing the filter pack to produce a range of colors. Another effect is created when you expose an area with one filter pack and another area with a different filter pack. Also, try using an electronic flash, filters, or transparent plastic to color the light. Another technique is to employ a penlight as the source of exposure. It can also be used to draw with and to emphasize certain areas. Attach it to a string and swing it above the paper to make an unusual exposure effect. Filters can be placed in front of it to color the light, too.

● To maintain a naturalistic color balance when printing on negative paper (RA-4), put a clear, processed piece of negative film in the enlarger to make use of its orange mask.

● Combine a negative that has been made with a camera with one or more

of the cameraless techniques.

● Rephotograph or scan the photogram and incorporate it with another camera or cameraless image.

● Remember, all the regular guidelines for printing apply. This means areas may be burned and dodged during exposure.

● Challenge yourself to find interesting materials to experiment with. Use the open nature of the photogram to explore as many arrangements and uses of the materials as possible.

Chemograms

A variation of the photogram is the chemogram, which involves applying photographic chemicals to a camera or cameraless image with a brush, or by dribbling (figure 16.6). Begin with a photogram on black-and-white paper. Selectively paint the developer on the paper with a brush. By permitting time to elapse between exposure, painting, and fixing, limited color effects (yellow and reddish tones) can be produced as the photochemicals and the components of the emulsion oxidize. Another option is to use a strong reducing agent such as thiourea and a base such as sodium carbonate as a painting medium before the image is fixed. Mixing these two chemicals produces a silver sulfide stain. This can create unusual juxtapositions in image makeup, contrast, and spatial relationships. Normal fixing and washing should render the image and colors permanent. Further effects can be achieved by toning. Consider scanning the final result and then use image software to continue to manipulate the image.

Cliché-Verre

Cliché-verre combines the handwork of drawing with the action of the light-sensitive materials of the photographic process to make a picture. Shortly after William Henry Fox Talbot made public his photogenic drawing, three English artists and engravers, John and William Havell and J.T. Wilmore, devised this method of working. In their technique a piece of glass was covered with a dark varnish and allowed to dry. A needle was then employed to etch through the varnish to the glass. The glass was used as a negative and contact-printed onto photographic paper. They exhibited prints from their process in March 1839, making it one of the first spin-off methods to come from the invention of the photographic process.

In France the process was "reinvented" in 1851, when Adalbert Cuvelier used the glass collodion plate method. He introduced it to Jean-Baptiste-Camille Corot, who made it popular. It was employed by many other artists of the Barbizon school and proved to be an accurate, easy, and inexpensive way to make monochrome prints.

The process was revived again in the United States in the late 1960s and early 1970s. At this time there was renewed interest in nontraditional approaches to the photographic medium, which got a boost in part from the effects of the counterculture and its interest in alternative modes of expression.

Making a Cliché-Verre

Begin making a cliché-verre by getting a piece of glass and covering it with an opaque paint or varnish. Black spray paint works well. The glass can be smoked instead of painted to make a different type of visual effect by creating uneven densities. One method to smoke the glass is to hold it over the chimney of a lighted kerosene lamp. A sheet of film that has been exposed to white light and developed to maximum density can be used instead of glass. Scratching on a photographic emulsion generally produces a more ragged-edged line than that obtained with a coated piece of glass.

Once the glass is dry, a drawing is made with a stylus (needle, X-Acto knife, razor blade, piece of bone, or whatever you can imagine) by scratching through the coating to the glass. The glass can now be used as a negative to make a contact print or enlargement on a piece of photographic paper.

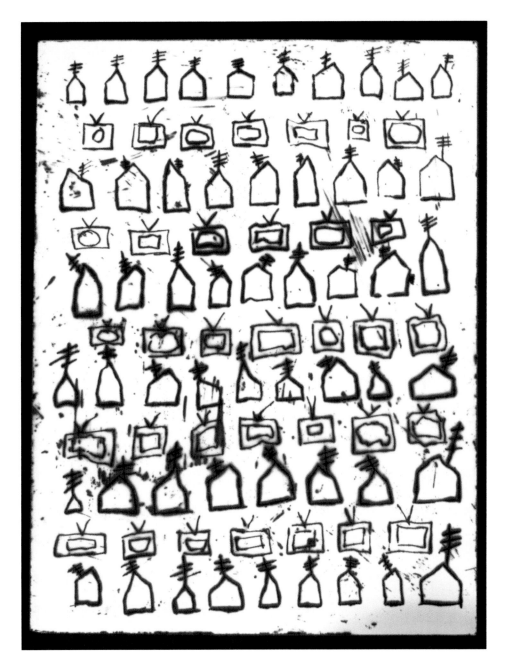

According to a recent A.C. Nielsen survey, American households annually watch a total of 224,372,599,000 hours of television. The cliché-verre technique is applied here to lampoon the influence that television has come to have in our society.

© Robert Hirsch. *Television Land*, 1986. 20 x 16 inches. Chromogenic color print. Courtesy of CEPA Gallery, Buffalo, NY.

Traditionally only black-and-white prints were made with this technique, but by using color photographic paper and dialing in different filter pack combinations it is possible to achieve a wide range of colors (see figure 16.8). Color can be used in a variety of ways for different effects:

● Use colored inks to opaque the glass. Applying a series of different-colored inks and not scratching down all the way to the glass can provide a multilevel color effect.
● Apply translucent colored inks to the glass or plastic negative as a way to introduce different colors into the final print.

- Combine the cliché-verre method with a camera-made negative. Scratch directly onto the camera-made negative and then make the print.
- Combine the use of colored inks and scratching onto a camera-made negative. Scan the completed work and continue making alternations with digital imaging software.

Hand-Altered Negatives and Prints

The first color photographs made their appearance in the form of hand-colored daguerreotypes. This was done to correct for the fact that all the early photographic processes lacked the ability to record color. The demand for color was greatest in portrait work. Miniature painters, who found themselves instantly unemployed by Daguerre's process, met the need by tinting daguerreotypes and painting over calotypes (the first photographic negative/positive process done on paper). In Britain the public seemed to have a preference for the "two penny coloured" pictures as opposed to the "penny plain." The hand coloring of black-and-white photographs continued to be widely practiced by commercial photographers for over the next 100 years.

Today hand altering a negative or print allows you to circumvent and to explore ideas that would not normally find their way into current photographic processes. It lets you introduce nonrepresentational colors, lines, patterns, and toshapes into a photograph. It pushes the boundaries and limits of photography, enabling you to achieve a unification of materials, practice, and vision that is not possible to achieve in standard practices. It interjects a physical presence into the work and also alters the sense of time, because hand alterations expand and prolong the interaction of the imagemaker within the process.

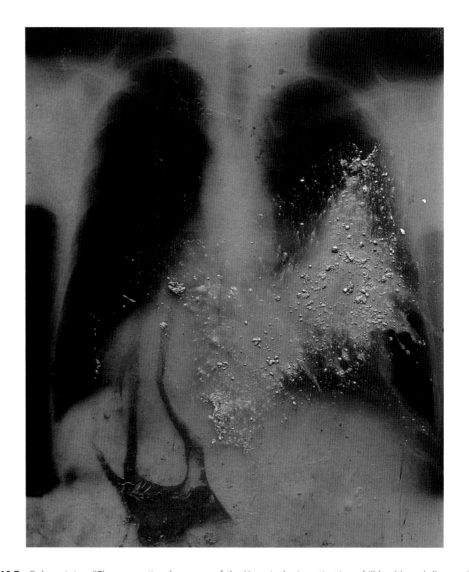

16.7 Cohen states: "The conventional purpose of the X-ray is the investigation of ill health and disease. I have chosen to hand-alter the X-ray with color in order to expose and undermine this purported neutrality of use. The mediums I employ react chemically and physically with the film, producing changes in color and consistency, making the unseen visible. Decomposing the X-ray, these actions parallel the decay and evaporation of the body [this X-ray is of a person with AIDS]. They also invoke an empathic response to its transience. The colors become metaphors for the noncorporal, the immaterial, those aspects of the person the X-ray as a diagnostic device circumvented. The X-ray's power to make the internal visible is not neutral; it invokes terror. I do not allow the scientific/diagnostic to abolish the possibility of ecstasy which is on the other side of terror."

© Cora Cohen. *R8*, 1993. 17 x 14 inches. Exposed roentgenograph film with mixed media.

Methods

Some of the methods of modification of the negative and/or print include scraping or scratching with a stylus and drawing or painting directly onto the image surface. This can be done with a brush, spray paint, an airbrush (see next section), cotton balls, or other means of application. Colors can be either transparent or opaque. The medium can be acrylics, food coloring, dyes, ink, oil paint, or watercolors (figure 16.7). Heat can be selectively applied to distort or destroy part of the image. Chemicals or chemical processes can be used to physically alter the appearance of the image (figure 16.8). Optical distortion materials can be placed in front of lenses or light sources to dramatically change the image. Electronic signals can be employed to create a pattern on a screen that is photographed or used to directly expose the film or the paper. The photo-based image can be combined with other media, such as engraving, lithography, silkscreening, or one of the many forms of printmaking (figure 16.9).

Airbrushing

The airbrush, invented in 1882, is a small, handheld spray gun able to transmit a precise mixture of fluid (dye, ink, or paint) and air to a specific surface location. A dual-action, internal mix brush with a fine head assembly is a good choice for most photographic applications. It permits the operator to do detailed work and alter the width of the line and the value or opaqueness of the fluid without having to stop and make adjustments. The use of an optional bottle container is recommended to extend the normal spraying range without having to stop and refill. The airbrush is powered through a flexible hose by pressurized canned air, such as Badger Propel, or by a compressor with an air-pressure regulator. Being able to adjust the air pressure from 10 to 100 pounds per square inch (psi) gives extra control over the line quality and intensity. Start at about 20 psi and add pressure at the rate of about 5 psi to see how it affects the character of the spray line.

The fluid medium needs to be thin. Typical starting places are one part water to one part nonclogging ink or watercolor, seven parts water to one part acrylic, or one part enamel to one part enamel thinner. Spraying requires a constant steady motion to avoid dips, runs, and sags. Work rapidly to avoid having the head clog. After each operation, spray clean water or solvent through the airbrush until all the color is out. Most technical difficulties, that is equipment failures, are due to improper cleaning. Follow the manufacturer's cleaning and maintenance instructions. Airbrushing must be done, following all safety guidelines, in a well-ventilated area with an

16.8 A slide-projected image was directed onto the model and photographed. Prints were made from slide film that was processed in C-41 chemicals. These were collaged onto clear acrylic with a matt gel. A sharp object was used to scratch patterns directly into the emulsion of the prints.

©Joyce Roetter. *Split Triptych*, 1990. Each 12 x 96 inches. Chromogenic color prints on acrylic.

16.9 As a printmaker and painter, Henderson uses photo-based techniques whenever it is necessary to serve a particular image. In this piece the background was created with ink brayers, the red "lifesaver" was painted in oils, and the drawings were appropriated from eighteenth-century medical texts with the aid of a copy machine. Copiers can be used to create an image that will accept ink and can then be printed to any absorbent or semiabsorbent surface. For Henderson: "The process becomes a mode of inquiry, an open-ended dialectic that bears directly on the formal content. A discourse is formed between the handmade and the reproduced, the pictorial sources and their signifiers, and between the tradition of painterly expressiveness and postmodern strategies of appropriation and representation."

© Adele Henderson. *Ontogeny No. 5*, 1995. 40 x 30 inches. Acrylic, oil, litho ink transfers from electrostatic prints on gesso panel.

exhaust fan and with the operator wearing a double-cartridge respirator.

For additional detailed information on many hand-altered methods see HIRSCH, ROBERT. *Photographic Possibilities: The Expressive Use of Ideas, Materials & Processes*, 2nd ed. Boston, MA: Focal Press, 2001.

Toning for Color

Toning is a method of adding to or altering the color of a black-and-white photograph. The following are commercially available ways of affecting the color of a print.

Development

The combination of paper developer and printing paper offers the most subtle way to control color through chemical manipulation of the emulsion. The age, dilution, temperature, time, and type of paper developer all affect the final tone of the print. Silver bromide papers usually produce a cool neutral to green color while silver chloride emulsions make warmer tones. The combination of both the type of developer and kind of paper also has an effect on the tones produced if any other method of toning is employed later.

Replacement

Process the print with a nonhardening fixer, such as Kodak Rapid Fix, without adding Solution B. Now the silver compounds in the emulsions can be converted with inorganic compounds—that is, gold, iron, selenium, and sulfur—to produce a wide range of muted and subtle colors. Factors influencing the color are the metallic compound used, the degree of toner dilution, the type of paper and developer, the temperature of the solution, and the length of toning.

Dye Toning

Dye toning produces the most vivid and widest range of colors. The dye base is usually attached to the silver in the

A black-and-white print was made from a negative etched with a knife. Acrylic paint, ink, and Gesso were applied with a Badger dual-action airbrush and a handbrush. Selected areas were colored with Prismacolor pencils. Materials, appropriated from magazines, were glued onto the print with TALAS archival white glue. This composite, layering approach allows nonlinear thinking and feeling to influence events in time and space.

© Robert Hirsch. *Remembering and Forgetting: A New Way of Seeing*, 1991. 16 x 20 inches. Gelatin-silver print with paint, colored pencil, and collage materials. Courtesy of CEPA Gallery, Buffalo, NY.

emulsion through the action of a mordanting chemical. Mordants such as potassium ferrocyanide act as a catalyst and combine with the dye to fix it in place. This prevents it from bleeding or migrating within the dyed area. The print is placed in the dye solution. The dye is deposited in the emulsion in direct proportion to the density of the ferrocyanide image.

A variety of colors can be achieved by mixing dyes, immersing the image in consecutive baths of different dye, and selectively masking parts of the print with a frisketlike rubber cement. There are also straight dye applications in which the silver is not converted, but the toner simply dyes all parts of the image equally. Dyes often lack long-term stability and fade when exposed to any type of UV light. Dyes often leave residues that can be seen in the base of the paper even after complete washing.

Safety

Many of the toning compounds are extremely toxic. Before using any toner read the directions and follow the safety procedures outlined by the manufacturer

Brose has developed a complex series of uncommon hand-photochemical processes that use bleach and toner to infuse images of early gay male erotica with color. Brose states: "the altered images wrestle the original footage from the arena of traditional representation by subverting the time and space experience through compression and fragmentation while exploiting the effects of the vintage film's deterioration. This hybrid process is an organic result of translating moving images into a seemingly static medium."

© Lawrence Brose. *Untitled, Agnes Brooklyn Bridge #1*, 2001, from Brose's film *De Profundis*, 1997. 46 x 34 inches. Inkjet print. Courtesy of CEPA Gallery, Buffalo, NY

Towery combines pinhole photography with digital by attaching a cap with a pinhole in it to a digital camera in place of a traditional lens. With this body of work, Towery likens the circles of confusion involved in the way a pinhole makes an image to the current state of photography, which he feels is also in a state of confusion. The traditional view of photography as being linked to ultimate truth, evidence, and proof, is challenged by the ability of digital technology to manipulate any image. "Now that Photoshop has become a verb, the nature of the medium is confused."

© Terry Towery. *Final Tuscan Sunflowers*, from *Circles of Confusion*, 2003. 12 x 18 inches. Inkjet print.

and in the addendum on safety (see page 344). Always wear rubber gloves and work in a well-ventilated space.

For additional information see: Rudman, Tim. *The Photographer's Toning Book: The Definitive Guide*. NY: Amphoto Books, 2002. If you are interested in making your own toners the Photographers Formulary (www.photoformulary.com) offers a complete range of materials for the photographic chemist.

Color Pinhole Photographs

Go into a dark room and make a small, round hole in the window shade that looks out onto a bright outside scene. Hold a piece of translucent paper six to 12 inches from the hole and you will see what is outside. This optical phenomenon, which dates back to the ancient Greeks, provides the basis for making pinhole photographs. Note: The image will be upside down, the same as in our eyes. Our brain turns it right side up.

Birth of the Camera

The camera obscura (Latin for "dark room") is a drawing device used to project an image onto a flat surface where it can be traced. It is based on the same principle that underlies pinhole photography. By the sixteenth century the camera obscura was in common use by artists such as Leonardo da Vinci. In 1658 Daniello Barbaro placed a lens on the camera obscura. It was this device that helped to work out the understandings and uses of perspective, which had been baffling artists, scientists, and scholars for centuries. Daguerre's camera was a simple camera obscura with a lens.

How the Camera Works: the Circle of Confusion

An optical image is made up of what is known as tiny circles of confusion. Technically, the circle of confusion is the size of the largest circle with an open center, that the eye cannot distinguish from a dot, a circle with a filled-in center. It is the major factor that determines the sharpness of an image and the limiting factor of depth of field. When these circles are small enough to form an image they are called "points" and the image is considered to be in focus. The pinhole camera has infinite depth of field, because it creates circles of confusion that are about the same size as the pinhole all over the inside of the camera. This means that these tiny circles of confusion are small enough to be considered points of focus with enough resolution to become a coherent image. If you add a lens, it makes smaller points of focus and the image is sharper and more coherent.

Pinhole Camera Building Materials

These items are needed to make a pinhole camera:

● A sheet of stiff mat board or illustration board at least 1/16 inch thick. One side of the board should be black. This will be the inside of the camera. The black helps to reduce internal reflection.

● A sharp X-Acto (number 11 blade is good) or mat knife.

● A 2- x 2-inch piece of brass shim or aluminum. An offset plate, obtained from a printer, is ideal. You can also use an aluminum pie pan or TV dinner tray.

● Glue. Any household white or clear glue is fine.

● A steel-edged or plain straight-edged ruler will deliver a far more accurate and close cut than a cheap wooden or plastic ruler.

● A number 10 or number 12 sewing needle (see table 16.2).

● A small fine file or number 0000 sandpaper.

● A ballpoint pen.

● Black photographic pressure tape or black electrician's tape.

● A changing bag (optional).

● A piece of black-and-white, single-weight, fiber-based enlarging paper.

Using a pinhole camera with an extremely short focal length, Ess exposed 4- x 5-inch Polaroid positive negative film. Ess uses filters to produce "psychological colors" suitable for her image content. To create these two monochrome colors Ess "blocked out the top part of the image with a customized dodging tool. I then exposed the bottom part of the paper using filtration to create the greenish, yellowish gray of the bottom. I changed the filtration and then blocked out the bottom and exposed the top to get the purplish blue. The theme of my work is the subjective relationship of the self to the phenomenal world and the fact that our memories, emotions, and thoughts determine how and what we see."

© Barbara Ess. *Untitled*, 1993. 39 ½ x 27 ¼ inches. Chromogenic color print. Courtesy of Curt Marcus Gallery, New York, NY.

● Polaroid Time-Zero film and SX-70 camera for color pictures.
● The blueprint of an adjustable focal-length pinhole camera provided in figure 16.10.

A 35-mm camera can be converted into a pinhole camera. Cover a UV filter with black (opaque) construction paper with a good pinhole in the center. Place it on a 35-mm camera and it becomes a pinhole camera. A body cap with a pinhole constructed in its center can also be used.

Zero Image Company (www.zeroimage.com) makes a modified body cap, called a Zone Plate, for various cameras, which has a laser-cut pinhole. The same company also makes wooden pinhole cameras. Polaroid also makes a pinhole camera kit.

Variable Focal-Length Pinhole

The focal length of a pinhole camera is determined by the distance of the pinhole from the light-sensitive material. Building a camera with a variable focal length gives you the flexibility similar to that of having a zoom lens. The adjustable focal-length camera should be built to the dimensions given in the blueprint in figure 16.10 if you plan to shoot any Polaroid film. You can use the film pack as a movable focal plane or make one out of cardboard. If you make one, be sure to glue on an upside-down set of cardboard steps to hold the paper flat during exposure. Save the used film packs because they make excellent ready-made holders for any other materials you want to expose. They are structural and can be easily moved forward or backward inside the camera to vary the focal length. As the focal plane is moved closer to the pinhole, the angle of view becomes wider and the exposure time drops as needed.

Pinhole Camera Construction

Following the blueprint in figure 16.10, lay out the dimensions on the board. Carefully cut out all the pieces, using a sharp knife and a straightedge. Sand any rough areas. Now proceed to the next two sections, making the pinhole and the shutter. After this is done, glue all the pieces together. Do not rush; allow the glue to dry. Finally, use the black tape to make all the seams light-tight. Mark both the right and left sides of your camera clearly in the number of inches the focal point is from the pinhole. This is to give you more accurate and repeatable results. The closer to the pinhole, the wider the angle of view and the shorter the exposure will be.

Special Color Materials, Practices, amd

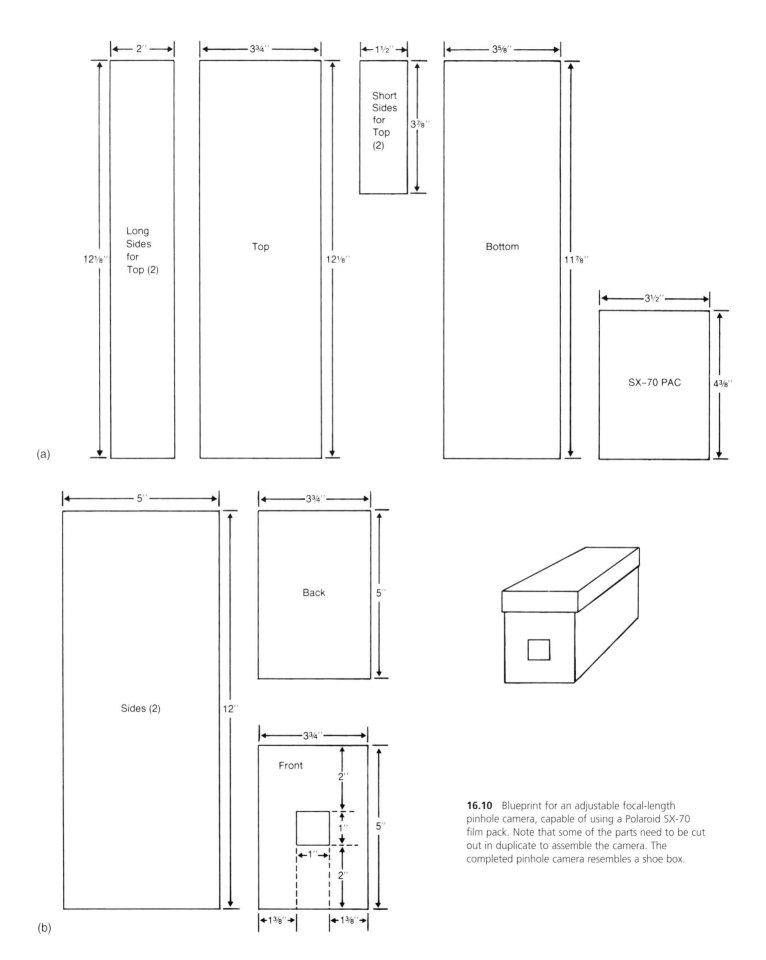

(a)

(b)

16.10 Blueprint for an adjustable focal-length pinhole camera, capable of using a Polaroid SX-70 film pack. Note that some of the parts need to be cut out in duplicate to assemble the camera. The completed pinhole camera resembles a shoe box.

Making the Pinhole

Do not stab a hole in the metal; gently drill it with the needle on one side and then the other (see table 16.2). Sand or file. Repeat until the hole is as perfectly round and as free from defects as possible. With aluminum you can increase image sharpness by thinning the metal around the pinhole. This can be done by placing the metal on a book and punching it lightly in the center with a ballpoint pen and then smoothing the back with a file. Then make the hole with the needle.

Now find the center of the front end of the camera. Cut a square opening equal to half the diameter of the metal pinhole material and glue or tape it into place.

The Shutter

You can create a simple shutter by making a sliding door in front of the pinhole with some thin board, or save the piece you cut out of the center of the camera front for the pinhole. Darken the sides with a marker and use a piece of tape to build thickness and to act as a handle. This creates a trapdoor-type shutter. Another option is to simply use the black plastic top from a film container and hold it in place with your hand or tape. Aluminum foil and tape also work.

Exposure

If you know the needle number you can figure out what f-stop will be used to make the pinhole, based on the focal length. A light meter can be used to give a ballpark exposure figure, provided you know the speed of the light-sensitive material being exposed.

The Aperture Formula

The f-stop is a simple ratio expressing the relation of the size of the opening that emits light, the pinhole, to the distance from the opening to film plane (table 16.2). Therefore, a one-inch opening and a seven-inch focal length gives a ratio of 1:7, or an f-stop of f/7. A num-

Table 16.2
Standard Needle Sizes and Their Diameters

Needle Number	Diameter
4	.036 inches
5	.031 inches
6	.029 inches
7	.026 inches
8	.023 inches
9	.020 inches
10	.018 inches
12	.016 inches
13	.013 inches

ber 10 needle makes a pinhole diameter of .018 inches with a five-inch focal length and would make an f-stop of f/277, which can be rounded off to f/280 (.018 divided into 5 is 277.777).

Starting Exposure Times

Outdoor exposure times run between one and 15 seconds, depending on quality of light and the focal length. Trial and error will provide a starting point for acceptable exposure.

Getting the Hang of It

If you have never worked with a pinhole camera, begin by exposing black-and-white photographic paper. Process the paper following standard black-and-white procedures. If it is too light, give it more exposure; if it is too dark, give it less exposure. When you get a good negative, dry it and make a contact print. After experience is gained it is possible to expose any type of photographic material in the pinhole camera.

Pinhole SX-70 Film Exposure

After learning the basics of the pinhole camera, you will be ready to start with color materials. SX-70 Time-Zero film offers a quick entrance with color. SX-70

follows the same basic rules as color slide film. If the print is too light, it means it has been given too much light, so cut back on the exposure. Should it be too dark, this indicates it was not given enough light. To correct this, increase the exposure time.

SX-70 Filtration

With the SX-70 film, prints are often too "cool" looking, having either a blue or cyan cast. This can be corrected by using plastic color-compensating filters. To make the print warmer, use yellow or magenta plus yellow filters to correct. Twenty points of filtration is a good starting place. Use yellow to reduce blue and magenta plus yellow to reduce cyan.

You can also use the color filters to experiment in purposely altering the color to change the mood or feeling of

---

a s s i g n m e n t

MAKE THE FOLLOWING PINHOLE PICTURES:

1. A portrait of one person that makes a statement about that person. Go beyond a pinhole mug shot.
2. A group portrait of two or more people. This compounds the problems of composition and technical limitations.
3. An architectural study (portrait of a building). Show how this building is unique and what made you stop and photograph it.
4. An object from nature. Show the lifeforce at work.
5. A human-made object. Show why it is important to you.
6. A self-portrait. Tell something about yourself.

In the course of creating these six pinhole pictures, change the focal length. Have a minimum of one wide-angle view, one normal view, and one telephoto view. List the focal length and other exposure information on the back of every print.

Babcock, who likes to build cameras, has converted a VW van and an Airstream motorhome into giant cameras. The exposures are made on color mural paper (which could be used as a negative), but Babcock prefers the negative image because it "represents the photographic process" and delivers an "expressively convincing post-nuclear frame-of-mind."

© Jo Babcock. *Intersection Rocks*, 1993. 40 x 65 inches. Chromogenic color print.

---

a scene. Filters create added density, and you may have to increase the exposure time.

What next? Go on and expose color negative material or Ilfochrome Classic paper, or even modify the camera to take a Polaroid 4-x 5-inch back.

For more detailed information read SHULL, JIM. *The Beginners Guide to Pinhole Photography*. Buffalo, NY: Amherst Media, 1999; RENNER, ERIC. *Pinhole Photography: Rediscovering a Historic Technique*, 2nd ed. Boston: Focal Press, 2000; or contact Eric Renner at: www.pinholeresource.com.

Nonsilver Approaches and Color

The majority of the material covered thus far, with the exception of digital imaging, has its foundation in silver-based photographic methods. In these methods, silver is used as the prime light-sensitive material in the chemical formation of the photographic image. There are other ways in which a photographic image can be formed. This section provides an introductory overview of a few of the major methods. There are older, commercially obsolete processes such as blue printing and gum printing. Many artists combine old and new technologies by digitizing their negatives and adjusting them to the older processes to produce better prints. These techniques permit the exploration and extension of the demarcation between the photographer, the subject, and the process of photography. The ensuing images can expand the scope of photographic vision by opening new pathways in both ideas and working methods.

Before working with any new process, read and follow all safety recommendations supplied by the manufacturer, as well as those in the safety addendum (see page 34). Processes that make use of potassium ferricyanide, ferric ammonium citrate, or ammonium and potassium dichromates can be disposed of by pouring them into a plastic bag filled with kitty litter. This bag can then be sealed and placed in a protected outside trash container.

Cyanotypes: Blueprint Process

The cyanotype (aka the blueprint) enables the photographer to make prints without a darkroom, an enlarger, or special developing chemicals. Images can be

put on a variety of material. The final picture is quite permanent and it is simple and fun to do.

Blueprinting is one of the easiest and most versatile of the nonsilver approaches to working with color and a photographic process, but there are other processes, including carbon, gum, and Vandyke printing. It is possible to combine different nonsilver methods, creating a new personal blending of the processes tailored to suit your own vision.

History of Blueprints

The process known as cyanotype was invented in 1842 by the distinguished English astronomer and scientist Sir John Herschel (1792–1871) as a way to make fast copies of his notes and sketches.

Herschel made a number of important contributions to photography, including the discovery that sodium thiosulfate would act as a fixing agent for silver-based photographs and the first photograph on a glass plate. He introduced the terms "photography," "negative," "positive," and "snapshot" into our vocabulary. It was not until the 1880s that the process caught on with the introduction of precoated cyanotype paper for use by architects and shipbuilders, who nicknamed the process "blueprinting."

How It Works

The cyanotype does not rely on silver salts but on ferric salts to form an image. A salt is the result of the mutual action of an acid with a base. Some salts of iron are reduced to ferrous salts when exposed to light in the presence of organic matter. These fer-

rous salts act as powerful reducers of other metallic salts that are not affected by the ferrous salts. Ferric ammonium citrate gets broken down by the action of light to a ferrous salt. The ferrous salts react as reducers on the potassium ferricyanide. The areas not exposed to light remain in their ferric state and are washed away during development.

Paper

Cyanotypes can be made on a variety of paper surfaces and cloth. The Rives BFK paper is a good one to start with for general applications. Arches's watercolor 130-lb paper gives a more textured image with a loss of detail. Any type of paper, from a grocery bag to copying paper, offers possibilities. However, improper paper selection results in discouragement due to failure to produce good image quality.

Sizing

Sizing is not critical but some sizing is needed for this process. It supplies the organic material that is needed for the reduction of the ferric salts to ferrous

salts, and it helps to keep the image on the top of the paper, which prevents it from appearing flat. Many papers, such as Rives BFK, have enough sizing, but others may require additional sizing to produce a good print. Sizing can be applied and allowed to dry before the paper is coated. It is available in liquid form at grocery stores and can be brushed on (see section on gum bichromate printing below).

Sensitizing Solution

There are numerous formulas, but a basic sensitizing solution can be made from just two chemicals. Ferric ammonium citrate (the green granular form is the most sensitive and stable) is mixed 50 grams (1.76 oz) to 250 milliliters (8.45 oz) of distilled water. In a separate container mix potassium ferricyanide, 35 grams (1.23 oz) with 250 milliliters (8.45 oz) of distilled water. Be sure the potassium ferricyanide crystals appear bright orange before use. If they look rusty red they will not be effective. Mix only enough solution for your immediate needs. Store each separately in a dark

with newspaper underneath to avoid staining the floor. Use a hair dryer on the low setting to speed the drying.

In the second method, the chemicals are applied to the paper with a polyfoam brush. Dip the brush into a tray of emulsion, press the brush onto the side of the tray to get rid of the excess, and apply it to the paper, being careful to get an even coat.

Blueprint paper can also be purchased precoated from various sources. It is often called by a different name, such as solar paper or sun paper. The quality and sensitivity vary greatly; check them out carefully before purchasing large amounts of paper.

What to Shoot

When selecting subjects for this process remember that the final image will be cool and that midtonal range details tend to get lost. Simple, strong graphic images with a minimum of clutter work well.

Printing

Take the dry paper and place your negative over it (emulsion to emulsion) in a contact printing frame, or cover with a piece of clean glass and a backing board. Take this sandwich outside and expose to bright sunlight. This nonsilver printing-out process is fairly fast, but exposure times vary greatly depending on how the material was coated, the time of day, the time of year, and the location.

brown plastic container with the air squeezed out. Combine the two solutions right before you are ready to coat the paper. Discard the solutions by pouring them into kitty litter, placed inside a plastic bag. Seal the bag and put it into an outside trash container. Coated paper can be stored like regular photographic paper, but it is most sensitive right after it has been coated.

The Coating Process

The entire coating process should be carried out in a safelight darkroom if possi-

ble. It can be done in a dimly lit room, but some sensitivity will be lost. When you are ready to sensitize the paper, mix the two solutions together. There are two methods for accomplishing this.

In the first method, the paper is floated in a tray of solution for about three minutes. Tap the paper with a print tong very gently to dispel any air bubbles. Also use the tong to agitate the paper in the solution, taking care not to get any of the solution on the back of the paper. Use the print tong to carefully remove the paper, letting the excess drip into the tray, and hang the paper to dry

Gum printing has a distinct physical presence and offers an array of synthetic color possibilities. Osinski's photograph from a model train setup displays a "duplicate reality" in miniature to the lifesize "reality" it mimics. "Printing in gum bichromate can cause a dislocation of scale," says Osinski. "Is it a human-sized world, or miniature? Is it a familiar landscape or a strange world?"

© Christine Osinski. *Ronnie's Train*, 1980. 11 x 14 inches. Gum Bichromate print.

Exposure times can vary from as short as three minutes to as long as eight hours. Test strips can be made to determine exposure, but visual inspection is reliable and faster. The print is properly exposed when it appears about 20 percent darker than the final image is intended to be. The highlights will look glazed and possess a metallic sheen. The paper will change color from a yellow-green to a blue-gray as the image appears. Typical sunlight exposures are between three and 15 minutes.

If artificial light is used for exposure, be certain it is an ultraviolet source such as carbon arc lamps, mercury vapor lamps, or sunlamps. The exposure times

are usually longer than with sunlight. Start at 15 minutes with the lamp about 24 inches from the print frame.

After properly exposing the print, remove it in dim light and wash in running water until the highlights clear (look white), then dry it.

Handle the paper from the back or the corners. You will leave fingerprints if you touch the surface.

Spotting and Storage

Cyanotypes can be spotted with watercolor, Prussian blue, or Marshall's photo pencils.

Cyanotypes are a very stable process. For maximum life, they should be treated following the suggestions for color materials in the preservation section of chapter 9, page 193. Nonbuffered board is recommended for matting cyanotypes.

Troubleshooting

If you get muddy blues or cloudy whites, try blueprint intensification. After the picture is processed, soak it in a 4 percent solution of fresh hydrogen peroxide and distilled water. Mix 1 ounce (29 ml) of hydrogen peroxide with 25 ounces (740 ml) of distilled water. Soaking time is determined by visual inspection, but it is generally brief. This should intensify the blue and make it richer, and at the same time clean up the white highlight areas. When the picture looks good, rewash it for at least five minutes.

The Gum Bichromate Process

Gum bichromate printing is a simple process that uses a pigment (water colors or tempera), a liquid gum to carry the pigment, and a light-sensitive chemical (ammonium dichromate or potassium dichromate) to produce a nonnaturalistic color image from a contact negative. The softening of the photographic image and the subjective use of color allow the photographer a great amount of freedom in the creation of the print.

The first workable gum process was developed by an Englishman, John Pouncy, in 1856. It was made popular in the 1890s by Robert Demachy and Alfred Maskell, who renamed the process photo aquint.

There are many different recipes for making gum prints. This simple recipe is presented as a starting place and to show how the basic process works. Feel free to make adjustments and personalize the process. Much of what is discussed in the blueprint section can be applied to the making of gum prints, including the safety rules.

Selection, Presoaking, and Sizing

Pick a high-quality etching or watercolor paper, since it must be able to withstand being soaked and dried many times. Rives BFK and Arches's watercolor paper offer good starting points and are widely available. The more texture the paper possesses, the less detail there will be in the final image.

The selected paper should be presoaked in hot water (100°F, 38°C) for 15 minutes and hung up to dry. Without a presoak, the paper will shrink after the first time it is processed, making accurate registration of all the following exposures impossible.

Next, the presoaked paper must be sized to seal the pores of the paper. This step may be skipped if the paper has been presized by the manufacturer. Some printmakers carry out this step even if the paper has been presized in order to maintain better control over the pigment in the highlight areas. Sizing is accomplished by soaking the paper in a solution of gelatin to minimize pigment staining in the highlight areas.

Knox gelatin, available in most grocery stores, works well. Stir one packet into a quart of hot water (100°F) until it is dissolved, then pour it into a tray. Put the paper in the tray of dissolved gelatin and leave for two minutes. Squeegee the paper and hang it up to dry. Some people give the paper a second coat of sizing after the first one has dried.

Preparing the Sensitizer, Gum, and Pigment

Mix one ounce (29 ml) of ammonium dichromate, which is twice as sensitive to light as potassium dichromate, with 10 ounces (296 ml) of water and set it aside. The dichromate and dry gum can be purchased at a chemical supply company.

The gum is available as premixed lithographer's gum or dry powder acacia gum. The lithographer's gum can be obtained at a graphic arts or printing supplier. It lasts a long time provided it contains an antibacterial agent. The dry gum solution is made by mixing two ounces (57 g) of dry gum to four ounces (118 ml) of water. Stir it until it is dissolved, and set it aside.

Next, place about a half-inch (1.3-cm) ribbon of pigment in a baby food jar and mix it together with one ounce (29 ml) of the liquid gum. Tube watercolors are easy to begin with. Put the lid on and shake until the solution is completely mixed. The amount of pigment used varies with the brand and color. Experience will guide you with future mixing. Now combine one ounce (29 ml) of the liquid dichromate to make a working solution. The gum and dichromate are generally mixed together in equal amounts.

Preparing the Paper for Printing

Tape or pin the prepared paper by its corners to a flat board. Brush the working solution as quickly as possible onto the paper in long, smooth, horizontal strokes and then in vertical ones, slightly overlapping the previous strokes. Make a complete stroke without redipping the brush in the emulsion. Disposable polyfoam brushes work well. Do not oversoak the paper or let the solution puddle. Coat an area larger than the negative that will be used to make the contact print. Let the paper dry in a darkened room. It is not sensitive to light until it has dried. Drying time can be reduced by using a hair dryer on a low heat setting. Expose the paper as soon as it is dry, because it will not keep for more than about 24 hours.

Registration and Making the Print

One approach to making gum prints is to print the negative a number of times using different colors. To ensure each exposure lines up with the previous one, a system of registration is helpful. This can be done visually or by gently outlining all four corners of the negative on the paper with a soft-leaded pencil before the first printing. If critical registration is a must, a punch and registration buttons (available at graphic arts suppliers) should be used.

After the registration method has been selected and carried out, put the negative on the dry-coated paper and cover with a clean piece of glass, or place in a printing frame. When sunlight is not abundant and consistent, a daylight

photoflood or sunlamp can be used to make the exposure. With the light source at a distance of 24 inches (61 cm) from the paper, starting exposure time should be about 10 minutes. Different-colored pigments require different exposure times. Most of the exposures should be in the range of five to 20 minutes.

A blowing fan will lengthen the life of the light source and keep the print from getting too hot. Too much heat can produce a pigment stain on the print.

Developing the Print

After the exposure is made there should be a distinct image where the light has darkened the gum bichromate on the paper. Remove the negative and store it safely. Place the paper face down in a tray of water that is between 70° and 80°F (21° and 26°C). Let it soak for a minute or two. Turn the paper face up and gently wash the loosened solution away. Hang the paper up to dry.

Multiple Printing

After the paper has dried, additional colors and coats of emulsion may be applied and the paper reprocessed. This can create depth, increase color saturation, extend the overall tonal range, and produce a sense of the surreal. One negative can be used for many different exposures. A wider variety of results can be produced by making negatives that possess different densities (such as those used in making posterization prints) or by using entirely different negatives.

For more information on nonsilver processes read CRAWFORD, WILLIAM. *The Keepers of Light.* Dobbs Ferry, NY: Morgan & Morgan, 1979; JAMES, CHRISOPHER. *The Book of Alternative Photographic Processes.* Clifton Park, NY: Delmar Learning, 2001; and HIRSCH, ROBERT. *Photographic Possibilities: The Expressive Use of Ideas, Materials and Processes,* 2nd ed. Boston, MA: Focal Press, 2001.

For additional information and supplies of numerous nonsilver and alternative processes contact Bostick and Sullivan at: www.bostick-sullivan.com and Photographers' Formulary, www.photoformulary.com; for papers and brushes contact Daniel Smith, www.danielsmith.com.

The Dye-Transfer Process

The invention of films such as Kodachrome, Agfacolor, and Ektachrome provided solutions for an accurate, easy-to-use, nonscreen, and integral method of making color transparencies. A problem that all these processes shared was the lack of a way to make prints from slides.

Prints had to be made by a commercial lab that used the carbro process, an improved version of Thomas Manly's 1899 Ozotype and his 1905 Ozobrome processes.

The carbro process used carbon tissue in conjunction with a bromide print, not silver, to make an image of permanent pigment. In the carbro process black-and-white prints were made from each of the three separation negatives made from the original transparency through red, green, and blue filters. The gelatin emulsions were stripped from each of the prints after development and dyed cyan, magenta, and yellow. They were then superimposed on a new paper base. The carbro process offered excellent control in the making of the print but was complex, costly, and not suitable for assembly-line production of photographs. The dye-transfer process grew out of these techniques.

The dye-transfer process was originally introduced in 1935 as the Eastman Wash-off Relief process. It was replaced by the improved Kodak Dye-Transfer process in 1946 and discontinued in 1993.

In the dye-transfer process, separation negatives were made by photographing the original transparency or print on black-and-white film through red, green, and blue filters. If archivally processed, these negatives could be used to make new prints at a future date, long after the original color image disappeared. These negatives were used to expose special matrix films that would in turn transfer the dyes in printing.

Dyes of any color could be employed, but the subtractive system (magenta, yellow, and cyan) was used when a normal full-color print was required. The matrix made from the blue separation was dyed yellow, the matrix from the green separation was dyed magenta, and the matrix from the red separation was dyed cyan. The print was made on a special receiving paper, which was attached face up on a smooth surface. Each of the matrices was squeegeed face down against it and allowed to remain until the dye was absorbed. The dyes were transferred in the order of cyan, magenta, and yellow. Accurate registration was necessary to avoid blurred outlines and color fringing.

A subjective variation of this process entails making a single black-and-white matrix from a black-and-white negative and then selectively hand coloring the matrix with colors mixed from the subtractive dyes. It was a technically demanding process that required careful attention to detail. It provided the photographer with extra control over color, contrast, and density while making the print in full room light. The dyes used in this process were more stable than those in the conventional chromogenic processes, giving the print a longer life.

Until the 1980s, most color work was rejected as vulgar, gaudy, or too technically unstable for serious noncommercial work. The use of the dye-transfer process by such photographers as Eliot Porter has helped to legitimize the use of color in all areas of photography.

The Fresson Process: Carbon Process

The Fresson process, invented by Theodore-Henri Fresson at the turn of the century, uses a "secret" carbon printing technique to create a pointillistic print from colored pigments. The Fresson Studio (www.atelier-fresson.com), which is in France, currently produces only a few thousand color prints each year. It requires about six hours to make each print. The Fresson process offers its own unique color look and excellent image control, and it is said to be one of the most archival of any of the commercial procedures in use today.

To make a Fresson print, four color separations are made from an original color transparency. A separate exposure is then made for the cyan, magenta, yellow, and black separations, using a carbon arc light source, onto the special Fresson paper, which is made up of pigments similar to those used in oil painting. The paper has to be coated, exposed, developed, and dried four consecutive times, once for each of the separations.

During the exposure, the pigment is hardened in proportion to the amount of light it has received. Now the print is "developed" using a solution of water and sawdust. During the development process, the pigment that has not been hardened by the action of light is softened by the water and removed by the

16.11 This is how the carbon print appeared after the cyan pigment was transferred to the white receiving paper.

16.12 This is how the carbon print looked after the black pigment was transferred on top of the cyan pigment.

16.13 This is how the carbon print evolved after the magenta pigment was transferred on top of the cyan and black pigments.

16.14 The yellow pigment was applied last to create the final four-color carbon image.

© Tod Gangler. *Mars in the Land of Venus*, 2003. Carbon pigment prints.
Courtesy of Art & Soul Studio, Seattle, WA

sawdust, which acts as a mild abrasive. What remains after this operation makes up the final color image. This unusual developer permits local control of the image by pouring varying amounts of sawdust onto the print. It is possible to use this sawdust developer anytime in the future, after the initial

image has been created, to make alterations to the print.

Presently other small companies utilize a digital version of Ducos du Huron's tricolor carbon process to produce color photographic prints. Pigment images are much less fugitive than dyed ones and thus provide an unusual

16.11-16.14 Based on Charles Berger's UltraStable system, a few studios, such as Gangler's Art & Soul, continue to blend nineteenth- and twenty-first-century technologies to make modern carbon prints.

degree of permanence. Since the colors are stacked on top of the support, rather than developed within the emulsion, the final print has a unique sharpness and three-dimensional quality that cannot be seen in regular four-color reproduction such as that used in this book (figures 16.11–16.14).

16.15 and **16.16**   In the 1970s Wolf started making an edition of April Fool's cards by using an electrostatic copy machine as a camera. "They are very different from my documentary work. There was and is no established aesthetic, no 'right way' of making work, which I find liberating and fun. It gives me reason to experiment and not worry about making art. I still make pictures by laying objects on glass, but now I do it on a flatbed scanner."

© Lloyd Wolf. *April Fools*, 1980. 11 x 8 ½ inches. Color electrostatic print.

© Lloyd Wolf. *April Fools*, 2003. 11 x 8 ½ inches. Inkjet print.

Color Electrostatic Processes

Using a color electrostatic photocopier such as a Canon, 3M, Sharp, or Xerox lets the photographer investigate a combination of manual, mechanical, and electric processes for imagemaking with instant feedback. Typically they work on a subtractive method. Magenta, yellow, and cyan pigments, similar to those found in acrylic paints, are coupled with a polymer resin in the toner. This makes a filmy layer of color that is electronically fused onto the paper, thereby producing a permanent image. The lens on the copier acts like a simple camera without a bellows so there is only one focal range possible, providing a very limited depth of field (¼ to ½ inches above the copier glass). This type of system offers the creative user great flexibility and many possibilities in the making of a print.

Digital copiers that scan an original and encode the pictorial information into a binary code of digital data are the current standard and can reproduce up to 256 gradations of each color at up to 600 dpi.

Electrostatic Experiments

Consider using a color photocopying machine to make these pictures:

● Have an enlarged Xerox color print made from a slide. This is performed by a copying machine with a special attachment for making prints from a slide.

- Make a color copy of one of your regular color prints.
- Now perform at least one of the following methods. Compare the results with the original and note what changes have taken place.
- Have a print made on a good-quality drawing paper. Hand color all or part of it with colored pencils, inks, or watercolor paints.
- Cut out a series of images, arrange them on the copier glass, and make a print. Try combining both two-dimensional and three-dimensional objects.
- Explore a theme, such as food. Collect various items that are central to the theme—beans, bread, fruit, grains, leaves, nuts, pasta, seeds, and spices. They may be whole, broken, or cut up. Compose them on the copier glass and explore their color and spatial and textural relationships.
- Combine a series of electrostatic prints to form larger images. Start with a group of four prints that visually connect and expand it into a mural.
- Place a live model on the copy glass. Pose the model so that the changes in the model's position on the copy glass can be combined to form a whole image. Sequence the prints as you proceed to ensure that the visual mosaic being produced is coming together in the desired manner. Redo any prints that are not properly positioned. Try incorporating colored acetate and/or cloth into blank areas for added color, depth, and textural variation.

Future Developments

During its brief history, photography has subverted the hypothesis that art was fundamentally immersed with the imitation of appearances. Photography has disrupted the single, ordered, consistent style of traditional classicism. By familiarizing us with a worldwide range of art and culture, photography has enlarged our realm of aesthetic experiences beyond those directly observed in nature.

As the technical barriers between analog and digital continue to fall away, photography can make the most of its democratic tradition. People with a variety of voices will be able to interact more easily with the medium, enhancing its aesthetic concerns and growth. Photographers should be open to saying yes to a multitude of working practices. The underpinnings of photography's future potency lie in our willingness to tolerate the messiness of diversity.

Valentino tells us: "the title comes from the Bible (Deuteronomy): 'And you shall enjoy, together with the Levite and the stranger in your midst, all the bounty that the Lord your God has bestowed upon you and your household.' This reference established a framework for how a community should relate to one another and especially to those on the fringes. The figure and walls were created in a 3D modeling program, surrounded by scanned images of a fourteenth-century Christian manuscript. The torah scroll was printed front and back on a seven-foot sheet of paper and displayed on a wooden spool."

© John Valentino. *Mishpatim*, From the series: *Stranger in Our Midst*, 2003. 60 x 50 inches. Inkjet print and mixed media.

1800-

1800	Thomas Jefferson elected president
1803	United States buys large tract of land from France (Louisiana Purchase).
	Robert Fulton propels a boat by steam power
1807	Street lighting by gas in London

1802 Thomas Young puts forth the idea that all colors can be formed with three primary colors (additive color synthesis).

1810 Johann Seebeck discovers silver chloride assumes natural spectral colors when exposed to white light.

1810-

1812 United States declares war on Britain
1814 British burn Washington, DC; Treaty of Ghent ends war

1816 Niépce brothers begin experiments to obtain images using light-sensitive materials.
1819 Sir John Herschel discovers that hyposulphite of soda dissolves silver salts.

1820-

1821 Principles for the electric motor discovered by Michael Faraday.
1824 Beethoven's Symphony No. 9 in D major is performed in Vienna.
1829 William B. Burt obtains first U.S. patent for a typewriter ("Typographer").

1829 Louis-Jacques-Mandé Daguerre enters into a partnership with Joseph Nicéphore Niépce.

1830-

1833 British abolish slavery in their colonies.
1839 Britain and China fight Opium War.
Abner Doubleday lays out first American baseball field and conducts first game.
Kirkpatrick Macmillian builds first bicycle.

1839 Daguerre makes public his daguerreotype process. William Henry Fox Talbot announces his paper positive/negative process.

1840-

1841 First University degrees granted to women in the U.S.
1846 *Communist Manifesto* written by Karl Marx.
1847 Gold Rush begins in California.
1848 First Women's Rights convention held in Seneca Falls, NY.
1849 Singer sewing machine invented.

1840 Sir John Herschel records colors on silver chloride-coated paper.
1848 Edmond Becquerel makes color impressions on silver-chloride plates (Heliochromy).

Unidentified Photographer. *Bomb Basket and Shells*, La Faux, France, Circa 1918. 4 x 5 inches. Autochrome. Courtesy of Mark Jacobs Collection.

1850-	1851	*The New York Times* begins publication.	1851	Levi Hill announces his Hillotype but never reveals the details of his process.
	1857	E.G. Otis installs first safety elevator.	1855	James Clerk Maxwell suggests color images can be produced by using filters according to Young-Helmholtz theory and recorded by photographic means.
	1859	Charles Darwin writes *Origins of the Species*.	1856	Alphonse Poitevin discovers two ways of printing with potassium bichromate, which launches carbon printing and photolithography.
1860-	1861	American Civil War begins.	1861	James Clerk Maxwell makes the first three-color projection.
	1865	American Civil War ends, Lincoln assassinated, Ku Klux Klan founded.	1862	Louis Ducos du Hauron describes methods of producing color photographs and patents the first one-shot color camera.
			1867	Niépce de Saint-Victor demonstrates an improved Heliochromy process but is still unable to make permanent images.
			1869	Louis Ducos du Hauron publishes *Photography in Color*. Charles Cros declares the theory of three-color separation printing.
1870-	1876	Alexander Graham Be invents the telephone.	1871	Richard Leach announces his dry-plate process (not perfected until 1878).
	1877	Thomas Edison invents the phonograph.	1873	Hermann W. Vogel discovers dye added to photographic emulsion can make it sensitive to other colors.
			1878	Louis Ducos du Hauron publishes his description for making color images.
1880-	1880	First practical electric lights invented by Edison and J.W. Swan.	1880	Charles Cros describes the "hydroptypie" or dye-transfer printing method. Photographic halftone appears in New York newspaper.
	1883	First skyscraper of ten stories is built in Chicago. Brooklyn Bridge is opened.	1881	Frederick Ives invents trichromate halftone plates for making color reproductions.
	1884	Sir Charles Parsons invents first practical steam turbine engine.	1882	First orthochromatic plates are manufactured.
			1886	Frederick Ives unveils halftone process enabling photographs to be reproduced in the same operation as printing text.
			1888	The Kodak camera is marketed by George Eastman.

© Maggie Talylor. *Southern Gothic*, 2001. 15 x 15 inches. Inkjet print.

1890-			
	1892	Rudolph Diesel patents internal combustion engine	
	1893	Karl Benz and Henry Ford make their first cars.	
	1896	A.H. Becquerel discovers radioactivity.	
	1898	U. S. declares war on Spain.	

1890-
1892 Rudolph Diesel patents internal combustion engine
1893 Karl Benz and Henry Ford make their first cars.
1896 A.H. Becquerel discovers radioactivity.
1898 U. S. declares war on Spain.
Spain cedes Cuba, Puerto Rico, Guam, and the Philippines.
Pierre and Marie Curie discover radium and polonium.
1899 Sigmund Freud's *The Interpretation of Dreams*.

1890 The *Illustrated American*, the first U.S. photojournalism magazine, begins publication.
1891 Gabriel Lippmann invents a color interference process.
Frederick Ives invents first practical one-shot color camera.
1894 John Joly patents the first line-screen process for additive color images.
1896 Joly Color process is introduced. James McDonough patents a color line-screen process.

1900-
1900 Max Planck formulates quantum theory.
R.A. Fessenden transmits human voice via radio waves.
First flight of Count Ferdinand von Zeppelin's airship.
1901 Guglielmo Marconi transmits first transatlantic telegraphic radio messages.
Oil drilling begins in Persia. Instant Coffee debuts.
1903 Orville and Wilbur Wright fly a self-propelled airplane.
1905 Albert Einstein formulates Special Theory of Relativity.
Revolution Russia.
1906 San Francisco earthquake.
First music radio program broadcast in the U.S..
1907 First exhibition of cubist painters in Paris.
1908 Ford produces first Model T cars.
1909 Vassily Kandinsky's first abstract paintings.
Age of Plastic begins with the manufacture of L.H. Baekeland's Bakelite.

1900 The $1 Brownie, designed by Frank Brownell, is marketed by Kodak.
1904 Lumiére brothers patent an additive-color plate with an integral mosaic screen (Autochrome).
Dr. J. H. Smith's bleach-out process (dye-destruction), Uto paper introduced.
1905 Thomas Manly patents the Ozobrome process (carbo process).
1906 First fully panchromatic plates are sold by Wratten and Wainwright.
Clare L. Finlay patents improved additive line screen called Finlay Colour.
1907 Lumiére Autochrome plates marketed.
1908 Thames Colour screen, based on Finlay Colour, is introduced.
1909 Thames Colour Plate released.

1910-
1911 Ernest Rutherford formulates his theory of atomic structure.
1912 S.S. *Titanic* sinks.
1914 World War 1 begins.
1915 Einstein formulates his General Theory of Relativity.
Aspirin available.
1917 Lenin heads Bolshevik Revolution in Russia.
U.S. enters World War 1.
1918 WW 1 ends (8.5 million dead).
Influenza epidemic starts (22 million die).

1910 Louis Dufay's Dioptichrome Platye is unveiled.
1912 Rudolph Fisher and H. Siegrist patent tripack process with color couplers in three-layered emulsion.
1914 Kodachrome two-color process for portraiture introduced.
National Geographic begins publication of color halftones from Autochrome plates.
1916 Agfa Colour plates introduced.

© Stephen Marc. *Untitled from Passage on the Underground Railroad* [03MS], 2002. 9 x 26 inches. Inkjet print.

1920-	1920	League of Nations forms without the U.S. Nineteenth Amendment gives American women right to vote.	1923	Keller-Dorian, Berthon lenticular color movie process demonstrated.

1920-

1920 League of Nations forms without the U.S.
       Nineteenth Amendment gives American women right to vote.
1921 First transmissions of regular radio programs in the U.S.
1925 John Logie Baird transmits recognizable human features via television.
       Heisenberg, Bohr, and Jordan develop quantum mechanics theory.
1927 *The Jazz Singer*, first full-length commercial "talkie" released.
1929 New York stock market crashes.
       Museum of Modern Art opens

1923 Keller-Dorian, Berthon lenticular color movie process demonstrated.
1924 Leopold Mannes and Leopold Godowsky Jr. patent two-layer color process.
1925 Jos Pé Company introduces dye-imbibition process.
       Oskar Barnack markets first Leica camera.
       Anatol Josepho patents first photo booth.
1926 First underwater Autochromes made.
1928 Kodacolor lenticular film introduced for movies.
       Leitz markets 35-mm filmstrip projector for lenticular color films.
1929 Finlay Colour plate process introduced.

1930-

1930 Worldwide economic depression begins.
1931 Empire State Building opens.
1933 Adolf Hitler appointed German chancellor.
       First Nazis concentration camps erected.
       All modern and Jewish art suppressed in Germany; about sixty thousand emigrate.
       Franklin Roosevelt inaugurated as President of U.S.
1936 Mussolini and Hitler proclaim Rome-Berlin Axis, sign Anti-Comintern pact with Japan.
       BBC London begins television service.
1939 World War II starts.
       Computer experiments begin at Harvard.
       RCA introduces television at the World's Fair in New York.

1930 Mannes and Godowsky join Kodak Research Lab.
1932 Technicolor produces the first three-color Disney cartoon.
       Agfa introduces 35-mm lenticular film.
       Lumiére Autochrome glass plates are replaced by Filmcolor.
1933 Gasparcolor process, first commercial dye-destruction process, launched.
1934 Technicolor produces first "live" three-color film.
1935 16-mm Kodachrome movie film introduced.
       Eastman Wash-Off Relief process marketed.
1936 Kodachrome roll film introduced.
       Agfacolor Neu, integral tripack film unveiled.
       Life magazine beings publishing.
1938 Kodachrome ready-mounting service started.
1939 Agfacolor provides a monopack color negative and paper for negative/positive printing.

1940-

1941 Japan attacks Pearl Harbor, United States enters World War II.
1942 Ernico Fermi splits the atom.
1945 World War II ends. U.S. drops atomic bombs on Hiroshima and Nagasaki.
       Thirty-five million war dead, plus 10 million in Nazi concentration camps.
1946 United Nations formed.
       Nuremburg war trials begin.
1947 Bell Labs invents the transistor.
       Jackie Robinson becomes the first black baseball player in the major leagues with the Brooklyn Dodgers.
1948 Gandhi assassinated.
       The State of Israel is proclaimed by the United Nations.
       Peter Goldmark invents the long-playing records.
1949 Communists under Mao Tse-tung take control of China.

1940 Sakura Natural Color film made in Japan.
       Museum of Modern Art in New York opens its Department of Photography.
1942 Kodacolor films and papers unveiled.
1945 Kodak's Dye Transfer process replaces Wash-off Relief.
1946 Ektachrome color sheet film, processable by the photographer, introduced.
1947 Polaroid 60 second process invented by Dr. Edwin Land.
1948 Nikon 35-mm camera introduced.

1950-

1950	Korean War starts.
1952	U.S. explodes hydrogen bomb.
1954	U.S. Supreme Court rules racial segregation in schools unconstitutional.
	Dr. Jonas Salk begins inoculating schoolchildren with antipolio serum.
1956	Elvis Presley releases *Blue Suede Shoes*, *Hound Dog* & *Don't be Cruel*.
1957	USSR launches *Sputnik* satellites.
	Jack Kerouac publishes *On the Road*.
1959	Fidel Castro becomes premier of Cuba.
	Hawaii becomes fiftieth U.S. state.

1950	Xerox copying machine produced.
1954	Eastman Kodak signs consent decree after antitrust action by U.S. government, ending monopoly on photofinishing.
1955	Kodak releases their color processes to photofinishers in U.S., marking the beginnings of the modern photofinishing industry.
1958	Kodacolor film available in 35-mm cassettes.
1959	Nikon F 35-mm SLR introduced.

1960-

1960	U.S. scientists develop laser device.
1961	Bay of Pigs invasion of Cuba.
	USSR launches first manned space craft.
1962	Cuban Missile crisis.
1963	President John F. Kennedy is assassinated.
1964	Gulf of Tonkin resolution signals major U.S. involvement in Vietnam War.
	Beatles release "I Want to Hold Your Hand."
1965	Malcolm X is assassinated.
	Regular color television programming begins.
1966	National Organization for Women founded.
1967	Six Day Israeli-Arab War.
	Black ghetto riots begin in U.S. cities.
1968	Martin Luther King and Robert F. Kennedy are assassinated.
1969	Neil Armstrong becomes first man to walk on the moon.

1962	Polaroid launches Polacolor peel-apart (diffusion transfer) film and camera.
1963	Kodak unveils the Instamatic.
	Cibachrome prints exhibited at Photokina.
1965	3M announces Electrocolor process.
1968	Kodak makes resin-coated paper (Ektacolor 20) available to photofinishers.

© Jessica Todd Harper. *Becky with Mom*, 2001. 32 x 40 inches. Inkjet print.

1970-		
	1970	448 U.S. colleges are closed or on strike as result of Vietnam War protest; 4 students killed by National Guard at Kent State University.
	1972	Watergate break-in Democratic party headquarters.
	1973	Cease-fire agreement signed in Vietnam War. Yom Kippur War between Israel and Arabs; Arabs begin oil embargo of nations that supported Israel.
	1974	Nixon resigns as president over Watergate scandal.
	1975	Communists seize Saigon, end 20 years of U.S. military involvement in Vietnam. BETA and VHS formats introduced.
	1972	Polaroid SX-70 marketed. First drive-through Fotomat. Color CAT scans made.
	1973	Kodacolor processing changed to C-41.
	1976	Viking I sends first color images of another planet (Mars) back to earth.

1980-		
	1981	MTV goes on the air 24 hours a day.
	1983	Internet (ARPANET) starts operations.
	1984	Megabit memory chip invented.
	1981	Electronic still (digital) camera demonstrated by Sony. Agfa and Ilford introduce black-and-white chromogenic films.
	1986	Manufacturers establish standards for electronic still photography and still video equipment. Canon introduces professional still video camera system.
	1989	Fuji unveils Velvia, an extremely high-resolution E-6 film.

1990-		
	1991	Iraqi invasion force in Kuwait is destroyed by U.S.-led Allied Forces.
	1995	U.S.-led NATO peace-keeping forces begin mission in Bosnia.
	1992	Kodak markets Photo CD.

2000-		
	2001	World Trade Center destroyed by terrorists.
	2002	U.S. overthrows Taliban regime in Afghanistan.
	2003	U.S. invades Iraqi.
	2003	Kodak introduces affordable digital camera that equals 35mm film.

© Gregory Crewdson. *Untitled* [woman in flowers], 1998. 50 x 60 inches.
Chromogenic color print.
Courtesy of Luhring Augustine, New York, NY.

Historical Events in the Development in Color Photography ● 349

© Deena des Rioux. *Family Portrait Series: Family Reunion*, 2002.
41 x 30 inches. Inkjet print.

Safety in the Color Darkroom

Safety in the color darkroom is a concern that must be introduced into a photographer's daily routine. Here des Rioux presents a scenario of "a future view of the

past when zero air quality is the norm. In a nostalgic setting, the human subjects are inaccessible: in their place are framed portraits that show 'the family' in protective gear where a breathing apparatus is an everyday accessory."

It is of vital importance that all photographers assume responsibility for protecting themselves when working with any photo-based process in either the analog or digital darkroom. Learning all safety precautions and guidelines before beginning to work with any process will help to ensure a long and safe relationship between you and the practice of making images.

Guidelines for Chemical Handling and Mixing

Every photographer working in a color darkroom needs to be aware of specific health and environmental concerns to ensure and promote safe working conditions. Before working with any process mentioned in this book, it is necessary for each photographer to become familiar with and observe the following basic precautions and guidelines:

1 *Before* carrying out any process, including mixing, handling, disposal, and storage, read all safety material provided by the manufacturer and in this book. Read and follow all instructions and safety recommendations on Material Safety Data Sheets (MSDS) and product literature, which are provided with each product by its manufacturer. Obtain any special safety equipment, such as gloves, goggles, and facemask, *before* using the materials you have purchased. MSDS were created by the U.S. Occupational Safety and Health Administration (OSHA) and are available from the manufacturers of each product, usually on a company's website. Each manufacturer prepares its own MSDS, which typically provide additional ecological, disposal, transport, and regulatory information. Websites containing general information such as *www.ilpi.com/msds/index.html,* which will allow you to find specific details and even has a "Demystify" feature to explain data that you do not understand.

2 Become familiar with all the inherent dangers associated with any chemicals used. When acquiring any chemicals or when working with a new process, ask about proper handling and safety procedures. Obtain MSDS for all chemicals used, which can usually be found on the manufacturer's website. Keep them available in a notebook for easy reference. Learn how to interpret the MSDS. Right-to-know laws in the United States and Canada require all employers to formally train workers to read MSDS. Certain color chemicals are more dangerous than others. Paraphenylenediamene and its derivatives, found in some color developers, and formaldehyde and its derivatives, found in stabilizers, are two of the most toxic.

3 Know the first-aid and emergency treatment for the chemicals with which you are working. Keep the telephone numbers for poison control and emergency treatment prominently displayed in your working area and near the telephone. Each MSDS has the manufacturer's emergency number on it.

4 Many chemicals may be flammable. Keep them away from any source of heat or open flame to avoid possible explosion or fire. Keep an ABC-type fire extinguisher in the darkroom, which can be used for ordinary combustibles (wood and paper), solvent, grease, and electric fires in the work area.

5 Protect chemicals from low temperatures (lower than 40°F, or 4.4°C). They may freeze, burst in their containers, and contaminate your working environment. Chemicals that have been frozen may also be damaged and deliver unexpected and faulty results.

6 Work in a well-ventilated space (see the ventilation section). Hazardous chemicals should be mixed in a vented hood or outdoors. Check MSDS or the manufacturers for recommended ventilation guidelines for the chemicals you are using.

7 Avoid contamination problems by keeping all working surfaces clean, dry, and free of chemicals. Use polystyrene mixing rods, funnels, graduates, and pails. Use separate mixing containers for each chemical, and do not interchange them. Label them with a permanent marker. Thoroughly wash all equipment used in chemical mixing. Keep floors dry to prevent slips and falls.

8 Protect yourself. Wear disposable, chemical-resistant gloves, safety glasses, and plastic aprons. Find a glove maker who gives information that indicates how long the glove material can be in contact with a chemical before it becomes degraded or permeated. Degradation happens when the glove deteriorates from being in contact with the chemical. Permeation occurs when molecules of the chemical penetrate the glove material. Permeated gloves often appear unchanged and wearers may be unaware they are being exposed to the chemical. Some chemicals can penetrate chemical gloves in minutes and begin to affect the skin. Barrier creams, which can protect the skin from light exposure to specific chemicals, can be applied to your skin. Choose the right cream to block acids, oils, or solvents, and use it exactly as directed. Do not use harsh soaps or solvents to wash your hands. After washing, apply a high-quality hand lotion to replace lost skin oils.

9 Consult the MSDS for the proper type of protection required with each chemical or process. When mixing powdered materials, use an NIOSH-approved (National Institute of Occupational Safety and Health) mask for toxic dusts. When diluting concentrated liquid chemicals containing solvents, acetic acid, and sulfites, use a combination organic vapor/acid gas cartridge. Ideally all mixing should be done in a local exhaust system. If you have any type of reaction, immediately suspend work with all photographic processes and consult with a knowledgeable physician. Once an allergic reaction has occurred, you should avoid the chemicals unless your physician approves the use of a respirator. Employers of workers who wear respirators, including dust masks, are required by OSHA to have a written respirator program, formal fit testing, and worker training. People with certain diseases and some pregnant women should not wear them. Check with your doctor.

10 Follow mixing instructions. Mix chemicals in order and precisely according to directions, including the mixing times. Improper mixing procedures can produce dangerous chemical reactions or give undesirable results.

11 Keep all chemicals off of your skin and out of your mouth. If you get any chemicals on your skin, flush immediately with cool, running water.

12 Do not eat, drink, or smoke while handling chemicals. Wash your hands thoroughly after handling any chemicals. OSHA forbids the consumption or storage of food or drink wherever toxic chemicals are in use or stored. Food should not be stored in the refrigerator next to chemicals and paper.

13 Always pour acids slowly into water; never pour water into acids. Do not mix or pour any chemical at eye level because a splash could prove harmful. Wear unvented chemical splash goggles when mixing acids.

14 Label each solution container to reduce the chance of contamination and/or using the wrong solution.

15 Avoid touching any electrical equipment with wet hands. Install shockproof outlets (ground fault interrupters) in your own darkroom. Make certain all equipment is grounded. Keep the floor dry. When designing a darkroom, plan to separate wet and dry areas.

16 Follow the manufacturer's instructions for proper disposal of all chemicals. Bleach and fix should be filtered through a small, inexpensive silver-recovery unit. This silver can be sold to recoup the cost of the unit. The concentration of silver in such a unit can be highly toxic and must be handled with caution. Each local water treatment facility has its own rules. Photographers need to find out what they are. Since household septic systems use bacteria to break down waste they can be easily damaged by photographic chemistry disposal. Most septic systems can handle a few pints of chemistry at any one time. If you are using larger quantities it is advisable to go to another location. Purchase spill-control centers, which contain special "pillows" or other devices that can be dropped on acids, solvents, or caustic chemical spills to immediately absorb them. They are sold by safety supply companies.

Wash yourself and any equipment that has come into contact with any chemicals. Launder darkroom towels after each session. Specific questions about Kodak products can be answered by their Environmental Technical Services at (716) 477–3194. Ilford provide a similar service at (201) 265–6000.

These drawings illustrate how the placement of ventilation inlets and outlets affects a local exhaust system in a photographic darkroom.

17 Keep all chemicals properly stored. Use safety caps and/or lock chemicals to prevent children, friends, and pets from being exposed to their potential dangers. Store chemicals in a cool, dry area away from any direct sunlight.

18 People have varying sensitivities to chemicals. Reduce your risk by keeping exposure to all chemicals to a minimum. Some chemicals cause an immediate and identifiable effect, while others, such as a skin allergy, can take years to develop. Consult your physician if you have a reaction while working with any chemicals. Be prepared to tell your doctor precisely what you were working with and what your symptoms are. Follow the physician's advice about reducing chemical exposure, using respiratory protection, and other precautions. Photographers should consult physicians who are board certified in occupational medicine or toxicology for such advice.

19 If you are planning a pregnancy, are pregnant, are breast-feeding, or have any pre-existing health problems, consult your physician. Share with the physician any information from the MSDS, from this book, or from other sources about possible adverse reactions before undertaking any photographic process. Children, senior citizens, allergy sufferers, smokers, heavy drinkers, and those with chronic conditions and diseases are considered to be most susceptible to the hazards of photographic chemicals.

Specific safety measures and reminders are provided throughout this book whenever there is a deviation or exception from these guidelines. These instructions are not designed to produce paranoia but to ensure that you have a long and safe adventure in exploring color photography. Remember your eyes, lungs, and skin are porous membranes and can absorb chemical vapors. It is your job to protect yourself.

Disposing of Chemicals

As environmental regulations are made stronger, what may have been acceptable to pour down the drain ten years ago may not be permissible today. As the

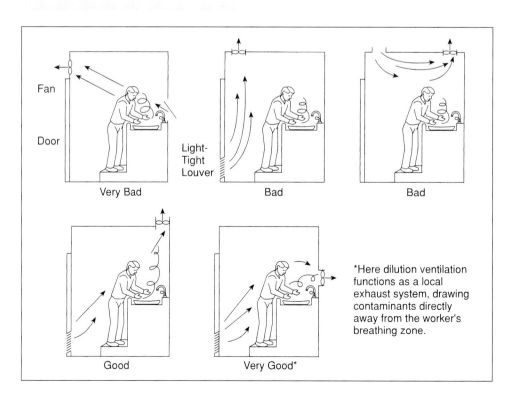

*Here dilution ventilation functions as a local exhaust system, drawing contaminants directly away from the worker's breathing zone.

beneficiaries of cleaner air and water, photographers are responsible for following local regulations.

Municipal waste-treatment plants can handle most photo chemical solutions under a certain volume and concentration. Local sewer authorities regulate the concentrations and the volume of chemicals released per day into sewer systems. Normally most individual home photographic processing will not exceed these regulations. Before setting up a darkroom contact the local sewer authority for information about disposing of your photographic solutions.

Ventilation

It is advisable to work in a space that has a light-tight exhaust fan and an intake vent for fresh air. Exhaust fans are rated by their ability to remove air in cubic feet per minute (cfm). A 10-x-20-foot darkroom with a 10-foot ceiling would require an exhaust fan rated at 500 cfm (against ¼- to ½-inch static pressure) to do fifteen air exchanges per hour. Fans that do 500 cfm just sitting on the floor will *not* provide proper ventilation. The amount of ventilation needed varies depending on what chemicals are used, room size, and conditions. Read the MSDSs or contact the manufacturer for suggested ventilation guidelines for chemicals. The illustration below shows how air inlets and outlets should be positioned for maximum effect. This type of ventilation, known as general or dilution, is designed to dilute the contaminated air with large volumes of clean air to lower the amounts of contaminants to acceptable levels and then exhaust the diluted mixture from the work area. Dilution ventilation does not work with highly toxic materials or any particle materials that form dusts, fumes, or mists. These materials require what is referred to as local exhaust ventilation, such as a table slot or fume hood, to capture the contaminants at the source before they escape into the room air. Refer to the references at the end of this swction to carefully research this area before constructing a system.

Water for Photographic Processses

Water makes up almost two-third of the human body, and three-quarters of our planet's surface, and is the key ingredient in most predigital photographic processes. Although water itself does not create a safety issue, it is included here because its purity can affect your processing results. The following information applies whenever water is called for in any process discussed in this book.

Use a source of "pure" water. The chemical and mineral composition and pH of your local water source can affect processing results. Color developers are most sensitive to these factors. You can eliminate this variable beforehand by making certain your water source is pure or by using water processed by reverse osmosis. Distilled water often has had certain components (calcium) removed that are required for proper chemical reactions to take place. Water that has gone through a softening process is not recommended for any photographic chemical mixing. This is because water is generally softened by passing it through a treatment tank that contains high amounts of salts. This process alters the chemical composition of the water and can lead to processing irregularities.

References

Arts, Crafts and Theater Safety (ACTS), 181 Thompson Street #23, New York, NY 10012. (212)777–0062. ACTS will answer questions about chemicals, workspace design, and doctor referral.

The Center for Occupational Hazards, 5 Beekman Street, New York, NY 10038, (212)227–6220 answers questions concerning safety in artists' working spaces by letter or telephone.

CLARK, N., CUTTER, T., MCGRANE, J. A. *Ventilation: A Practical Guide.* New York: Nick Lyons Books, 1987.

Eastman Kodak Co. *Photolab Design.* Kodak Publication K-13. Rochester, NY: Eastman Kodak, 1989.

Eastman Kodak Co. *Safe Handling of Photographic Chemicals.* Kodak Publication J-4. Rochester, NY: Eastman Kodak, 1979.

FREEMAN, VICTORIA AND HUMBLE, CHARLES G. *Prevalence of Illness and Chemical Exposure in Professional Photographers.* Durham, NC: National Press Photographers Association, 1989.

MCCANN, MICHAEL, *Artist Beware,* 2nd ed. New York: Watson-Guptill, 1992.

The National Press Photographers' Association, 3200 Croasdaile Drive, Suite 306, Durham, NC 27705.

OSHA's Publications Office, Room N-3101, 200 Constitution Ave., N.W., Washington, DC 20210; (202) 523–9667.

Emergency Telephone Numbers

Numbers for the local poison control hotline are usually listed in the first few pages of your telephone directory. Keep this number along with the phone numbers listed below close to the telephone in case of an emergency.

Questions about photographic chemicals can be answered by telephoning the following health and safety numbers, some of which operate 24 hours a day:

Agfa (303) 623–5716

Ilford Medical Emergency, North America, 24-hour hotline, (800) 842-9660

Kodak, North America, 24-hour hotline, (716) 722-515

Kodak, Australia/Asia/Western Pacific, 24-hour hotline, 03-350-1222

Kodak, United Kingdom/Europe/Africa, 24-hour hotline, 01-427-4380

Your Local Poison Control Center: . . . .
. . . .

REMPEL, SIEGFRIED AND WOLFGANG REMPEL. *Health Hazards for Photographers*. New York: The Lyons Press, 1993.

ROSSOL, MONONA. *The Artist's Complete Health & Safety Guide*, 2nd edition. New York: Allworth Press, 1994.

SPANDORFER, MERLE, JACK SNYDER and DEBORAH CURTISS. *Making Art Safely: Alternative Methods and Materials in Drawing, Painting, Printmaking, Graphic Design, and Photography*. New York: John Wiley & Sons, 1995.

SHAW, SUSAN, and ROSSOL, MONONA. *Overexposure: Health Hazards in Photography*, 2nd ed. New York: Allworth Press, 1991.

TELL, JUDY, ed. *Making Darkrooms Saferooms*. Durham, NC: National Press Photographers' Association, 1988.

Safety in the Digital Studio

Protecting Yourself and Your Computer

While the computer does not expose the user to possibly hazardous chemicals or fumes, an artist working at a computer should be aware of the possible health effects.

Monitor Emissions: ELF/VLF

Extremely Low Frequency (ELF) and Very Low Frequency (VLF) emissions are types of electromagnetic radiation created by monitors. Some research studies have linked these emissions to an increased risk of cancer or miscarriage. Keep your eyes at least 18 inches away from the screen and avoid prolonged exposure. Low emissions monitors are available as well as filters for the screen.

Eye strain

Eye strain can be reduced by working in a well-lit room and by keeping the screen free of dust and clear of reflections.

Taking Breaks

Take a 15-minute break every one or two hours to help maintain your sanity and prevent fatigue. Try mixing non-computer related activities into your digital routine. Consider exercises designed to be done while you are at your desk.

Carpal Tunnel Syndrome

Carpal Tunnel Syndrome, caused by repetitive movements and improper keyboard and mouse use, is characterized by numbness and tingling in the wrists and hands. In advanced stages, the syndrome can cause permanent nerve damage. Keeping your wrists flat, straight, and at a height equal to your elbows will help prevent injury. Learning how to operate the mouse with your non-dominant hand can also help reduce repetitive movement stress.

Proper Posture/Lower Back Problems

Sit in a fully adjustable ergonomic chair with your feet flat on the floor or on a footrest. Periodically make slight adjustments to your chair's settings so your body is not always in the same position. The top of the monitor should be at eye level.

Power Surge Protection

Use a surge-suppression device to protect a computer and peripherals from a spike. Power surges, called spikes, occur when the power to your home or studio is restored after an interruption. These surges can damage the sensitive circuitry in your computer.

© Koya Abe. *Beyond Culture*, 2000. 30 x 40 inches. Chromogenic color print.

Index